NAILING
1Z0-808

Practical Guide
to
Oracle Java SE8 Programmer I Certification

by Igor Soudakevitch

2nd Edition

NAILING 1Z0-808:
Practical Guide to
Oracle Java SE8 Programmer I Certification
by Igor Soudakevitch

Copyright © 2017 by Igor Soudakevitch. Second edition
www.igor.host
ISBN-13: 978-1548193980
ISBN-10: 1548193984

Java and the Java logo are registered trademarks of Oracle Corporation; Microsoft, Windows and Windows Server are registered trademarks of Microsoft Corporation in the United States and/or other countries. Other product and company names such as NetBeans, IntelliSense, etc. mentioned herein may be the trademarks of their respective owners. The author of this publication is not associated with any product or vendor mentioned in this book.

The example companies, organizations, products, domain names, email addresses, logos, people, places, and events mentioned herein are fictitious. No association with any real company, organization, product, domain name, email address, logo, person, place, or event is intended or should be inferred.

This book expresses the author's views and opinions. The information contained in this book is provided without any express, statutory, or implied warranties. Neither the author nor his resellers or distributors will be held liable for any damages caused or alleged to be caused either directly or indirectly by this book.

Interior and cover design: Igor Soudakevitch
Illustrations: Raphael Krivonogov

About the Author

Igor Soudakevitch never thought of writing this book; he sort of plunged into it headfirst when Providence gave him a mighty slap on his rump. And yet, however strange it may sound, *Nailing 1Z0-808* is a labor of love; for Igor cannot live without coding. He wrote his first program at the tender age of eleven, and still keeps that old, yellowish roll of perforated tape.

Igor relocated to Japan in 1990 to work as a researcher at Tokyo Institute of Technology, in the field that is known nowadays as Applied Nanotechnology and Nanoscience, but then changed lanes in order to fully embrace another passion of his life, namely translation and study of foreign languages.

After spending fourteen unforgettable years in the Land of Rising Sun and Blooming Robotics he returned to his native Moscow where he continues to live with his family, all the while rendering children's – and Nobel Prize winners' – books from English, French and Japanese into his mother tongue, tinkering with Raspi and Arduino, and writing articles on the art of what he enjoys most: coding and translating.

I am nothing without you, Tamaki.
Thank you for being in my life.

ACKNOWLEDGEMENTS

I have not attempted to cite in the text all the authorities and sources consulted in the preparation of this guide. To do so would require more space than is available.

There are, however, certain individuals without whom writing this book would be simply impossible. My special thanks go to Simon Roberts for his outstanding Live Lessons, Paul Anilprem and his colleagues at Enthuware for their exceptional product not to mention ever-present support, and all the good folks at the CodeRanch who helped me see the Java light and get to where I am now.

- *Mommy? Why did you marry an idiot?*

- *How could you say that?! Our Daddy is smart! Look, he's studying for his Java certification right now!*

- *Yes, I know... But why he laughs hysterically and screams "I'm an idiot!" every other minute?*

AUTHOR'S NOTE

As this is an account of personal experience, it is highly prejudiced and opinionated. If some of what follows sounds too categorical, it is based on the notes that were written *in extremis*. The author would not like to have on his conscience anything that may happen to the reader who puts blind trust into everything that the book recommends – or advises against.

Contents

Target Audience

Given the following class definitions (disregard line numbers):

In file C:\Try_Java\tempa\Exam.java:

```
1 package tempa;
2 import tempb.*;
3
4 public class Exam {
5     protected Exam(Examinee e){}
6 }
```

In file C:\Try_Java\tempb\Examinee.java:

```
1 package tempb;
2 import tempa.Exam;
3
4 public class Examinee {
5     String str;
6     protected Examinee(){
7         this.str = "1Z0-808 is tricky!";
8     }
9     protected void exclaim(){
10         System.out.println(str);
11     }
12 }
```

In file C:\Try_Java\org\xlator\TargetAudience.java:

```
1 package org.xlator;
2 import tempa.*;
3 import tempb.Examinee;
4
5 public final class TargetAudience extends Examinee {
6     String str = "Then again, maybe not...";
7     TargetAudience(){
8         exclaim();
9     }
10     @Override
11     public void exclaim(){
12         System.out.println(str.substring(0, str.length()));
13     }
14     public static void main(String[] args) {
15         Examinee ta = new TargetAudience();
16         new Exam(ta);
17     }
18 }
```

What is the result when we attempt to compile and run the TargetAudience class from C:\Try_Java?

    A.   1Z0-808 is tricky!
    B.   Then again, maybe not...
    C.   Compilation fails
    D.   StringOutOfBoundsException is thrown at run time

See the correct answer overleaf.

Answer to the 'Target Audience' question:

The correct answer is option C for the code does not compile.

The fail-safe way to solve problems on the exam is to read question first, then glance at the available choices to see if some of them can be eliminated immediately because options are syntactically invalid quite often, and only after that start analyzing code. Let me do it for you:

> Prints this, prints that... hmm, a possible comperr... what? *StringOutOfBoundsException*?! Nah, I don't think so, **java.lang** has no such thing: it should've been SIOOBE → option D is out. Damn, three more to go. To the code, then.

> Line numbers start with 1; full contents, then → need to verify if imports are listed *after* packages... check → all three classes live in different packages → RED ALERT! RED ALERT! some class members or constructors along the inheritance chain may be inaccessible... → aha! **TargetAudience** does extend another class! something fishy must be going on... → now to the **main()** method... right, an object... hmm, reftype differs from actype... oh, we're calling another class' constructor, aren't we now? in a different package, no less? well, you know, that ctor better be `public`, otherwise no go... → yeap, just as I expected: it's `protected` → LOC16 in **TargetAudience** won't work. Done!

And here's the actual error message produced by the compiler:

```
C:\Try_Java\org\xlator\TargetAudience.java:16 error: Exam(Examinee) has protected access in Exam
        new Exam(ta);
        ^
1 error
```

The entire chain of reasoning takes but twenty seconds, and this is what you too will be able to pull off every single time on the exam regardless of the problem you're facing – after you worked your way through this OCA bootcamp with all its obstacle courses, that is.

This book has one sole purpose: to hone your skills for solving exam questions both reliably and quickly; as such, it doesn't even attempt to replace a full-fledged Java study guide. Ideally, *Nailing 1Z0-808* should become the beachhead from which you'll be launching your final offensive to conquer the coveted 'Oracle Certified Programmer I' title. This entire tune-up, refueling and ammo-stocking phase won't take more than three weeks. However, to benefit from it fully you should already know your way around Java basics so grab a solid tutorial, study online or watch[1] video lessons and so on; *Preface* lists some reliable titles.

I'd be very much interested in hearing how you fared on the exam. Do find a minute to tell me your score and what objectives you missed. Comments and suggestions are welcome.

Visit www.igor.host for online tests. E-learning course **Enrollment Key**:   Ld2W$,eK=&Q^ha

---

[1] You can find free Java online courses at MIT, UC Berkeley, etc. Stay away from YouTube, though: it has no QC.

Abbreviations and Acronyms

actype – actual object's type at run time

assop – assignment operator; mostly used metonymically, in the sense of assignment statement

castype – data type specified inside the parentheses for an explicit cast

comperr – compilation error

ctor – constructor

def – definition

dim – dimension

initer – initializer

initing – initializing

op – operator

paramlist – list of formal parameters in a lambda expression

preditype – data type specified inside the angle brackets of a generified **Predicate**

reftype – reference type

refvar – reference variable

sout – any printing statement such as **System.out.println()**, etc.

stat – statement

ternop – ternary operator; often used metonymically to denote a ternary statement

var – variable

AIOOBE – `ArrayIndexOutOfBoundsException`

CCE – `ClassCastException`

ChE – checked exception

CSR – the Catch-or-Specify Requirement

DTPE – `DateTimeParseException`

E – an exception (regardless of the type)

IAE – `IllegalArgumentException`

IOE – `IOException`

IOOBE – `IndexOutOfBoundsException`

LDT – any of the new date/time classes in Java 1.8 (such as `LocalDate`, `LocalTime` or `LocalDateTime`)

LOC – line of code

NFE – `NumberFormatException`

NPE – `NullPointerException`

RTE – `RuntimeException`

SIOOBE – `StringIndexOutOfBoundsException`

TCF – `try-catch-finally` construct (not necessarily containing either `catch` or `finally`)

Preface

T his story does end happily, with data types flowing smoothly across the screen, almost nodding at me like old trusted friends. There was a moment, however, when it wasn't at all that enjoyable; in fact, everything looked downright depressing.

This is what the author posted on the CodeRanch forum on May 20, 2016 (edited slightly for better readability):

A few days ago I failed my 1Z0-808 at 62%.

[This should] serve as a warning to those who dream about becoming Oracle-certified in a snap. Alright, here it goes:

I started preparing in the earnest six months ago. The first thing I did was quitting my job, quite literally.

After burning the proverbial bridges behind me I watched... no, that's a wrong word; I worked painstakingly through the entire video course, a.k.a. *Live Lessons*, on 1Z0-803 by Simon Roberts. Was spending on that ten to twelve hours daily. Took me three weeks; no holidays, no weekends, no nothing... Why this long? Because I was hitting *Pause* every few seconds to write notes, think over what Simon was talking about and, most importantly, put all of it out in code. By using Notepad++. Yes, that's right. For the first two months I wasn't letting myself fire up an IDE.

Soon running my tiny 'javalets' directly from the CLI became so tedious that I hacked the Registry and wrote a minimalist launcher to run the code by right-clicking on the .java file in the Explorer window. This trick alone allowed me to write and test well over a hundred javalets a day, all the while learning new, even more mind-boggling rules from the JLS.

By my rough estimation, by the mid-January, 2016, I had thought up, tested, twisted, tortured, tormented, and otherwise tweaked with over 3,000 javalets while listening to and watching Simon. (Mind you, not because watching him makes you do all those unspeakable things, no. He did an outstanding work. The best there is. I'm going to write an extensive review about his video course, although not right now. Right now I don't have the right. Right...)

And then I hit the books. Oh boy, did I hit 'em... Here's the list:

- the ubiquitous *OCA: Oracle Certified Associate Java SE 8 Programmer I Study Guide. Exam 1Z0-808* by Jeanne Boyarsky & Scott Selikoff (loved it; positively loved it! granted, it's ridden with typos but still makes a great read; in fact, THE greatest);

- *OCA Java SE 7* by Mala Gupta (liked it, especially all those tightly packed Review Notes; btw, her new book, this time on 1Z0-808, will be released very soon);

- *Head First Java* by Kathy Sierra & Bert Bates (dropped it after a couple of weeks; reason: the delivery grated on my nerves; in my eyes, it'll make a perfect present to one's worst enemy but that's just me; anyhow, all my comments are highly subjective);

- *Thinking in Java* by Bruce Eckel (6th ed.) (not everything, of course; I didn't touch collections, inner classes, threads, and other advanced topics that are not on the exam; I am awed by this book; a few pieces of code resemble poems, even; then again, it's just me);

- few chapters from *Effective Java* by Joshua Bloch (am going to read it ten more times; pure pleasure);

- *Java 8. Pocket Guide* by Robert & Patricia Liguori (I always keep this book within my reach and consult with it dozens of times daily);

- *Java in a Nutshell* by Benjamin Evans & David Flanagan (6th ed., which covers JSE8) (I think I did find a typo in their code but the book itself is undeniably excellent; helped me to look at certain concepts from a different angle; would love to translate it if I only had a chance...);

- *Exercices en Java* par Claude Delannoy (4e éd., couvre JSE8 aussi) (I certainly enjoyed it; would've gladly recommended it to any of my friends);

- *La programmation objet en Java* par Michel Divay (apparently, he teaches this very course at the Univ.of Rennes; the book itself is as dry as moon dust and bo-oring but it has one major advantage: it makes use of simple UML diags, which I find helpful when solving problems);

- and three more books in Russian, which are too obscure to talk about here.

Naturally, just reading books won't cut it so I did exercises. As Jeanne Boyarsky loves to repeat, "Practice!" And so I practiced. It looked like this: read Chapter 1, do the exercises to that Chapter, do not check answers but read Chapter 2 instead, come back and repeat the exercises to Chapter 1, compare your own answers (to see if they are the same, otherwise it would mean that you are unsure about certain points) and finally check them against the key. Loop in the same fashion to finish the book. Cover all the books that have exercises. Then do it again and again until your score becomes at least 90% at every single pass.

Boyarsky & Selikoff's book alone contains 345 exercises if we count in the three mock up exams; I did the whole cycle three times (and read the book itself four times, from cover to cover; now I'm reading it for the fifth time; I did quit my job, remember?). Mala Gupta's book gives a lot of practice, as well...

I also enrolled for a four-week-long course on Java 8 that they teach at Bauman's Technical University here, in downtown Moscow. Three hours of brain wracking practice in class, then solving all those home assignments until four o'clock in the morning. For twenty days.

Attended JPoint, a Java conference for students organized by the local JUG. Was reading all Java-related magazines I could get my hands on in all the languages I'm familiar with. Sat for hours cracking Java Interview questions that can be found on so many sites in India...

The idea was to saturate myself with Java code, until I puke blood or drop dead. Or both. Didn't happen, though.

This epic picture will not be complete without me squinting at my screen while working through emulated exams; I had plenty of those, too:

- two 60-question-long practice exams that are bundled with *OCA SE7 Programmer I & II* by Kathy Sierra, et al.;

- over 600 questions in the Enthuware Question Bank;

- Kaplan Self-Test with its 180 questions;

- as for the testing software that comes with the B&S book, I stopped using it after seeing how many errors it contains; preferred pen and paper instead.

Kathy Sierra's quizzes are tough. Enthuware's even harder – and thoroughly enjoyable. The explanations alone are worth the buck; they are first rate, hands down.

As for Kaplan's... I wish I could sue that sorry bunch. Their so-called 'self-test' (for which I paid over $80 and which is even advertised on the Pearson Vue[2] site as a part of the official Oracle Certification Bundle, of all things) is the worst piece of software workmanship that I have ever seen in my entire life.

In case someone is curious why I resent them that much, here are the reasons; there are two of them... hold it! three![3]

---

[2] And on Oracle University site, too...

[3] Come to think of it, I can add one more: Kaplan SelfTest website misleads the prospective buyers into thinking that these mock-up tests mimick "the actual test environment perfectly" (I took this expression right from the Testimonials section on their landing page.) Mildly put, it isn't true. In fact, none of the simulated 1Z0-808 prepware suits reproduce the look and feel of the *actual* test envionment – which puzzles me to no end. After all, it's just GUI; no changes to the business logic are needed to recreate the atmosphere of the real exam...

Firstly, the desktop version's GUI is full of visual bugs that literally clutter the screen (seriously!) and it is only the web-based version that works as advertised. Secondly, their flash cards contain errors and ambiguities in the explanations, and finally, the questions are simply... well, too simple. I took their mock-up exam in the so-called Certification Mode and got 96%. Without breaking a sweat, with tons of time to spare, without even reviewing my answers...

Now, about Enthuware. My scores were 77% on Foundation, 74-79-75-81-74-80 on Standard Tests 1 thru 6, and 78% on the Last Day Test. The Enthuware developers have a sort of a running scoreboard on their site; it says that the average Standard Tests score from thousands of users is 74.8% while the actual exam score is 88%. My avscore was 77.2... so I thought I had this exam, this damned 1Z0-808 thingy in my pocket... Over 800 hours of reading, plus coding, plus cracking puzzles, plus almost 9000 lines of review notes that weren't merely copied&pasted from anywhere but were indeed my own brainchildren... Notes to myself. Remember this, remember that... "Watch out for the wrappers' constructors! they accept either underlying primitives or Strings!"... "Be on guard for trim()! StringBuilder doesn't have it!"... "switch accepts compile-time constants only!"... Stuff like that. Even earned myself the 'dry eye' syndrome because of watching too many Simon Roberts videos, so now I'm dragging my sorry derrière around wiping tears from the corner of my right eye every few seconds. Like a fool. All those efforts... down the drain...

How do you call it? this strange, hollow feeling when you know, with a cold, calm, even serene and contented certainty know that you gave everything humanly possible – and yet it wasn't enough?

Do not worry, I am about to finish. I think I know what my problem was and still is. Am going to test this hypothesis next time, around June 17. Will report both the results and my findings.

Thanks for listening.
Signing off for now.

And then, on June 26, 2016...

This is a simple follow-up on my previous post:
I finally passed (98%); now to the 1Z0-809!

There was also one more post that I placed on amazon.com as a review for *OCA: Oracle Certified Associate Java SE 8 Programmer I Study Guide. Exam 1Z0-808* by Jeanne Boyarsky & Scott Selikoff:

Six weeks ago I failed my 1Z0-808 exam at 62%. Was too naïve, cocky and self-confident to the point of arrogance – and the exam creators taught me a lesson. Which I did learn because the day before yesterday I retook the exam and passed it with the 98% score. My study kit included three tools each of which, IMO, is a must for all those who need solid, certification-grade Java skills. Here's the list:

– this study guide, which will give you every single bit of the theoretical and practical knowledge required to pass the exam with flying colors;
– a video course on preparing for the Oracle JSE exams by Simon Roberts (the very person who developed the initial concept of the questions a couple of decades ago; his video course was *the* foundation upon which I built and expanded my knowledge base further by reading this book);
– and, finally, the 1Z0-808 Test Studio by Enthuware, with its 600+ questions, which will probe, drill, grind, boil, and pig-roast you on all possible aspects and nuances. When you are done with it, you will be seeing both Java and yourself in a completely new light.

Clench your teeth, bear the pain – a lot of it is coming your way, especially if you are new to Java as I was – but stick to these three tools, and you *will* get your certification.

Unfortunately, none of these fine instruments can give you the second key to the success: they all discuss in detail purely technical matters while the way you work through and with the questions during the actual exam is equally important. At what speed should you go through the test? Since many of the questions are booby-trapped, is it advisable to second-guess yourself and attempt to re-solve the problem some other way? When you immediately see the "correct" answer, should you check every other option? Or is it better to move on to the next question right away because this way you'll save time, and it is *time* that is the most precious resource during the exam... What about 'cherry picking'? What about the 'Review Later' check-marks? Just how restrained or generous should you be with them? Is it safe to trust your gut instincts rather than do things by the book, checking and re-checking every single LOC methodically? As I found out, and at a great cost, too, some of the answers to these and many other questions are, in fact, counterintuitive and even paradoxical.

Tactics, guys, I'm talking tactics here. All those study guides, video lessons, exam simulators, and testing suits crafted by talented people are a part of your winning strategy but – sorry for sounding like Captain Obvious – it's the execution that gets the job done. If you think this psychological cr*p is something that belongs to the 70s and that you'll never have use for it, be my guest. Just go ahead, I wish you all the luck. You'll need it. As for me, I had to learn this lesson the hardest way possible, for which I am actually grateful. The initial failure forced me to scrap and then rebuild my entire approach, devise a fool-proof plan of attack, invent shorthand notations for cracking loops, diagramming the objects' lifecycle dynamics, expressing inheritance, polymorphic behavior, etc. and even to formulate dozens of concise, easy-to-remember rules all the while saturating myself with the Java code until my eyes start hurting whenever I see an erroneous snippet. No study guide that I know of, no software and no Java coders' forum teach such skills, which I find quite puzzling because they are simply indispensable. To the extent that I am going to write a small book on the whole experience[4]...

Now, if I may, a direct advice: code. Code as much and as often as you can, immediately test all your ideas or doubts while reading, listening or simply thinking about what you've been learning AND DO NOT use an IDE for the first few weeks as the very minimum. Stick to your Notepad++ instead and run everything from the CLI. This will reveal your soft spots and the typical mistakes you tend to make.

Still reading? Hmm. Well, stop then and go get this study guide by Jeanne Boyarsky and Scott Selikoff, the test suite by Enthuware and the video course by Simon Roberts. Best of luck! I actually envy you: you still have your chance to score the perfect 100% :)

You know the saying, "*Practice makes perfect?*" It isn't true. Only perfect practice makes perfect. To know syntax rules, principles of overriding and so on isn't enough; I witnessed it firsthand. You need to learn how to apply them under stress, when everything works against you.

The pages that follow contain every single trick, approach, or technique I had been using while both preparing for and taking the actual exam. I will tell you *all of it*, down to the most boring and even embarrassing detail – because tactics *is* about details.

There is one problem, though. I did sign the NDA[5] before taking the exam, so I can't possibly give you a laundry list of correct answers to the real questions; often you'll have to figure them out on your own by *inferring*: the very concept that we will meet again when working with generics and lambdas. But do not worry: I'll be at your side all along, dropping hints now and then, and generally helping as much as humanly possible – and permissible by law.

Let me show you an example right away. Why am I reusing my old posts in this section of the book? Because this approach illustrates the principle that you will – you *will*! – encounter in one of the textual questions[6] on the real exam. Can you name it, this principle? It is one of the benefits of polymorphism.

Hint: the preceding paragraph mentions the correct answer in the open. And here's another hint, which is more like a reminder: the Test Studio by Enthuware has it all. *All the answers*. You just have to dig for them a little deeper.

---

[4] This very book you are reading.

[5] Non-Disclosure Agreement; we sign these whenever we are about to sit an Oracle cert exam.

[6] Half a dozen of questions will have no code in them; they are included to test your knowledge of the most basic concepts of the object-oriented programming (OOP).

PART I
Know Your Enemy

- *Young man! Don't you know that the Department of Public Health warns about dangers of smoking?*
- *It's OK. I'm a programmer, after all.*
- *?!*
- *We spit on warnings and care about errors only.*

I.0   Toe Suckers and Guinea Pigs

O nce nailed, this certification is supposed to become our closest ally – if not a friend. Right now, however, it seems more like an uphill battle. This being said, let's start by taking a closer look at the adversary's stronghold.

As you probably remember, B&S[7] contains a brief description of the history of OCA exams and what they are for. How about using another angle to better appreciate what's in store for us?

This is what was published in the *Fix It* section of *Java Magazine*, July-August 2015 (pp.14-15):

> ([...] The purpose of this certification [1Z0-808 – *I.S.*] is to enable beginners to demonstrate their knowledge of fundamental Java concepts. The certification is designed for beginners in programming and/or those with a nonprogramming background who have basic mathematical, logical, and analytical problem-solving skills and who want to begin to learn the Java programming language; and for novice programmers and those program-mers who prefer to start learning the Java programming language at an introductory level.
>
> After successfully completing this certification, candidates can confidently utilize their knowledge on Java datatypes, operators, statements, arrays, lists, and exception-handling techniques.)
>
> Naturally, these questions have small embedded traps that spring open if you rush through without consider-ing exactly what the code is doing. [...]

Got the picture? In my eyes, it basically says the OCAJSE8 exam – with all its "small" traps – is meant for toddlers if not toe-sucking infants.

Ready? then asks the column in a silver-haired mentor's tone – and produces this (Q3, 2nd part):

```
//fix this /


        }
    }
```

And this content from Shop.java:
```
package shop;
public class OnlineCart extends Cart{
    public static void main(String[] args) {
        Cart c = new OnlineCart();
    }
}
```

Which code fragment can be inserted at `line n1` to enable the Shop class to compile?
a. `final class Cart`
b. `public class Cart`
c. `private class Cart`
d. `protected class Cart`

Solutions

Question 1. The correct java.util.List is an replaces the element at element. The add() me position in the list.

Question 2. The correct At line 4, the code create ence variable.
At line 5, e1 is another are two reference variab accessible by using both At line 6, the assignme object inaccessible throu Option A is incorrect b

---

[7] Throughout this book, B&S stands for the OCA 1Z0-808 Study Guide by Jeanne Boyarsky and Scott Selikoff. Its OCP sibling, the study guide for 1Z0-809, will be referred to as B&S809.

Take a good look at the highlighted area; hopefully, you can spot the problem right away. If not, re-read the quiz and its LOCs – unhurriedly and *subvocalizing*; this is how you should work through the code whenever you suspect it might be booby-trapped. What are the telltale signs that can arouse such a suspicion in you, how do you apply this technique in different scenarios – all this will be illustrated later; right now I am drawing your attention to something else entirely.

Alright, by now you should have it. Being `public`, **OnlineCart** class cannot possibly be declared in the file **Shop.java**, which makes all those options **a** through **d** simply irrelevant. In other words, while lying a bear trap for us toddlers, the quiz creator[8] shot herself in the foot.

Now, I'm neither saying nor implying she is insufficiently qualified; there's no doubt in my mind she is thoroughly professional: after all, her employer is Oracle Univ., and this credential alone is enough for me. But this example is as real as it gets, and by using it I mean to say that there are so many rules, nuances and subtleties to Java that even the most knowledgeable person might slip occasionally. Unfortunately for us, the exam itself is not that understanding and neither it is forgiving. Paraphrasing Forrest Gump, 1Z0-808 is like a box of chocolates: *ya never know what ya gonna get*. But twenty[9] strikes out of seventy seven, and you are done for.

The exam is delivered from a remote server; it doesn't live on the local machine. (I actually asked the exam administrator in my test center about this and she confirmed that it is so.) The machine was a peculiar looking flat-case desktop PC, deep-space black with no markings, it had a lockable CD/DVD-drive and no USB connectors on the front panel. The rear panel was well out of reach; I didn't managed to get a look at it. To be honest, I didn't even try…

The machine was connected to a small bluish box that looked like a regular Ethernet hub to me. The test room had one more computer, a twin to mine; it was also connected to the hub.

The most unusual feature of the whole setup was the monitor: it was square. Not the usual 4:3, 16:10 or 16:9 aspect ratio, no. It was 1:1. I've only seen such things twice in my entire life, and both times it was on the OCA exam.

Some test centers run their exams on Mac but in my case the OS was Windows-based; probably, some flavor of MS Windows Server because its flash screen had the Windows logo. According to my observations, the access to the exam is protected by a double-authentication protocol.

It seems that each exam is unique in the sense that the questions are most probably taken from a larger bank in a quasi-random order. The available answers (a.k.a. options) among which we have to choose the correct one(s) are shuffled each time the exam subset is being generated.

By 'quasi-random' I mean the following: it looks like[10] that the exam is made up of three major sections:

- a Core section, which contains questions that appear always, on each exam, for every candidate regardless of the date or location; in other words, these questions aren't randomly chosen from the question bank and will be present in every case;

- an Advanced section whose questions test our knowledge on a higher level of comprehension; close to Tough / Very Tough classification by Enthuware; these are the questions that are chosen randomly;

---

[8] Sushma Jagannath of Oracle University.

[9] Later I'll show you how I arrived at this number. Then again, my logic can be totally bogus. You still have your own head. (EDIT: In the mid-December, 2016, Oracle again changed the number of questions; now there are eighty of them.)

[10] The only way to ascertain this is to ask Oracle – and those guys ain't talking.

- a 'Guinea Pig' section, which is made up of the questions that Oracle tests on us. As you know after reading B&S, these questions are not graded. At all. Unfortunately, there is no way to tell if your current question is of the ungraded variety, otherwise it would mean that you can spit it in the face, kick its butt and then skip it altogether – and get away with it...

I think this general layout is more or less correct because I met core questions both times, the tough ones were different, and there were some average looking problems that I met only once. I have this feeling that the core questions make up 70 to 80% of the whole set. I can be wrong, though.

When looking up your score, you'll see a list of the objectives that you have missed; after the second sitting my list contained a single item – "Create and overload constructors; including impact on default constructors" – and since my score was 98%, it appears that a single objective is worth 2%. On the other hand, the failed attempt (62%) gave me a list with 21 items; now you know why I think that the game is over after twenty strikes.

This math, however, does not mean much because we can answer wrongly for a completely different reason that has nothing to do with the objective that we are being tested for. 'Spooked-by-a-shadow' sort of thing.

An illustration. Do you remember the **TargetAudience** example? Admittedly, that was a shamelessly contrived piece of code, but still, how many objectives does it incorporate? Let's count:

- applying access modifiers such as `public` and `protected`;
- applying non-access modifiers such as `final`;
- applying `this` keyword;
- initing[11] of fields in constructors;
- using method overloading;
- working with methods defined in some of the core Java API classes.

At least six, and if we count in `package` and `import` declarations, general class design principles, rules for valid identifiers... Too many. While the code actually tests us on the proper use of constructors, it also throws a lot of dust into our eyes.

Apparently, designing test quizzes is an art in itself, and that's precisely why Oracle has this 'Guinea Pig' section on the exam.

Let's have another illustration. The same quiz block that appeared in Java Magazine (July-Aug 2015), contained one more somewhat ambiguously formulated question. Please look it up on your own; it concerns garbage collection, which is on the list of the exam objectives, too. Try to figure out what's wrong with the wording, then refer to the **Quizzical Quiz Questions** in the *Letters to the Editor* column (p.7) in the Nov-Dec 2015 issue (External Resources).

Very well; so Oracle tests new questions on us toe suckers and guinea pigs all in one – and we don't even get credit for this – but why do they need new questions in the first place? I suspect it's a defensive mechanism against braindumps. No more on this subject you shall hear from me.

Now, back to the test rig. It may sound silly at first but I strongly advise you to take a long, hard look at the keyboard. See if it has a **Sleep / Hibernate / Power Off** key on it. Now imagine what happens when you accidentally hit it during the exam.

---

[11] Please refer to the Abbreviations and Acronyms section.

Worst case scenario: game over. Like, totally. The session with remote server has been abruptly terminated, and you're out for good. Best case scenario: the connection can be restored, and you are able to continue right from the point of premature termination.

In fact, when I asked the exam admin about this, she replied that the best case scenario is exactly what would happen. But she wasn't at all sure about the timer...

My keyboard did not have potentially suicidal keys on it. And neither did mouse[12].

Good. Now, to the battlefield, that is, the screen. As I've told you, it was square, and most of the time the picture looked pretty much like this:

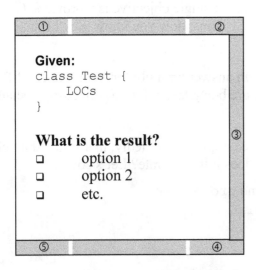

Legend:

① – Exam taker's name
    Oracle Testing ID

② – Countdown timer, 02:30:00 → 0:00:00
    ☐ 'Flag for Review' checkbox

③ – Vertical scrollbar

④ – **Review / Previous / Next** buttons

⑤ – **Help** button

It wasn't the usual, maximized window that takes up almost entire screen leaving accessible just the Taskbar; no, there was no Taskbar, not even a collapsed one – which means no Start button. As for the Ctrl+Alt+Del combo to access the Task Manager with its plethora of interesting options, I think it would have worked but I didn't try it. Neither did I hit Win+R or other hot-key combinations to see if it would be theoretically possible to gain access to the command line, PowerShell, ports, and so on. Most probably, would not have worked; too obvious.

I also think they have disabled the Clipboard; same goes for the PrintScreen key (at least that's how I would have gone about it if someone asked me to harden the exam environment against casual attacks.) Apart from taking the buffer out of the picture, they apparently took care of the selection event handler because the displayed text itself is not selectable.

Pearson Vue suggests that in order to familiarize themselves with the look and feel of the exam software, candidates should visit the following link: http://www.pearsonvue.com/demo/. To be honest, I don't think it is terribly important in our case because the 1Z0-808 GUI is quite simple and straightforward. It's up to you.

Do watch, however, 'What to expect in a Pearson VUE test center' video; it is close to what I have observed (https://home.pearsonvue.com/test-taker/security.aspx). One comment, though: they are checking now our watches. When I asked the administrator if it is because the modern wearable gizmos have built-in cameras and whatnots, she just smiled sweetly and said nothing. Draw your own conclusions.

---

[12] No, I didn't check the mouse pad – because there was none! Otherwise... ☺

Before taking the exam, you are supposed to sign some papers including the NDA and Oracle Certification Terms & Conditions; you'll see this legal stuff again, this time right on the screen. As soon as you click 'I accept', the clock starts ticking.

Now, pay close attention to what I'm saying: **this trick**[13] **alone can save you up to TEN minutes**… and oh boy, if you only knew how precious becomes time during the exam… but you'll need to be prepared to benefit from it fully.

You see, there are TWO clocks on the exam. As I've just said, the first one commences its countdown when you click 'I accept'. After that you'll have 10 minutes to calm down, get a grip of yourself, concentrate, switch to full combat mode and/or read the Instructions (like clicking Help brings up the Help screen, clicking Next forwards to the next question while clicking Previous… I think, you got the picture.) So, you can skim all this self-explanatory stuff and then do whatever takes your fancy during those 10 minutes – which should be writing down some really important things that will help you crack the questions.

Now, what are they, these 'really important things'? Do you remember the following little passage from B&S (page 363)?

> If there's a particular facet of the Java language that you have difficulty remembering, try memorizing it before the exam and write it down as soon as the exam starts.[…] For example, you may have trouble remembering the list of acceptable data types in `switch` statements. If so, we recommend you memorize that information before the exam and write it down as soon as the exam starts for use in various questions.

This is it – with one correction: NOT as soon as the exam starts but *before* it. I repeat, you'll have as much as 10 minutes to do it. But do remember: you are supposed to click Start within those 10 minutes – and only then the SECOND timer will begin its 2h30m countdown…

B&S mentions the data types for `switch`. IMO, there are two more items that you might be writing down before the actual exam: the table of modifiers and an extract from the operator precedence chart. Maybe even the list of the most 'popular' ChEs + RTEs plus five major cases when an NPE gets thrown. Again, it's up to you. Anyway, we'll talk about all these in Part 2, Exam Objectives, or *Pater Noster*.

Perhaps, the only really helpful bit of info in the Instructions is the fact that you can strike out wrong answers right on the screen. Now, B&S809 says that

> You can right-click questions to cross out answers. This lets you mark answers as incorrect as you go so that you have less to think about as you read. It also helps you remember what you've eliminated when you go back to questions.

True, true – but again, with one minor correction: to do so you'll need to keep the Ctrl key pressed. So, Ctrl+right-clicking will eliminate a particular choice. Remember me mentioning a **Sleep / Hibernate / Power Off** button? Now you know you'll may need to use the keyboard after all, so watch out.

<u>Another time-saving tip</u>: to cross out incorrect answers do NOT click on the O or □ symbols in the list of the available options, it won't work, you'll be just wasting precious seconds; click instead right on the words / code. This particular option will immediately gray out and become stricken-through. The state is persistent, so when reviewing your answers, you'll see those grayed out lines of text/code as you have left them.

---

[13] Yeah, it is a bit sneaky, I admit that much; on the other hand, they themselves say it in the open: we have prepared curved balls plus a minefield for you. So I think it's just fitting; after all, in love and war, etc…

When you finish answering the questions, a table will appear on the screen containing a list of all those questions that you have marked for Review plus, supposedly, those questions that you have forgotten to answer (or ticked off insufficient number of times, like two instead of three, etc.) I say 'supposedly', because I did not test this function. On the other hand, the Instructions did promise it. In any case, do whatever it takes but do not leave any question unanswered or answered incompletely. Make double sure of it, the penalty is just too harsh.

One more thing of equal importance. You will need to take all the precautions so as not let anything disrupt your concentration. Both B&S and B&S809 contain many really helpful, practical suggestions in this department, like dressing in layers, using earplugs and so on. All of it solid, all of it true. Here I'd like to share with you a few of my own observations:

- ❑ If the test center permits bringing in drinks, do not use caffeinated beverages: they'll most probably make you jumpy and even more thirsty (which did happen to me.) Bring in just plain water in a fully transparent plastic bottle with no markings (basically, just strip off the label).

- ❑ Have on you a couple of glucose tablets in case of hypoglycemia because of all this nervousness, otherwise you risk becoming listless.

- ❑ Watch out for uncapped markers. In all probability, you will be given a couple of felt tip pens (I've got one, blue, on the first sitting, and two, green and red, on the second.) Well, it turned out that because of all the excitement I forgot to cap my single pen – and its tip dried up. *Oops!* can write no more. So I dipped the pen into my coffee, and the trick worked. But I lost almost ten seconds – and got seriously distracted, it broke my concentration even more…

- ❑ Count the steps between the office and the test room. Sounds mysterious but tell me, can you guess why I didn't call the exam admin by waiving at the CCTV camera with my dried-up pen? Because I counted the time it took us to move from the office (where they checked my IDs and I signed all those legal papers and so on) to the test room: almost 50 seconds. Add here the time it would have taken the admin to understand the meaning of my wild grimaces, find a fresh pen and bring it in. Best case scenario – close to a couple of minutes, wouldn't you say? While I solved my silly problem in ten seconds. It didn't help pass the exam, though…

Alright, back to our little story. Well, during the first sitting I hadn't realized that I could have benefited from extra 10 minutes, so after clicking 'I accept' I spent thirty or so seconds scrolling through Instructions and then, right before clicking 'Start', I just sighed heavily and murmured 'Hit me'.

And so it did.

Entire 1Z0-808 at a glance. What does it tell you?

Chapter

I.1 Taking the Heat

I mmediately one thing became apparent – and I was utterly unprepared for it. This was of *immense* importance, but even more serious were consequences. Naturally, you may be of a completely different opinion; I am simply sharing my experience with you, that's all.

Now, what is it, this hellishly important thing? Take a deep breath, then read slowly:

THE CODE IS PRETTY-TYPED

All of it. Every frigging LOC[14]. And what are the consequences of this momentous discovery?

Since the code is properly formatted, we can stop counting curly braces… Guys! *We can stop counting those pesky things and waste time on them*!

I dunno, maybe it's just me but before the exam I took for granted that one of the possible traps could be a missing or misplaced brace. Besides, a string of them may get in the way obscuring the meaning, the clarity of code. "Get used to those horrible braces", warns the study guide by Kathy Sierra and Bert Bates referring, for example, to this curly brace parade on the same line: }}}}}. Or take B&S (p.33):

> Identifying blocks needs to be second nature for the exam. The good news is that there are lots of code examples to practice on. You can look at any code example in this book on any topic and match up braces.

But now all the initialization blocks, all the method and constructor bodies and so on can be grasped at a glance. I suspect that the Oracle cert team simply got tired of all the complaints (in a couple of days after successfully passing the exam you'll get an email asking you to participate in a survey) and finally gave in making all code pretty-typed.

I, however, couldn't believe my eyes and continued, stubbornly and stupidly, match the braces just *wasting time*. A lot of it. On the second sitting it was altogether different: I simply took them all in at a glance, just making sure that all the method bodies, initers, etc. are properly enclosed. But no counting this time! That was a *major* time saver.

Alas, this is perhaps the only piece of good news about the code being pretty-typed on the exam because when you properly format your LOCs, with most of the closing braces on fresh lines, with indentations and all, the listing becomes *lo-ong*.

Combined with the fact that the font size is rather big (I think it is around 18 points), it means that many questions – not to mention answer options! – cannot fit on a single screen thus forcing you to scroll up and down incessantly and desperately. Damn! That threw me out of synch[15] with the code, I was out of the groove – and got real nervous.

And what happens when you are nervous? Some people (me included) start second-guessing themselves. Doubt sneaks in and fogs your mind, you become tense, edgy… The vicious circle at its worst.

---

[14] This, however, I fully realized only near the end of the exam.

[15] To tell the truth, I'm fairly surprised that none of the software-based mock up exams that I'm familiar with (such as Kaplan's, Enthuware, etc.) simulate this particular feature. After all, it is harder to crack problems when you can't see *entire* code and *all* available options…

So I committed another hideous error: after checking off the option(s) I thought to be correct, I began to re-read the code looking for previously unnoticed traps. Each and every time.

That was most foolish of me. But wait, there was another deadly mistake: being full of doubts, I started marking up *too many* questions for Review…

Stop here for a sec and think what reviews are meant for. To check your answers in case you missed something, right? Like re-running calculations for nested loops, for example, just to see if you got everything correctly the first time. Or to take another look at the code for which you couldn't decide between two options, something like that[16]. And when you mark almost every other question… What would *that* mean? It would mean that you'll be practically taking the same exam once again. Still within the allotted time. Which is already running out because of multiple re-readings…

When I went through all the questions, I had only 15 minutes left, and the Review list contained some thirty items. And I didn't even remember which were the most difficult ones; those that really needed my attention…

Another psychological trap I let myself in is that I was expecting nasty tricks in every single question. The thing is, many questions don't even try to deceive you; they are straight as an arrow. Tell me, can you spot anything even remotely suspicious about this one (something to this tune *is* on the real exam):

Given in the file HiThere.java:

```
class HiThere {
    public static void main(String[] args) {
        System.out.print("Hi there" + args[0]);
    }
}
```

Which set of commands prints Hi there! in the console?

A. javac HiThere
   java HiThere !
B. javac HiThere.java
   java HiThere !
C. javac HiThere.java !
   java HiThere
D. javac HiThere.java
   java HiThere.class !

I didn't see anything out of the ordinary, either. But spent on this one a few minutes instead of few seconds stubbornly resisting to trust my own eyes and instincts. All because I was wound up for devilishly clever trickery – where there was none…

We have already covered the make up of the exam questions according to their basic functions (the 'Core', 'Advanced' and 'Guinea Pig' types). Another possible classification is based on the inclination of the question to deceive you, to run the proverbial red herring across your path. Viewed from this angle, a question can be:

- ❑ a straight arrow,
- ❑ a curved ball to throw you off balance, and
- ❑ a caltrop that is meant to cripple you.

The class **HiThere** is, obviously, of the first type. Let's have a curved ball:

---

[16] B&S mentions some other techniques that you can use during Review like applying context clues from other questions, etc.

```
List<Integer> l = new ArrayList<>();
l.add(42);
l.add(null);
for (int i = 0; i<l.size();i++) System.out.print(l.get(i));    // line 1
for (Object i : l) System.out.print(i);                         // line 2
for (int i : l) System.out.print(i);                            // line 3
```

Does the code compile? If it does, what is the result? If not, what is the reason for the comperr? And if the code throws an RTE, what is the reason for that?

The answer is this: the code does compile, both line 1 and line 2 print 42null each, and line3 prints 42 then throws an NPE because we attempt to unbox an **Integer** by implicitly calling **Integer.intValue()** on a `null` object.

Please don't be alarmed; in all probability, you will not get such a question on the exam: it is more of the OCP realm. But there are at least three questions in our OCA 1Z0-808 that relate to the behavior of `null`, which includes several scenarios – and this is your curved ball: you'll be needing to keep track of a number of things at the same time. We'll cover these scenarios when discussing NPE.

How about meeting a simple yet nasty caltrop? Here you go:

Given:

```
int a = 0;
String str = new String("Yell");
str = str.replace("Yell", "Hell");
str = str.insert(4,"o");
if ("Hello" == str && a++ == 0) str = null;
System.out.println(a);
```

What is the result?

   A.   The code prints 1
   B.   The code prints 0
   C.   Compilation fails
   D.   The code throws an exception at run time

The correct answer is C: compilation fails.

The exam knows that we got used to see **insert()** rather often – and catches us off guard[17].

And now I am going to confide to you THE mistake I made. The real one. All-embracing. The mother of all mistakes. Ready?

I didn't read the questions. Hah! how about that? Bet you didn't see it coming. Me neither :(

But fact is a fact is a fact. I did not read the textual part properly, that is, carefully. Was too anxious to get to the 'meat', the code itself. On my way home from the exam I was, naturally, thinking about the questions while writing them down from memory – and suddenly saw that a lot of times I tried to mark as correct the lines that would compile while the question must have been asking for the lines that wouldn't, and vice versa. "Ah, so that's why I couldn't get the right number of options so many times! The question asked for two but I found three… And since the GUI wouldn't allow me to checkmark so many, I relied on my blind luck and did it for only two. Both incorrect ones…"

Line from "The Rainmaker". "*You must be stupid, stupid, stupid!*"…

---

[17] **insert(**int offset, String str**)** belongs to the class **StringBuilder** rather than **String**.

After failing the first sitting, after spending weeks recalling and reconstructing the exam questions, analyzing my own behavior and realizing what I have done, a set of most simple rules formed in my mind:

- Don't jump to the code. Read – the question – first. *Force yourself to read it.*
- Give the problem your best shot at the very first pass.
- Do it unhurriedly and never let yourself re-read what you have already read carefully.
- Take the code at its face value. Not every snippet is meant to deceive you.
- No cherry picking; do the questions as they come in.
- Treat your Review marks as gold.
- Trust your gut feelings.
- Resist the temptation to redo calculations right away, leave it for the Review.

In hindsight, it all became so painfully apparent: I did not clearly think my approach through *beforehand*. Despite the fact that it is so uncomplicated… Take, for example, the 'Review marks' rule. If certain questions are too tough for you, if you are barely sure of what the code is doing, marking the problems for Review won't help much – especially when you mark too many of them: you simply won't have time to do a decent job. On the other hand, when you go through the questions like an ice-breaker, without dwelling on them too much, when you completely unleash your instincts as a coder and let them work for you… then you will have tons of time left and, therefore, stand a good chance of catching mistakes and disarming previously unnoticed traps on the Review. Not to mention gathering context clues during the initial pass…

But enough of this fountain of words, let's have hard facts. Here's the timeline for my second sitting:

Initial pass – 77 questions – 40 minutes. Yes, I did say forty. Not 2h15m like before. ("Wow… I'm sorta flying through all this like a Greek god or something…")

1st Review – a dozen of marked up questions (half of them loops, nested or otherwise) – 18 minutes. ("Damn, they were right, after all. It *is* kiddies stuff…") Swiftly found and corrected two silly mistakes.

1st *complete* Review – all 77 questions – 35 minutes. ("Day-dreaming on a golden cloud…") After recalling a puzzle in the Enthuware, changed one of the answers.

2nd complete Review – ditto – 22 minutes. ("Bo-oring…") No mistakes spotted this time.

Seeing that I still have a good half an hour left and no more interesting things to do, I decided to call it a day.

My final conclusions after two sittings:

All things considered, I must say that the most important, overarching rule that leads to success is also the simplest and most logical one:

Read the question first, then options and then code *carefully*. Subvocalize, even.

For example, take a look at this:

```
int[][] arr2D = new int[][] { { 0, 1, 2, 3 } { 4, 5 } };
```

Monospaced fonts are notoriously hard on eyes, particularly when the font size is unusually large – as it is on the actual exam. It is surprisingly easy to overlook a missing comma in the above LOC *especially* when you're tired after, say, fifty or so questions and time is already pressing because:

a) you have, most probably, marked up a good dozen of questions for Review (which means you'll need more time for them), and

b) there may be some frustratingly time-consuming loop(s) ahead…

Another important guideline: if you see more correct answers than the question asks for, and you still can't find what is wrong with the options you're ready to tick off, review <u>the most 'obvious' choice</u> extra carefully: it just may contain a trap.

Never assume that the exam creators made a mistake.[18]

I also noticed this: **weird looking, overly complex code**[19] **is most likely to be booby-trapped** on a fairly *simple concept* such as (listed in the order of prevalence):

–   out-of-scope vars;
–   invalid syntax;
–   unreachable stats.

---

[18] Unbelievable as it may sound, they do have a typo in one of their questions (which has to do with the class **LocalDate**): it lists a misspelled `DateParseExcpetion` as one of the options. I met this typo both times…

[19] Particularly involving loops or post-decrement/post-increment notation.

Chapter

I.2   Lock and load[20]

A lright, so far we've been talking about tactics and now it's time to lay out the winning strategy against 1Z0-808.
Nothing can be simpler:

- ❑ follow up on what you're learning by coding as much as you can, and
- ❑ solve as many practice question as possible.

From this point on our discussion is going to be fairly technical; we're leaving behind all this psychological stuff – but I hope that you do see now just how important it is. This being said, let us move closer to the drawing board, so to speak.

You probably remember from *Preface* that using an IDE is not advisable (for at least the first few weeks.) Running programs from the command line, however, requires a lot of typing thus tempting you to abandon the whole idea and switch back to your favorite IDE. Resist the temptation. The point is, no one expects from you highly polished typing skills. It's more about writing clean code without the help on the part of IntelliSence (in its concrete implementation, of course, such as Eclipse, NetBeans, Android Studio and so on.)

This will pay off a hundredfold when you are dealing with the questions that rely on the interaction between and among the data types located in different packages. This approach – writing code in Notepad++[21] and then running it from the CLI – truly helps master access modifiers and imports, not to mention learning to be on alert for your most typical mistakes.

In order to save time on typing commands in the console, I invite you to try out my solution of how to teach the machine to run a **.java** file by right-clicking it in the Windows Explorer.

The solution requires two steps: 1) hacking the Windows Registry, and 2) writing a launcher, which is even easier than it sounds.

Step 1: Hacking Registry

Add the following key to your Registry: **HKEY_CLASSES_ROOT*\\shell\\Run with Java** and then specify its command (default value): **C:\\JC\\RWJ.bat %1**

The easiest way to do it is to create a plain ASCII file (let's call it **RWJ.reg**) and fill it with the following code (also downloadable from External Resources):

```
Windows Registry Editor Version 5.00
[HKEY_CLASSES_ROOT\*\shell\Run with Java]
[HKEY_CLASSES_ROOT\*\shell\Run with Java\command]
@="C:\\JC\\RWJ.bat %1"
```

Double-clicking **RWJ.reg** will import the keys into the Registry.

---

[20] Most people nowadays associate this immortal phrase with John Wayne whose nickname was Duke. Our exam also has a question with a Duke in it. And just as the heroes John Wayne portrayed, the question is honest and straightforward, without any traps.

[21] Or JEdit, etc.

Step 2: Writing a Launcher

In the **C:\JC**[22] folder create a text file[23] named **RWJ.bat** and fill it with the code from **Appendix B** (or jump to External Resources for a download link.) Below is the same code but with line numbers in it because we'll be needing them for the discussion that follows.

```
 1 echo off
 2 rem ********************************************************************************
 3 rem *              RWJ.bat: Compiles Java classes and launches JVM                *
 4 rem *                 Coded by Igor Soudakevitch; www.igor.host                   *
 5 rem *              Distributed under the terms and conditions of the GPL          *
 6 rem ********************************************************************************
 7 rem ver.0.18 / Jan.24, 2016 /
 8
 9 rem ----------------- Just a reminder: javac & JVM invocation ---------------------
10 rem      javac -encoding UTF-8 -d C:\Garbage\classes org\xlator\_main_class_.java
11 rem      java -cp C:\Garbage\classes org.xlator._main_class_
12
13 rem Resulting cp dir structure: C:\Garbage\classes\org\xlator
14
15 rem Suppose we've got RunMe.java with a reference to ClassA, which is defined in
16 rem ClassA.java located in the same dir. Both classes belong to the same package
17 rem org.xlator, and are located in the _whatever_dir_\org\xlator.
18 rem In this case run from _whatever_dir_:
19 rem              javac .\org\xlator\RunMe.java     where .\ is actually redundant
20 rem              java org.xlator.RunMe
21
22 rem Source files should be UTF-8 encoded to correctly support Unicode output
23 rem ----------------- End of introductory comments --------------------------------
24
25
26 rem      This is THE ONLY place to mutate settings; refer to 'RULES' below
27
28                 set args=1234 1Z0-808 5678
29                 set packaged=ON
30                 set javac_d_switch_cp=C:\Garbage\classes
31                 set package_name=org.xlator
32                 set pack_root_dir=C:\Try_Java
33                 set dos_pack_path=org\xlator
34
35                 set added_path1=tempa
36                 set added_path2=tempb
37                 set all_added=.\%added_path1%;.\%added_path2%
38
39                 set enc=-encoding UTF-8
40 rem             set enc=
41                 set enc_type=UTF-8
42 rem             set enc_type=
43 rem             set Xlint=
44                 set Xlint=-Xlint:unchecked
45                 set warn=
46 rem             set warn=-nowarn
47 rem             set Xdiags=
48                 set Xdiags=-Xdiags:verbose
49                 set add_cp=;%CLASSPATH%
50 rem             set add_cp=
51                 set removal=ON
52 rem             set removal=NO
53
```

---

[22] Naturally, the folder's name can be entirely different; just take good care of the command line in Registry.

[23] Preferably, in the 'ANSI as UTF-8' encoding (a.k.a. 'UTF-8 without BOM') but, strictly speaking, it is not necessary unless you are planning to use charset encodings other than plain ANSI.

```
54 rem                              RULES:
55 rem     Added paths must be present BELOW %pack_root_dir%, e.g.:
56 rem     C:\
57 rem     |--- .........
58 rem     |--- Try_Java
59 rem     |       |
60 rem     |       |--- org
61 rem     |       |      |--- xlator
62 rem     |       |
63 rem     |       |--- tempa
64 rem     |       |--- tempb
65 rem     |--- .........
66
67 rem --- 'packaged' var defines whether the source files contain the package statements
68
69 rem --- If packaged==NO then classes will be compiled and run according to
70 rem --- the 'simple_process' section (i.e., within the current dir)
71
72 rem --- If packaged==YES then the compiled classes will be placed inside
73 rem --- the javac_d_switch_cp dir that is to be used with -d switch (ref.to javac -help)
74
75 if "%enc%" == "" (
76         set enc_flag=OFF
77         ) ELSE (
78         set enc_flag=ON
79         )
80 if "%add_cp%" == "" (
81         set add_cp_flag=OFF
82         ) ELSE (
83         set add_cp_flag=ON
84         )
85 if "%warn%" == "" (
86         set warn_flag=ON
87         ) ELSE (
88         set warn_flag=OFF
89         )
90 if "%Xlint%" == "" (
91         set Xlint_flag=OFF
92         ) ELSE (
93         set Xlint_flag=ON
94         )
95 if "%Xdiags%" == "" (
96         set Xdiags_flag=OFF
97         ) ELSE (
98         set Xdiags_flag=ON
99         )
100 if "%packaged%" == "ON" (
101         goto packaged_process
102         ) ELSE (
103         goto simple_process
104         )
106 :simple_process
107 echo.
108 echo.
109 echo --------------------------- FYI -----------------------------------
110 echo.
111 echo     args                        : %args%
112 echo     main class package          : void
113 echo     package path                : void
114 echo     referenced class package(s) : void
115 echo     javac -d switch classpath   : void
116 echo     appended CLASSPATH env var  : void
117 echo     forced encoding             : %enc_flag% (%enc_type%)
118 echo     -Xlint:unchecked            : %Xlint_flag%
119 echo     -Xdiags:verbose             : %Xdiags_flag%
120 echo     warnings                    : %warn_flag%
121 echo     *.class removal             : %removal%
122 echo.
123 echo ------------------- End of batch file messages -----------------------
124 echo.
125 echo.
126 echo.
127 javac %enc% %Xlint% %Xdiags% %1
```

```
128 java -cp . %~n1
129 echo.
130 echo **********************************************************************
131 echo *   all classes in the current dir(s) will be removed now; hit ^^C to abort   *
132 echo **********************************************************************
133 echo.
134 if "%removal%" == "ON" del *.class
135 pause
136 exit
138 :packaged_process
139 cls
140
141 rem    The following 'if' checks whether the specified dir exists
142 rem    because a special file named 'nul' is present in every dir.
143 rem    And one more thing: the 'exist' test only checks for *files*;
144 rem    that's precisely why we have to use \nul
145
146 if exist %javac_d_switch_cp%\nul goto get_to_it
147     echo *
148     echo *
149     echo *********************************************************
150     echo *           Packaged mode is ON but
151     echo *              %javac_d_switch_cp% dir doesn't exist
152     echo *********************************************************
153     echo *
154     echo *
155     set /p answer=Do you want to create it now (Y/N)?
156     if /i "%answer:~,1%" EQU "Y" goto create_dir
157     if /i "%answer:~,1%" EQU "N" goto exiting
158
159 :create_dir
160 md %javac_d_switch_cp%
161 echo.
162 echo.
163 if not errorlevel 1 (
164         echo %javac_d_switch_cp% dir created successfully.
165         ) ELSE (
166         echo Couldn't create %javac_d_switch_cp% dir!
167         echo.
168         echo.
169         pause
170         exit
171 )
172 goto get_to_it
173
174 :exiting
175 echo.
176 echo.
177 echo I ain't got nothing to do then. Bye.
178 echo.
179 echo.
180 pause
181 rem   to set errorlevel, use '\b' switch on exit, like this:   exit \b
182 exit
183
184 :get_to_it
185 echo.
186 echo.
187 echo ----------------------------- FYI -----------------------------------
188 echo.
189 echo     args                          :    %args%
190 echo     main class package            :    %package_name%
191 echo     package path                  :    %pack_root_dir%\%dos_pack_path%
192 echo     referenced class package(s)   :    %pack_root_dir%\%added_path1%;%pack_root_dir%\%added_path2%
193 echo     javac -d switch classpath     :    %javac_d_switch_cp%\%dos_pack_path%
194 echo     appended CLASSPATH env var    :    %add_cp_flag%
195 echo     forced encoding               :    %enc_flag% (%enc_type%)
196 echo     -Xlint:unchecked              :    %Xlint_flag%
197 echo     -Xdiags:verbose               :    %Xdiags_flag%
198 echo     warnings                      :    %warn_flag%
199 echo     *.class removal               :    %removal%
200 echo.
201 echo -------------------- End of batch file messages ----------------------
```

```
202 echo.
203 echo.
204 echo.
205 cd %pack_root_dir%
206 javac %enc% -cp %all_added%%add_cp% -d %javac_d_switch_cp% %Xlint% %Xdiags% %1
207 java -cp %javac_d_switch_cp%%add_cp% %package_name%.%~n1 %args%
208 echo.
209 echo **************************** CLEANING UP *****************************
210 echo *   all classes in -d cp dir(s) will be removed now; hit ^^C to abort   *
211 echo *********************************************************************
212 echo.
213 pause
214 if "%removal%" == "ON" (
215 del %javac_d_switch_cp%\%dos_pack_path%\*.class
216    if exist %javac_d_switch_cp%\%added_path1%\*.class del %javac_d_switch_cp%\%added_path1%\*.class
217    if exist %javac_d_switch_cp%\%added_path2%\*.class del %javac_d_switch_cp%\%added_path2%\*.class
218 )
```

Now let's run a test and see how the whole idea works:

1) Create the folder **C:\Try_Java** with three more subfolders in it:

> **org**
> **tempa**
> **tempb**

2) In the subfolder **org** create one more subfolder named **xlator**; the final result should resemble this tree:

```
56 rem     C:\
57 rem     |--- ..........
58 rem     |--- Try_Java
59 rem     |       |
60 rem     |       |--- org
61 rem     |       |     |--- xlator
62 rem     |       |
63 rem     |       |--- tempa
64 rem     |       |--- tempb
65 rem     |--- ..........
```

3) Go to **C:\Try_Java\org\xlator** and create **HelloWorld.java** there with the help of Notepad++, etc. Use the 'ANSI as UTF-8' encoding. If you absolutely sure that your Java classes do not output Unicode characters, you can flip `rems` to comment out lines 39 and 41 instead of lines 40 and 42. This will disable the forced encoding switch of the Java compiler. By default, the forced encoding is ON because lines 39 and 41 are uncommented:

```
39              set enc=-encoding UTF-8
40 rem          set enc=
41              set enc_type=UTF-8
42 rem          set enc_type=
```

4) Fill **HelloWorld.java** with any valid Java code you want. Just make sure of two things:
   - the file starts with valid `package` declaration;
   - even if the class isn't `public`, its name and the **.java** file's name must be the same.

It is possible to dispense with the `package` declaration altogether and compile and then run the **.java** file right from inside the folder the source file lives in. This practice is not recommended, though, because, after all, we must learn how to work with several packages at once.

By default, the package declaration is `package org.xlator;` (which reflects one of my websites' URL); naturally, you can be using something else; simply search and replace all instances of `org` and `xlator` in **RWJ.bat** with whatever you need; right now, however, I suggest you use the following code just to test the launcher and see how it works on your machine:

```
package org.xlator;
public class HelloWorld{
    public static void main(String[] args) {
        System.out.println("Hello, hello...");
    }
}
```

5) Right-click **HelloWorld.java** in the Windows Explorer to open the context menu and select 'Run with Java' option.

6) **RWJ.bat** will launch `javac` and then JVM so you are going to see something close to this:

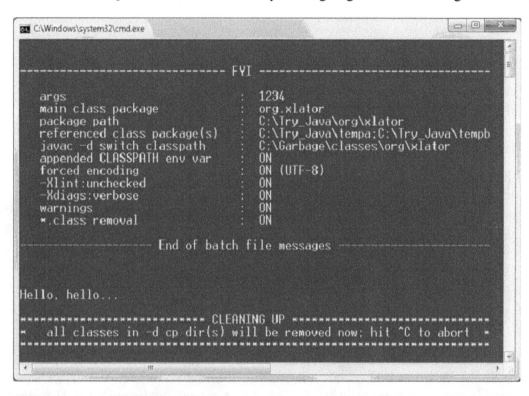

Basically, this is it. The rest of the discussion concerns simple details like what and how should be changed to accommodate your particular needs.

First of all, let's strip the launcher down to the most basic code possible and take a look at its beating heart. Here it is:

```
javac %1
java %~n1
```

Yes, it's that simple: first we pass our **.java** file to `javac` by invoking `javac %1` and then we pass the class name to JVM. This trick, however, works **only if** the class name is exactly the same as the filename without the extension – which is removed with the help of ~n switch.[24]

Let me repeat; this is important. The above requirement – the class name must be exactly the same as the filename without the extension – **has nothing to do with** the JLS rule on naming files that contain a `public` class. It is there because of the ~n switch, that's all[25].

---

[24] So if you don't like **RWJ.bat** – maybe it's too limited by your standards – now you can build your own launcher.

[25] I am saying it just in case: the switch ~n is passed to cmd rather than to `java`; it is called a 'CMD variable edit'; you can read more on this fascinating stuff in *Windows XP Under the Hood: Hardcore Windows Scripting and Command Line Power* by Brian Knittel.

Here's an illustration. Rename **HelloWorld.java** to **Brass.java**, then change the class name to **Brass**; you can also make it package-`private` (leave the package declaration in place, though):

```
package org.xlator;
class Brass{
    public static void main(String[] args) {
        System.out.println("Hello, hello..."); }
}
```

Run **Brass.java** by right-clicking it. Works fine, right? Now change class name to **Glass** and run the file. *Oops!* "Error: could not find or load main class org.xlator.Brass". Rename the class **Glass** back to **Brass**, and it will work again.

Now let's address the execution flow. Depending on whether the package declaration is present, the flow forks on line 100 by checking the `packaged` flag declared on line 29:

```
 29         set packaged=ON

100 if "%packaged%" == "ON" (
101        goto packaged_process
102        ) ELSE (
103        goto simple_process
104        )
```

We are going to leave out the `simple_process` section (which is reserved for **.java** files without the package declaration in them; naturally, in this case you'll also need to flip the `packaged` flag) and concentrate instead our attention on the generalized case, which is represented by the `packaged_process` section.

Once the `packaged_process` section has been entered on line 138, the code on line 146 checks if the directory specified on line 30 for the `javac -d` switch exists:

```
 30          set javac_d_switch_cp=C:\Garbage\classes

138 :packaged_process
146 if exist %javac_d_switch_cp%\nul goto get_to_it
```

The `javac -d` switch defines where the compiler should place the compiled classes. In all probability, your machine doesn't have the **C:\Garbage\classes** directory, so – after asking your permission, of course (lines 147 through 157) – this directory will be created for you by running lines 159 through 172:

```
147    echo *
148    echo *
149    echo ********************************************************
150    echo *         Packaged mode is ON but
151    echo *         %javac_d_switch_cp% dir doesn't exist
152    echo ********************************************************
153    echo *
154    echo *
155    set /p answer=Do you want to create it now (Y/N)?
156    if /i "%answer:~,1%" EQU "Y" goto create_dir
157    if /i "%answer:~,1%" EQU "N" goto exiting
158
159 :create_dir
160 md %javac_d_switch_cp%
161 echo.
162 echo.
163 if not errorlevel 1 (
164        echo %javac_d_switch_cp% dir created successfully.
165        ) ELSE (
166        echo Uh-huh! Couldn't create %javac_d_switch_cp% dir!
167        echo.
168        echo.
169        pause
170        exit
171 )
172 goto get_to_it
```

If you decide against creating **C:\Garbage\classes** directory, the execution terminates by falling through into the `exiting` section on line 174:

```
174 :exiting
175 echo.
176 echo.
177 echo I ain't got nothing to do then. Bye.
178 echo.
179 echo.
180 pause
181 rem   to set errorlevel, use '\b' switch on exit, like this:   exit \b
182 exit
```

The real job is done in the section `get_to_it`, which starts on line 184. The batch file first prints out supplementary info like what arguments will be passed to JVM, what is the package name of the class that contains the entry point, and so on (lines 187 through 201):

```
184 :get_to_it
185 echo.
186 echo.
187 echo --------------------------- FYI ----------------------------------
188 echo.
189 echo    args                      :  %args%
190 echo    main class package        :  %package_name%
191 echo    package path              :  %pack_root_dir%\%dos_pack_path%
192 echo    referenced class package(s) : %pack_root_dir%\%added_path1%;%pack_root_dir%\%added_path2%
193 echo    javac -d switch classpath  :  %javac_d_switch_cp%\%dos_pack_path%
194 echo    appended CLASSPATH env var :  %add_cp_flag%
195 echo    forced encoding           :  %enc_flag% (%enc_type%)
196 echo    -Xlint:unchecked          :  %Xlint_flag%
197 echo    -Xdiags:verbose           :  %Xdiags_flag%
198 echo    warnings                  :  %warn_flag%
199 echo    *.class removal           :  %removal%
200 echo.
201 echo -------------------- End of batch file messages ----------------------
```

Then we enter (line 205) the package directory from where we invoke first the compiler (line 206) followed by passing the main class to JVM on line 207. If the program runs successfully, we'll be given a chance to retain the compiled classes in place, otherwise they will be deleted (lines 214 – 218). The `pause` statement on line 213 is indispensable as it allows us to see compiler messages, our program's output, a stack trace, etc. If you want to keep the compiled classes, press **^C** at this point; if not, hit **Space**.

```
202 echo.
203 echo.
204 echo.
205 cd %pack_root_dir%
206 javac %enc% -cp %all_added%%add_cp% -d %javac_d_switch_cp% %Xlint% %Xdiags% %1
207 java -cp %javac_d_switch_cp%%add_cp% %package_name%.%~n1 %args%
208 echo.
209 echo *************************** CLEANING UP ***************************
210 echo *   all classes in -d cp dir(s) will be removed now; hit ^^C to abort  *
211 echo ******************************************************************
212 echo.
213 pause
214 if "%removal%" == "ON" (
215 del %javac_d_switch_cp%\%dos_pack_path%\*.class
216 if exist %javac_d_switch_cp%\%added_path1%\*.class del %javac_d_switch_cp%\%added_path1%\*.class
217 if exist %javac_d_switch_cp%\%added_path2%\*.class del %javac_d_switch_cp%\%added_path2%\*.class
218 )
```

Right now **RWJ.bat** lets us work with three different packages: our main class lives in `org.xlator`, two more packages are **tempa** and **tempb**. This packaged structure is reflected in the **C:\Try_Java** directory's file structure.

Why *three* packages and not four or even more? It's because study guides and question banks rarely use four; besides, it seems that the real exam never uses more than three (at least I met only three; yes, in both sittings.)

Other switches like `Xlint` or `Xdiags` you can look up on your own[26], and as for flags, here is a brief description:

```
28              set args=1234 1Z0-808 5678      ← args for psvm's String[] array
29              set packaged=ON                  ← is ON when .java file has package declaration
30              set javac_d_switch_cp=C:\Garbage\classes   ← dir to store classes
31              set package_name=org.xlator      ← main class's package
32              set pack_root_dir=C:\Try_Java     ← dir we compile & run from
33              set dos_pack_path=org\xlator     ← path to package in DOS notation
34
35              set added_path1=tempa            ← second package
36              set added_path2=tempb            ← third package
37              set all_added=.\%added_path1%;.\%added_path2%   ← path to 2nd & 3rd pckgs
38
39              set enc=-encoding UTF-8          ← .java file encoding (if encoding is ON)
40  rem         set enc=                         ← void if no encoding needed
41              set enc_type=UTF-8               ← encoding type (if encoding is ON)
42  rem         set enc_type=                    ← void if no encoding needed
43  rem         set Xlint=
44              set Xlint=-Xlint:unchecked       ← enables recommended warnings
45              set warn=                        ← warnings are ON
46  rem         set warn=-nowarn                 ← won't generate warnings
47  rem         set Xdiags=
48              set Xdiags=-Xdiags:verbose       ← verbose diag messages
49              set add_cp=;%CLASSPATH%          ← compiler uses CLASSPATH environment var
50  rem         set add_cp=        ← void if compiler doesn't look into CLASSPATH[27]
51              set removal=ON     ← compiled classes will be deleted after termination
52  rem         set removal=NO     ← compiled classes will be left in javac_d_switch_cp dir
```

Alright, let's have another example, this time with three packages and command line arguments – and then we really should move on, to the essential and much more interesting things.

1)   Create three **.java** files and fill them with the following pieces of code:

In file **ClassA.java** (to be located in **C:\Try_Java\tempa**):

```
package tempa;
public class ClassA{
    public String name;
    public ClassA(){
        name = this.getClass().getSimpleName();
    }
    public ClassA(String name) {
        this.name = name;
    }
}
```

In file **ClassB.java** (to be located in **C:\Try_Java\tempb**):

```
package tempb;
import tempa.*;

public class ClassB extends ClassA{
    public ClassB(String name){
        super(name);
    }
}
```

---

[26] For example, here: http://docs.oracle.com/javase/7/docs/technotes/tools/solaris/javac.html#nonstandard
[27] Control Panel ► System ► Advanced System Settings ► System Properties ► Advanced ► Environment Variables

In file **MyClass.java** (to be located in **C:\Try_Java\org\xlator**):

```
package org.xlator;
import tempa.*;
import tempb.*;

class MyClass {
    public static void main(String[] args) {
        ClassA ca = new ClassA();
        ClassB cb = new ClassB("ClassB");
        System.out.println(ca.name + ", " + cb.name + ", " + args[1]);
    }
}
```

2) Make double sure that line 28 in **RWJ.bat** contains *at least* two command line args, e.g.:

```
28      set args=1234 1Z0-808 5678
```

3) Run **MyClass.java** by right-clicking it and selecting 'Run with Java'[28]:

```
C:\Windows\system32\cmd.exe

------------------------------- FYI -------------------------------
    args                           :  1234 1Z0-808 5678
    main class package             :  org.xlator
    package path                   :  C:\Try_Java\org\xlator
    referenced class package(s)    :  C:\Try_Java\tempa;C:\Try_Java\tempb
    javac -d switch classpath      :  C:\Garbage\classes\org\xlator
    appended CLASSPATH env var      :  ON
    forced encoding                :  ON (UTF-8)
    -Xlint:unchecked               :  ON
    -Xdiags:verbose                :  ON
    warnings                       :  ON
    *.class removal                :  ON
------------------- End of batch file messages -------------------



ClassA, ClassB, 1Z0-808

************************* CLEANING UP *************************
*  all classes in -d cp dir(s) will be removed now; hit ^C to abort  *
********************************************************************
```

As we can see, **RWJ.bat** works and, apart from the practice test software and study guides mentioned in *Preface*, this is basically all you'll ever need to get prepped for the 1Z0-808 exam.

Final Remarks on Dilemma '2IDE | !2IDE'

We will still use an IDE occasionally in order to, say, look into the source code for the core Java classes (refer, for example, to the discussion of Problem 1.15).

---

[28] At this point I'd recommend to hit ^C and peek into the **C:\Garbage\classes** folder to see how the compiler places compiled classes. Besides, we'll need a **.class** file for a decompilation exercise in a few minutes.

What's more, an IDE such as NetBeans may allow to run uncompilable code by clicking the "Run Anyway" button in the error notification dialog. Let's take a brief look at this interesting feature. What follows is a snapshot of a most simple class in the NetBeans environment:

```
 1      package garbage;
 2
 Q  ⊞   import  ...27 lines    variable str not initialized in the default constructor
30                             ----
31      class Test {           (Alt-Enter shows hints)
 ●          final String str;
33  ⊟      public static void main(String[] args){
34              System.out.println("Hi there!");
35          }
36      }
```

As we can see, the code is clearly uncompilable (BTW, there *is* a question on the exam that will test you on the mandatory initing of `final` fields) and, therefore, won't run from inside the CLI. After asking the IDE to run it anyway, we'll see the code producing "Hi there!" in the console… Amazing. How is it ever possible?

Whenever Java code runs, it means there's a **.class** file for it, so let's decompile the bytecode[29]:

```
/*
 * Decompiled with CFR 0_117.
 */
package garbage;
import java.io.PrintStream;
class Test {
    final String str;
    Test() {
        throw new RuntimeException("Uncompilable source code - variable str not
                                    initialized in the default constructor");
    }
    public static void main(String[] args) {
        System.out.println("Hi there!");
    }
}
```

There! NetBeans simply added a no-arg constructor with a `throw` clause in it. Naturally, this is not always possible; for example, as soon as we make the var **str** `static`, the trick stops working. To make it work again, we'll have to explicitly define a no-arg ctor:

```
class Test {
    final static String str;
    Test(){}        // comperr on this line: var str might not have been inited
    public static void main(String[] args){
        System.out.println("Hi there!");
    }
}
```

Only after that the IDE will be able to insert the `throw` clause to make the code compilable. The decompiled class will look exactly as the previous case except for the variable **str**: it will be declared `final static` and not just `final`.

---

[29] This is a very simple case so the Class File Reader by Lee Benfield (http://www.benf.org/other/cfr/) will suffice.

External Resources

The two issues of *Java Magazine* that were mentioned in the text + **RWJ.bat**, **RWJ.reg**, the lambda-related **Filter.java** and all practice questions to Chapters II.1 through II.9 can be downloaded here: www.igor.host\nailing1z0-808\Nailing_1Z0-808_Resources.zip.

You may want to visit www.igor.host to take a look at the Errata list, write a comment, etc.

PART II
Exam Objectives, or *Pater Noster*

We gonna be rich! Daddy says he's got entire Java inheritance practically in his pocket!

Chapter
II.0   Opening Remarks

This part is arguably the most important section of the book – and it is also the longest – as it deals with virtually every rule from the JLS and javadocs for the core Java classes[30] you will be applying during the exam.

These rules cover practically all questions that belong to the Core section, and that's why this part is called *Pater Noster*: you need to know it by heart. Yes, you do; at least the Core Rules. As for the Extra Rules, they concern more advanced subjects, which are less likely to appear on the actual 1Z0-808 yet provide more insight into the Exam Objectives.

The Rules are listed according to the official **Oracle 1Z0-808 Exam Topics**[31] (nine categories of 42 topics in total.)

Apart from the Core Rules, you should memorize (and maybe even write down within the additional 10 minutes right before the actual exam) a couple of tables:

Table 1   Java Access Modifiers (extract)

Modifier	Classes	Interfaces	Constructors	Methods	Data Members
Access modifiers					
package-private	✔	✔	✔	✔	✔
private	✘	✘	✔	✔	✔
protected	✘	✘	✔	✔	✔
public	✔	✔	✔	✔	✔
Other modifiers					
abstract	✔	✔	✘	✔	✘
final	✔	✘	✘	✔	✔
static	✘	✘	✘	✔	✔

Table 1 does not list all the modifiers that are available in Java; it is limited to those that are within the scope of the official Oracle 1Z0-808 Exam Topics. A checkmark means that this particular data type or class/interface member[32] accepts this particular modifier.

To memorize the table, we can use mnemonics, visual patterns or just good old logic. Since we spare no efforts in preparation, let's have all of it[33]:

---

[30] Within the scope of OCAJP8 objectives, of course, since Java 1.8 API contains 4240 classes in 217 packages, and we cannot be reasonalbly expected to master them all.

[31] http://education.oracle.com/pls/web_prod-plq-dad/db_pages.getpage?page_id=5001&get_params=p_exam_id:1Z0-808

[32] Incidentally, constructors are *not* class members (JLS, §8.2, *Class Members*).

[33] The stranger the association, the better the mental hooks and anchors; some parallels might sound silly but this is the whole point... You may want to experiment with your own mnemonic formulas, the ones that work best for *you*.

- take a closer look at the leftmost column and you'll see that modifiers are listed *alphabetically*[34] within their groups (pa-pri-pro-pu & a-f-s) – and the groups are also given alphabetically (A followed by O);

- now examine the title row: as classes are the root of all evil in 1Z0-808, we start with them…

- … and continue with the behavior-defining interfaces…

- … which are followed – in the order of importance from the class design point of view – by constructors who have the final say in the state of objects…

- …then we have methods who just love to be overridden and overloaded…

- …and lastly, there is an assorted bunch of mischievous – although sometimes primitive – data members, a.k.a. variables;

- the right-hand part of the title row forms something close to 'Cl_I_C (click) Me, Data' (not to mention CIC for 'kick'), which, of course, is *the* way to greet our fellow Java coders who happen to be Star Trek fans;

- when tabled as pictured, the crossmarks form three distinct areas:

  ❑ a Lone Star on the right, which reminds us that – if the spaghetti westerns are to be believed – neither a sheriff in Texas nor a variable in Java can be abstract; they are always painfully real;

  ❑ a square island of four crosses, the burial ground for those top-level classes and interfaces who foolishly believed they were private and even protected citizens. Basically, the whole upper part of the table says that we are free to use whatever access modifier we want EXCEPT for the classes or interfaces of the upper crust; how sad: despite all their importance they can afford neither complete privacy nor protection…

  ❑ and a triangle (The Ramp of Doom? as for Biblical allusions, I leave them to you) of six crosses, which rests on the bottom line of the table; the easiest way to memorize it is probably by its visual pattern.

Then again, it's only natural that a top-level class cannot be `static` as a static entity is something that belongs to a class[35]; for example, we access static members by appending the dot operator to their data type names… Following this line of reasoning, we arrive at the conclusion that inner classes and interfaces can be `static` – and indeed they can!

Interfaces cannot be `final` because this would strip them of their ultimate *raison d'être* for what good is an interface if no one can extend or implement it?

As for the constructors, they are rather sneaky in following both static and non-static semantics (on the one hand, we can't call them on an instance, they are neither overridable nor inheritable, which resembles static methods, while on the other hand, their bodies can contain, for example, `this`, which implies a non-static concept…)

Since constructors aren't inherited, there is no way to implement an abstract constructor.

A constructor is always invoked in respect to an object, and since a static member *must* be accessible even in the absence of any object of this particular data type, there can be no constructors without objects, hence no static constructors may exist.

---

[34] Or lexicographically, if you want to split hairs.

[35] Did you notice that the compiler sometimes calls an interface a class? Declare a public interface in a wrongly named file (like `public interface I{}` in the file **File.java**) and observe this error: "class I is public, should be declared in a file named I.java".

Finally, no constructor can be `final` (no pun intended) because it "…is not inherited, so there is no need to declare it `final`" (JLS, §8.8.3).

One last thing – which, unfortunately, is not apparent from the table – concerns local variables: the only modifier that is allowed inside methods, constructors or initers is `final`. You *will* have a question on the exam that tests you on this particular subject.

– If you digest information better through code than words, here's the same table:

(in file I6.java)

```
interface I1 {}
// private interface I2 { }          // top-level, hence INVALID
// protected interface I3 { }        // top-level, hence INVALID
// final interface I4 { }            // INVALID
// static interface I5 {}            // INVALID
public interface I6 { }
abstract interface I7 { }            // abstract keyword is redundant
```

(in file C6.java)

```
class C1 { }
// private class C2 { }              // top-level, hence INVALID
// protected class C3 { }            // top-level, hence INVALID
final class C4 { }
abstract class C5 { abstract void run5(); }

public class C6 {
    int a;
    private int b;
    protected int c;
    public int d;
    static int e;
    final int f = 0;
    // abstract int g;               // INVALID
    private class C7 { }             //
    protected class C8 { }           // all six are VALID
    static class C9 { }              // but inner classes and interfaces
    private interface I8 { }         // are not on the 1Z0-808 exam
    protected interface I9 { }       //
    static interface I10 { }         //
    // final interface I11 { }       // INVALID
    C6(){ }
    private C6(int a){ }
    protected C6(int a, int b){ }
    public C6(int a, int b, int c){ }
    // abstract C6(){ }              // INVALID
    // final C6(){ }                 // INVALID
    // static C6(){ }                // INVALID

    void run1(){
        int a;
        final int f;
        // private int b;            // INVALID
        // protected int c;          // INVALID
        // public int d;             // INVALID
        // static int e;             // INVALID
        // abstract int h;           // INVALID
    }

    private void run2(){ }
    protected void run3(){ }
    public void run4(){ }
}
```

The pattern on the right is probably the easiest way to memorize and quickly write down the whole table for the exam.

The second table, which concerns the priority of operators, is harder by far to master; luckily for us, we'll be needing only a part of it for the exam:

	C	I	C	M	D
pa					
pri	✖	✖			
pro	✖	✖			
pu					
a				✖	✖
f		✖	✖		
s	✖	✖	✖		

Table 2.1 Priority of Operators (full form)

Priority	Operator	Operation	Associativity[36]
1	[ ]	array index	left to right
	( )	method call	
	.	member access	
2	++	postfix or prefix increment	right to left
	--	postfix or prefix decrement	
	+ -	unary plus, unary minus	
	~	bitwise complement (bitwise **NOT**)	
	!	boolean **NOT** (inverter)	
	(type)	type cast	
	new	class instantiation (object creation)	
3	* / %	multiplication, division, remainder	left to right
4	+ -	addition, subtraction	left to right
	+	string concatenation	
5	<<	signed bit shift left	left to right
	>>	signed bit shift right	
	>>>	unsigned bit shift right	
6	< <=	less than, less than or equal to	left to right
	> >=	greater than, greater than or equal to	
	instanceof	reference test	
7	==	equal to	left to right
	!=	not equal to	
8	&	bitwise **AND**	left to right
	&	boolean **AND** (conjoiner)	
	^	bitwise **XOR**	
	^	boolean **XOR** (exclusive disjoiner)	
	|	bitwise **OR**	
	|	boolean **OR** (inclusive disjoiner)	
9	&&	boolean **AND** (conditional-**AND**)	left to right
	||	boolean **OR** (conditional-**OR**)	
10	? :	ternary conditional	right to left
11	=	simple assignment	right to left
	*= /= += -= %= <<= >>= >>>= &= ^= |=	compound assignment (operation and assignment)	
12	->	lambda token	left to right

---

[36] Determines how ops of the same precedence are grouped in the absence of parentheses. Consider, for example, int a=3-2-1; this might produce either 0 (if evaluated from left to right) or 2 (right to left). The answer is 0.

Aside from the basic arithmetic rules (*/ *vs.* +–), the most important points to remember for the exam are these:

❏ postfix / prefix increment / decrement operators are of the top priority;
❏ all arithmetic ops including comparison come before equality testing;
❏ assignment, including its compound forms, is of the lowest priority.

Now let's have only the part that is really needed for the exam (I don't remember meeting either `instanceof` or the comparison operators or XOR but who knows what your particular set of questions will contain…):

Table 2.2 Priority of Operators (extract to memorize for the exam)

Priority	Operator	Operation
↑	`[ ]( ).`	array index – method call – member access
↑	`++ -- ! (type) new`	post/prefix incr/decr – **NOT** – cast – instantiation
↑	`* / %`	multiplication, division, 'remainder'
↑	`+ -`	addition, subtraction – string concatenation
↑	`< <= > >= instanceof`	comparison ops – reference test
↑	`== !=`	equality
↑	`& ^ |`	**AND – XOR – OR**
↑	`&& ||`	short-circuiting **AND – OR**
↑	`? :`	ternary conditional
↑	`= *= /= += -= %= ...`	assignment in all its forms

As for the data types that are acceptable by `switch`, or a list of the NPE-throwing scenarios mentioned in *Preface*, they will be covered in the chapters that follow. Naturally, it's up to you to decide which concrete tables (if any) you are going to write down before the exam.

Now let's briefly discuss certain assumptions that, according to Oracle University[37], you'll need to make in order to correctly interpret the context of a question:

Assume the following:

❏ <u>Missing package and import statements</u>: If sample code does not include `package` or `import` statements, and the question does not explicitly refer to these missing statements, then assume that all sample code is in the same package, and import statements exist to support the code. ← *This is a typical situation; happens in most of the questions that use core Java classes defined outside of the **java.lang** package such as **java.io.IOException**, **java.util.List**, **java.util.function.Predicate** and so on.*

❏ <u>No file or directory path names for classes</u>: If a question does not state the file names or directory locations of classes, then assume one of the following, whichever will enable the code to compile and run: ← *Also quite common.*
    ■ All classes are in one file;
    ■ Each class is contained in a separate file, and all files are in one directory.

❏ <u>Unintended line breaks</u>: Sample code may have unintended line breaks. If you see a line of code that looks like it has wrapped, and this creates a situation where the wrapping is significant (for example, a quoted string literal has wrapped), assume that the wrapping is an extension of the same line, and the line does not contain a hard carriage return that would cause a compilation failure. ← *Didn't meet this one. At all. Just as I've said, the entire code was pretty-typed.*

---

[37] http://education.oracle.com/pls/web_prod-plq-dad/db_pages.getpage?page_id=5001&get_params=p_exam_id:1Z0-808

- ❑ <u>Code fragments</u>: A code fragment is a small section of source code that is presented without its context. Assume that all necessary supporting code exists and that the environment fully supports the correct compilation and execution of the code shown and its omitted environment. ← *A good half of the questions contain such code fragments.*

- ❑ <u>Descriptive comments</u>: Take descriptive comments, such as "setters and getters go here," at face value. Assume that correct code exists, compiles, and runs successfully to create the described effect. ← *Met it once, in the form "setter and getter methods go here".*

Word of caution:

It can be very tempting to actively use web resources to prepare for the exam. This can also lead to a dismal failure for most of those resources aren't subject to rigorous quality control. They are just like people: can't trust 'em all, can we?

For example, you may have come across something like this: "For convenience, the Java compiler automatically imports three entire packages for each source file: (1) the package with no name, (2) the **java.lang** package, and (3) the current package (the package for the current file)."

What's interesting, this phrase comes directly from an official Java SE tutorial – but is badly outdated. The current JLS8 (Chapter 7, *Packages*, preamble) clearly states that

> «A package consists of a number of compilation units. A compilation unit automatically has access to all types declared in its package and also automatically imports all of the public types[38] declared in the predefined package **java.lang**»,

so now it's *two* packages, not three.

Apparently, some sites for Java students just don't bother with keeping their pages up to date… I would recommend not to rely on Web but use instead solid study guides and tools from reputable authors / vendors.

<u>A few suggestions on how to work through the chapters that cover exam objectives</u>:
- – keep a written record of your errors;
- – start and finish your day by going through this list of failures;
- – use colors, invent mnemonic formulas, draw pictures on paper and in your mind (as you know, funny ones work the best) and so on; do whatever helps commit the rules to memory[39]; you'll be amazed what results it brings in a very short time.

And on a final note:

> **Do not worry much about 'Extra' stuff;**
> **concentrate instead on the 'Core Rules' and related problems because**
> **you *will* encounter something close to them during the actual test.**

---

[38] **java.lang** contains `public` types only so that's why we usually hear a shorter phrase like '**java.lang** is the only package that is imported implicitly'. Although a tiny bit redundant, the JLS's wording is a good reminder that "A top level type is accessible outside the package that declares it only if the type is declared `public`" (JLS, Ch.7).

[39] You may want to read or watch something on stage magicians' mnemonic technique; this stuff definitely works…

Chapter
II.1

EXAM OBJECTIVES – Group One:
Java Basics

The 1Z0-808 objectives within this group:

1.1 Define the scope of variables
1.2 Define the structure of a Java class
1.3 Create executable Java applications with a main method; run a Java program from the command line, including console output
1.4 Import other Java packages to make them accessible in your code
1.5 Compare and contrast the features and components of Java such as: platform independence, object orientation, encapsulation, etc.

 CORE RULES (with some Extras):

1.1 Scope of variables:

- ❑ Basically, scope refers to that portion of code where a variable is visible, in other words, can be accessed.

- ❑ Variables can operate on different levels and, therefore, they can have multiple scopes:
    - class-level variables,
    - instance variables,
    - local variables (including loop vars), and
    - method arguments.

- ❑ Local variables are most often defined within the body of a method/constructor and in sub-blocks.

- ❑ The scope of a variable is limited by the nearest pair of matching curly braces, {}. For example, the scope of a local variable is less than the scope of a method if the variable was declared within a sub-block inside the method. This sub-block can be an `if` statement, a `switch` construct, a loop, a TCF construct, or just a group of assorted stats enclosed by a matching pair of braces.

- ❑ Local variables are not visible (*read*: they cannot be accessed) outside the method or sub-block in which they're defined.

- ❑ Instance variables are defined and accessible within an object, which effectively means we need a valid object to work with them. Any instance method of the same class can access these instance variables.

- ❑ Class-level variables, a.k.a. `static` variables, are shared by all of the instances of the class; what's more, they can be accessed even if there are no objects of the class.

- ❑ Method arguments are used by a method that accepts parameters. Their scope is confined to the method within which they're defined.

- ❑ A method argument and a local variable cannot share the same identifier, that is, name.

- Same goes for <u>class</u> and <u>instance</u> variables: they can't be defined using the same name.

- On the other hand, <u>local</u> and <u>class/instance</u> vars may be defined using the same name. If a method defines a local var that shares the same name with an class/instance variable, the local var shadows the class/instance var (in other words, makes it invisible.)

- Sometimes the variables' scopes overlap with each other; the only way to be sure if a variable is accessible is to identify the block it belongs to (by looking at braces).

- Loop variables are local to the loop within which they're defined.

- All variables go into scope as soon as they get declared.

- Class variables remain in scope as long as the program is running.

- Instance variables go out of scope when the object is garbage collected.

- Local variables go out of scope when the block they are declared in ends.

Putting out these rules in code:

```
1  class VarScope{
2      static int x = 4, y;
3      static{
4          x = 44;
5      }
6      int a = 1, b;
7      {
8          b = 11;
9      }
10     void run(int b){
11         int a = b;
12         int c;
13         {
14             // int c = 666;                // INVALID
15             int x = 444;
16         }
17         for (int d = 0; d < 3; d++){
18             // int a = 3;                  // INVALID
19             int e = 5;
20             e++;
21             System.out.println("e = " + e);    // prints 6 repeatedly
22         }
23     }
24     public static void main(String[] args) {
25         int a = 3;
26         new VarScope().run(a);
27     }
28 }
```

Line 2 declares `static` variables, which exist on the class level[40]. These variables are visible inside all methods and class-level blocks. Being class members, these fields do not require explicit initialization; the `static int` **y** automatically receives the value of 0.

---

[40] Some people also refer to them as *class fields* but we won't. After all, the JLS has no notion of 'class fields'; it mentions only '*super*class fields', and from the context it becomes clear that the term means instance fields defined in the supertype.

Lines 3–5 define a static initialization block, which deals with static members only. This block fires only once, at the moment when the class is loaded. Please note that the assignment statement on line 4 executes *outside* any method.

Line 6 declares non-static, that is, instance variables (a.k.a. *instance* or *object fields*), which are known to all methods and class-level blocks UNLESS they are shadowed by other variables that happen to have the same name (which is unwise at it leads to much confusion). Instance vars also do not require explicit initialization, and **b** on line 6 automatically receives the value of 0.

Next comes the instance initialization block (lines 7–9), which fires every time an object is being created (naturally, after the very first initialization of the var at the point of its declaration); as the result, line 8 assigns the value of 11 to **b**, which used to be 0 when freshly declared. Similarly to static initers, the stats inside an instance initer execute outside any method.

Line 10 declares a method argument, `int` **b**, which is a local variable known only inside its method. Please note that this local var **b** doesn't clash with the instance var **b**; instead, it shadows the instance var **b**. Same goes for `int` **a** declared and assigned the value of the arg **b** on line 11; this particular var is also a 'shadow-caster' and known only inside its method.

Local variable `int` **c** exists only inside **run()**; unlike `static` and instance vars, local vars are not automatically inited thus requiring an explicit initing BEFORE they may be used. There is at least one question on the exam that arms a bear trap based on this concept.

The sub-block on lines 13–16 attempts to declare two more vars that share names with previously declared vars: `int` **c** and `int` **x**. Line 14, however, does not compile since the scope of `int` **c**, declared two LOCs before, overlaps with that of the second `int` **c**, and Java does not allow multiple declarations of the same var. As for `int` **x** on line 15, this var is known only to its method, so there's no problem. `int` **x** from line 15 ceases to exist after line 16.

As we can see, the scope of a var is limited by a pair of braces. There is, however, an exception to this rule, namely, `for` loops: their local vars (a.k.a. *loop vars*) are defined *before* the opening brace (refer to line 17 or to this example of a `for-each` loop: `for(int i : intArray){}`).

Line 18 foolishly attempts to re-declare already known local var `int` **a** whose scope starts on line 11 and ends after line 23. (Just a reminder: being shadowed, the instance var `int` **a** from line 6 is still out of the picture at this point.)

The local var `int` **e** from line 19 is visible only inside the `for` loop on lines 17–22. The exam creators are truly in love with this trap so be warned. Both **d** and **e** cease to exist after line 22.

The fourth and final attempt to re-declare `int` **a**, which is used as a param for **run()**, is met with success on line 25 because we are inside a different method whose matching braces limit this var's scope... *Whew!* Half a thousand words to describe twenty or so simple LOCs... All in all, shadowing should be used sparingly. Mildly put.

1.2 Structure of Java class:

❏ The structure and functions of Java class are defined in a source code file (**.java** file).

❏ The compiler creates a single Java bytecode file (**.class** file) for each compiled class, even if it is nested. As for the **.class** files themselves, they are not on the 1Z0-808 exam.

❏ A class can define multiple components, such as:
  - `package` and `import` declarations,
  - comments,
  - variables,
  - methods,
  - constructors,
  - initialization blocks,
  - *nested classes,* ⎫
  - *nested interfaces,* ⎬ these data types
  - *annotations,* and ⎭ are not on the 1Z0-808 exam
  - *enums.*

❏ A single **.java** file can define multiple classes and/or interfaces.

❏ A `public` class can be defined only in a source code file with the same name.

❏ The structure of the source code file can have direct impact on the compilability of a Java class (something that you will be tested for), so it is important to be able to recognize misplaced statements in a class:

  ■ Java classes are kept inside packages, which group together related classes and interfaces. The packages also provide access protection and namespace management.

  ■ The `import` stat is used to import `public` classes and interfaces from other packages.

  ■ EXTRA: If a needed `import` statement is missing, classes and interfaces should be referred to by their fully qualified names (in the form of *pack.[subpack.]type_name*).

  ■ Classes can be imported by class name or wildcard. Wildcards do not make the compiler look inside subpackages (which are mapped to the local file system as subfolders).

  ■ EXTRA: In the event of a conflict, class name imports take precedence over wildcards.

  ■ `package` and `import` statements are optional. If present, they apply to all the classes and interfaces defined in the same **.java** file.

  ■ Fields and methods are also optional but, unlike the `package` and `import` stats that must precede the class declaration, they may be placed in any order within the class;

  ■ If a class defines a `package` statement, it should be the first statement in the **.java** file. It is a comperr if the `package` stat appears inside or after the class declaration;
    Corollary: If a class has a `package` statement, all the `imports` should follow it.

  ■ A class can contain exactly one `package` statement;

  ■ A class can include multiple `import` statements;

  ■ The `import` statement uses simple names of classes and interfaces from within the class.

  ■ The `import` statement cannot be applied to multiple classes or interfaces with the same simple name;

  ■ Redundant imports are allowed.

  ■ EXTRA: The `import` statement requires the dot operator.

- ❏ Comments are another component of a class: they are used to annotate Java code and can appear anywhere within the source code file.
- ❏ EXTRA: Comments can contain any characters from the entire Unicode charset.
- ❏ There are three types of comments:
  - ▪ a single-line comment // (a.k.a. 'end-of-line comment'), which hides from the compiler anything that is present to the right-hand side of it;
  - ▪ a multiline comment /* */, and
  - ▪ EXTRA: a Javadoc comment /** */, which is not on the exam.
- ❏ A comment can appear in multiple places, before or after a `package` statement, before, within, or after the class definition, and before, within, or after the bodies of methods, constructors, blocks, loops and so on.
- ❏ A Java class may define zero or more members such as `static` fields, instance variables, methods, or constructors[41] whose definitions can be placed in any order within the class.

  Corollary: Since the declaration order does not matter, a method may use, for example, an instance variable even before it has been declared in the file.

Putting out these rules in code:

```
1  /* File: Test.java
2   * This is a simple illustration of the rules
3   * that concern Java class structure
4   */
5
6  package org.xlator;
7  import java.lang.*;
8  // package org.xlator;          // INVALID
9  // import java.util.*;          // VALID but the code uses another approach
10 import java.util.ArrayList;
11 import java.util.Date;
12 // import java.sql.Date;        // INVALID
13
14 interface I1{}
15 // public interface I2{}        // INVALID
16
17 class C1{ }
18 public class Test {
19     public static void main(String[] args) {
20         System.out.println(new Test().list.add("Hello"));   // prints true
21     }
22     java.util.List<String> list = new ArrayList<String>();
23 }
```

Lines 1 through 4 are self-explanatory as they make use of the multiline comment syntax.

Line 7 imports all the classes (including **String**, which is the data type for the string literal "Hello" and the objects to be contained within the **ArrayList** referred to by the var **list**) from the **java.lang** package – which is already visible to the compiler, thus making this `import` statement redundant; this doesn't throw a comperr, though. Line 8 is invalid as the `package` statement must precede `imports` and may appear only once. Lines 10 and 11 can be replaced with a single statement: `import java.util.*;` as shown on the commented-out line 9.

---

[41] Okay, okay, so constructors aren't class members, I admit. Let's pretend they are for the sake of brevity.

Line 12 throws a comperr: "a type with the same simple name is already defined by a single-type-import of Date".

Line 15 is invalid because the source code file is named wrongly (it should have been **I2.java**). It follows that a single **.java** file cannot contain more than one `public` class or `public` interface.

Line 20 uses the variable **list**, which is declared later, on line 22, but there's no comperr since the declaration order of the class or instance vars does not matter.

Line 22 specifies the fully qualified name of the interface **List** used as the reftype of the var **list**. We could also uncomment line 9, and there would be no conflict because fully qualified names take precedence over wildcards.

EXTRA: Perhaps, the only surprise is that line 20 prints **true** instead of the half-expected **Hello**; it's because the class **ArrayList**'s **add()** method (inherited from the interface **List**, which, in its own turn, extends the interface **Collection**) returns a `boolean` (**true** if the collection changed as a result of the call). This stuff, however, is not on the exam; in fact, even the Exam Objective 9.4, *Declare and use an ArrayList of a given type*, doesn't go to such depth… Would make a nice little trap, though.

1.3   Create executable Java applications with a main method; run a Java program from the command line, including console output:

❑   Before any Java class can be used by the JVM, it must be compiled into bytecode:
   `javac MyClass.java`   →   creates the bytecode file **MyClass.class**

❑   Java classes can be either executable or non-executable. An executable Java class runs when its class name (together with optional parameters) is handed over to the JVM:
   `java MyClass 1 2 3`   →   no extension! it's our class name, not the filename!

❑   To be executable, the Java class must define the **main()** method, a.k.a. 'entry point', at which the JVM begins program execution.

❑   The most commonly used signature of the **main()** method is:
   `public static void main(String[] args)`

❑   EXTRA: also acceptable are the varargs: `public static void main(String... args)`

❑   To make the class executable, its **main()** method must be both `public` and `static`.

❑   A class can define multiple methods with the name **main()**, provided that their signatures do not match the signature of the **main()** method defined as the program's entry point.

❑   The 'entry-point' **main()** accepts an array of type **String** that will contain the parameters specified on the command line after the class name. In fact, the **main()** method uses copies of these parameters as its arguments[42].

❑   Arguments are referenced starting with **args[0]**. An attempt to access an argument that wasn't passed in causes an RTE, namely, AIOOBE.

❑   EXTRA: **String[] args** in `public static void main()` is never `null`. If the program is run without any command line arguments, **args** points to a **String** array of zero length.

---

[42] Although these terms are mostly used interchangeably, parameters in a strict sense are the variables in a method declaration. Arguments are the actual values that are passed in when the method is invoked. Many people don't see or care about the difference; the OCA exam won't test you on this, either; needed for OCP, though.

1.4   Import other Java packages to make them accessible in your code:

Many rules concerning importing Java packages have been already covered in Item 1.2, *Structure of Java class*, because these objectives are closely related. Now let's take another look at these principles while paying attention to a number of important details:

❏   Java code is commonly organized into packages, which resemble file system folders.

❏   To reference public classes or interfaces contained in other packages, we can use:
   −   either an `import` statement, or
   −   the fully qualified name of the class/interface.

❏   No `import` statement can be placed before a `package` declaration.

❏   An `import` statement can end with either simple name of the class or a wildcard symbol, that is, asterisk *.

❏   If an `import` statement ends with the asterisk, it means that the code wants to have access to all `public` data types in that particular package.

❏   On the other hand, the wildcard symbol does not provide access to any of the subpackages that may exist inside that one.

❏   The **java.lang**[43] package is the only package the compiler imports automatically.

❏   Packages can contain multiple subpackages depending on how programmers organize their classes and interfaces.

❏   By default, classes and interfaces in different packages and subpackages aren't visible to each other.

❏   On the other hand, all classes and interfaces within the same package are visible to each other.

❏   The package and subpackage names are chained together with the dot operator.

❏   An `import` statement is nothing but a handy way to tell the compiler where to look for a specific `public` class or interface; it does not 'import' anything[44] but makes our life easier by allowing to use simple names for the `public` classes and interfaces defined in other packages.

   Corollary: Instead of using an `import` stat, we can always write the fully qualified name of the `public` class or interface right in our code – but it soon becomes tedious.

❏   EXTRA: It also follows that `import` statements can't be used to access multiple classes or interfaces that share the same simple name but reside in different packages. This problem can be solved, for example, by using an `import` stat for one conflicting class and the fully qualified name for its competitor. Another approach is to re-think the entire architecture of your namespace.

❏   An `import` stat allows to gain access to either a single `public` member of the package, or to all of them (by using the abovementioned wildcard symbol).

---

[43] It provides language support by making available fundamental types, system methods, widely used classes such as **String**, **StringBuilder**, **Math** and so on, threads, and exceptions. Contains 104 data types (at least in 1.8).

[44] Unlike the #include directive in C/C++ that makes the compiler look into the standard library and copy code from the header files into the program (thus increasing the program size, which wastes memory and the CPU time), the `import` stat makes the JVM look into the Java standard library, execute code there, and substitute the result into the program. As no code is copied and there is no waste of memory or processor's resources, Java's import can be considered as more efficient mechanism than #include.

- ❑ **Known trap on the exam**   If a data type isn't `public`, it cannot be imported:

```
package pack1;
class A {}

package pack2;
import pack1.*;
// import pack1.A;              // INVALID: "A is not public in pack1; cannot
                                            be accessed from outside package"
// class B extends A {}        // INVALID: ditto
// class C extends pack1.A {}  // INVALID: ditto
```

- ❑ Unlike the asterisk used to access file system subfolders, `import` stat's wildcard symbol does not work in a similar fashion with subpackages. In other words, * does not import subpackages.

- ❑ EXTRA: If the source code file does not contain a `package` declaration, the class / interface is considered to be a member of the so-called default package.

- ❑ EXTRA: The default package's members are accessible only to the classes or interfaces defined in the same directory that contains the default package.

- ❑ EXTRA: A class belonging to a default package can't be used in any named packaged class regardless of whether it is defined within the same directory, or not.

- ❑ It is possible to import an individual public *static* member of a class or all of its public static members by using an `import static` declaration.

- ❑ To import a `static` method, we must use its name only, that is, without parentheses.

- ❑ If the code appears clean and the LOCs are numbered, be on guard for missing imports – especially when you see:
    - ■ lists (**List** and **ArrayList**)
    - ■ predicative lambdas
    - ■ LDT-related LOCs
    - ■ **Arrays** (e.g., **Arrays.asList()**)[45]
    - ■ **Collections** (e.g., **Collections.sort()**)

1.5 Compare and contrast the features and components of Java such as platform independence, object orientation, encapsulation, etc.:

- ❑ Java is a computer programming language that is concurrent, class-based and object-oriented[46]. The advantages of object-oriented software development:
    - ■ Modular development of code, which improves its robustness;
    - ■ Reusability of code;
    - ■ Code is more flexible and dynamic at run time;
    - ■ Better maintainability of code.

- ❑ The OOP-based development is supported by a number of built-in features, such as encapsulation, inheritance, polymorphism, and abstraction.

---

[45] BTW, I didn't meet the **Arrays.binarySearch()** method on the exam; that's why this guide doesn't cover it.

[46] Alan Key – who invented the term 'object-oriented' – reportedly remarked once that the term is actually a misnomer: it should have been something like 'message-oriented'…

- Encapsulation allows objects to hide their internal characteristics and implementation details. Each object can provide a number of methods, which are accessible to other objects thus permitting them to read and/or change its internal state.

- Encapsulation is realized through the use of access modifiers.

- Some of the advantages of encapsulation:
  - The internal state of every object can be protected;
  - Encapsulation improves usability and maintainability of code because the behavior of an object can be modified independently of other data types;
  - Encapsulation decreases coupling, that is, interaction between and among classes thus improving modularity of the design.

- Polymorphism is the ability to realize behavior depending on the underlying data type. A polymorphic data type is the type whose methods can also be applied to variables of some other related type. In other words, we can use the same variable to refer to different types and thus a method call can perform different tasks depending on the type of the actual object.

- Polymorphism makes the code more dynamic at run time and also improves its flexibility and reusability.

- Inheritance provides an object with the ability to acquire the fields and methods of its parent class, also called superclass or base class. Inheritance further enhances reusability of code by adding new features to an existing data type without modifying it.

- Java does not support multiple inheritance. Each class is permitted to extend only one class, but can implement multiple interfaces.

- EXTRA: Abstraction allows to develop data types in terms of their own functionality instead of implementation details. Java provides support for abstract classes that expose interfaces to the outside world without including the actual implementation of all methods. Basically, abstraction aims to separate the implementation details of a class from its behavior.

- EXTRA: Difference between abstraction and encapsulation:
  - Abstraction and encapsulation are complementary concepts: while abstraction deals with the behavior of an object, encapsulation concerns the implementation details of this behavior.
  - Encapsulation is usually achieved by hiding information about the internal state of an object and thus can be seen as a way to realize abstraction.

- Java is platform independent, meaning that it allows to develop applications that can run, without having to be rewritten or recompiled, on any platform that has Java Runtime Environment.

Problem 1.1   Given:

```
class Parser {
    String input = "0123";
    public void parseMe(String str) {
        int output = 0;
        try {
            String input = str;
            output = Integer.parseInt(input);
        } catch (IllegalArgumentException iae) {
            System.out.println("Wrong argument!");
        }
        System.out.println(
            "input: " + input + ", output: " + output);
    }
    public static void main(String[] args) {
        Parser p = new Parser();
        p.parseMe("2013");
    }
}
```

What is the result?

    A. input: 0123, output: 0123
    B. input: 2013, output: 2013
    C. input: 0123, output: 2013
    D. Wrong argument!
    E. None of the above because compilation fails

Problem 1.2   Given the contents of three files:

A.java:

```
import java.lang.*;
import java.lang.String;
public class A {
    public void runMe(String str) {}
    String a = str;
}
```

B.java:

```
public class B {
    public void answer() {
        private String p = "protected";
        System.out.println("This StackOverflow question is " + p);
    }
}
```

C.java:

```
import java.io.FileNotFoundException;
package mypack;
interface FileReader {
    String readFromFile(String fname) throws FileNotFoundException;
}
```

Which statement is true?

    A. Only A.java compiles successfully.
    B. Only B.java compiles successfully.
    C. Only C.java fails compilation.
    D. All three files fail compilation.

Problem 1.3 Given the code from the PinkFloyd_Wall_SideB_7.java file:

```
public class PinkFloyd_Wall_SideB_7 {
    public static void main(String[] args) {
        System.out.println("Goodbye " + args[0] + " " + args[1]);
    }
}
```

Which set of commands prints Goodbye Cruel World?

A. javac PinkFloyd_Wall_SideB_7
   java PinkFloyd_Wall_SideB_7 Cruel World
B. javac PinkFloyd_Wall_SideB_7.java Cruel World
   java PinkFloyd_Wall_SideB_7
C. javac PinkFloyd_Wall_SideB_7.java
   java PinkFloyd_Wall_SideB_7 Cruel World
D. javac PinkFloyd_Wall_SideB_7.java
   java PinkFloyd_Wall_SideB_7.class Cruel World

Problem 1.4 Given the code from the Eat2GetFit.java file:

```
public abstract class Eat2GetFit {                              // line 1
    static double caloriesPerNight = 0f;                        // line 2
    public static void main(String[] args) {
        int weight, height, age;
        if (  !(args.length < 3)  )  {                          // line 3
            weight = Integer.parseInt(args[0]);
            height = Integer.parseInt(args[1]);
            age = Integer.parseInt(args[2]);
        } else {
            System.out.println(
                "State patient's weight, height and age!\n" +
                "(use metric units: kg and cm)");
        }
        caloriesPerNight = weight * height / age * (int)100;     // line 4
        System.out.println(
            "Stay below " + caloriesPerNight + " cals per night!");
    }
}
```

And given the following set of commands:

javac Eat2GetFit.java
java Eat2GetFit 100 100 100

What is the result?

A. Stay below 10000 cals per night!
B. Compilation fails on line 1
C. Compilation fails on line 2
D. Compilation fails on line 3
E. Compilation fails on line 4

Problem 1.5   Given the file WhichOne.java:

```
public class WhichOne {
    public static void main(Object[] args) {
        System.out.println(args[0] + " is an Object!");
    }
    public static void main(Number[] args) {
        System.out.println(args[0] + " is a Number!");
    }
    public static void main(String[] args) {
        System.out.println(args[0] + " is a String!");
    }
    public static void main(int[] args) {
        System.out.println(args[0] + " is an int!");
    }
}
```

and commands:

javac WhichOne.java
java WhichOne 1234

What is the result?

- A.   1234 is an Object!
- B.   1234 is a Number!
- C.   1234 is a String!
- D.   1234 is an int!
- E.   Compilation fails
- F.   An ArrayIndexOutOfBoundsException is thrown at run time

Problem 1.6   Given:

```
public class OpenSesame {
    public static void main(String... args) {                 // line 1
        if (args[4].equals("password") ? false : true) {       // line 2
            System.out.println("Access denied!");
        } else {
            System.out.println("Access granted!");
        }
    }
}
```

And given the commands:

javac OpenSesame.java
java OpenSesame My voice is my password

What is the result?

- A.   Access denied!
- B.   Access granted!
- C.   Compilation fails on line 1
- D.   Compilation fails on line 2
- E.   An ArrayIndexOutOfBoundsException is thrown at run time

Problem 1.7   Given the contents of four files:

Janitor.java:

```
package office;
public class Janitor {
    // some valid code
}
```

BroomCloset.java:

```
package office;
public class BroomCloset {
    // lot and lot of valid code
}
```

Broom.java:

```
package office.broomcloset;
public class Broom {
    // even bigger amount of valid and astonishingly crafty code with all
    // necessary constructors and even a mahogany handle for the broom
}
```

AngryBoss.java:

```
package empirestatebuilding;

// INSERT your code here

public class AngryBoss {
    public Broom fetchBroom(Janitor j, BroomCloset bc) {
        // valid code
        return new Broom();
    }
}
```

Which LOC(s), when inserted in AngryBoss.java, shall enable the code to compile?

A. `import office.*.*;`

B. `import office.broomcloset.*;`

C. `import office;`
    `import office.broomcloset;`

D. `import office.BroomCloset;`
    `import office.broomcloset.Broom;`

E. `import office.*;`
    `import office.broomcloset.*;`

Problem 1.8 Which three statements describe the object-oriented features of the Java language?

A. Objects cannot be reused.
B. A subclass can inherit from a superclass.
C. Objects can share behavior with other objects.
D. A package must contain more than one class.
E. Object is the root class of all other objects.
F. A main method must be declared in every class.

Problem 1.9   Which of the following best describes encapsulation?

A. Encapsulation ensures that certain fields and methods of an object can be made inaccessible to other objects.
B. Encapsulation ensures that classes can have abstract fields and methods.
C. Encapsulation ensures that data types can have inheritable methods.
D. Encapsulation ensures that data types can be designed in such a way so that if a method has an argument DataTypeOne dto, any subclass of DataTypeOne can be passed to that method.

Problem 1.10 Which one is true about Java byte code?

A. It can run on any platform.
B. It can run on any platform provided the byte code was compiled for that platform.
C. It can run on any platform that has the JRE (Java Runtime Environment).
D. It can run on any platform that has javac.exe (that is, a Java compiler).
E. It can run on any platform provided this platform has both the JRE and javac.exe.

Problem 1.11 Given the contents of two Java source files:

```
package hackathon.hacker;
public class Hacker {
    public void hack() {
        System.out.println("Done!");
    }
}
1 package hackathon;
2 public class Hackathon {
3     public static void main(String[] args) {
4         System.out.println("Ready... set... go!");
5         new Hacker().hack();
6     }
7 }
```

What three modifications, made independently to the class Hackathon, will enable the code to compile and run?

A. Replace line 5 with new hackathon.hacker.Hacker().hack();
B. Replace line 5 with new hackathon.*.Hacker().hack();
C. Add import hackathon.hacker.*; before line 1
D. Add import hackathon.hacker.*; after line 1
E. Add import hackathon.hacker.Hacker; after line 1

Problem 1.12 Given:

```
class C {
    static void m(int i) {
    }
    public static void main (String[] args) {
        int a = 18;
        m(a);
        System.out.println(a);
    }
}
```

What is the result?

  A. 17
  B. 18
  C. 19
  D. Compilation fails
  E. An exception is thrown at run time

Problem 1.13 Given:

```
public class Test {
    public static void main(String[] args) {
        doStuff();                              // line 1
        int x1 = x2;                            // line 2
        int x2 = a;                             // line 3
    }
    static void doStuff() {
        System.out.println(a);                  // line 4
    }
    static int a;
}
```

Which line causes a compilation error?

  A. line 1
  B. line 2
  C. line 3
  D. line 4

Problem 1.14 Given:

```
class Vars {
    int j, k;
    public static void main(String[] args) {
        new Vars().doStuff();
    }
    void doStuff() {
        int x = 1;
        doStuff2();
        System.out.println("x");
    }
    void doStuff2() {
        int y = 2;
        System.out.println("y");
        for (int z = 0; z < 3; z++) {
            System.out.println("z");
            System.out.println("y");
        }
    }
}
```

Which two items are fields?

  A. j
  B. k
  C. x
  D. y
  E. z

Problem 1.15

Which two classes compile and can be run successfully using the command:

```
java RunMe hello goodbye
```

A.
```
class RunMe{
    public static void main (String args) {
        System.out.println(args[1]);
    }
}
```

B.
```
class RunMe{
    public static void main (String[] args) {
        System.out.println(args[2]);
    }
}
```

C.
```
class RunMe{
    public static void main (String[] args) {
        System.out.println(args);
    }
}
```

D.
```
class RunMe{
    public static void main (String[] args){
        System.out.println(args[1]);
    }
}
```

Problem 1.16

Given the complete contents of the file Jupiter.java:

```
 1 public class Jupiter {
 2     public static void main (String[] args) {
 3         System.out.print("Welcome " + args[1] + "!");
 4     }
 5 }
 6 class Juno {
 7     public static void main (String[] args) {
 8         Jupiter.main(args);
 9     }
10 }
```

And the commands:

```
javac Jupiter.java
java Juno Jupiter Juno
```

What is the result?

A. Welcome Jupiter!
B. Welcome Juno!
C. Compilation fails because a source file can contain only one main() method
D. An ArrayIndexOutOfBoundsException is thrown
E. Run-time error is thrown because we run wrong class: it should've been Jupiter

Problem 1.17 Given:

```
public class Test { }
```

Which package is automatically imported by the Java compiler?

    A. java.lang
    B. javax.swing
    C. javax.net
    D. java.*
    E. The package with no name

Problem 1.18

Which three are benefits of encapsulation?

    A. Encapsulation allows to change the class implementation without changing the clients.
    B. Encapsulation prevents leakage of confidential data out of the objects.
    C. Encapsulation prevents code from causing exceptions.
    D. Encapsulation enables the class implementation to protect its invariants.
    E. Encapsulation allows classes to be combined into the same package.
    F. Encapsulation enables multiple instances of the same class to be created safely.

Problem 1.19 Given:

```
class Vars {
    int z;
    public static void main(String[] args){
        Vars obj = new Vars();
        int z = 3;
        System.out.print(z);
        obj.doStuff();
        System.out.print(z);
        System.out.print(obj.z);
    }
    void doStuff() {
        int z = 2;
        doStuff(z);
        System.out.print(z);
    }
    void doStuff(int zzz) {
        z = 1;
    }
}
```

What is the result?

    A. 3 2 3 1
    B. 3 2 3 0
    C. 3 1 3 1
    D. 3 1 3 0

Problem 1.20 Given:

```java
class Looper {
    public static void main(String[] args) {
        for (int kk = 0; kk < 4; kk++) {
            System.out.print("kk = "+ kk + ", ");
            kk = kk + 1;
        }
        System.out.println("kk = "+ kk + ", ");
    }
}
```

What is the result?

    A. kk = 0, kk = 2, kk = 0,
    B. kk = 0, kk = 2, kk = 2,
    C. kk = 0, kk = 2, kk = 4,
    D. Compilation fails.

Problem 1.21 Which three statements are true about the structure of a Java class?

    A. Only one private constructor is allowed per class.
    B. A class can have overloaded static methods.
    C. A field and a method can share the same name.
    D. A public class must have a main method.
    E. No class can be declared without methods.
    F. Fields do not need explicit initialization before use.

Problem 1.22 Given:

```java
class TestingMain {
    void main() {
        System.out.println("one");
    }
    static void main(String args) {
        System.out.println("two");
    }
    public static void main(String[] args) {
        System.out.println("three");
    }
    void main(Object[] args) {
        System.out.println("four");
    }
}
```

What is the output?

    A. one
    B. two
    C. three
    D. four

Problem 1.23 Given the contents of three files:

Peripherals.java:

```
package peripherals;
public class Peripherals{
    void attach(){
        /* connecting LCD, keyboard, mouse, WiFi dongle */
        System.out.print("OK... ");}
    public Peripherals(){ attach(); }
}
```

microSD.java:

```
package microsd;
public class microSD{
    private String os;
    private String card = "Transcend 16GB Class10";
    public static void writeImage(){
        new microSD().os = "Raspbian";
        System.out.print("OK... ");
    }
}
```

Raspi.java:

```
package raspi;
public class Raspi{
    void assemble(){
        new Peripherals();                          // line r1
        writeImage();                               // line r2
    }
    void powerOn(){ System.out.println("It works!"); }
    public static void main(String[] args) {
        Raspi raspi = new Raspi();
        raspi.assemble();
        raspi.powerOn();
    }
}
```

Which snippet will allow the code to compile and run successfully?

A. Add to class **Raspi**:
```
import peripherals.*;
import microsd.microSD;
```

B. Add to class **Raspi**:
```
import peripherals.Peripherals;
import microsd.microSD.*;
```

C. In class **Raspi**:
add `import peripherals.*;`
replace line r2 with `microSD.writeImage();`

D. In class **Raspi**:
add `import static microsd.microSD.writeImage;`
replace line r1 with `new peripherals.Peripherals();`

E. Add to class **Raspi**:
```
import peripherals.Peripherals;
import static microsd.microSD.writeImage();
```

Problem 1.1 – C

Given:

```
class Parser {
    String input = "0123";                              // line p1
    public void parseMe(String str) {
        int output = 0;
        try {
            String input = str;                         // line p2
            output = Integer.parseInt(input);
        } catch (IllegalArgumentException iae) {
            System.out.println("Wrong argument!");
        }
        System.out.println(
            "input: " + input + ", output: " + output); // line p3
    }
    public static void main(String[] args) {
        Parser p = new Parser();
        p.parseMe("2013");
    }
}
```

What is the result?

   A.   input: 0123, output: 0123
   B.   input: 2013, output: 2013
   C.   input: 0123, output: 2013
   D.   Wrong argument!
   E.   None of the above because compilation fails

The var `input` declared on line p2 inside the `try` block shadows the instance field of the same name declared on line p1. The scope of this local var, however, is limited to the `try` block only so that's why the **println()** method on the line p3 uses the instance field's value. In addition, since **parseMe()** is invoked with a valid parameter, the `catch` block has no chance to run.

Problem 1.2 – A

Given the contents of three files:

A.java:

```
import java.lang.*;                                 // line X1
import java.lang.String;                            // line X2
public class A {
    public void runMe(String str) {}
    String a = str;
}
```

B.java:

```
public class B {
    public void answer() {
        private String p = "protected";             // line X3
        System.out.println("This StackOverflow question is " + p);
    }
}
```

C.java:

```
import java.io.FileNotFoundException;
package mypack;
interface FileReader {
    String readFromFile(String fname) throws FileNotFoundException;
}
```

What is the result?

    A. Only A.java compiles successfully.
    B. Only B.java compiles successfully.
    C. Only C.java fails compilation.
    D. All three files fail compilation.

The file **A.java** has two redundant `import` statements on lines X1 and X2 but this does not produce a compile-time error because redundant imports are allowed.

The class **B** says that the local var **p** declared on line X3 is `private` thus leading to a comperr because the only modifier allowed inside methods is `final`.

The file **C.java** has its sequence of `package` and `import` statements wrong: `import` may never precede `package`.

Problem 1.3 – C

    Given the code from the PinkFloyd_Wall_SideB_7.java file:

```
public class PinkFloyd_Wall_SideB_7 {
    public static void main(String[] args) {
        System.out.println("Goodbye " + args[0] + " " + args[1]);
    }
}
```

    Which set of commands prints Goodbye Cruel World?

    A. javac PinkFloyd_Wall_SideB_7
       java PinkFloyd_Wall_SideB_7 Cruel World
    B. javac PinkFloyd_Wall_SideB_7.java Cruel World
       java PinkFloyd_Wall_SideB_7
    C. javac PinkFloyd_Wall_SideB_7.java
       java PinkFloyd_Wall_SideB_7 Cruel World
    D. javac PinkFloyd_Wall_SideB_7.java
       java PinkFloyd_Wall_SideB_7.class Cruel World

This is an example of a 'straight arrow': the question is both simple and harmless. You will meet a good dozen of them on the actual exam so don't waste time desperately searching for traps in each and every case.

Option A omits **.java** file extension in the call to **javac.exe**; option B displaces command-line arguments for **java.exe**, and D specifies **.class** file instead of the class name.

Problem 1.4 – E

    Given the code from the Eat2GetFit.java file:

```
public abstract class Eat2GetFit {                          // line 1
    static double caloriesPerNight = 0f;                    // line 2
    public static void main(String[] args) {
        int weight, height, age;
        if ( !(args.length < 3) ) {                         // line 3
            weight = Integer.parseInt(args[0]);
            height = Integer.parseInt(args[1]);
            age = Integer.parseInt(args[2]);
        } else {
```

```
        System.out.println(
            "State patient's weight, height and age!\n" +
            "(use metric units: kg and cm)");
    }
    caloriesPerNight = weight * height / age * (int)100;      // line 4
    System.out.println(
        "Stay below " + caloriesPerNight + " cals per night!");
    }
}
```

And given the following set of commands:

```
javac Eat2GetFit.java
java Eat2GetFit 100 100 100
```

What is the result?

- A. Stay below 10000 cals per night!
- B. Compilation fails on line 1
- C. Compilation fails on line 2
- D. Compilation fails on line 3
- E. Compilation fails on line 4

It's OK if an `abstract` class has no `abstract` methods so line 1 compiles, and although `abstract` classes by definition cannot be instantiated, the code never attempts to create an object of type **Eat2GetFit** → hence the program is potentially executable.

The integer literal 0 on line 2 has an **f** appended which makes it a `float`. A `float` is perfectly assignable to a `double` so there's no comperr.

The expression `!(args.length < 3)` on line 3 produces a `boolean`, hence line 3 compiles, too.

The real problem is on line 4, which attempts to use the vars `weight`, `height` and `age`. Since these vars are local, they must be inited before being used yet their initing is not guaranteed (specifically, if the `args` array has two slots in it or less). The compiler realizes it and throws an error.

Problem 1.5 – C

Given the file WhichOne.java:

```
public class WhichOne {
    public static void main(Object[] args) {
        System.out.println(args[0] + " is an Object!");
    }
    public static void main(Number[] args) {
        System.out.println(args[0] + " is a Number!");
    }
    public static void main(String[] args) {
        System.out.println(args[0] + " is a String!");
    }
    public static void main(int[] args) {
        System.out.println(args[0] + " is an int!");
    }
}
```

and commands:

```
javac WhichOne.java
java WhichOne 1234
```

What is the result?

    A.   1234 is an Object!
    B.   1234 is a Number!
    C.   1234 is a String!
    D.   1234 is an int!
    E.   Compilation fails
    F.   An ArrayIndexOutOfBoundsException is thrown at run time

The code does compile.

The class **WhichOne** declares four overloaded **main()** methods but only one of them has a valid entry point's signature (which uses an array of type **String** as its argument).

Although the JVM is passed just a single arg, the code uses the very first slot in the array so there's no run-time error.

Problem 1.6 – B

    Given:

```
public class OpenSesame {
    public static void main(String... args) {                    // line 1
        if (args[4].equals("password") ? false : true) {         // line 2
            System.out.println("Access denied!");
        } else {
            System.out.println("Access granted!");
        }
    }
}
```

    And given the commands:

```
javac OpenSesame.java
java OpenSesame My voice is my password
```

    What is the result?

    A.   Access denied!
    B.   Access granted!
    C.   Compilation fails on line 1
    D.   Compilation fails on line 2
    E.   An ArrayIndexOutOfBoundsException is thrown at run time

The code does compile.

Line 1 is valid because a vararg is acceptable as the **main()** method's argument. In fact, the compiler translates a vararg into an array of type **String**.

Line 2 also has a valid ternop syntax thus producing no compile-time error.

When the program is run, the **args** array fills with five **String** values and the code uses the last one of them, so there's no AIOOBE.

The ternary op on line 2 is straightforward despite its seemingly inverted logic: as **args**[4]'s value matches the string "password", the ternary operator returns `false` and the `else`-branch is therefore executed.

Problem 1.7 – E

Given the contents of four files:

Janitor.java:

```
package office;
public class Janitor {
    // some valid code
}
```

BroomCloset.java:

```
package office;
public class BroomCloset {
    // lot and lot of valid code
}
```

Broom.java:

```
package office.broomcloset;
public class Broom {
    // even bigger amount of valid and astonishingly crafty code with all
    // necessary constructors and even a mahogany handle for the broom
}
```

AngryBoss.java:

```
package empirestatebuilding;

// INSERT your code here

public class AngryBoss {
    public Broom fetchBroom(Janitor j, BroomCloset bc) {
        // valid code
        return new Broom();
    }
}
```

Which LOC(s), when inserted in AngryBoss.java, shall enable the code to compile?

A. `import office.*.*;`

B. `import office.broomcloset.*;`

C. `import office;`
   `import office.broomcloset;`

D. `import office.BroomCloset;`
   `import office.broomcloset.Broom;`

E. `import office.*;`
   `import office.broomcloset.*;`

Another typical example of what you should expect on the actual exam: a couple of screens filled with garbage through which you'll have to waddle by scrolling up and down. While rather time consuming and therefore frustrating, the problem itself is quite simple and contains no serious traps.

Options A and C are syntactically invalid as only one asterisk is both *required* and *allowed* inside a generalized `import` stat.

Option B imports source files from the package **office.broomcloset** only thus leaving the classes **Janitor** and **BroomCloset** inaccessible since they live inside the package **office** rather than **office.broomcloset**.

And finally, although option D uses fully qualified names for the classes, it forgot to summon **Janitor**. Replacing **office.BroomCloset** with **office.*** fixes this error.

Problem 1.8 – BCE

Which three statements describe the object-oriented features of the Java language?

    A. Objects cannot be reused.
    B. A subclass inherits non-private fields and methods from a superclass.
    C. Objects can share their behavior with other objects.
    D. A package should contain at least two classes.
    E. Object is the root class for every object in Java.
    F. Every class must declare its own main method.

Option A is incorrect since reusability is one of the cornerstones of the object-oriented design.

Packages does not prescribe the number of classes they can contain, so the option D is not correct, either. And finally, classes can be totally void of members, which makes option F incorrect.

Problem 1.9 – A

Which of the following best describes encapsulation?

    A. Encapsulation ensures that certain fields and methods of an object can be made inaccessible to other objects.
    B. Encapsulation ensures that classes can have abstract fields and methods.
    C. Encapsulation ensures that data types can have inheritable methods.
    D. Encapsulation ensures that data types can be designed in such a way so that if a method accepts an argument of type DataTypeOne, any subclass of DataTypeOne can be passed to that method.

The actual exam has at least two questions related to encapsulation; one is completely textual like this Problem 1.9; the other one is code-based and contains a simple trap (or even two, depending on how you look at it). We'll meet and disarm those nasties soon enough, in Exam Objective 6.5, *Apply encapsulation principles to a class*, which belongs to Group 6, *Working with Methods and Encapsulation*.

As for the solution to the current Problem, options B, C and D do not concern encapsulation.

Problem 1.10 – C

Which one is true about Java byte code?

    A. It can run on any platform.
    B. It can run on any platform provided the byte code was compiled for that platform.
    C. It can run on any platform that has the JRE (Java Runtime Environment).
    D. It can run on any platform that has javac.exe (that is, a Java compiler).
    E. It can run on any platform provided this platform has both the JRE and javac.exe.

I met two versions of this question on the exam; both didn't mention either byte code or **javac.exe** specifically but did talk about Java compiler and Java programs in general. Expect no traps in this one.

Option A is way too general, B doesn't understand the meaning of byte code, option D specifies unrelated requirement, and E builds on D.

Problem 1.11 – ADE

Given the contents of two Java source files:

```
package hackathon.hacker;
public class Hacker {
    public void hack() {
        System.out.println("Done!");
    }
}
```

```
1 package hackathon;
2 public class Hackathon {
3     public static void main(String[] args) {
4         System.out.println("Ready... set... go!");
5         new Hacker().hack();
6     }
7 }
```

What three modifications, made independently to the class Hackathon, will enable the code to compile and run?

    A. Replace line 5 with `new hackathon.hacker.Hacker().hack();`
    B. Replace line 5 with `new hackathon.*.Hacker().hack();`
    C. Add `import hackathon.hacker.*;` before line 1
    D. Add `import hackathon.hacker.*;` after line 1
    E. Add `import hackathon.hacker.Hacker;` after line 1

This is an example of a question that uses certain assumptions; for example, both classes are `public` but we are not provided with filenames → hence we get to assume that the filenames are immaterial in this case.

Option A correctly makes the class **Hacker** accessible to the class **Hackathon** by using the fully qualified name during the creation of the object on which we then call the method **hack()**.

Option B has an asterisk before the class name and therefore violates syntactic rules.

Option C wants to place an `import` stat before `package`, which is not allowed.

As for option D, it imports entire package `hackathon` while option E imports a single class only, the very one that we actually need.

Problem 1.12 – B

Given:

```
class C {
    static void m(int i) {
    }
    public static void main (String[] args) {
        int a = 18;
        m(a);
        System.out.println(a);
    }
}
```

What is the result?

    A. 17
    B. 18
    C. 19
    D. Compilation fails
    E. An exception is thrown at run time

Remember me saying that we should take the questions at their face value? This one can be – and should be – cracked in two seconds: the printing stat is well within the scope of **a**, **m()** is static and accepts an int → done! As for those two inexplicable values of 17 and 19, they were put there simply to confuse you. Expect the same treatment from the 1Z0-808 creators.

Problem 1.13 – B

Given:

```
public class Test {
    public static void main(String[] args) {
        doStuff();                              // line 1
        int x1 = x2;                            // line 2
        int x2 = a;                             // line 3
    }
    static void doStuff() {
        System.out.println(a);                  // line 4
    }
    static int a;
}
```

Which line causes a compilation error?

    A. line 1
    B. line 2
    C. line 3
    D. line 4

Line 1 compiles because **doStuff()** is static and its invocation meets the method's signature. Line 3 is valid since the class declares its static field **a** even though the declaration comes after the body of **doStuff()**. This does not throw a comperr because the order of class member declaration does not matter. Line 4 compiles for exactly same reason: the printing stat is within the var **a**'s scope, which makes **a** accessible.

Line 2, however, attempts to assign the not-yet-existing local var **x2**'s value to **x1**. It's only class members[47] that can be declared in any order; local vars do not work this way.

Problem 1.14 – AB

Given:

```
class Vars {
    int j, k;
    public static void main(String[] args) {
        new Vars().doStuff();
    }
    void doStuff() {
        int x = 1;
        doStuff2();
        System.out.println("x");
    }
    void doStuff2() {
        int y = 2;
        System.out.println("y");
```

---

[47] Plus constructors plus static and instance initers, although these guys are not class members (JLS, §8.2).

```
        for (int z = 0; z < 3; z++) {
            System.out.println("z");
            System.out.println("y");
        }
    }
}
```

Which two items are fields?

    A. j
    B. k
    C. x
    D. y
    E. z

Since fields are not local variables, options CDE are incorrect (**x** and **y** are regular locals, and **z** is the so-called loop var, also very much local).

Problem 1.15 – CD

Which two classes compile and can be run successfully using the command:

```
java RunMe hello goodbye
```

A.
```
class RunMe{
    public static void main (String args) {
        System.out.println(args[1]);
    }
}
```

B.
```
class RunMe{
    public static void main (String[] args) {
        System.out.println(args[2]);
    }
}
```

C.
```
class RunMe{
    public static void main (String[] args) {
        System.out.println(args);
    }
}
```

D.
```
class RunMe{
    public static void main (String[] args){
        System.out.println(args[1]);
    }
}
```

All classes are compilable except the one in option A: its printing stat wants to access a slot in an array while the method's signature doesn't provide for array-type args. What's more, even if the printing stat were using just the refvar rather than a slot (like option C does), the method's signature wouldn't make it a valid entry point: it still needs a **String** array.

Option B throws an AIOOBE at run time because the command line specifies only two arguments while the printing stat wants to access the third slot. Option D is a textbook case of the classic HelloWorld-type program, and as for option C, it produces a rather unpalatable output ([Ljava.lang.String;@2a139a55 on my machine).

This is due to the fact that arrays do not provide their own implementation of the **toString()** method, which they inherit from the root class **Object**.

To see what's going on and what **toString()** has to do with all this, we need to dig into the source code for the core Java class **PrintStream** that lives in the **java.io** package (which is zipped and placed into the file **rt.jar** inside your JDK 1.8 dir). The easiest way to look at it is to open an IDE such as NetBeans, place the cursor on **println()** and press Ctrl-B (or use Navigate | Go to Declaration in the context menu).

The IDE should teleport you to this point inside the file **PrintStream.java**:

```
public void println(Object x) {
    String s = String.valueOf(x);                      // next jumping board
    synchronized (this) {
        print(s);
        newLine();
    }
}
```

Now, as we can see, the method **println()** invokes the class **String**'s static **valueOf()** method to make the representation of the object **x** that was passed to it; let's jump to the point of **valueOf()** declaration in the file **String.java**:

```
public static String valueOf(Object obj) {
    return (obj == null) ? "null" : obj.toString();
}
```

So, if the object is `null`, the method returns a **String** var whose value is literally "null", and if not... To see what happens in this non-trivial case, we boldly go to the declaration of **toString()** in the class **Object**:

```
public String toString() {
    return getClass().getName() + "@" + Integer.toHexString(hashCode());   }
```

Now it's clear how we got the sequence of symbols 2a139a55: it's the hashcode of our object, namely array **args** of type **String**. As for **java.lang.String**, it's self-explanatory, and the prepended [L means a one-dim array of reference types while [[F would have meant a two-dim array of `floats` and so on – but this stuff isn't on the exam.

What follows, however, *IS* on the exam (you'll have at least one Core question about it). Borrowing directly from the javadoc[48] on **Object**:

> In general, the toString method returns a string that "textually represents" this object. The result should be a concise but informative representation that is easy for a person to read. It is recommended that all subclasses override this method.

The key point to remember here is that you have to be on high alert whenever you see a user-defined data type used as a param for **println()** or **print()** invocation: unless the class defines its own implementation of the **toString()** method, the output will look like garbage.

And one more thing which you *will* be tested on. It's about one of the NPE-throwing scenarios; a perfect trap for us exam takers. Go back a little and take another look at the body of the **valueOf()** method defined in **String**:

```
return (obj == null) ? "null" : obj.toString();
```

_____

[48] It's a matter of personal preference, of course, but for those with poor eyesight – take me, for example – I'd recommend to download the whole bunch of javadocs from Oracle and keep them on your local drive. Not just because of speed; it'll become a lot easier on your eyes if you tweak the root-level style-defining file (lives inside <your_jdk_1.8_path>\docs\api dir; in my case it's C:\Program Files\Java\jdk1.8.0_66\docs\api\stylesheet.css) to change typefaces, font sizes and colors for different tags, etc. It really helps to decrease the strain, believe me.

Retreat again and then jump to the declaration of **print()** inside the **PrintStream** class:

```
public void print(String s) {
    if (s == null) {
        s = "null";
    }
    write(s);
}
```

Now we see why it is perfectly safe to invoke printing stats such as **println()** or **print()** on a `null` object: these methods never throw a **NullPointerException** because of the built-in protection mechanism. And yes, I did meet a question on the exam asking me exactly this…

Problem 1.16 – B

Given the complete contents of the file Jupiter.java:

```
 1 public class Jupiter {
 2     public static void main (String[] args) {
 3         System.out.print("Welcome " + args[1] + "!");
 4     }
 5 }
 6 class Juno {
 7     public static void main (String[] args) {
 8         Jupiter.main(args);
 9     }
10 }
```

And the commands:

```
javac Jupiter.java
java Juno Jupiter Juno
```

What is the result?

A. Welcome Jupiter!
B. Welcome Juno!
C. Compilation fails because a source file can contain only one main() method
D. An ArrayIndexOutOfBoundsException is thrown
E. Run-time error is thrown because we run wrong class: it should've been Jupiter

This problem does not test your knowledge of the **main()** method's signature: it asks if you know that however many data types a source file contains, the compiler always places them into separate **.class** files → meaning that you can run any class you want as long as it has the executable **main()** method.

So this is exactly what happens here: **javac.exe** compiles both classes into separate files (**Jupiter.class** and **Juno.class**), places them into the source dir, then we nonchalantly pass the class **Juno** to the JVM – and it runs it for us because both classes have their own executable **main()** methods. **Juno**'s **main()** calls the **Jupiter**'s **main()** passing to it a valid array of the command line args. All in all, nothing surprising.

Now, let's look at the whole setup from a different angle; please note the wording of the problem: "Given the <u>complete contents</u> of the file **Jupiter.java**". Indeed, the class declaration starts right on the first line; there's no package declaration. What would've happened if we added a package declaration without changing anything else? The answer is, the classes would have compiled just fine but the JVM would've thrown a run-time error: "Could not find or load main class Juno". Interesting, wouldn't you say? The required **Juno.class** file apparently exists but the virtual machine can't see it…

This happens because the compiler automatically 'expands' the data type names during compilation to their fully qualified form (that is, with their package name prepended) – and the JVM can't then find **Juno.class** because it is forced to look into a wrong directory.

How to fix this problem? Suppose, the source code says that the classes belong to the package named **org.xlator**:

```
1 package org.xlator;              // ← this is the only change in our code
2 public class Jupiter {
3     public static void main (String[] args) {
4         System.out.print("Welcome " + args[1] + "!");
5     }
6 }
7 class Juno {
8     public static void main (String[] args) {
9         Jupiter.main(args);
10     }
11 }
```

Let's assume further that this package is mapped to the local file system as follows:

C:\Try_Java\org\xlator

This means that in the simplest case when we don't move the compiled classes to a dedicated directory (which can be done by using the compiler's **-d** switch), the **.class** files will be stored in the same dir, **C:\Try_Java\org\xlator**.

Now it becomes obvious that in order to run a **.class** file successfully, we simply should move into the appropriate dir within the file system's hierarchy and do our job from there:

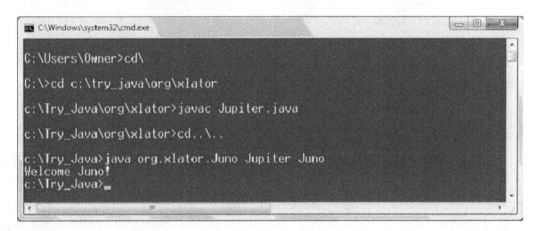

Problem 1.17 – A

Given:

```
public class Test { }
```

Which package is automatically imported by the Java compiler?

    A.   java.lang
    B.   javax.swing
    C.   javax.net
    D.   java.*
    E.   The package with no name

We have already mentioned that the option E is outdated so what remains is just option A. This problem can be presented in a different wording on the exam but the implied meaning is essentially the same. Expect no traps here.

Problem 1.18 – ABD

Which three are benefits of encapsulation?

    A. Encapsulation allows to change the class implementation without changing the clients.
    B. Encapsulation prevents leakage of confidential data out of the objects.
    C. Encapsulation prevents code from causing exceptions.
    D. Encapsulation enables the class implementation to protect its invariants.
    E. Encapsulation allows classes to be combined into the same package.
    F. Encapsulation enables multiple instances of the same class to be created safely.

If I remember correctly, there was just a couple of questions related to encapsulation: one code-based and another one textual. What I don't remember is what the textual question was asking: about benefits or the meaning of encapsulation… Probably, both; this is why I give you a combination of these variants which should cover all possible aspects. Hopefully…

Option C is out because exceptions are irrelevant to encapsulation, and E and F also miss the point.

Problem 1.19 – A

Given:

```
class Vars {
    int z;
    public static void main(String[] args){
        Vars obj = new Vars();
        int z = 3;                          // line 1
        System.out.print(z);                // line 2
        obj.doStuff();
        System.out.print(z);                // line 3
        System.out.print(obj.z);            // line 4
    }
    void doStuff() {
        int z = 2;                          // line 5
        doStuff(z);
        System.out.print(z);                // line 6
    }
    void doStuff(int zzz) {
        z = 1;
    }
}
```

What is the result?

    A. 3 2 3 1
    B. 3 2 3 0
    C. 3 1 3 1
    D. 3 1 3 0

We can see right from the beginning that this problem contains no traps related to compilation errors, and that's a good news as we don't have to watch out for something non-`static` in `static` context, incompatible assignments and whatnots. A good third of the questions on the actual exam are like this, which makes our life easier.

Now, the code declares a local var (on line 1) that shadows the instance field **z** → hence line 2 outputs 3. Then the code invokes **doStuff()** that declares another shadow-casting local var on line 5, which gets printed on line 6 and produces 2 because the second, overloaded **doStuff()** changes the instance field rather the local var's value. When we add here one of the most important rules for the exam – local vars are visible only inside the methods they are declared in – it becomes obvious that line 3 prints 3, and then line 4 prints the value of the instance field that was changed by the overloaded **doStuff**(int), namely 1.

Problem 1.20 – D

Given:

```
class Looper {
    public static void main(String[] args) {
        for (int kk = 0; kk < 4; kk++) {
            System.out.print("kk = "+ kk + ", ");
            kk = kk + 1;
        }
        System.out.println("kk = "+ kk + ", ");        // line 1
    }
}
```

What is the result?

A. kk = 0, kk = 2, kk = 0,
B. kk = 0, kk = 2, kk = 2,
C. kk = 0, kk = 2, kk = 4,
D. Compilation fails.

One of the most 'popular' traps on 1Z0-808; fortunately for us, it's also quite simple. All you have to remember is that local vars are visible inside the nearest[49] matching pair of braces – and loop vars are not exempted from this rule despite the fact they are declared *before* the braces → meaning that the second printing stat throws a comperr since **kk** isn't visible anymore on line 1.

You would have remembered this little peculiarity exhibited by loop vars if you watched Simon's *Live Lessons*: he briefly mentions it when talking about loops. In fact, I can tell you in retrospect that when someone like Simon Roberts calls our attention to certain subtleties, we can be pretty sure to meet them on the actual exam.

Problem 1.21 – BCF

Which three statements are true about the structure of a Java class?
A. Only one private constructor is allowed per class.
B. A class can have overloaded static methods.
C. A field and a method can share the same name.
D. A public class must have a main method.
E. No class can be declared without methods.
F. Fields do not need explicit initialization before use.

The question is as straightforward as it can be. The only item worthy of spending a minute on is, perhaps, option C.

---

[49] Nearest to the local var's declaration point, that is.

The possibility for a field (can be either a class or an instance var) and a method to share the same name is due to the fact that Java has *four* namespaces: for fields, methods, data types, and packages, hence no conflict. Other languages can have a radically different view on this; for example, Scala recognizes just two namespaces: for values (fields, methods, packages, and singleton objects), and for types (class and trait names).

Four namespaces in Java can provide endless hours of amusement for the whole family, pets included; consider, for example, the following class:

```
1 class String{
2     String(){}
3     String(String String){}
4     String String(){ return new String(); }
5     public static void main(String[] string) {
6         String String = new String(new String().String());
7         System.out.println("String!");
8     }
9 }
```

This little bundle of mischief compiles without a hitch but the JVM then chokes on **main()**:

The code happily prints "String!" as soon as we refine the reference to the **String** array **string** by stating the fully qualified name for the needed data type, which used to be obscured:

```
5     public static void main(java.lang.String[] string) {
```

Problem 1.22 – C

Given:

```
class TestingMain {
    void main() { System.out.println("one"); }
    static void main(String args) { System.out.println("two"); }
    public static void main(String[] args) { System.out.println("three"); }
    void main(Object[] args) { System.out.println("four"); }
}
```

What is the output?

    A. one
    B. two
    C. three
    D. four

This one is just a simpler variant of Problem 1.5 as the exam creators sometimes repack their questions to test related concepts from different angles. There's no trap; all the question does is innocently asking if we know the **main()** method's signature...

Problem 1.23 – D

Given the contents of three files:

Peripherals.java:

```
package peripherals;
public class Peripherals{
    void attach(){
        /* connecting LCD, keyboard, mouse, WiFi dongle */
        System.out.print("OK... ");}
    public Peripherals(){ attach(); }
}
```

microSD.java:

```
package microsd;
public class microSD{
    private String os;
    private String card = "Transcend 16GB Class10";
    public static void writeImage(){
        new microSD().os = "Raspbian";
        System.out.print("OK... ");
    }
}
```

Raspi.java:

```
package raspi;
public class Raspi{
    void assemble(){
        new Peripherals();                          // line r1
        writeImage();                               // line r2
    }
    void powerOn(){ System.out.println("It works!"); }
    public static void main(String[] args) {
        Raspi raspi = new Raspi();
        raspi.assemble();
        raspi.powerOn();
    }
}
```

Which snippet will allow the code to compile and run successfully?

    A.   Add to class **Raspi**:
```
import peripherals.*;
import microsd.microSD;
```

    B.   Add to class **Raspi**:
```
import peripherals.Peripherals;
import microsd.microSD.*;
```

C.   In class **Raspi**:
     add `import peripherals.*;`
     replace line r2 with `microSD.writeImage();`

D.   In class **Raspi**:
     add `import static microsd.microSD.writeImage;`
     replace line r1 with `new peripherals.Peripherals();`

E.   Add to class **Raspi**:
     `import peripherals.Peripherals;`
     `import static microsd.microSD.writeImage();`

Available options strongly hint on problems with `imports`; what's more, the class **Raspi** lacks any of them so the nature of our task is apparent. On the other hand, the exam just loves to palm off redundant or syntactically incorrect `imports` on us, so in the questions that concern interaction among data types located in different packages, it is much safer to start with **main()** and go with the execution flow.

Raspi's **main()** calls **assemble()** who references a constructor in **Peripherals** and a certain **writeImage()** method, which is not defined in **Raspi** → this is a telltale sign that **writeImage()** is `static` – provided, of course, its invocation is valid in the first place → a glance at **microSD** confirms: yeap, the method *is* `static` → we'll only need to look for `import static`[50] in the given options → A, B and C are instantly eliminated.

Now, option D quite correctly imports a `static` method → we can even contrast it with option E, which tries to do the same but uses () after the method's name – and that's not allowed → done.

At the Review stage we check the second LOC in option D → oh yes, it uses a fully qualified name so there's no need to import anything from the package **peripherals**. Now let's make double sure all other options are indeed incorrect.

E is wrong, we already know that. What about A? Its second LOC is valid but the invocation of **writeImage()** still needs the class name – or an object – and we have none.

Option B is out because its second `import` uses a wildcard after the class name as if it were a package.

Option C does reference the class name for **writeImage()** but the compiler still has no idea where to look for this class as its `import` is missing.

When everything is in place, the program outputs OK... OK... It works!

---

[50] Why `import static` and not just `import`? Because the call omits the class name.

Chapter
II.2

EXAM OBJECTIVES – Group Two:
Working With Java Data Types

The 1Z0-808 objectives within this group:

2.1 Declare and initialize variables (including casting of primitive data types)
2.2 Differentiate between object reference variables and primitive variables
2.3 Know how to read or write to object fields
2.4 Explain an object's lifecycle (creation, "dereference by reassignment" and garbage collection)
2.5 Develop code that uses wrapper classes such as **Boolean**, **Double**, and **Integer**

CORE RULES (with some Extras):

As the first two objectives are closely related, we will cover them in a single block.

2.1 <u>Declare and initialize variables (including casting of primitive data types)</u> +

2.2 <u>Differentiate between object reference variables and primitive variables:</u>

❑ Declaring a variable is done by stating the data type and giving the variable a valid identifier, in other words, name.

❑ The exam uses identifiers that contain – using regex for brevity – only [a-zA-Z$_][51]. Identifiers are not limited in their length.

❑ Identifiers may not begin with a digit. As for the underscore _ and the dollar sign $, they are allowed in the starting place. There's one question on the exam that has a var's name that starts with a digit. As soon as you find it, you can forget about traps in identifiers.

❑ Java keywords such as `switch` and so on, may not be used as identifiers.

❑ A literal is a fixed value that doesn't need further calculations to be assigned to any variable provided the variable is of a compatible type.

❑ Numeric literals, which are used to represent numeric values, may contain underscores between digits and begin with 1–9, 0, 0x, 0X, 0b, or 0B (where 0 stands for zero).

❑ When several variables share a type, they can be declared and initialized in the same statement.

❑ ***Non-final*** non-local variables do not require explicit initialization: they are inited automatically to their corresponding default value (which depends on the data type in question) during object instantiation (for instance fields) or class initialization (for `static` fields). ***final*** vars mandate explicit initing (discussed in more detail in the Exam Objective 6.3, *Create and overload constructors, including impact on default constructors*).

---

[51] I'm saying this simply because Java recognizes almost entire Unicode charset as valid characters for identifiers; for example, £var or ¥var are OK, too; they're just not on the exam, that's all.

EXTRA: Methods in a `final` class are effectively `final` since it's obviously impossible to override or hide them; as for fields, they aren't implicitly `final`:

```
final class One { int a = 10; static int b = 20; }
class Test {
    public static void main(String[] args) {
        One o = new One();
        o.a = 30; o.b = 40;                        // compiles just fine
        System.out.println(o.a + " " + o.b);       // 30 40
    }
}
```

❑ Local variables (including loop vars) must be explicitly initialized before use.

❑ The basic building blocks of Java types are the so-called primitive types, which are predefined by the language. Java doesn't allow user-defined primitive types.

❑ The language defines eight primitive data types – `byte`, `short`, `int`, `long`, `float`, `double`, `char`, and `boolean` – which can be classified as follows:

  ■ numeric:
      – integral types
      – floating-point types
  ■ boolean

❑ Numeric types:

  ■ Numeric types can store either integer or floating-point values.

  ■ `byte`, `short`, `int`, and `long` can be used to store integers.

  ■ `byte`, `short`, `int`, and `long` allocate 8, 16, 32, and 64 bits, respectively, to store their values.

  ■ `float` and `double` can be used to store floating-point values.

  ■ `float` and `double` allocate 32 and 64 bits, respectively, to store their values.

  ■ The default data type for integral literals is `int`.

  ■ To designate an integer as `long`, we append L or l to the literal value.

  ■ Numeric values can be stored in binary, octal, decimal, and hexadecimal formats.

  ■ Decimal literals use digits from 0 to 9. Octal literals use digits from 0 to 7 (a total of 8 digits). Hexadecimal literals use digits from 0 to 9 and letters from A to F. Binary literals use digits 0 and 1.

  ■ Octal literals must be prefixed with 0 (zero), hex literals start with the prefix 0x or 0X, and binary literals begin with 0b or 0B.

  ■ The default data type for floating-point values is `double`.

  ■ To designate an integral or floating-point value as `float`, we add the suffix F or f to the literal value.

  ■ The suffixes D and d can be used to mark a literal as a `double` value.

  ■ The `char` data type is stored as an unsigned positive integer.

- char can store a single 16-bit Unicode character, from '\u0000' (or 0) to a maximum of '\uffff' (or 65,535) inclusive.

- When a symbol gets assigned to a char, Java stores its integer equivalent value. It is therefore allowed to assign a positive integer value to a char instead of a symbol (for example, char ch = 97 to store the letter 'a').

- To assign a symbol to a char variable, we use single quotes: char ch = 'a';

❑ The data type boolean:

- boolean can store data with only two possible values, true and false, which are also used as literal values.

- Unlike some other programming languages, Java does not recognize the numeric literals 1 and 0 as valid boolean values.

❑ Casting:

- Casting is the process of forcefully making a variable behave as a variable of another type. Casting applies to both primitive and reference variables, and can be implicit or explicit.

- Automatic casting done by the Java compiler internally is called implicit casting. Implicit casting is performed to convert a narrower data type to a wider data type.

- The casting done by the programmer is called explicit casting. Explicit casting is mandatory to convert a wider data type to a narrower data type.

- Converting a narrower data type into a wider data type is called widening while converting a wider data type into a narrower type is called narrowing. Widening is safe so the Java compiler does not flag any error even if the programmer did not use the cast operator (T). Narrowing is intrinsically unsafe, hence the programmer should explicitly use the cast operator in narrowing.

❑ Reference types:

- Primitive types, which represent single values, can be assembled into reference types, which represent a group of values.

- Apart from this, reference types can also have methods.

- Unlike primitive types, reference types can be null.

❑ Default values for primitive numeric types are their corresponding 'zeroes' (that is, 0 or 0.0) and false for boolean.

❑ Reference types default to null.

Extra Practical Rules:

- Both f/F and d/D can be used not only on floating-point literals, so float f = 10F is VALID.

- ANY integral literal (incl. in binary, hex or octal notation) is assignable to `long` w/o l/L.

- <u>ATTN</u>: `char` literals (such as 'a', etc.) are assignable to `long` BUT w/o l/L ONLY.

- The underscores in numerical values can appear ONLY between digits or be chained like

    1____2__3 (same as 123)[52]. They can be used in the floating point literals, too:

    ```
    double d = 0_1234.567;              // 1234.567
    ```

- `floats` with floating-point literals should have f/F appended → be attentive to the cases when they are passed to methods that expect `floats`.

<u>Using Exponent</u>:

The exponent is used with the floating-point literals only (e or E for decimals, or p or P for hexes):

```
double d1 = .2e2;
double d2 = 2.e2;
double d3 = 2.0e2;
//  double d4 = 2.0e2.0;        // INVALID; the exponent must be an integer
double d5 = (long) .2e2;
//  double d6 = (Long) .2e2;    // INVALID; two-step transformation
double d7 = 0E0D;              // obfuscated 0.0
int    a  = 0X0E0D;           // nothing fancy, just 3597 in hex notation
```

<u>Octal Notation</u>:   A floating point number cannot be written in octal (it gets interpreted as decimal, instead):

```
class Octal{
    public static void main(String[] args) {
    double x1 = 01234.;
    double x2 = 01234;
    System.out.println(x1 + " " + x2);       // 1234.0 668.0
    }
}
```

<u>Casting to `char` and back</u>:   What it boils to, `char` is unsigned whereas `byte`, `short`, etc. can be negative, so **char = short** and so on *won't compile*.

Also, `char` can hold up to 65535 while `short` maxes out at 32767, so **short = char** *won't compile*, either. An explicit cast to the rescue!

- Implicit narrowing occurs only for `byte`, `char`, `short`, and `int` → it does not occur for `long`, `float`, or `double`.

  So, this will not compile:

  ```
  int i = 129L;
  char ch = 30L; will fail, too, even though 30 is representable in char.
  ```

  However:

  ```
  final int s = 10;
  char c = s;     // OK as s is a constant (it's final) and its value fits into a char.
  ```

---

[52] The use of underscores is better to be left to declarations only: there are cases when underscores are simply not allowed (for example, the **Integer.decode()** method does not accept underscores between digits).

Combat Rule:

No *VARIABLE* other than `char` can be assigned to a `char` without an explicit cast whereas a *CONSTANT* can be assigned to a `char` only if the value fits into `char`.

Converting from `int` or `long` to `float` or from `long` to `double` can lead to loss of precision.[53]

`char` behaves almost as an unsigned `short`[54], e.g.:

`sout('a' +1)` prints 98

A floating-point literal written in **binary** or **hex** cannot use any suffix denoting the floating-point notation (**other wording**: the floating-point suffixes f, F, d, and D are applicable only to decimal notation.)

Known trap on the exam: Watch out for casts: they act on the nearest right-side neighbor only.

`null` can be cast to any reference type: `"Hello".equals((String)null);` is perfectly valid.

---

[53] https://www.securecoding.cert.org/confluence/display/java/NUM13-J.+Avoid+loss+of+precision+when+converting+primitive+integers+to+floating-point

[54] It is not a two's-compliment integral type, though…

Problem 2.1   Given:

```
class Test {
    public static void main(String[] args) {
        String[][] astr = new String[2][];
        astr[0] = new String[2];
        astr[1] = new String[3];
        int a = 42;
        for (int i = 0; i < astr.length; i++) {
            for (int j = 0; j < astr.length; j++) {
                astr[i][j] = "" + a;
                a++;
            }
        }
        for (String[] e : astr) {
            for (String c : e) {
                System.out.print(c + " ");
            }
            System.out.println();
        }
    }
}
```

What is the result?

A.   42 43
      44 45 null
B.   42 43
      44 45 46
C.   Compilation fails
D.   A NullPointerException is thrown at run time
E.   An ArrayIndexOutOfBoundsException is thrown at run time

Problem 2.2   Given the code fragment:

```
3. public static void main(String[] args)  {
4.         float fVar = 123.123f;
5.         double dVar  = 123;
6.         short sVar = 123;
7.         int iVar = 123;
8.         long lVar = 123;
9.         iVar = fVar;
10.        fVar = iVar;
11.        dVar = fVar;
12.        lVar = sVar;
13.        fVar = dVar;
14.        dVar = iVar;
15.        iVar = dVar;
16. }
```

How many LOCs fail to compile?

A.   one
B.   two
C.   three
D.   four

Problem 2.3   Given the following code:

```
package periodictable;
class Element {
    public String name;
    public int electrons;

    public Element(String name, int electrons) {
        this.name = name;
        this.electrons = electrons;
    }
}
```

And the following main method inside another class in the same package:

```
public static void main(String[] args){
    Element[] AlkaliMetals = {
        new Element("Lithium", 3),
        new Element("Sodium", 11),
        new Element("Potassium", 19),
        new Element("Rubidium", 37),
        new Element("Caesium", 55),
        new Element("Francium", 87),
    };

    System.out.println("Group:\t\t\t" + AlkaliMetals);
    System.out.println("Element:\t\t" + AlkaliMetals[3]);
    System.out.println("Number of electrons:\t" + AlkaliMetals[3].electrons);
}
```

Assuming that the hash codes are correct, what is the result?

A.   Group: AlkaliMetals
     Element: Rubidium
     Number of electrons: 37

B.   Group: [Lperiodictable.Element;@2a139a55
     Element: Rubidium
     Number of electrons: 37

C.   Group: [Lperiodictable.Element;@2a139a55
     Element: periodictable.Element@15db9742
     Number of electrons: 37

D.   Group: [Lperiodictable.Element;@2a139a55
     Element: periodictable.Element@15db9742
     Number of electrons: Electrons@372sf871

E.   Group: [Lperiodictable.Element;@2a139a55
     Element: Rubidium
     Number of electrons: null

Problem 2.4   Which two code fragments are illegal?

A.   abstract int MyVar = 42;
B.   private final static String str = "?!";
C.   byte b1 = 1, b2, b3 = 3;
D.   short s1 = 10, int i1 = 123;
E.   double d1 = 0f;

Problem 2.5 **Given:**

```
public static void main (String [] args){
    int a, b, c = 0;                         // line 1
    int a, b, c;                             // line 2
    int g, int h, int i = 0;                 // line 3
    int d, e, FIELD;                         // line 4
    int k = l = m = 0;                       // line 5
}
```

Which two declarations compile?

    A. On line 1
    B. On line 2
    C. On line 3
    D. On line 4
    A. On line 5

Problem 2.6 **How many illegal statements are in the following code fragment?**

```
byte myByte = 128;
byte yourByte = (byte) 128;
byte hisByte = (short) 128;
byte herByte = (int) 128;
```

    A. One
    B. Two
    C. Three
    D. Four
    E. None

Problem 2.7 **Which declaration correctly initializes a** `boolean` **variable?**

    A. boolean flag1 = 1;
    B. boolean flag2 = 0;
    C. boolean flag3 = null;
    D. boolean false = false;
    E. boolean True = 1 < 2;

Problem 2.8 **Which code fragment causes a compilation error?**

    A. float f3 = 1000;
    B. float f1 = 1000F;
    C. float f2 = (float) 1_000.0;
    D. double f4 = 1000.0;
    E. float f5 = 1000.0;
    F. float f7 = (float) f4;

Problem 2.9   Given:

```
class Choices {
    private boolean flag;
    private int number;
    public void show() {
        while (flag) {
            if (number % 2 == 0){
                number += 4;
                System.out.print(number + " ");
            } else {
                number *= 2;
                System.out.print(number + " ");
            }
            if (number > 16) break;
        }
    }
    public static void main (String[] args) {
        new Choices().show();
    }
}
```

What is the result?

    A. 0 4 8 12
    B. 0 2 6 10 14
    C. Compilation fails
    D. The program enters an endless loop
    E. The program prints nothing

Problem 2.10 Given:

```
public class Slope {
    public static void main(String[] args) {
        int bottom;
        int ridge = 5;
        while ( ridge-- > 0 ) ++bottom;
        System.out.print("Result: " + bottom);
    }
}
```

What is the result?

    A. Result: 4
    B. Result: 5
    C. Result: 6
    D. The program enters an endless loop
    E. Compilation fails

Problem 2.11 Given:

```
public class Test {
    public static void main(String[] args) {
        double[] darr = {11, 22.0, 'a', 33.0f};
        for (double e : darr) {
            e = e + 10;
            System.out.print(e + " ");
        }
    }
}
```

What is the result?

      A. 21.0 32.0 107.0 43.0
      B. 21.0 32.0 a10 43.0
      C. Compilation fails
      D. An exception is thrown at run time

Problem 2.12 Given:

```
package test;
class Parent {
    public static void main(String[] args){
        Child c = new Child();
        Parent p = new Parent();
        p = c;
        System.out.println("parent: " + p.getClass());
        System.out.println("child: " + c.getClass());
    }
}
class Child extends Parent{}
```

What is the result?

      A. parent: class test.Object
          child: class test.Child
      B. parent: class test.Parent
          child: class test.Child
      C. parent: class test.Child
          child: class test.Parent
      D. parent: class test.Child
          child: class test.Child

Problem 2.13 Given:

```
public class Arr {
    public static void main(String[] args) {
        int [] arr = null;
        System.out.println(arr);
    }
}
```

What is the result?

      A. 0
      B. null
      C. Compilation fails
      D. java.lang.NullPointerException is thrown

Problem 2.14 Given:

```
class A {
    static void run (int[] a) {
        a[0] += 10;
    }
    public static void main (String[] args) {
        int[] a = new int[1];
        a[0] = 5;
        run(a);
        System.out.println(a[0]); } }
```

What is the result?

 A. 5
 B. 10
 C. 15
 D. Compilation fails
 E. An exception is thrown at run time.

Problem 2.15 Given:

```
public class Test {
    public static void main (String[] args) {
        int arr1[] = {1, 3, 5, 7, 9};
        int arr2[] = {0, 2, 4, 6};
        arr2 = arr1;
        for (int e : arr2) {
            System.out.print(e + " ");
        }
    }
}
```

What is the result?

 A. 0 2 4 6
 B. 0 2 4 6 9
 C. 1 3 5 7
 D. 1 3 5 7 9
 E. Compilation fails
 F. An exception is thrown at run time

Problem 2.16 Given:

```
class NegativeModulo {
    static void getModulo(float f){
        System.out.println(-f%-f);
    }
    public static void main(String[] args) {
        getModulo(2.0);
    }
}
```

What is the result:

 A. 0
 B. 0.0
 C. -0.0
 D. Compilation fails
 E. An IllegalArgumentException is thrown at run time

Problem 2.17 Given the following code fragment:

```
char c = Byte.MAX_VALUE + 1;
byte b = c;
if (b >= 0) System.out.println("pos");
else System.out.println("neg");
```

What is the result?

    A. pos is printed
    B. neg is printed
    C. Compilation fails
    D. An ArithmeticException is thrown

Problem 2.18 Given the following:

```
 1 package mypack;
 2 import static java.lang.Double.parseDouble;
 3
 4 class Square {
 5     final static float squareIt (String str){
 6         return (float) parseDouble(str) * parseDouble(str);
 7     }
 8     public static void main(String[] args) {
 9         System.out.println(new Square().squareIt("2.0"));
10     }
11 }
```

What is the result?

    A. The code prints 4.0
    B. Compilation fails on line 2
    C. Compilation fails on line 6
    D. Compilation fails on line 9

2.3   <u>Know how to read or write to object fields</u>:

❑   An object field is another name for an instance variable defined in a class.

❑   Access modifiers[55] determine if the object fields can be read and written to directly by using instance variables.

❑   <u>Accessing object fields</u>:

■   Reading:

– by directly accessing the field (its access modifier permitting), or
– by using a method that returns the field's value.

■   Writing:

– by directly accessing the field (its access modifier permitting), or
– by using constructors or methods that assign a value to the field.

 EXERCISES (for Key Summary ref.to App.D):

Problem 2.19   Given:

```
public class Report {
    int sizeMB;
    String title;
    public Report(int sizeMB, String title) {
        this.sizeMB = sizeMB;
        this.title = title;
    }
}
```

And given the code fragment:

```
Report r1 = new Report(25, "Report");
Report r2 = new Report(25, "Report");
Report r3 = r1;
boolean b1 = r1 == r2;
boolean b2 = r2.title.equals(r3.title);
System.out.print(b1 + " : " + b2);
```

What is the result?

A.   true : true
B.   true : false
C.   false : true
D.   false : false

---

[55] The use of access modifiers is covered by Exam Objective 6.5, "Apply encapsulation principles to a class".

Problem 2.20   Given:

```
class ExamTaker {
    public String name;
    protected int score;
    private boolean passed;
    public void show() { System.out.println(
            "Name: " + this.name + ", Passed: " + isPassed(score));
    }
    public boolean isPassed(int score) {
        return passed = score >= 65;
    }
    public void setScore(int score){
        this.score = score;
    }
}
class OCAJP8 {
    public static void main(String[] args) {
        ExamTaker alice, bob;
        alice = bob = new ExamTaker();
        alice.name = "Alice";
        bob.name = "Bob";
        bob.setScore(62);                       // Bob failed the exam...
        alice.setScore(100);                    // but Alice got the perfect score!
        bob.show();
    }
}
```

What is the result?

A. Name: Alice, Passed: true
B. Name: Alice, Passed: false
C. Name: Bob, Passed: true
D. Name: Bob, Passed: false
E. Compilation fails

Problem 2.21   Given the class:

```
class ObjectFields {
    int iVar;
    static int cVar;
    void setFields(){
        this.iVar = 22;
        this.cVar = 22;
    }
    public static void main(String[] args) {
        ObjectFields of = new ObjectFields();
        of.iVar = 100;
        ObjectFields.cVar = 200;
        iVar = 200;
        cVar = 300;
        this.iVar = 200;
        this.cVar = 400;
        of.iVar = 100;
        of.cVar += 200;
        ObjectFields.cVar += 300;
        of.setFields();
        System.out.println("iVar=" + of.iVar + ", cVar=" + of.cVar);
    }
}
```

What is the result if we comment out all those LOCs that do not compile?

    A. iVar=22, cVar=22
    B. iVar=200, cVar=300
    C. iVar=400, cVar=700
    D. iVar=600, cVar=1100

Problem 2.22   Given:

```
class Q {
    String str = "null";
    int a = 12;
    Q(String String) {
        str = String;
    }
    Q(int a) {
        this.a = a;
    }
    void println() {
        System.out.print(str + " " + a + " ");
    }
    public static void main(String[] args) {
        new Q("Hi!").println();
        new Q(123).println();
    }
}
```

What is the result?

    A. null 12 null 123
    B. Hi! 12 null 12
    C. Hi! 12 null 123
    D. Compilation fails

Problem 2.23   Given:

```
class Engine {
    int hp;
    String model;
    Engine() {
        hp = 80;
        model = "Junior";
    }
}
public class Test {
    public static void main(String[] args) {
        Engine e1 = new Engine();
        Engine e2 = test1(e1);
        test2(e2);
        System.out.println(e1.hp + " " + e2.model);
    }
    public static Engine test1(Engine e) {
        e.model = "Senior";
        e.hp = 120;
        return e;
    }
    public static void test2(Engine e) {
        e.model = "Grandpa";
        e.hp = 170;
        return;
    }
}
```

What is the result?

    A. 80 Junior

    B. 120 Senior

    C. 170 Grandpa

    D. Compilation fails

Problem 2.24   Given:

```
class NetBeans {
    private String theme;
    public String getTheme() {
        return theme;
    }

    public void setTheme(String theme) {
        this.theme = theme;
    }

    public static void main (String[] args) {
        NetBeans nb1 = new NetBeans();
        NetBeans nb2 = new NetBeans();
        nb1.setTheme(null);
        nb2.setTheme("Darcula");
        System.out.print(nb1.getTheme() + " : " + nb2.getTheme());
    }
}
```

What is the result?

    A. : Darcula

    B. null : Darcula

    C. Darcula : Darcula

    D. A NullPointerException is thrown at run time

Problem 2.25   Given:

```
class Char {
    char var;
    public static void main (String[] args) {
        char var1 = 'a';
        char var2 = var1;
        var2 = 'b';
        Char c1 = new Char();
        Char c2 = c1;
        c1.var = 'c';
        c2.var = 'd';

        System.out.print(var1 + ", " + var2);
        System.out.print(c1.var + ", " + c2.var);
    }
}
```

What is the result?

    A. a, bc, d

    B. a, bd, d

    C. c, bd, d

    D. b, cc, d

Problem 2.26   Given the following classes:

```
class Student {
    private int age;
    private String name;
    public String getName() { return name; }
    public void setName(String name) { this.name = name; }
    public int getAge() { return age; }
    public void setAge(int age) { this.age = age; }
}

public class Test {
    public static void main(String[] args) {
        Student std = new Student();
        // insert code here
    }
}
```

Which statement sets the field `name` of the object `std`?

    A.   std.setName() = "John Smith";

    B.   setName("John Smith");

    C.   Student.setName("John Smith");

    D.   std.setName("John Smith");

CORE RULES (with some Extras):

2.4 Explain an object's lifecycle (creation, "dereference by reassignment" and garbage collection):

- ❑ Object's lifecycle:

    - ■ It begins when the object is initialized and ends when the object goes out of scope or is no longer referenced;

    - ■ A live object can be referenced by a var to make available its methods and fields to other objects;

    - ■ Simply declaring a reference var does not imply that a new object will be created.

    - ■ Out of several practical ways[56] to create a new object in Java only two are needed for the 1Z0-808 exam:

        - by using the keyword `new`   ← universal method[57]
        - by using double quotes   ← this shorthand is available only for **String**.

    - ■ An object becomes eligible for garbage collection when it can no longer be accessed.

    - ■ An object becomes inaccessible when no reference variable points to it any longer because:

        - the reference variable was re-assigned to another object,
        - the refvar was set to `null`, or
        - went out of scope

- ❑ The inaccessible objects are removed from memory by the so-called garbage collection mechanism. The purpose of garbage collection is to identify and remove the objects that are no longer needed by a program so that their resources can be reclaimed and reused.

- ❑ EXTRA: **OutOfMemoryError** is thrown by the JVM when it's unable to create objects on the heap and the garbage collector cannot free more memory for the JVM.

- ❑ EXTRA: The programmer can attempt to call the garbage collector by calling the method **System.gc()** or **Runtime.getRuntime().gc()** but the fact is the garbage collector is invoked fully automatically and it is not guaranteed that the GC process will ever run during a program's lifecycle. All we can be sure about is whether objects are eligible for being garbage collected.

---

[56] 1) `new`, 2) clone(), 3) Class.forName(), 4) newInstance(), 5) by deserialization, 6) thru the class **Constructor**.

[57] Although it does look like the LDT-related classes don't use `new`, they simply define no `public` constructors; that's why we need to use `static` methods to create, say, a **LocalDate** object by calling **LocalDate.of()**, which invokes **create()** who then calls `private` **LocalDate**(int year, int month, int dayOfMonth) constructor, and so on.

Problem 2.27   Given:

```
public class ObjectsGalore {
    static ObjectsGalore obj1, obj2, obj3, obj4;
    int numberOfObjects;
    public static int addObject(ObjectsGalore obj4) {
        return obj4.numberOfObjects *= 2;
    }
    public static void main(String[] args) {
        obj1 = obj2 = obj3 = new ObjectsGalore();
        obj4 = obj2;
        addObject(obj4);
    }
}
```

How many objects of the class ObjectsGalore are created in memory at run time?

A. 1
B. 4
C. 8
D. Compilations fails

Problem 2.28   Given:

```
public class ExamTaker {
    private String name;
    private int score;
    private String exam;
    private boolean passed;
    ExamTaker(){}
    ExamTaker(String name, int score, String exam){
        this.name = name;
        this.score = score;
        this.exam = exam;
    }
    public void show() {
        System.out.println("Name: " + name + ", passed: " + passed);
    }
    public boolean isPassed() {
        return passed = score >= 65;
    }
    public static void main(String[] args) {
        // line X
    }
}
```

Which statement, when inserted at line X, correctly initializes an ExamTaker instance?

A. ExamTaker examTaker = "Bob";
B. ExamTaker examTaker = ExamTaker.new("Bob", 100, "1Z0-808");
C. ExamTaker examTaker = new ExamTaker();
D. ExamTaker examTaker = ExamTaker("Bob", 100, "1Z0-808");
E. None of the above

Problem 2.29   Given:

```
1.  class Student {
2.      String name;
3.      Student(String name){
4.          this.name = name;
5.      }
6.  }
7.    public class Test {
8.        public static void main (String[] args) {
9.            Student s1 = new Student("Alice");
10.           Student s2 = new Student("Bob");
11.           Student s3 = new Student("Carol");
12.           s1 = s3;
13.           s3 = s2;
14.           s2 = null;
15.       }
16.   }
```

Which statement is true?

    A.   After line 14, three objects are eligible for garbage collection.
    B.   After line 14, two objects are eligible for garbage collection.
    C.   After line 14, one object is eligible for garbage collection.
    D.   After line 14, none of the objects is eligible for garbage collection.

Problem 2.30   Given:

```
1.  class A {
2.     String name;
3.     A obj;
4.     A(String name){
5.         this.name = name;
6.     }
7.  }
8.
9.  class B extends A {
10.    B(String name) {
11.        super(name);
12.    }
13. }
14.
15. class Test {
16.    public static void main(String[] args) {
17.        A aa = new A("AA");
18.        A ab = new B("AB");
19.        B bb = new B("BB");
20.        aa.obj = ab;
21.        ab.obj = bb;
22.        ab = bb;
23.        bb = null;
24.        ab = null;
25.
26.    }
27. }
```

When the object ab, created by LOC18, becomes eligible for GC?

    A.   After line 22
    B.   After line 23
    C.   After line 24
    D.   Never in this program

2.5 Develop code that uses wrapper classes such as **Boolean**, **Double**, and **Integer**:

❏ What are wrapper classes?

Java provides specialized classes corresponding to each of the primitive data types:

byte ↔ **Byte**, short ↔ **Short**, int ↔ **Integer**, long ↔ **Long**,

float ↔ **Float**, double ↔ **Double**,

char ↔ **Character**,

boolean ↔ **Boolean**

These are called wrapper classes.

❏ Why do we need wrapper classes?

Sometimes it becomes easier to handle primitives if they were objects. For example, the wrapper classes provide many useful methods for such occasions but these methods expect objects as their arguments. Now and then it is simply required: say, being a **Collection**, an **ArrayList** is not allowed to contain primitives. In this case, Java can autobox the passed primitive parameters into the proper wrapper types – and we then can use on them handy methods from the **java.util** package such as **Collections.sort()** and so on.

❏ What is autoboxing?

Autoboxing refers to converting primitive data types into objects (that is, instances of the corresponding wrapper classes) automatically by the compiler.

❏ What is unboxing?

Converting an object into its underlying primitive data type is called unboxing.

EXTRA:

❏ More on wrappers:

■ All primitive wrappers' constructors EXCEPT **Character** (which has only one constructor: **Character**(char value)) accept a null treating it as a null **String** but they then throw an NFE (or NPE in case of **Float** and **Double**) EXCEPT the **Boolean**(null) constructor, which returns FALSE (in contrast to the primitive false).

■ None of the primitive wrapper classes has a no-arg constructor.

■ ALL wrappers (except **Character**) accept a **String** and ALL (no exceptions) accept their underlying primitives;

■ Most popular methods:

valueOf(): STATIC! returns a **Wrapper** object; accepts both **String** and primitive
static Integer valueOf(int i)   Returns an Integer instance representing the specified int value.
static Integer valueOf(String s)   Returns an Integer obj holding the value of the specified String.

*prim***Value():** NON-STATIC! returns an underlying primitive; is a no-arg instance method;
int intValue()   Returns the value of this **Integer** as an int.

parse*Prim***():** STATIC! returns a primitive that represents the passed-in String; accepts String by def
static int parseInt(String s)   Parses the string argument as a signed decimal integer.

■ **Boolean**.FALSE is an **Object** (same for **Boolean**.TRUE).

□ **Constructors: in most cases two constructors** (except **Character** and **Float**)

Boolean(boolean value)
Boolean(String s)   ←   case-insensitive!
                                          most importantly: if String = **null** OR **not a valid keyword:**
                                          → Boolean.FALSE (obj corresponding to the primitive `false`)
Integer(int value)   - - - - - - }   no traps here
Integer(String s)   - - - - - - }
Byte(byte value)   ←   TRAP: <u>accepts only byte!</u> new Byte(1) won't work; needs cast
Byte(String s)   ←   TRAP: new Byte("128") throws an NFE
Short(short value)   - - - - - - }   accepts both `short` and `byte` (will be widened)
Short(String s)   - - - - - - }
Long(long value)   - - - - - - }   accepts any integral two's-compliment type → no `char`
Long(String s)   - - - - - - }
Character(char value)   ←   accepts only 'apostrophed' args such as 'a' or '\u0123'
                                          or a cast (e.g., Character c = new Character((char)1);
Float(double value)   ←   strange but true… syntax sugar?
Float(float value)
Float(String s)   ←   Float("1"), Float("1f") and Float("1d") are OK
                                          Float("1L") throws an NFE
                                          Float("01"), Float("01F") and Float("01D") are OK
                                          Float("0x…[F/D]") and Float("0b…") throw an NFE
Double(double value)
Double(String s)   ←   similar to Float

□ primitive == wrapper works; the right-hand side gets unboxed.

□ A primitive passed to a **List**<Wrapper> will autobox.

However – WATCH OUT! – the compiler will perform **only a single-step** conversion on its own! can't add, say, a `byte` or `short` to **List**<Integer>):

```
byte b = 10;
short s = 20;
List<Integer> l = new ArrayList<>();
//    l.add(b);                        // won't compile
//    l.add(s);                        // won't compile, either
l.add( (int)b );                       // VALID
```

□ Parsers of the wrapper classes accept only **String**s (or **String**, radix).

□ **Boolean.valueOf**(String**)** and its overloaded **Boolean.valueOf**(boolean) version return a reference to either **Boolean.**TRUE or **Boolean.**FALSE wrapper obj, and do NOT create a new **Boolean** object; they simply return the `static` constants **TRUE** or **FALSE** defined in the **Boolean** class.

□ All wrapper classes are immutable.

□ Although the wrappers extend **Number**, there's no IS-A relation between any two of the wrapper classes. So, casting an **Integer** to, say, **Long** won't work. **Byte** == **Short**, etc. throws a comperr, too.

□ **Byte**, **Short**, **Integer** and **Long** use the same numerical pool (similar to **String** case) up to `byte`'s boundaries (-128 … 127), hence == evaluates to `true` when the values are the same and do not overshoot this range. Beyond those boundaries, the operator 'double equals' compares just object references.

Problem 2.31   **Given:**

```
public class Book {
    String title;
    boolean secondHand;
    double price;
    Book() {
        // line b1
    }
    public String toString(){
        return title + ", new: " + !secondHand + ", price: " + price;
    }
    public static void main(String[] args) {
        Book b = new Book();
        // line b2
        System.out.print(b);
    }
}
```

Which two modifications, made independently, enable the code to print Gone with the Wind, new: true, price: 9.5?

  A. Replace line b2 with:
```
b.title = "Gone with the Wind";
b.secondHand = false;
b.price = 9.5;
```
  B. Replace line b2 with:
```
this.title = "Gone with the Wind";
this.secondHand = false;
this.price = 9.5;
```
  C. Replace line b1 with:
```
this.title = new String("Gone with the Wind");
this.secondHand = new Boolean(false);
this.price = new Double(9.5);
```
  D. Replace line bl with:
```
title = "Gone with the Wind";
secondHand = FALSE;
price = 9.5f;
```
  E. Replace line b1 with:
```
this("Gone with the Wind", false, 9.5);
```

Problem 2.32   **Given:**
```
public class BoolArray {
    public static void main(String[] args) {
        Boolean[] barr = new Boolean[3];
        barr[0] = new Boolean(Boolean.parseBoolean("tRUE"));
        barr[1] = new Boolean("True");
        barr[2] = new Boolean(false);
        System.out.println(barr[0] + " " + barr[1] + " " + barr[2]);
    }
}
```

What is the result?

  A. true false false
  B. true true false
  C. false false false
  D. An IllegalArgumentException is thrown at run time
  E. A NullPointerException is thrown at run time

Problem 2.33   Given:

```java
class Parser {
    String input = "2013";
    public void parseMe(String str) {
        int output = 0;
        try {
            String input = str;
            output = Integer.parseInt(input);
        } catch (IllegalArgumentException iae) {
            System.out.println("Wrong argument!");
        }
        System.out.println(
            "input: " + input + ", output: " + output);
    }
    public static void main(String[] args) {
        Parser p = new Parser();
        p.parseMe("0123");
    }
}
```

What is the result?

    A.   input: 0123, output: 0123
    B.   input: 2013, output: 0123
    C.   input: 2013, output: 83
    D.   Wrong argument!
    E.   None of the above

Problem 2.1 – A

Given:

```
class Test {
    public static void main(String[] args) {
        String[][] astr = new String[2][];              // line t1
        astr[0] = new String[2];
        astr[1] = new String[3];
        int a = 42;
        for (int i = 0; i < astr.length; i++) {
            for (int j = 0; j < astr.length; j++) {      // line t2
                astr[i][j] = "" + a;
                a++;
            }
        }
        for (String[] e : astr) {
            for (String c : e) {
                System.out.print(c + " ");
            }
            System.out.println();
        }
    }
}
```

What is the result?

A. 42 43
    44 45 null
B. 42 43
    44 45 46
C. Compilation fails
D. A NullPointerException is thrown at run time
E. An ArrayIndexOutOfBoundsException is thrown at run time

The refvar **astr** declared on line t1 is local and needs explicit initing before use. The next example throws a comperr saying that variable **myStr** 'may not have been initialized':

```
public static void main(String[] args) {
    String myStr;
    System.out.println(myStr);          // INVALID
}
```

This restriction becomes painfully evident in case of primitives, which you have doubtlessly observed many times. In our problem, however, we are dealing with an array, which is a reference type whose value gets inited at the point of allocation (an object gets created → the refvar that points to it is assigned a value that holds this object's address). The following compiles but throws an **ArrayIndexOutOfBoundsException** when the JVM attempts to access the first slot in the array **astr**:

```
public static void main(String[] args) {
    String myStr = "hello";                 // shorthand to create a String obj
    System.out.println(myStr);
    String[] myArr = new String[0];
    System.out.println(myArr);              // [Ljava.lang.String;@2a139a55
    System.out.println(myArr[0]);           // throws AIOOBE
    int b = 123;
    System.out.println(b);    }
```

Still, the reference var **myArr** is inited even if its length is zero. But what about the values that an array's slots hold when the array's length isn't zero? The JLS8, §4.12.5, says that

> Each class variable, instance variable, or <u>array component</u> is initialized with a default value when it is created.

From here follows that since our array is of type **String**, each slot gets inited with a `null` as the same §4.12.5 stipulates that "For all reference types, the default value is `null`".

Now, the code in Problem 2.1 uses a nested `for` loop to assign some other values to the second dimension of the array **astr** but takes the *first* dimension's length as the criterion for its conditional expression on line t2. Since the array is jagged (its 2nd dim is longer than the 1st dim), the last slot in the 2nd dim is left out of the loop and retains its initial value, that is, `null`. Should the conditional expression on line t2 be rewritten as `j<astr[0].length`, the 2nd dim wouldn't have contained `null`s at all.

Problem 2.2 – C

Given the code fragment:

```
3. public static void main(String[] args)  {
4.          float fVar = 123.123f;
5.          double dVar  = 123;
6.          short sVar = 123;
7.          int iVar = 123;
8.          long lVar = 123;
9.          iVar = fVar;
10.         fVar = iVar;
11.         dVar = fVar;
12.         lVar = sVar;
13.         fVar = dVar;
14.         dVar = iVar;
15.         iVar = dVar;
16. }
```

How many LOCs fail to compile?

- A. one
- B. two
- C. three
- D. four

The floating-point literals are treated as `double`s by default but line 4 works because 123.123 has the suffix **f** appended to it; otherwise it wouldn't have compiled.

Line 5 compiles because floating-point variables accept integer constants.

Line 6 is OK, too, since the value 123 – which is an `int` by default – is automatically narrowed to `short` and 123 is within the range for a `short`.

Line 7 is just trivial and doesn't throw a comperr, either.

On line 8 we have an automatic widening to a `long`.

Line 9, however, attempts to assign a floating-point variable to an `int`, so the compiler complains of 'a possible lossy conversion from `float` to `int`'. An explicit cast to `int` would have worked here, although it can lead to a loss of precision.

The assignments on lines 11 through 12 are all valid because the right-hand sides are narrower than the left-hand sides, but the next LOC attempts to perform a lossy conversion from `double` to `float`. An explicit cast `fVar = (float)dVar` would force the LOC to compile.

And finally, line 15 wants to assign a wider `double` to a much narrower `int`, which flags a comperr. Naturally, `iVar = (int)dVar` would make the line valid.

Taking all this into consideration, we can conclude the current exercise by formulating the following rule: explicit casts between <u>primitive numeric</u> types always compile. By the way, Problem 2.6 addresses some interesting variations of this tune.

Problem 2.3 – C

Given the following code:

```
package periodictable;
class Element {
    public String name;
    public int electrons;

    public Element(String name, int electrons) {
        this.name = name;
        this.electrons = electrons;
    }
}
```

And the following main method inside another class in the same package:

```
public static void main(String[] args){
    Element[] AlkaliMetals = {
        new Element("Lithium", 3),
        new Element("Sodium", 11),
        new Element("Potassium", 19),
        new Element("Rubidium", 37),
        new Element("Caesium", 55),
        new Element("Francium", 87),
    };

    System.out.println("Group:\t\t\t" + AlkaliMetals);
    System.out.println("Element:\t\t" + AlkaliMetals[3]);
    System.out.println("Number of electrons:\t" + AlkaliMetals[3].electrons);
}
```

Assuming that the hash codes are correct, what is the result?

A. Group: AlkaliMetals
    Element: Rubidium
    Number of electrons: 37

B. Group: [Lperiodictable.Element;@<hash_value>
    Element: Rubidium
    Number of electrons: 37

C. Group: [Lperiodictable.Element;@<hash_value1>
    Element: periodictable.Element@<hash_value2>
    Number of electrons: 37

D. Group: [Lperiodictable.Element;@<hash_value1>
    Element: periodictable.Element@<hash_value2>
    Number of electrons: Electrons@<hash_value3>

E. Group: [Lperiodictable.Element;@<hash_value>
    Element: Rubidium
    Number of electrons: null

This problem contains a small trap that tests our knowledge of the fact that primitive and reference variables behave differently in many aspects. For example, even if a reference variable has been initialized, there's no guarantee that its string representation is always meaningful.

In this particular case we are dealing with an array of nameless objects, and arrays do not override the method **toString()**, which they inherit from the class **Object**. Something similar goes for user data types: they all should override **toString()**. If we added, say, the following declaration to the definition of the class **Element**

```
public String toString(){ return this.name; }
```

the code's output would have been option B.

Problem 2.4 – AD

Which two code fragments are illegal?

    A.   abstract int myVar = 42;
    B.   private final static String $tr = "?!";
    C.   byte b1 = 1, b2, b3 = 3;
    D.   short s1 = 10, int i1 = 123;
    E.   double d1 = 0f;

Option A is correct because no variable (either of primitive or reference data type) may be declared abstract in Java[58]. Option D is correct, too, as multiple declaration of variables of different data types is not allowed in one statement (the comma should have been replaced with the semicolon). Potentially problematic B is out since the Problem doesn't say **$tr** is local.

Problem 2.5 – AD

Given:

```
public static void main (String [] args){
    int a, b, c = 0;                          // line 1
    int a, b, c;                              // line 2
    int g, int h, int i = 0;                  // line 3
    int d, e, FIELD;                          // line 4
    int k = l = m = 0;                        // line 5
}
```

Which two declarations compile?

    A.   On line 1
    B.   On line 2
    C.   On line 3
    D.   On line 4
    E.   On line 5

Option A is correct because we have three vars of the same data type declared within a single stat, and the fact that only one of them gets inited is irrelevant because those vars are never used.

---

[58] This subject has been already addressed in Table 1 (Chapter II.0, *Opening Remarks*). Nevertheless, the concept of abstract variables is theoretically solid (refer, for example, to *Deductive Verification of Object-Oriented Software* by Benjamin Weiß, p.6).

Line 2 does nothing criminal in itself and would have compiled when placed before line 1 but the problem is these two LOCs declare the same local vars → they are mutually exclusive.

Option C fails compilation because the syntax does not allow repetition of data types within a single declaration stat (and commas make this entire LOC a single stat.)

Option D is OK, although Java Code Conventions[59] recommends to reserve fully capitalized identifiers for constants only (and **FIELD** looks particularly odd here as the var is local). It's not a felony, though... yet[60].

And finally, option E is invalid as it attempts to assign an undeclared **l** to **k** and undeclared **m** to **l**. If the code declared both **l** and **m** before this line, it would have compiled:

```
int l, m;
int k = l = m = 0;          // now it's VALID
```

Problem 2.6 – C

How many illegal statements are in the following code fragment?

```
byte myByte = 128;                  // line 1
byte yourByte = (byte) 128;         // line 2
byte hisByte = (short) 128;         // line 3
byte herByte = (int) 128;           // line 4
```

    A. One
    B. Two
    C. Three
    D. Four
    E. None

Line 1 is illegal because 128 is an `int` by default; actually, it wouldn't be a problem thanks to implicit narrowing but the value exceeds `byte`'s range → this LOC requires an explicit narrowing cast → and this is exactly what line 2 does; note, however, that the most significant bit gets lost in the process thus giving us an interesting result at run time.

Line 3 fails compilation because casting an `int` to `short` explicitly still doesn't address implicit lossy conversion to `byte`. What we can do here is step down one more time by adding another narrowing cast.

As for line 4, it wants to redundantly cast an `int` to `int`, which still gets assigned to a much narrower `byte` thus flagging a comperr.

Here's how we could re-write the currently illegal LOCs to make them compile:

```
byte myByte = (byte)128;               //
byte hisByte = (byte)(short) 128;      // all three vars will store -128
byte herByte = (byte)(int) 128;        //
```

[59] http://www.oracle.com/technetwork/java/codeconvtoc-136057.html
[60] Feeling tired? Take a coffee break and re-motivate yourself by reading *Imprisonment for Irresponsible Coding* by Yegor Bugayenko, http://www.yegor256.com/2015/11/24/imprisonment-for-irresponsible-coding.html

Problem 2.7 – E

    Which declaration correctly initializes a `boolean` variable?

        A. boolean flag1 = 1;
        B. boolean flag2 = 0;
        C. boolean flag3 = null;
        D. boolean false = false;
        E. boolean True = 1 < 2;

Literals 1 and 0 are not recognized by Java as valid `boolean` values so options A and B are incorrect.

The var **flag3** is declared as `boolean`, which is a primitive data type whereas `null` can be assigned to a reference type only. If **flag3** were a **Boolean**, the LOC would have compiled.

Option D illegally uses the keyword `false` as an identifier.

Option E is valid since 1) the identifier **True** is not a keyword in Java, and 2) the expression 1<2 returns a `boolean`.

Problem 2.8 – E

    Which code fragment causes a compilation error?

        A. float f3 = 1000;
        B. float f1 = 1000F;
        C. float f2 = (float) 1_000.0;
        D. double f4 = 1000.0;
        E. float f5 = 1000.0;
        F. float f7 = (float) f4;

Option A assigns an `int` to a `float`, which is valid.

Option B does the same, and the suffix F is actually redundant here.

Option C uses a mandatory narrowing cast and an underscore, which is placed correctly: between digits.

Option D is trivial because floating-point literals are `double` by default.

Option F explicitly downcasts (in other words, performs a narrowing conversion of) a `double` to a `float`, which is valid.

So this leaves us only option E: it doesn't compile because 1000.0 is `double` by default. To make this LOC compile, we could either employ a narrowing cast or add the suffix F (or f).

Problem 2.9 – E

Given:

```
class Choices {
    private boolean flag;
    private int number;
    public void show() {
        while (flag) {
            if (number % 2 == 0){
                number += 4;
                System.out.print(number + " ");
            } else {
                number *= 2;
                System.out.print(number + " ");
            }
            if (number > 16) break;
        }
    }
    public static void main (String[] args) {
        new Choices().show();
    }
}
```

What is the result?

    A. 0 4 8 12
    B. 0 2 6 10 14
    C. Compilation fails
    D. The program enters an endless loop
    E. The program prints nothing

The var **flag** is an instance field and as such does not need explicit initing; it simply gets assigned the default value, that is, `false` → so the code never enters the `while` loop and the printing stats never fire.

Problem 2.10 – E

Given:

```
public class Slope {
    public static void main(String[] args) {
        int bottom;
        int ridge = 5;
        while ( ridge-- > 0 ) ++bottom;
        System.out.print("Result: " + bottom);
    }
}
```

What is the result?

    A. Result: 4
    B. Result: 5
    C. Result: 6
    D. The program enters an endless loop
    E. Compilation fails

The var **bottom** is local and needs an explicit initing before the `while` loop may increment it. The printing stat also wants to use this uninited var, so the code actually contains two invalid LOCs.

Problem 2.11 – A

Given:

```
public class Test {
    public static void main(String[] args) {
        double[] darr = {11, 22.0, 'a', 33.0f};
        for (double e : darr) {
            e = e + 10;
            System.out.print(e + " ");
        }
    }
}
```

What is the result?

    A.   21.0 32.0 107.0 43.0
    B.   21.0 32.0 a10 43.0
    C.   Compilation fails
    D.   An exception is thrown at run time

The easiest way to tame `chars` is to remember that these sneaky things behave almost as unsigned `shorts`; take them at their numeric face, so to speak, by forcing yourself to see them as mere numbers.

Viewed from this angle, it should come as no surprise that, say, `char c = 'a' + 10` compiles just fine and that the array **darr** also gets valid primitives in each of its slots.

So, both eleven and 'a' (whose numeric value is 97) get promoted to corresponding `doubles`, and 33.0f is just a `float` that is perfectly assignable to a `double`.

Problem 2.12 – D

Given:

```
package test;
class Parent {
    public static void main(String[] args){
        Child c = new Child();
        Parent p = new Parent();
        p = c;
        System.out.println("parent: " + p.getClass());
        System.out.println("child: " + c.getClass());
    }
}
class Child extends Parent{}
```

What is the result?

    A.   parent: class test.Object
          child: class test.Child
    B.   parent: class test.Parent
          child: class test.Child
    C.   parent: class test.Child
          child: class test.Parent
    D.   parent: class test.Child
          child: class test.Child

Both **c** and **p** are reference vars, so the assop p = c simply 'dereferences' **p** to **c**, that's all. The **Parent** object gets lost as the result, and what's left is just a single object of the type **Child** – plus two distinct references that point to it.

Hm-m... Alright, one more thing: it is probably worth to note here that 'dereferencing' does not mean setting a reference var to `null` (at least not in Java); it's just a popular misconception. What really puzzles me is why the exam lists "dereference by reassignment" as one of its objectives while neither Java Lang Specs or JVM Specs define any dereference in the first place; they merely use the term...

Problem 2.13 – B

Given:

```
public class Arr {
    public static void main(String[] args) {
        int[] arr = null;
        System.out.println(arr);
    }
}
```

What is the result?

A. 0
B. null
C. Compilation fails
D. java.lang.NullPointerException is thrown

The var **arr** is of a reference type (arrays are **Object**s), so it's only natural to set it to `null`. As to why the printing stat doesn't throw an NPE when its arg is `null` and obediently outputs "null" instead, we have already covered it when discussing Problem 1.15.

Problem 2.14 – C

Given:

```
class A {
    static void run (int[] a) {
        a[0] += 10;
    }
    public static void main (String[] args) {
        int[] a = new int[1];
        a[0] = 5;
        run(a);
        System.out.println(a[0]);
    }
}
```

What is the result?

A. 5
B. 10
C. 15
D. Compilation fails
E. An exception is thrown at run time

This exercise relates to two exam objectives at once: 2.2, *Differentiate between object reference variables and primitive variables*, and 6.6, *Determine the effect upon object references and primitive values when they are passed into methods that change the values*.

This is what happens here: we pass **a** to the method **run()** → the method gets a copy of this reference var → then accesses the first slot of the array and increases it by ten.

Yes, the copy of **a** is a local var and dies when the method completes its work, but – unlike primitive vars – the changes made through a copy of an object reference get reflected in the object itself.

If you still feel confused by this difference, I suggest you look up the remote controller analogy[61]; personally, I know of no better explanation: it is concise, hits the bull's-eye, pretty vivid and clear. Soon we'll meet it again.

Problem 2.15 – D

Given:

```
public class Test {
    public static void main (String[] args) {
        int arr1[] = {1, 3, 5, 7, 9};
        int arr2[] = {0, 2, 4, 6};
        arr2 = arr1;
        for (int e : arr2) {
            System.out.print(e + " ");
        }
    }
}
```

What is the result?

A. 0 2 4 6
B. 0 2 4 6 9
C. 1 3 5 7
D. 1 3 5 7 9
E. Compilation fails
F. An exception is thrown at run time

There's no trap here, just a simple case of 'dereference by reassignment': as the code assigns **arr1** to **arr2**, the object, which **arr2** was pointing to, gets lost and forgotten.

Problem 2.16 – D

Given:

```
class NegativeModulo {
    static void getModulo(float f){
        System.out.println(-f%-f);
    }
    public static void main(String[] args) {
        getModulo(2.0);
    }
}
```

---

[61] *Data Structures and Algorithms in Java* by Michael T. Goodrich, Roberto Tamassia and Michael H. Goldwasser, 6th ed, 2014, p.7, or *Thinking in Java* by Bruce Eckel, the chapter "Everything is an Object".

What is the result?

    A. 0

    B. 0.0

    C. -0.0

    D. Compilation fails

    E. An IllegalArgumentException is thrown at run time

Whatever the modulo op does is immaterial in our case because the invocation of **getModulo()** is faulty in the first place: floating-point literals are `double` by default. On the other hand, `getModulo((float)2.0)` would have worked and produced -0.0. As to why the value is negative, please refer to the Core-Rules-plus-Extras section for Exam Objective 3.1, *Use Java operators, including parentheses to override operator precedence.*

Problem 2.17 – C

Given the following code fragment:

```
char c = Byte.MAX_VALUE + 1;
byte b = c;                              // line 1
if (b >= 0) System.out.println("pos");
else System.out.println("neg");
```

What is the result?

    A. **pos** is printed

    B. **neg** is printed

    C. Compilation fails

    D. An ArithmeticException is thrown

`char` can be as large as 65535 while `byte`'s range covers only -128 to 127 → the assignment on line 1 fails.

Problem 2.18 – C

Given the following:

```
1  package mypack;
2  import static java.lang.Double.parseDouble;
3
4  class Square {
5      final static float squareIt (String str){
6          return (float) parseDouble(str) * parseDouble(str);
7      }
8      public static void main(String[] args) {
9          System.out.println(new Square().squareIt("2.0"));
10      }
11 }
```

What is the result?

    A. The code prints 4.0

    B. Compilation fails on line 2

    C. Compilation fails on line 6

    D. Compilation fails on line 9

Line 2 is perfectly valid since Java allows redundant imports; just keep in mind that importing a `static` method is done without the parentheses (I met such a question on the second sitting).

The real problem lives on line 6 where each invocation of **parseDouble()** produces a `double`[62] but only the first value gets cast to `float` → the returned value is actually a `double` but the method **squareIt()** is supposed to return a `float`.

Problem 2.19 – C

Given:

```
public class Report {
    int sizeMB;
    String title;
    public Report(int sizeMB, String title) {
        this.sizeMB = sizeMB;
        this.title = title;
    }
}
```

And given the code fragment:

```
Report r1 = new Report(25, "Report");          // line t1
Report r2 = new Report(25, "Report");
Report r3 = r1;
boolean b1 = r1 == r2;
boolean b2 = r2.title.equals(r3.title);         // line t2
System.out.print(b1 + " : " + b2);
```

What is the result?

    A.   true : true
    B.   true : false
    C.   false : true
    D.   false : false

The code creates two distinct but identical objects, **r1** and **r2**, then declares another reference var and sets its value to **r1**. Since the `==` operator compares references, **b1** gets assigned `false` because the objects are different; on the other hand, **r1** `==` **r3** would yield `true`.

Finally, line t2 assigns `true` to **b2** since the field **title** is of type **String** and the class **String** overrides **equals()** so that the method compares not just references but actual contents.

And yes, some of the questions on the exam are *that* simple; just as I said, we should take them at their face value.

---

[62] Do remember that parsing methods in all wrapper classes produce underlying primitives.

Problem 2.20 – C

Given:

```
class ExamTaker {
    public String name;
    protected int score;
    private boolean passed;
    public void show() { System.out.println(
            "Name: " + this.name + ", Passed: " + isPassed(score));
    }
    public boolean isPassed(int score) {
        return passed = score >= 65;
    }
    public void setScore(int score){
        this.score = score;
    }
}
class OCAJP8 {
    public static void main(String[] args) {
        ExamTaker alice, bob;
        alice = bob = new ExamTaker();
        alice.name = "Alice";              // line o1
        bob.name = "Bob";                  // line o2
        bob.setScore(62);                  // Bob failed the exam...
        alice.setScore(100);               // but Alice got the perfect score!
        bob.show();
    }
}
```

What is the result?

   A.   Name: Alice, Passed: true
   B.   Name: Alice, Passed: false
   C.   Name: Bob, Passed: true
   D.   Name: Bob, Passed: false
   E.   Compilation fails

This problem uses comments to mislead you into believing that the code should print option D because "Bob failed the exam…" Personally, I didn't meet such a trap on my sittings but, if forum posts are to be believed, there are people who did – so be on alert just in case.

The real problem awaits us on the following line inside the definition of the class **OCAJP8**:

```
alice = bob = new ExamTaker();
```

This LOC blindly follows the pattern which should be reserved for initializing primitive vars only as it makes two distinct references point to the same object. While in case of primitives different vars would simply get the same values and further operations with one of the variables would not affect the other one, our situation is more complicated as we are dealing with references.

Following the analogy mentioned in the discussion to Problem 2.14, **alice** and **bob** are two distinct remote controllers that operate on the same TV set represented in our code by the object created with `new ExamTaker()`. At the moment of creation, the object was a nameless gadget, then line o1 slapped on it a sticker saying "Alice", then line o2 replaced it permanently with "Bob". After that the code pressed buttons on the remote controller named **bob** setting the TV to channel 62 (the var **score**'s value), then grabbed the remote controller named **alice** and changed the channel to 100. As the result, the output assures us that Bob passed the exam.

Problem 2.21 – A

Given the class:

```java
class ObjectFields {
    int iVar;
    static int cVar;
    void setFields(){
        this.iVar = 22;
        this.cVar = 22;
    }
    public static void main(String[] args) {
        ObjectFields of = new ObjectFields();
        of.iVar = 100;
        ObjectFields.cVar = 200;
        iVar = 200;
        cVar = 300;
        this.iVar = 200;
        this.cVar = 400;
        of.iVar = 100;
        of.cVar += 200;
        ObjectFields.cVar += 300;
        of.setFields();
        System.out.println("iVar=" + of.iVar + ", cVar=" + of.cVar);
    }
}
```

What is the result if we comment out all those LOCs that do not compile?

    A. iVar=22, cVar=22
    B. iVar=200, cVar=300
    C. iVar=400, cVar=700
    D. iVar=600, cVar=1100

Obviously, we should begin by investigating the reason(s) why the compilation fails in the first place. Scanning line after line, we find out pretty soon that the `static` method **main()** attempts to directly access the non-`static`, instance field **iVar**.

Now what? should we cross out all invalid LOCs and start adding numbers? but the exam software allows us to cross out only options and not the lines of code themselves → so most of the task must be performed mentally or at least on paper … the vars get reset occasionally… one of the fields is even static… wow, too many things to juggle and keep track of!

Fortunately, we are already armed with a handy practical rule – the 'hairier' the code, the simpler must be solution, – so let's not even waste time on computations and writing everything down. Just look closer: it's the very last statement that takes care of printing out the result; and what comes before it? A setter. Does the setter compile? Absolutely. It's 22-22, then. Takes all but twenty two seconds.

Another hint for the exam: leaving aside inheritance- and overriding-related questions, it's often printing stats that do something illegal or provide a key to instantly crack the problem, so pay close attention to **println()** and its cousins.

Problem 2.22 – C

> **Given:**
> ```
> class Q {
>     String str = "null";
>     int a = 12;
>     Q(String String) {
>         str = String;
>     }
>     Q(int a) {
>         this.a = a;
>     }
>     void println() {
>         System.out.print(str + " " + a + " ");
>     }
>     public static void main(String[] args) {
>         new Q("Hi!").println();
>         new Q(123).println();
>     }
> }
> ```

> **What is the result?**
>
> A. null 12 null 123
> B. Hi! 12 null 12
> C. Hi! 12 null 123
> D. Compilation fails

We have already seen how fields can be read from and written to by using either direct access or setters, a.k.a. mutators, and getters, a.k.a. accessor methods. This problem addresses one more way to set fields, namely by making use of constructors.

The code itself is as simple as ever can be; containing no traps, the question is a typical 'straight arrow'. The first nameless object has its **str** field inited in a constructor that doesn't touch the var **a**, while the second object mirrors the situation leaving **str** unchanged. In fact, as far as this particular class is concerned, there is no need to assign "null" to **str** at all as the var gets set to null by default, and the **println()** would then print null all by itself → no change in the output.

The **println()** method's invocation looks odd but since we defined it ourselves, there's no comperr, either.

Problem 2.23 – C

> **Given:**
> ```
> class Engine {
>     int hp;
>     String model;
>     Engine() {
>         hp = 80;
>         model = "Junior";
>     }
> }
> class Test {
>     public static void main(String[] args) {
>         Engine e1 = new Engine();                    // line t1
>         Engine e2 = test1(e1);                        // line t2
>         test2(e2);
>         System.out.println(e1.hp + " " + e2.model);
>     }
> ```

```
        public static Engine test1(Engine e) {
            e.model = "Senior";
            e.hp = 120;
            return e;                                    // line t3
        }
        public static void test2(Engine e) {
            e.model = "Grandpa";
            e.hp = 170;
            return;
        }
    }
```

What is the result?

    A.   80 Junior
    B.   120 Senior
    C.   170 Grandpa
    D.   Compilation fails

Another variation of the tune "How-to-set-fields-thru-object-reference". No surprises here; as for the empty `return` stat in the method **test2()**, it makes a weak, half-hearted attempt to throw a red herring across our path – and fails miserably as we do know how to read method signatures.

The most important thing about this code is that there's only one object, just two distinct references to it, so `System.out.println(e1 == e2)` returns `true`. It comes from the fact that neither method creates anything new, they just affect instance fields.

Line t1 creates an object **e1** whose fields read 80 and "Junior" because that's how they were set by the constructor **Engine()**. After that **test1()** changes them to 120 and "Senior" – and then what? What does the method assign to **e2** on line t2? a completely new object or a reference to what we already have? Think for a second.

OK, it's a reference to the original object; for to return a new object, line t3 should have read `return new Engine()`. Apply this change and test the refvars with 'double equals'... See? The output changes, too. All because we are dealing now with two distinct objects.

Alright, back to code; restore t3; next **test2()** – acting through **e2** – modifies our object by setting its fields to 170 and "Grandpa", which then get printed because **e1** and **e2** refer to the same... hm... entity. I'm objecting to saying 'object' all the time...

Problem 2.24 – B

    Given:

```
    class NetBeans {
        private String theme;
        public String getTheme() {
            return theme;
        }
        public void setTheme(String theme) {
            this.theme = theme;
        }
        public static void main (String[] args) {
            NetBeans nb1 = new NetBeans();
            NetBeans nb2 = new NetBeans();
            nb1.setTheme(null);
            nb2.setTheme("Darcula");
            System.out.print(nb1.getTheme() + " : " + nb2.getTheme());
        }
    }
```

What is the result?

    A.   : Darcula
    B.   null : Darcula
    C.   Darcula : Darcula
    D.   A NullPointerException is thrown at run time

Just a straightforward example of using setters and getters to access object fields. The exam contains half a dozen of questions that use the JavaBeans convention for the accessor/mutator method syntax – and not a single question that would test you exactly on that: all of them address completely different objectives. Come to think of it, it appears that the JavaBeans convention isn't on the exam, although many study guides and exam prepware do drill us on some basics. Then again, their authors apparently know what they are doing; after all, this book is based on my own experience, while they must have drawn feedback from the entire community of the former exam takers...

Problem 2.25 – B

Given:

```
class Char {
    char var;
    public static void main (String[] args) {
        char var1 = 'a';
        char var2 = var1;
        var2 = 'b';
        Char c1 = new Char();
        Char c2 = c1;
        c1.var = 'c';
        c2.var = 'd';
        System.out.print(var1 + ", " + var2);
        System.out.print(c1.var + ", " + c2.var);
    }
}
```

What is the result?

    A.   a, bc, d
    B.   a, bd, d
    C.   c, bd, d
    D.   b, cc, d

One more illustration of the difference between primitive and reference variables. While changes to **var2** don't affect **var1** in the slightest, making two different references point to the same object allows us to mutate the object's state through either of the refvars.

Problem 2.26 – D

Given the following classes:

```
class Student {
    private int age;
    private String name;
    public String getName() { return name; }
    public void setName(String name) { this.name = name; }
    public int getAge() { return age; }
    public void setAge(int age) { this.age = age; }
}
```

```
public class Test {
    public static void main(String[] args) {
        Student std = new Student();
        // insert code here
    }
}
```

Which statement sets the field name **of the object** std?

    A.   std.setName() = "John Smith";
    B.   setName("John Smith");
    C.   Student.setName("John Smith");
    D.   std.setName("John Smith");

Option A incorrectly uses the method **setName()**, which needs an argument of type **String**.

Option B is invalid because **setName()** is not `static` and, therefore, should be invoked on the **std** object.

And finally, option C is also incorrect because it invokes **setName()** by using the class's name, which is allowed for `static` members only.

Problem 2.27 – A

   Given:

```
public class ObjectsGalore {
    static ObjectsGalore obj1, obj2, obj3, obj4;
    int numberOfObjects;
    public static int addObject(ObjectsGalore obj4) {
        return obj4.numberOfObjects *= 2;
    }
    public static void main(String[] args) {
        obj1 = obj2 = obj3 = new ObjectsGalore();
        obj4 = obj2;
        addObject(obj4);
    }
}
```

How many objects of the class ObjectsGalore **are created in memory at run time?**

    A. 1
    B. 4
    C. 8
    D. Compilations fails

Although Java offers several ways to create objects, for 1Z0-808 we need to remember just a few: 1) with the help of the class instantiation expression that uses the keyword `new`, and 2) with a shortcut that is available for the class **String** only, that is, by using double quotes (with some unpleasant complications related to interned strings; unpleasant for us the exam takers, that is). There is also one more shortcut, which is used to allocate arrays, such as int[] a = {1,2,3}.

Fortunately, this problem does not contain **String**s or arrays, so we can with a clear conscience ask ourselves the only question that matters here: how many `new` ops does this code contain?

Just one → hence one object, and everything else is simply chaff. Do expect a similar question on the exam.

Problem 2.28 – C

> **Given:**

```
public class ExamTaker {
    private String name;
    private int score;
    private String exam;
    private boolean passed;
    ExamTaker(){}
    ExamTaker(String name, int score, String exam){
        this.name = name;
        this.score = score;
        this.exam = exam;
    }
    public void show() {
        System.out.println("Name: " + name + ", passed: " + passed);
    }
    public boolean isPassed() {
        return passed = score >= 65;
    }
    public static void main(String[] args) {
        // line X
    }
}
```

Which statement, when inserted at line X, correctly initializes an ExamTaker **instance?**

- A. ExamTaker examTaker = "Bob";
- B. ExamTaker examTaker = ExamTaker.new("Bob", 100, "1Z0-808");
- C. ExamTaker examTaker = new ExamTaker();
- D. ExamTaker examTaker = ExamTaker("Bob", 100, "1Z0-808");
- E. None of the above

The problem tries to mislead us by providing option E. Since options B and D are clearly invalid (as B uses new improperly and D omits new altogether) and option A can't compile, either (as the class **ExamTaker** isn't a **String**[63]), we are left with C and E.

Now, it may be tempting to select E because it looks like option C doesn't initialize the object – after all, it doesn't set the fields to some meaningful values, right? – but this is just an appearance. As a matter of fact, automatic initing of fields is implied by any object's lifecycle as Java guarantees that "each class variable, instance variable, or array component is initialized with a default value when it is created" (remember Problem 2.1?), so even an empty constructor cannot possibly mean that fields are left uninited: the no-arg **ExamTaker()** doesn't modify their default values, that's all.

Problem 2.29 – C

> **Given:**

```
1.  class Student {
2.      String name;
3.      Student(String name){
4.          this.name = name;
5.      }
6.  }
```

---

[63] In fact, it cannot extend **String** even if it wanted to. You will – hopefully – forgive me whenever I annoy you by repeating that the class **String** is not only immutable but also `final` as remembering these things is indeed important for the exam.

```
7.    public class Test {
8.        public static void main (String[] args) {
9.            Student s1 = new Student("Alice");
10.           Student s2 = new Student("Bob");
11.           Student s3 = new Student("Carol");
12.           s1 = s3;
13.           s3 = s2;
14.           s2 = null;
15.       }
16.    }
```

Which statement is true?

    A.   After line 14, three objects are eligible for garbage collection.
    B.   After line 14, two objects are eligible for garbage collection.
    C.   After line 14, one object is eligible for garbage collection.
    D.   After line 14, none of the objects is eligible for garbage collection.

Three new keywords, hence three objects. As LOCs 12 – 14 follow a sort of a zigzag pattern:

```
12.         s1 = s3;
13.         s3 = s2;
14.         s2 = null;
```

it might be tempting to view them simply as a single stat with chained assignments:

```
s1 = s3 = s2 = null;
```

Yes, this would set all three references to null thus making all three objects eligible for garbage collection – but our code works differently. To see the proof, replace line 15 with this:

```
System.out.println(s1.name + " " + s3.name); }     // Carol Bob
```

It's only an attempt to access s2.name that throws an NPE.

So, what's going on in Problem 2.29? Line 12 sets **s1** to point to the object referenced by **s3** (let's call it "Carol"), then line 13 re-assigns **s3** to point to the object referenced to by **s2** ("Bob") and lastly, **s2** is set to null. So it's only **s2** that is eligible for GC.

When studying for this objective, you should check your conclusions by trying to access objects' members after the critical point to see if you got it right as an NPE would mean that this particular object is ripe for harvest.

Problem 2.30 – D
    Given:

```
1.    class A {
2.        String name;
3.        A obj;
4.        A(String name){
5.            this.name = name;
6.        }
7.    }
8.
9.    class B extends A {
10.       B(String name) {
11.           super(name);
12.       }
13.   }
```

```
14.
15. class Test {
16.    public static void main(String[] args) {
17.        A aa = new A("AA");
18.        A ab = new B("AB");
19.        B bb = new B("BB");
20.        aa.obj = ab;
21.        ab.obj = bb;
22.        ab = bb;
23.        bb = null;
24.        ab = null;
25.
26.    }
27. }
```

When the object ab, created by LOC18, becomes eligible for GC?

    A.   After line 22
    B.   After line 23
    C.   After line 24
    D.   Never in this program

The problem seems a bit complicated with all those field assignments and setting refvars to `null`. As it is not immediately evident who depends on who and what exactly happens when someone is taken out of the equation, it is better to put the whole story into pictures.

After a lot of experiments, I have found that the following graphical representation of an object works best for me:

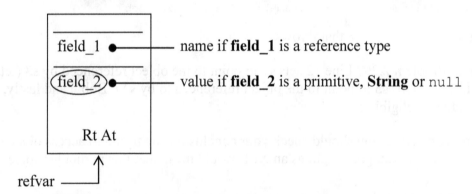

The end result resembles a crude UML diagram with some modifications, and every aspect is essential: the object is rectangular, the reference var (in other words, the object's name) is in the lower left corner, there is an open space near the top, fields are separated by lines, and the reftype-actype combo (i.e., Rt At) is at the bottom inside the object.

This little animal works equally well with both the GC- and inheritance-related questions. In cases where it is important to keep track of a `static` field's contents, I put the field inside an oval (although, as you probably know, the UML rules prescribe to underline `static` features).

As for representing behavioral features *inside* objects, I never needed this during the entire preparation period, so it's up to you to work out the best way to depict methods signatures…

Alright, let's apply all these little tricks to our problem and see how they work in practice.

LOCs 17 through 19 draw the following picture (to save time on the exam, the field names are written with their initial letters only, i.e. 'n' stands for **name** and 'o' stands for **obj**):

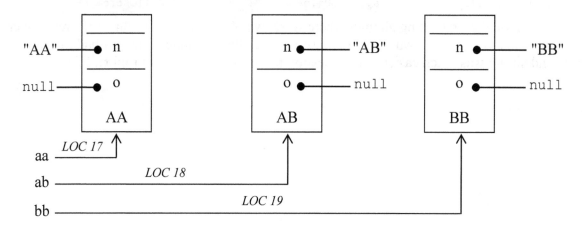

LOCs 20 through 22 change it into this:

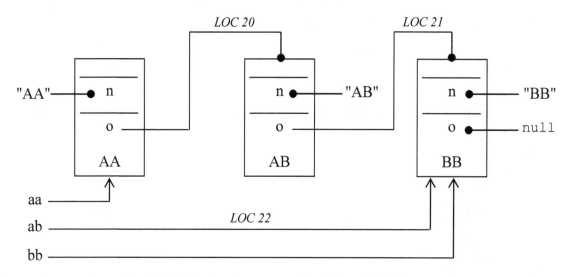

Please observe that after LOC 22 **ab** points not to **bb** (since **bb** is just a refvar) but to *the object* **bb** is referencing.

And finally, LOCs 23-24 set both **ab** and **bb** to null, so we are left with just a chain:

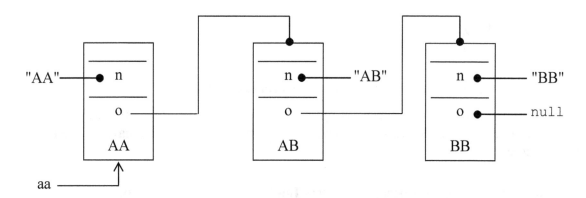

The drawing clearly shows that all three objects are alive and kicking till the very end. To see if this is indeed so, we can add the following stat on line 25 and run the code:

```
System.out.println("Hello from " + aa.obj.obj.name + "!");      // Hello from BB!
```

I met a similar question on the first sitting although there were two objects instead of three; if I remember correctly, one of them had itself as its own field; there were some other complications so I had to draw pictures. The second sitting was much easier as the question resembled the current Problem 2.30.

Problem 2.31 – AC

    Given:

```
public class Book {
    String title;
    boolean secondHand;
    double price;
    Book() {
        // line b1
    }
    public String toString(){
        return title + ", new: " + !secondHand + ", price: " + price;
    }
    public static void main(String[] args) {
        Book b = new Book();
        // line b2
        System.out.print(b);
    }
}
```

Which two modifications, made independently, enable the code to print Gone with the Wind, new: true, price: 9.5?

    A. Replace line b2 with:
```
b.title = "Gone with the Wind";
b.secondHand = false;
b.price = 9.5;
```
    B. Replace line b2 with:
```
this.title = "Gone with the Wind";
this.secondHand = false;
this.price = 9.5;
```
    C. Replace line b1 with:
```
this.title = new String("Gone with the Wind");
this.secondHand = new Boolean(false);
this.price = new Double(9.5);
```
    D. Replace line b1 with:
```
title = "Gone with the Wind";
secondHand = FALSE;
price = 9.5f;
```
    E. Replace line b1 with:
```
this("Gone with the Wind", false, 9.5);
```

Option B is incorrect as it places all three instance vars into a static context.

Option D won't compile, either, since it wants to assign FALSE to a primitive `boolean` var, and FALSE isn't a valid keyword for a `boolean` literal value. The following modification would have worked because **Boolean** unboxes:

```
secondHand = new Boolean("FALSE");
```

As for option E, it too throws a comperr because the class **Book** didn't define a corresponding three-arg constructor.

Problem 2.32 – B

    Given:

```
public class BoolArray {
    public static void main(String[] args) {
        Boolean[] barr = new Boolean[3];

        barr[0] = new Boolean(Boolean.parseBoolean("tRUE"));
        barr[1] = new Boolean("True");
        barr[2] = new Boolean(false);

        System.out.println(barr[0] + " " + barr[1] + " " + barr[2]);
    }
}
```

What is the result?

    A. true false false
    B. true true false
    C. false false false
    D. An IllegalArgumentException is thrown at run time
    E. A NullPointerException is thrown at run time

This problem tests if you know that the class **Boolean** has a case-insensitive constructor that accepts a **String** and allocates a **Boolean** object representing the value `true` if the input string reads "true" in any spelling, and a **Boolean** that represents `false` otherwise (like in case of "1", `null`, etc.) Same goes for the **parseBoolean(**String str**)** method.

What's more, similarly to all other wrapper classes, **Boolean** has another constructor that accepts an underlying primitive, that is a `boolean`.

Problem 2.33 – E

    Given:

```
class Parser {
    String input = "2013";
    public void parseMe(String str) {
        int output = 0;
        try {
            String input = str;
            output = Integer.parseInt(input);
        } catch (IllegalArgumentException iae) {
            System.out.println("Wrong argument!");
        }
        System.out.println(
            "input: " + input + ", output: " + output);
    }
    public static void main(String[] args) {
        Parser p = new Parser();
        p.parseMe("0123");
    }
}
```

What is the result?

    A. input: 0123, output: 0123
    B. input: 2013, output: 0123
    C. input: 2013, output: 83
    D. Wrong argument!
    E. None of the above

This problem wants to trick you by betting on two things: that you remember Problem 1.1 all too well and are going to follow the previous solution's steps purely mechanically (thus arriving at option B by simply swapping the values), or that, having noticed just how mighty out of place looks 83, you may start believing that the whole point of the exercise concerns octal notation.

Unfortunately, this is not the case as octal notation isn't even on the exam. The trap is built into the **Integer.parseInt()** method, of all things. Let's take another look at the documentation that comes with the core Java API:

```
static int parseInt(String s)          Parses the string argument as a signed decimal integer.
```

Decimal. Not octal. So the leading zero gets stripped off and the code prints:

input: 2013, output: 123

Which, of course, is option E.

Admittedly, this problem is way too tricky for the OCA exam, far-fetched and even insulting. By including it into this book, I wanted to remind you that there is a non-zero probability that the exam just might attempt to take an advantage of the way we tend to operate: when two things strongly resemble each another, we start thinking along similar lines. The exam will never test you on precisely same objective more than once, so stay focused and don't take anything for granted.

EXAM OBJECTIVES – Group Three:
Using Operators and Decision Constructs

The 1Z0-808 objectives within this group:

3.1 Use Java operators, including parentheses to override operator precedence
3.2 Test equality between **String**s and other objects using == and **equals()**
3.3 Create `if` and `if-else` and ternary constructs
3.4 Use a `switch` statement

CORE RULES (with some Extras):

3.1 <u>Use Java operators, including parentheses to override operator precedence:</u>

General Remarks:

❑ Naturally, all objectives are equally important since we need to pass the exam, but this one is simply indispensable because at least one of its aspects will appear in every question that contains sample code.

❑ A large number of questions on the exam concern the misuse of a particular operator leading to a compile-time error. Quite often these errors are caused by inappropriate data types which the operator accepts as its operands.

❑ Typical examples are control structures such as decision-making constructs, including `if-then`[64]`-(else)` and `switch` statements, as well as repetition handlers (`for`, enhanced `for`, `do-while`, and `while`). It is important to remember that, unlike most of these constructs, which evaluate `boolean` expressions, the `switch` statement is the only one that supports a variety of data types.

❑ Nested stats can be particularly tough, especially when they are used together with labels and/or `break` and `continue`. In fact, the exam pays special attention to such cases by including separate objectives to cover nuances.

❑ Some operators can be used only with numeric primitives, some apply only to `boolean` values, and some require objects only.

❑ Many Java operators are unary, meaning they accept a single operand, but the number of expressions they evaluate can often be greater than one. The order of evaluation plays therefore a crucial role. Spare no efforts memorizing at least Table 2.2 (ref.to Chapter II.0, *Opening Remarks*).

❑ Parentheses are used to override the default order of precedence. The exam includes at least two questions that will test you on this aspect in different scenarios.

---

[64] Although there's no `then` in Java, it *is* the official name of this stat (JLS, §14.9.1, *The if-then Statement*).

Java Operators At a Glance:

❏ The 1Z0-808 exam covers assignment, arithmetic, relational, and logical operators.

❏ Assignment operators:

■ The assignment operators store, or assign, a value into a variable. The left-hand operand must evaluate to an appropriate local variable, array element, or a field. The right-hand side can be any value of a type compatible with the variable.

■ Unlike all other binary operators, the assops are right-associative, which means that the chained assignments in a=b=c are performed in this fashion: a=(b=c).

■ The compound assops such as a+=smth and so on are equivalent to a=a+smth, etc. In other words, += can be interpreted as 'first add and then assign'.

■ EXTRA: The assignment is actually the *side effect* of the assignment expression evaluation[65]. Remembering this helps see that the following class does compile:

```
class Boo {
    public static void main(String[] args) {
        int a, b = 0;
        boolean boo;
        a = (boo = true) ? b = 10 : 11;
        System.out.println(a + " " + boo + " " + b);      // 10 true 10
    }
}
```

Look at the assop this way: when a value gets assigned to a var, the process doesn't stop at the variable; the value kind of 'bleeds' to the left thus becoming available to whatever sits further to the left of the var. The fact that some variable (like **boo** or **b** in the above example) gets assigned a value along the way is simply a side effect. Now it becomes clear that, as far as the ternop is concerned, **boo** = true is equivalent to true, and **b** = 10 also produces a value that can be assigned to **a**.

❏ Arithmetic operators:

■ Arithmetic operators do not accept the boolean data type. An attempt to do so results in a comperr.

■ ++ and -- are unary increment and decrement operators, which can be used in prefix or postfix notation.

■ In prefix notation, the value of the variable increments/decrements just before the variable is used.

■ The exam is particularly keen on testing us on postfix notation, wherein the value of the variable increments/decrements just after the variable is used.

■ Increment and decrement operators can be used only with variables and not with constants or expressions:

```
int x=0, a=1, b=2;
x++;
x = 5++;                  // INVALID
x = (a + b)++;            // INVALID
```

■ Unary operators have a higher precedence than multiplication and addition operators.

---

[65] It is interesting to note that many Java operators are used primarily because of their side effects. For example, the new operator has the profound side effect of creating a new object.

- **EXTRA**: There is a popular misconception that the % operator produces a reminder. Actually, what it computes is this:

  ```
  a % b = a - ( a / b ) * b
  ```

  Therefore,

5 % 3 = 2;	5 = 3*1 + 2	→	OK, it's a reminder
5 % (-3) = 2;	5 ≠ -3*1 + 2	→	not a reminder!
(-5) % (3) = -2;	-5 ≠ 3*1 + -2	→	not a reminder!
(-5) % (-3) = -2;	-5 = -3*1 + -2	→	a reminder

  So, we get the reminder only if both operands are of the same sign.

  <u>When it comes to %</u>: The first operand's sign is the sign of the result.

- **EXTRA**: JVM generates no **Throwable** on arithmetic overflow or underflow[66].

❏ <u>Relational operators:</u>

- Relational operators always produce a `boolean` value.

- Relational operators are used to compare values for equality (==) and nonequality (!=). To determine whether two numeric values are greater or less than each other, we use >, >=, <, and <=.

- It's a comperr to attempt to compare incompatible types. For example, an `int`, a `char`, or a floating-point value can't be compared with a `boolean`. On the other hand, we may compare an `int` and a `char` since `char` behaves almost as an unsigned `short`.

- The operators 'equal to' (==) and 'not equal to' (!=) can be used with any compatible primitive types.

- == returns `true` if the primitive values being compared are equal.

- != returns `true` if the primitive values being compared are not equal.

❏ <u>Logical operators:</u>

- Application of a logical operator always results in a `boolean` value.

- Logical operators are used in the decision-making structures to determine whether a set of conditions is `true` or `false`.

- Logical AND (&&) evaluates to `true` iff[67] all operands are `true`, and `false` otherwise.

- Logical OR (||) evaluates to `true` if any of the operands is `true`.

- Logical negation (!) inverts the `boolean` value.

- The logical operators && and || are also called short-circuit operators. If these operators can determine the output of the expression with the evaluation of the first operand, all subsequent operands are not evaluated.

EXTRA: De Morgan's Laws may come in handy, as well:

$\neg (P \wedge Q) \Leftrightarrow (\neg P) \vee (\neg Q)$ *translates in Java to*   `!(A&&B) == !A || !B; // true`

$\neg (P \vee Q) \Leftrightarrow (\neg P) \wedge (\neg Q)$ *translates in Java to*   `!(A||B) == !A && !B; // true`

---

[66] With one exception that concerns the class **StrictMath**: "In cases where the size is int or long and overflow errors need to be detected, the methods addExact, subtractExact, multiplyExact, and toIntExact throw an ArithmeticException when the results overflow" (ref.to the **StrictMath** API javadocs).

[67] 'if and only if'; the authors of the JLS love this abbreviation.

❑ Other useful rules to remember:

- `null` is the only literal value that can be assigned to a reference data type, such as **String**, etc. On the other hand, `null` cannot be assigned to a primitive var.

- If a **String** is `null` and then gets used with a + op, the result will be "null*smth*".

- Arithmetic ops turn everything into `int`s unless an operand is `long`, `float` or `double` (or a corresponding Wrapper, which unboxes first and then this rule will be applied again).

  (**other wording**: All operands of type `byte`, `short` or `char` are promoted AT LEAST to `int` before performing mathematical operations. If one of the operands is larger than `int` then the other one is promoted to the same type.)

  Illustration:

  ```
      Short ss = 10;
      Byte bb = 10;
      Long ll = 10L;
  //  byte b = ss + bb;     // "possibly lossy conversion from int to byte"
  //  byte b = ss % bb;     // ditto
  //  int c = ll / bb;      // "possibly lossy conversion from long to int"
  ```

- There is a question on the exam that asks – among other things – if Java allows operator overloading. The correct answer is 'No, it doesn't'. What's interesting, Java does use something that resembles operator overloading when it comes to the + op: it is overloaded for **String**.[68]

  Question: why this throws comperrs?

  ```
      String str = "";
      str = null + 'a';                    // INVALID
      str += 'a';
      str += null + 'a';                   // INVALID
      str = str + null + 'a';
  ```

  Let's apply the abovementioned rule: the + operator is overloaded for the cases where at least one of its operands is a **String**. So `null +'a'` will not compile because neither of the operands is a **String**.

  On the other hand, `str += 'a'` works because it translates to `str = str + 'a'` which means one of the operands *is* a **String**.

  Although the fourth LOC can indeed be re-written as `str=str+null+'a'` (which doesn't generate a comperr), the compiler first evaluates – and chokes on – the faulty `null + 'a'`. Expanding the expression to `str = str +` *whatever* comes later.

- It is important to remember that the types of the operands are determined at compile time. The third LOC in the next example won't compile even though the run-time type of the object referred to by **sobj** is **String**:

  ```
      Object sobj = "";
      String str = "";
      str = sobj + 'a';                    // INVALID
      str = (String) sobj + 'a';           // compiles and runs just fine
  ```

- An empty statement, represented by the semicolon, can appear in rather unexpected places making the code seem uncompilable while, in fact, it is perfectly legit:

  ```
      if (1 > 0);                          // VALID
  ```

---

[68] In the **String** API javadoc parlance: "The Java language provides special support for the string concatenation operator (+)".

EXERCISES (for Key Summary ref.to App.D):

Problem 3.1 Given the following code fragment:

```
class Answer {
    public static void main(String[] args) {
        int a = 42;
        if (a++ == 42) {
            System.out.println(
                   "The answer to Life, the Universe and everything is " + a);
        } else {
            System.out.println(
                   "The answer to Life, the Universe and everything is " + ++a);
        }
    }
}
```

What is the result?

A. The answer to Life, the Universe and everything is 42
B. The answer to Life, the Universe and everything is 43
C. The answer to Life, the Universe and everything is 44
D. Compilation fails

Problem 3.2 Given:

```
System.out.println("1 + 2 = " + 3 + 4);
System.out.println("1 + 2 = " + (3) + (4));
System.out.println("1 + 2 = " + (3 + 4));
```

What is the result?

A. 1 + 2 = 34
    1 + 2 = 7
    1 + 2 = 7
B. 1 + 2 = 7
    1 + 2 = 34
    1 + 2 = 7
C. 3 = 34
    3 = 7
    3 = 7
D. 1 + 2 = 34
    1 + 2 = 34
    1 + 2 = 7

Problem 3.3 Given the code fragment:

```
System.out.println(2 + 3 + 4 + "!");
System.out.println(2 + 3 * 4 + "!");
```

What is the result?

A. 27!
    212!
B. 234!
    212!
C. 9!
    14!
D. 54!
    14!
D. Compilation fails

Problem 3.4 Given the code fragment:

```
public static void main(String[] args) {
    int a = 0;
    System.out.println(a + a++ - a-- + " " + a);
}
```

What is the result?

- A. -1 0
- B. -1 -2
- C. 0 1
- D. 1 0

Problem 3.5 Given the fragment:

```
Integer aa = 42;
aa--;
System.out.print(--aa + " ");
System.out.print(aa);
```

What is the result?

- A. 40 40
- B. 39 40
- C. 38 40
- D. Compilations fails

Problem 3.6 Given:

```
int a = 19;
boolean bool1 = false, bool2 = true;
bool1 = ( 1.5 != (float) 1.5 ) || ( bool1 = true );
bool2 = ( ++a == a++ ) && ( !bool1 );
System.out.println("bool1:"+ bool1 + ", bool2:" + bool2);
```

What is the result?

- A. bool1:true, bool2:false
- B. bool1:true, bool2:true
- C. bool1:false, bool2:true
- D. bool1:false, bool2:false

Problem 3.7 Given:

```
int score = 80;
boolean passed = !((score < 80) || (score >= 100));
System.out.println(passed);
```

Which one is false?

- A. The code prints true
- B. The code prints false

Problem 3.8 Given:

```
System.out.println( 10 + 5 == 4 + 11);
System.out.println( 10 + (5 == 4) + 11);
System.out.println( "" + (5 <= 4) + "" );
System.out.println( "" + 10 + 5 == 4 + 11 + "");
```

How many statements fail compilation?

    A. One
    B. Two
    C. Three
    D. None

Problem 3.9

The very first exercise in *The Art of Computer Programming*, Vol.1, "Fundamental Algorithms" by Donald Knuth[69] reminds the reader that

> ...the text showed how to interchange the values of variables *m* and *n*, using the replacement notation, by setting $t \leftarrow m$, $m \leftarrow n$, $n \leftarrow t$.

You decided to beat Knuth himself at his game by devising a way to switch any two integer variables *without* using a temporal storage, and this is what you came up with:

```
class MemorySaver {
    public static void main(String[] args) {
        int a = 123;
        int b = 321;
        System.out.println("a=" + a + ", b=" + b);          // a=123, b=321
        a = a + b;
        b = a - b;
        a = a - b;
        System.out.println("a=" + a + ", b=" + b);          // a=321, b=123
    }
}
```

Suppose, we declare

```
int a = Integer.MAX_VALUE;
int b = Integer.MIN_VALUE;
```

What will happen?

    A. The algorithm will continue to work correctly
    B. Both a and b will flip their signs
    C. Compilation will fail
    D. The code will throw an ArithmeticException

---

[69] page 9 in the 3rd ed. (1997).

3.2 Test equality between **String**s and other objects using `==` and **equals()**:

❑ While `==` between two comparable primitive values checks whether they are equal, the very same operator between two reference vars checks whether these references point to the same object.

❑ The method **equals()** checks the equality of objects depending on its implementation by the particular data type it is being called on.

❑ For example, calling `==` on **String**s checks if they point to the same object within the common pool of strings while calling **equals()** on the same objects will check whether the sequence of characters is the same.

❑ On the other hand, since the class **StringBuilder** – unlike the class **String** – does not override **Object**'s **equals()** with its own implementation, calling **equals()** on **StringBuilder** objects is the same as using the `==` operator: it will check if they are pointing to the same object rather than peek at the values inside.

> **Corollary**: The easiest way to compare the *contents* rather than references of two **StringBuilder** objects, is to call **equals()** on the values returned by the **toString()** method.

❑ The **String**s created with double quotes get interned into a common pool unlike the **String**s computed at run time or created with the keyword `new`.

Expressing the same rules in code:

```java
class MyClass { String field = "Hello"; }

class TestEquality{
    public static void main(String[] args) {
        String str1 = "Hello";
        String str2 = "Hello";
        String str3 = new String("Hello");
        System.out.println(str1 == str2);                       // true
        System.out.println(str1 == str3);                       // false
        System.out.println(str1.equals(str2));                  // true

        StringBuilder sb1 = new StringBuilder("Hello");
        StringBuilder sb2 = new StringBuilder("Hello");
        System.out.println(sb1 == sb2);                         // false
        System.out.println(sb1.equals(sb2));                    // false
        System.out.println(sb1.toString().equals(sb2.toString())); // true

        MyClass mc1 = new MyClass();
        MyClass mc2 = new MyClass();
        System.out.println(mc1 == mc2);                         // false
        System.out.println(mc1.equals(mc2));                    // false
    }
}
```

❑ Other useful rules to remember:

▪ Even though integral and floating-point primitives are not always assignable to each other (thus requiring explicit casts), they may be freely compared with `==`:

```java
short s = 10;
double d = 10.;
if (s == d) System.out.println("=="); // prints ==
```

- `null == null` returns `true`.

- Question: Will `==` compile between 'covariant' operands?

  Answer: Yes, because there exists an IS-A relationship. An attempt to use `==` between unrelated reference types leads to a comperr:

```
Number n = 1.;
// Double d = 1;       // REMINDER:
// Double d = 1.f;     // these two LOCs are INVALID because they need
                       // a 2-STEP conversion: first to a primitive
                       // double and only then to a Double

Double d = 1.;
if (n == d) System.out.println("!");          // VALID; prints nothing

String s = new String("");
StringBuilder sb = new StringBuilder("");
// if (s == sb) System.out.println("?");       // INVALID:
                                               // "incompatible types"
```

Simple corollary: `==` between different Wrappers throws a comperr. It's only **equals()** that behaves itself.

EXTRA: It may look as if there's a way to trick the compiler into comparing two unrelated data types with the 'double equals' operator; this, however, is just an appearance since both objects are of the same reftype:

```
Boolean boo = new Boolean("false");
String str = new String("false");
//    System.out.println(boo == str);         // INVALID
Object[] array = {boo, str};
System.out.println(array[0] == array[1]);   // prints false
```

or even bolder and simpler:

```
Object boo = new Boolean("false");
Object str = new String("false");
System.out.println(boo == str);             // prints false
```

→ Reminder: the compiler always looks at reftypes and never cares about actypes.

- EXTRA: It is common to compare the values of the *instance* vars when testing two objects for equality because it is the instance vars that are used to store the state of a particular object at a particular point in time.

- EXTRA: **equals**(`null`) returns `false` on any object.

- EXTRA: The method **equals()** defined for a user data type should not modify any of the instance vars passed to it as its arguments; failure to do so will violate the contract for the method **equals()** defined by the Java API.

Problem 3.10   Given:

```
class Test {
    public static void main(String[] args) {
        StringBuilder sb = new StringBuilder("Same");
        String str = "Same";

        if (sb.equals(str)) {
            System.out.println("Same 1");
        } else if (sb.toString().equals(str)) {
            System.out.println("Same 2");
        } else {
            System.out.println("Different");
        }
    }
}
```

What is the result?

    A. Same 1

    B. Same 2

    C. Different

    D. A NullPointerException is thrown at run time

Problem 3.11   Given:

```
4.    StringBuilder sb1 = new StringBuilder("1Z0-808");
5.    String str1 = sb1.toString();
6.    // insert code here
7.    System.out.print(str1 == str2);
```

Which code fragment, when inserted at line 6, enables the code to print true?

    A. String str2 = str1;

    B. String str2 = new String (str1);

    C. String str2 = sb1.toString();

    D. String str2 = "1Z0-808";

Problem 3.12   Given:

```
public class Test {
    public static void main(String[] args) {
        String str1 = "Hello world!";
        String str2 = new String("Hello world!");
        if (str1 == str2) System.out.println("Same");
        if (str1.equals(str2))
        System.out.println("More of the same");
    }
}
```

What is the result?

    A. Same
          More of the same

    B. More of the same

    C. Same

    D. Nothing prints

Problem 3.13   Given the code fragment:

```
String str1 = "My String";
String str2 = new String("My String");
```

What is the proper way to check whether str1 and str2 have the same contents?

    A.   if (str1 == str2) { /* some code */ }
    B.   if (str1.equals(str2)) { /* some code */ }
    C.   if (str1 = str2) { /* some code */ }
    D.   if (str1.toString() == str2.toString()) { /* some code */ }

Problem 3.14   Given the following main method:

```
public static void main(String[] args) {
    StringBuilder sb = new StringBuilder("Inequality");
    String str = "Inequality matters";
    sb.append("matters");
    if (str == sb.toString()) {
        System.out.println("Same");
    }
    if (str.equals(sb.toString())) {
        System.out.println("More of the same");
    }
}
```

What is the result?

    A.   Same
         More of the same
    B.   More of the same
    C.   Same
    D.   Nothing prints
    E.   Compilation fails

Problem 3.15   Given:

```
class Twins {
    int age;
    Twins(int age) {
        this.age = age;
    }
}
class Test {
    public static void main (String[] args) {
        Twins t1 = new Twins(13);
        Twins t2 = new Twins(13);
        if (t1 == t2) {
            System.out.println("Identical");
        } else {
            System.out.println("Dissimilar");
        }
        if (t1.equals(t2)) {
            System.out.println("Identical");
        } else {
            System.out.println("Dissimilar");
        }
    }
}
```

What is the result?

A. Identical
   Dissimilar
B. Dissimilar
   Identical
C. Identical
   Identical
D. Dissimilar
   Dissimilar

Problem 3.16   Given:

```
class Twins {
    int age;
    String gender;
    Twins(int age, String gender) {
        this.age = age;
        this.gender = gender;
    }
    public boolean equals(){
        return this.age == age & this.gender == gender;
    }
}
class Test {
    public static void main (String[] args) {
        Twins t1 = new Twins(13, "Male");
        Twins t2 = new Twins(13, "Male");
        if (t1 == t2) {
            System.out.println("Identical");
        } else {
            System.out.println("Dissimilar");
        }
        if (t1.equals(t2)) {
            System.out.println("Identical");
        } else {
            System.out.println("Dissimilar");
        }
    }
}
```

What is the result?

A. Identical
   Dissimilar
B. Dissimilar
   Identical
C. Identical
   Identical
D. Dissimilar
   Dissimilar

3.3 Create `if` and `if-else` and ternary constructs:

❑ `if` and `if-else` constructs:

   ■ `if`'s logic is based on the result of a condition, which should evaluate to a `boolean` or **Boolean** value.

   ■ `if` constructs can be nested; theoretically, the depth is unlimited.

   ■ The `else` part isn't required.

   ■ Braces {} are not mandatory → watch out! only the nearest stat forms therefore a part of the `if` construct.

   ■ `if`'s expression doesn't accept a var declaration; it will, however, accept an assignment but only when the value is a `boolean` (or **Boolean**):

```
// if (boolean bb = true) System.out.println(":(");    // INVALID
boolean b;
Boolean boo;
if ( b = true ) System.out.println("Aha!");            // Aha!
if ( boo = Boolean.TRUE ) System.out.println("Mmm!");  // Mmm!
```

   ■ EXTRA: `if`'s body accepts a labeled `break`:

```
label: if (true) break label;                          // VALID
```

   ■ EXTRA: `if(false)` doesn't flag a comperr despite the fact that the nearest stat becomes unreachable.

   ■ EXTRA: Neither `if`- nor `else`-branch accepts a variable declaration:

```
if ( 1 > 0 )
    String str1 = "1 > 0";                             // INVALID
else
    String str2 = "?!";                                // INVALID
```

❑ Ternary constructs:

   ■ Ternary op does not require that its terms must be compile-time constant values.

   ■ When the ternop is used on the right-hand side of an assop, its (the ternop's) terms must 1) match or be numerically 'promotable', and 2) be compatible with the assop.

   ■ Both terms of the ternary op should return or evaluate to something. In the following example the code compiles because **test()** returns an `int`, `--res` evaluates to a value, and `for` is provided with a `boolean`:

```
class A {
    static int test(int a){return a*a;}
    public static void main(String[] args) {
        int res = 10, a = 0;
        if ((res > 10 ? test(a) : --res) < 10)
            System.out.println(res);               // prints 9
        for( ; Math.random()<.5? true : false ; ) { }  // VALID
    }
}
```

   Simple corollary: It's a comperr if either term consists of a `void` method such as **System.out.println()**, etc.:

```
String str = (1>0) ? "!" : System.out.println("?"); // INVALID
```

Problem 3.17   Given:

```java
class Test {
    public static void main(String[] args) {
        int x = 10;
        int y = x--;
        int z = --y;
        int a = x++;
        int b = x < y ? x < z ? x : y < z ? y : z;
        System.out.println(b);
    }
}
```

What is the result?

A. 16
B. 17
C. 18
D. 23
E. Compilation fails

Problem 3.18   Given the following:

As you are planning to sell your Android-based games, you need to calculate discount rates for bulk purchases using the following criteria:

– if someone buys three or four of your apps, you are willing to offer a 20% discount;
– buying five or more apps makes your clients eligible for a 50% discount;
– the miserly types who refuse to spend their ill-gotten money on more than two of your amazing games, will get no discount at all.

The following **main()** method should take care of the task:

```java
public static void main(String[] args) {
    double discount_rate = 0;
    int quantity = Integer.parseInt(args[0]);
    // line X;
}
```

Which two code fragments can be independently inserted at line X to meet the above criteria?

A. ```java
    if (quantity >= 5) { discount_rate = 0.5; }
    if (quantity == 3 || quantity == 4) { discount_rate = 0.2; }
    ```
B.  ```java
    discount_rate = (quantity >= 5) ? 0.5 : 0;
    discount_rate = (quantity >= 3) ? 0.2 : 0;
    ```
C. ```java
    discount_rate = (quantity >= 5) ? 0.5 : (quantity >= 3)? 0.2 : 0;
    ```
D.  ```java
    if (quantity >= 3 && quantity < 5) {
        discount_rate = 0.2;
    } else {
        discount_rate = 0;
    }
    if (quantity >= 5) {
        discount_rate = 0.5;
    } else {
        discount_rate = 0;
    }
    ```
E. ```java
    discount_rate = (quantity > 1) ? 0.2 : (quantity >= 5) ? 0.5 : 0;
    ```
    ```

Problem 3.19   **Given the following code fragment:**

```
public static void main(String[] args) {
    int value = 22;
    if (value >= 0) {
        if (value != 0)
            System.out.print("My ");
        else System.out.print("girl ");
        if (value < 10)
            System.out.print("wove ");
        if (value > 20)
            System.out.print("six ");
        else if (value < 30)
            System.out.print("dozen ");
        else if (value < 10)
            System.out.print("plaid ");
        else
            System.out.print("jackets ");
        if (value > 10)
            System.out.print("before ");
    } else {
        System.out.print("she ");
    }
        System.out.print("quit.");
}
```

What is the result?

A. My plaid jackets quit.
B. My six before quit.
C. six before she quit.
D. six dozen before quit.

Problem 3.20   **Given:**

```
String valid = "true";
if (valid) System.out.println("valid");
else System.out.println("not valid");
```

What is the result?

A. valid
B. not valid
C. Compilation fails
D. An IllegalArgumentException is thrown

Problem 3.21   **Given:**

```
int a = 5;

if ( !(a > 5)) {
    System.out.print("wow");
}{  System.out.print("zer"); }

System.out.print("!");
```

What is the result?

A. wow!
B. zer!
C. wowzer!
D. Compilation fails

Problem 3.22   Given:

```
public class Test {
    public static int runTest() {
        return 0;
    }
    public static void main (String[] args) {
        if (runTest()) {
            System.out.print("It works");
        }
        System.out.print("!");
    }
}
```

What is the result?

    A. It works!

    B. !

    C. Compilation fails

    D. An exception is thrown at run time

Problem 3.23   Given:

```
class Quantity {
    private boolean flag;
    public void show() {
        int qty = flag ? 1 : 100;
        System.out.print("How many? " + qty++);
    }
    public static void main (String[] args) {
        new Quantity().show();
    }
}
```

What is the result?

    A. How many? 1

    B. How many? 100

    C. How many? 2

    D. How many? 101

    E. Compilation fails

Problem 3.24   Given the code fragment:

```
String[] numbers = {"1", "2", "1", "1"};
int counter = 0;
```

And the following decision-making construct:

```
if ("1".equals(numbers[0])) { counter++;
} else if ("1".equals(numbers[1])) { counter++;
} else if ("1".equals(numbers[2])) { counter++;
} else if ("1".equals(numbers[3])) { counter++;
}
System.out.print(counter);
```

What is the result?

    A. 1

    B. 3

    C. Compilation fails

    D. An ArrayIndexOutOfBoundsException is thrown at run time

3.4 Use a switch statement:

- ❏ switch expression accepts all primitives and their wrappers (except boolean, long, float, and double with their corresponding wrappers) + **String** + enums[70].

- ❏ Every case constant expression in a switch block must be assignable to the type of switch expression.

  → The switch expression's type must be wide enough to hold all case values; the first case in the following example will not compile because 128 cannot be assigned to **b**, which can only hold values from -128 to 127 inclusive:

```
byte b = -128;
switch(b){
    // case 128:                    // comperr: possibly lossy conversion
                                     // from int to byte...
    case (byte)128:                  // ...while this monstrosity compiles
        System.out.println("!");     // and prints !
}
```

Corollary: if switch was promised, say, a byte, it will also accept certain chars (such as 'a' since the numerical value of 'a' (namely, 97) is within byte's range.) Same goes for a short.

Look at it this way: the flow isn't from top to bottom; just the opposite; it's not that byte can fit inside 128: it's 128 that can't fit inside byte.

Imagine that switch is a box with an opening on top (switch expression); we need to take an appropriate case value out of the box to perform our computations – but we can't do it if the value is larger than the opening: it simply won't get through! (Mental pic: a trapped monkey with its paw in a jar).

- ❏ No two identical case values are allowed in a switch.

  → pay attention to both literals and vars used as case values. Watch out for underscores in switch's cases that use integral types such as int, etc.; there can be identical twins lurking.

- ❏ EXTRA: The case value can't be the literal value null.

- ❏ EXTRA: The case value can define expressions that use literal values such as 1 + 2.

- ❏ switch requires curly braces but its body can be empty.

Alright, what follows isn't exactly about switch *per se* but we still need to review the rules that govern the use of braces anyway so let's do it right now:

The curly braces {} are required around method bodies, switch blocks, TCF constructs and lambdas with return and/or multiple stats; not required for ifs and loops (be careful with do-while, though; it will choke on more than one stat w/o braces).

---

[70] enum types aren't on the exam.

What's more, the TCF constructs are treated as a single statement, hence whatever surrounds them might not need braces, either:

```
class Test{
    public static void main(String args[]){
        do                                           // compiles just fine
            try{}
            catch(NullPointerException npe){}
            finally{}
        while(true);
//        do                                         // this do-while doesn't
//            System.out.println("");
//            System.out.println("");
//        while(true);
    }
}
```

❏   The `switch` expression does not accept declarations.

❏   The `switch`'s `cases` require constant expressions (in other words, they must be constant at run time)[71].

   Corollary: If a **case** expression uses a var, this var must be a **final primitive** because although `switch` does accept some wrappers, its **case** expressions must generate a constant value – and **wrappers aren't constants (not even final static ones**!)[72]

❏   The `default` section can be placed anywhere.

❏   Watch out for falling through due to missing `breaks`.

❏   EXTRA: Like any other block, the `switch` block can be labeled:

```
label: switch( doStuff() ) {
    default: break label;                           // VALID
}
```

❏   EXTRA: It is possible to initialize local vars in `switch`'s `default` section if this `default` is always accessible (like in the following example where the falling-through makes `default` reachable thanks to missing `breaks`):

```
class Test{
    public static void main(String[] args)  {
        new Test().test("test");       }
    public void test(String test){
        String var;
        switch(test){
            case "best":
            case "jest":
            case "rest":
            case "test":
            case "west":
            default:
                var = "protest";
        }
        System.out.println(var);                     // prints protest
    }
}
```

---

[71] Formal def: «A *constant expression* is an expression denoting a value of primitive type or a **String**» (JLS, §15.28)

[72] Because `switch` unboxes the wrapper, and autoboxing/unboxing happens only at run time…

EXERCISES (for Key Summary ref.to App.D):

Problem 3.25   **Given the code snippet:**

```
7.        boolean bool = true;
8.        switch (bool) {
9.           case true:
10.               System.out.print("True ");
11.               break;
12.            default:
13.               System.out.print("False ");
14.         }
15.         System.out.println("Blue");
```

Which option will allow the code snippet print True Blue?

    A. Remove the default section
    B. Replace line 7 with `String bool = "true";` and replace line 9 with `case "true":`
    C. Remove the `break;` statement at line 11
    D. Replace line 7 with `boolean bool = 1;` and replace line 9 with `case 1:`

Problem 3.26   **Given the code snippet:**

```
class Test {
    public static void main(String[] args) {
        // line X
        switch (a) {
            case 0:
                System.out.println("Zero");
                break;
            case 1:
                System.out.println("One");
                break;
        }
    }
}
```

Which three statements can be independently inserted at line X to enable the code to print Zero?

    A. short a = 0;
    B. Integer a = 0;
    C. Double a = 0;
    D. String a = "0";
    E. Byte a = new Byte("0");
    F. Long a = 0;

Problem 3.27   **Given the code snippet:**

```
class Modulo{
    public static void main(String[] args) {
        int a = 10;
        Short s = (short)(int)(long)(float) (a % 4.d);      // line 1
        switch(s) {                                         // line 2
            case 0:
                System.out.print("Divisible by 4");
                break;
            default:
                System.out.print("Not divisible by 4");
                break;
        }
    }
}
```

What is the result?

    A.   Compilation error on line 1
    B.   Compilation error on line 2
    C.   The code prints Not divisible by 4
    D.   The code prints Divisible by 4

Problem 3.28   Given:

```
String friend = "Alice";
switch(friend) {
    case "Alice":
        System.out.println("Hi Alice!");
    case "Bob":
        System.out.println("Hi Bob!");
        break;
    case "Carol":
        System.out.println("Hi Carol!");
        break;
    default:
        System.out.println("Hello stranger!");
}
```

What is the result?

    A.   Hi Alice!
    B.   Hi Alice!
          Hi Bob!
    C.   Hi Alice!
          Hi Bob!
          Hi Carol!
    C.   Hi Alice!
          Hi Bob!
          Hi Carol!
          Hello stranger!

Problem 3.29   Given:

```
class Week {
    public static void main (String[] args) {
        int day = 1;
        switch (day) {
            case "6": System.out.print("Saturday");
            case "7": System.out.print("Sunday");
            case "1": System.out.print("Monday");
            case "2": System.out.print("Tuesday");
            case "3": System.out.print("Wednesday");
            case "4": System.out.print("Thursday");
            case "5": System.out.print("Friday");
        }
    }
}
```

Which two modifications, made independently, enable the code to compile and run?

    A.   Adding a `break` statement after each print statement
    B.   Adding a default section
    C.   Removing the double quotes from each `case` label
    D.   Changing the type of the variable **day** to **String**
    E.   Arranging the `case` labels in ascending order

Problem 3.30   **Given:**

```
class Switcher{
    public static void main(String[] args) {
        final String str = "String ";
        switch ( str.trim() + "!" ) {                 // line 1
            case "String " + "!":                     // line 2
                System.out.println("String !");
                break;
            case "String" + "!" :                     // line 3
                System.out.println("String!");
                break;
        }
    }
}
```

What is the result?

    A.   String !
    B.   String!
    C.   Compilation fails on line 1
    D.   Compilation fails on lines 2 and 3

Problem 3.31   **Given:**

```
class Test {
    int test;
    int a = 10;
    int run(){ return 42; }
    void switchMe(){
        switch ( run() ) {}          // line 1
        switch ( test ) {            // line 2
            case a:                  // line 3
            default:
        }
    }
}
```

Which statement about this code is true?

    A.   Line 1 throws a comperr
    B.   Line 2 throws a comperr
    C.   Line 3 throws a comperr
    D.   There is nothing wrong with the code

Problem 3.32   **Given:**

```
class AnotherTest {
    int a, b;
    final int c = 0;
    void switchMe(){
        switch ( a = 0 ) {}          // line 1
        switch ( int d = 0 ) {}      // line 2
        switch ( 1 ) {}              // line 3
        switch ( a++ ) {             // line 4
            case a:                  // line 5
            case c:                  // line 6
        }
    }
}
```

Which two LOCs fail compilation?

A. Line 1
B. Line 2
C. Line 3
D. Line 4
E. Line 5
F. Line 6

Problem 3.33   Given:

```
class YetAnotherTest{
    final static int a1 = 0;
    final static Integer i1 = 1;
    public static void main(String[] args) {
        int x = 666;
        StringBuilder str = new StringBuilder("Java");
        switch (x) {
            case -123: str.append("S");
            case a1:   str.append("E");        // line 1
            case i1:   str.append("8");        // line 2
        }
        System.out.println(str);
    }
}
```

Which statement about the code is true?

A. The code compiles and prints Java
B. The code throws a comperr on line 1
C. The code throws a comperr on line 2
A. The code throws a RuntimeException

Keys & Discussion:

Problem 3.1 – B

Given the following code fragment:

```
class Answer {
    public static void main(String[] args) {
        int a = 42;
        if (a++ == 42) {                           // line 1
            System.out.println(
                "The answer to Life, the Universe and everything is " + a);
        } else {
            System.out.println(
                "The answer to Life, the Universe and everything is " + ++a);
        }
    }
}
```

What is the result?

   A. The answer to Life, the Universe and everything is 42
   B. The answer to Life, the Universe and everything is 43
   C. The answer to Life, the Universe and everything is 44
   D. Compilation fails.

Since the postfix notation means that the variable is used first and only then increments, the comparison between **a** and 42 on line 1 yields `true` and the control gets transferred to the `if`-branch rather than `else`-branch. By this moment, however, the value of **a** has been already incremented.

Mastering the postfix notation should be one of your top priorities since it is widely used on the exam. Let's have a few more examples to see how it works.

Example 1:

```
1. class PostFix {
2.     static int incr1(int x){ return x++; }
3.     static int incr2(int x){ x++; return x; }
4.     public static void main(String[] args) {
5.         int a, b, c;
6.         a = b = c = 0;
7.         System.out.println(a++);             // prints 0
8.         System.out.println(a);               // 1
9.         System.out.println(incr1(b));        // 0
10.        System.out.println(incr2(c));        // 1
11.    }
12. }
```

Lines 7 and 8 are easy. Line 2 mimics line 7 in its logic, and as for line 3, it uses the local var **x** twice, so the value it returns has been already incremented.

Example 2:

```
public static void main(String[] args) {
    int a = 0;
    System.out.println(a++ - a--);
    // System.out.println(a);   }
```

What is the result?

    A. -1
    B. 0
    C. 1

As I've got no control over what you are doing, there is no stopping you from reading any further without solving Example 2 first. If you're dead set on ruining everything, just go ahead; after all, passive learning is also a way to pass time. It's just not the way to pass an exam.

Alright, let's crack the sucker together:

The expressions involving arithmetic ops are evaluated left to right → so, how many times the var **a** gets used? → twice → and since by the second time the var's value has been already incremented, the answer is 0 - 1.

And now for the big finale: when we uncomment the last printing stat, it'll output... what?[73]

Problem 3.2 – D

Given:

```
System.out.println("1 + 2 = " + 3 + 4);
System.out.println("1 + 2 = " + (3) + (4));
System.out.println("1 + 2 = " + (3 + 4));
```

What is the result?

A. 1 + 2 = 34
    1 + 2 = 7
    1 + 2 = 7
B. 1 + 2 = 7
    1 + 2 = 34
    1 + 2 = 7
C. 3 = 34
    3 = 7
    3 = 7
D. 1 + 2 = 34
    1 + 2 = 34
    1 + 2 = 7

I had two different questions to this tune on different sittings; this one combines them all.

As we already know that the + op in Java is overloaded for **String**, here are the simplest formulas to remember:

❑   **String** with + (including +=) will take anything in any order; for example, `str += 'a'` or `str += false` or `str +=1` are all valid as well as `str = 'a' + str; str = 'b'+63+"a"`, `str = null + str`, and so on.

❑   If the expression contains a **String** that is followed by a +, whatever is to the right of the **String** becomes a string of **Strings**. Watch out for parentheses, though.

---

[73] The value of Dirac delta function $\delta(x)$ everywhere except at x = 0... No passive learning, remember?

Problem 3.3 – C

Given the code fragment:

```
System.out.println(2 + 3 + 4 + "!");
System.out.println(2 + 3 * 4 + "!");
```

What is the result?

    A. 27!
         212!
    B. 234!
         212!
    C. 9!
         14!
    D. 54!
         14!
    D. Compilation fails

The expression on the left-hand side of the **String** is evaluated first, then the **String** "!" makes the end result a **String**, too[74].

Problem 3.4 – A

Given the code fragment:

```
public static void main(String[] args) {
    int a = 0;
    System.out.println(a + a++ - a-- + " " + a);
}
```

What is the result?

    A. -1 0
    B. -1 -2
    C. 0 1
    D. 1 0

The whole chain is evaluated this way:

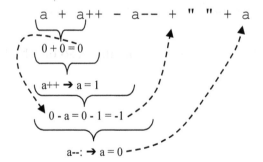

---

[74] §5.1.11, String Conversion (http://docs.oracle.com/javase/specs/jls/se8/html/jls-5.html#jls-5.1.11)

Problem 3.5 – A

Given the fragment:

```
Integer aa = 42;
aa--;                                   // line 1
System.out.print(--aa + " ");           // line 2
System.out.print(aa);                   // line 3
```

What is the result?

    A. 40 40
    B. 39 40
    C. 38 40
    D. Compilations fails

There's nothing illegal with using arithmetic ops on Wrappers: they simply unbox as needed and then autobox again, therefore the code compiles and option D is incorrect.

Line 1 decreases 42 by one resulting in **aa** = 41. Line 2 decrements the value further, combines it with the **String** " ", then prints 40 followed by a space. Line 3 just outputs the same value of **aa**.

Problem 3.6 – A

Given:

```
int a = 19;
boolean bool1 = false, bool2 = true;
bool1 = ( 1.5 != (float) 1.5 ) || ( bool1 = true );     // line 1
bool2 = ( ++a == a++ ) && ( !bool1 );                   // line 2
System.out.println("bool1:"+ bool1 + ", bool2:" + bool2);
```

What is the result?

    A. bool1:true, bool2:false
    B. bool1:true, bool2:true
    C. bool1:false, bool2:true
    D. bool1:false, bool2:false

Line 1 uses numerical promotions: first the `double` 1.5 is explicitly cast to the `float` 1.5, then this `float` is promoted to `double` again in order to compare these two values with the 'not equal' op thus resulting in the boolean `false`, which means `||` doesn't short-circuit; then the expression `bool1 = true` gets evaluated thus assigning true to **bool1** along the way.

Line 2 evaluates ++**a** == **a**++ resulting in `true` (and making **a** equal to 21 at the same time), so the short-circuiting AND still needs to evaluate !**bool1** thus resulting in `false`.

Problem 3.7 – A

Given:

```
int score = 80;
boolean passed = !((score < 80) || (score >= 100));
System.out.println(passed);
```

Which one is false?

    A. The code prints true
    B. The code prints false

Sometimes it is easier to apply De Morgan's Laws than evaluate each operand in a relational expression. Since NEG(A OR B) ≡ NEG(A) AND NEG(B), the stat on line 1 can be rewritten as

```
boolean passed = !(score < 80) && !(score >= 100);
```

To simplify it even more, we can mentally apply the negation operator:

```
boolean passed = score >= 80 && score < 100;
```

Problem 3.8 – A

Given:

```
System.out.println( 10 + 5 == 4 + 11);          // line 1
System.out.println( 10 + (5 == 4) + 11);        // line 2
System.out.println( "" + (5 <= 4) + "" );       // line 3
System.out.println( "" + 10 + 5 == 4 + 11 + ""); // line 4
```

How many statements fail compilation?

    A. One
    B. Two
    C. Three
    D. None

To crack this one, we need to recall that comparison ops have lower precedence than arithmetic ops. This is why line 1 is valid while line 2 fails compilation because it's illegal to add numeric types to a `boolean`.

The first "" in line 3 turns the `boolean` into a **String**, and then the same principle is applied once again on line 4 after the evaluation of the operands of the comparison op ==.

Problem 3.9 – A

The very first exercise in *The Art of Computer Programming*, Vol.1, "Fundamental Algorithms" by Donald Knuth reminds the reader that

> ...the text showed how to interchange the values of variables *m* and *n*, using the replacement notation, by setting $t \leftarrow m, m \leftarrow n, n \leftarrow t$.

You decided to beat Knuth himself at his game by devising a way to switch any two integer variables *without* using a temporal storage, and this is what you came up with:

```
class MemorySaver {
    public static void main(String[] args) {
        int a = 123;
        int b = 321;
        System.out.println("a=" + a + ", b=" + b);      // a=123, b=321
        a = a + b;
        b = a - b;
        a = a - b;
        System.out.println("a=" + a + ", b=" + b);      // a=321, b=123
    }
}
```

Suppose, we declare

```
int a = Integer.MAX_VALUE;
int b = Integer.MIN_VALUE;
```

What will happen?

    A.   The algorithm will continue to work correctly
    B.   Both **a** and **b** will flip their signs
    C.   Compilation will fail
    D.   The code will throw an ArithmeticException

Java has neither overflows nor underflows. If a value overflows, it goes back to the MIN_VALUE and continues from there, whereas if it underflows, it jumps back to the MAX_VALUE and continues from there.

The documentation for the class **Math** advises that

> The best practice is to choose the primitive type and algorithm to avoid overflow. In cases where the size is int or long and overflow errors need to be detected, the methods addExact, subtractExact, multiplyExact, and toIntExact throw an ArithmeticException when the results overflow.

java.math.BigInteger also throws **ArithmeticException** when the result is out of the supported range of $-2^{\text{Integer.MAX\_VALUE}}$ (exclusive) to $+2^{\text{Integer.MAX\_VALUE}}$ (exclusive).

Problem 3.10 – B

Given:

```
class Test {
    public static void main(String[] args) {
        StringBuilder sb = new StringBuilder("Same");      // line 1
        String str = "Same";

        if (sb.equals(str)) {                               // line 2
            System.out.println("Same 1");
        } else if (sb.toString().equals(str)) {             // line 3
            System.out.println("Same 2");
        } else {
            System.out.println("Different");
        }
    }
}
```

What is the result?

    A.   Same 1
    B.   Same 2
    C.   Different
    D.   A NullPointerException is thrown at run time

Object's **equals()** is defined simply as ==, and since the class **StringBuilder** does not override this method, we get if(false) on line 2, thus transferring control to the else-if branch.

As line 3 uses the **String**'s **equals()**, we get if(true) because both objects contain identical character sequences.

Problem 3.11 – A

Given:

```
4.    StringBuilder sb1 = new StringBuilder("1Z0-808");
5.    String str1 = sb1.toString();
6.    // insert code here
7.    System.out.print(str1 == str2);
```

Which code fragment, when inserted at line 6, enables the code to print true?

    A.   String str2 = str1;
    B.   String str2 = new String (str1);
    C.   String str2 = sb1.toString();
    D.   String str2 = "1Z0-808";

As **sb1** and **str1** are different reference types, comparing them with == would be illegal, that's why we need either another **String** object or another reference of type **String**, which is exactly those four options do. Further, to make the code print true, both references must point to the same object – and option A satisfies the requirement.

This problem demonstrates another practical principle of how to work during the exam: as soon as you find the answer you're looking for, move to the next question without even bothering with other options. You'll check them all during the complete Review.

Problem 3.12 – B

Given:

```
public class Test {
    public static void main(String[] args) {
        String str1 = "Hello world!";
        String str2 = new String("Hello world!");
        if (str1 == str2) System.out.println("Same");
        if (str1.equals(str2)) System.out.println("More of the same");
    }
}
```

What is the result?

    A.   Same
           More of the same
    B.   More of the same
    C.   Same
    D.   Nothing prints

Unlike **String** literals surrounded with double quotes, the **String** objects returned by methods or created with the keyword new are not interned, which means we are dealing here with two distinct objects.

Problem 3.13 – B

Given the code fragment:

```
String str1 = "My String";
String str2 = new String("My String");
```

What is the proper way to check whether str1 and str2 have the same contents?

A.   if (str1 == str2) { /* some code */ }
B.   if (str1.equals(str2)) { /* some code */ }
C.   if (str1 = str2) { /* some code */ }
D.   if (str1.toString() == str2.toString()) { /* some code */ }

The same problem, only paraphrased. Option A evaluates to `false` regardless of the contents while option C doesn't even compile because the assop produces a **String** and not a `boolean`. As for option D, it also evaluates to `false` regardless of the contents since the **String**s returned by methods don't get interned, so we would be trying to compare two distinct objects.

Problem 3.14 – D

Given the following main method:

```
public static void main(String[] args) {
    StringBuilder sb = new StringBuilder("Inequality");
    String str = "Inequality matters";
    sb.append("matters");
    if (str == sb.toString()) {
        System.out.println("Same");
    }
    if (str.equals(sb.toString())) {
        System.out.println("More of the same");
    }
}
```

What is the result?

A.   Same
       More of the same
B.   More of the same
C.   Same
D.   Nothing prints
E.   Compilation fails

Since the class **StringBuilder** doesn't override **Object**'s **equals()**, the **StringBuilder** objects must be first converted to **Strings**. As **sb.toString()** returns an object that is not kept in the pool, the first printing stat never fires. After the method **append()** returns "Inequalitymatters" (without a space), the second printing stat doesn't get executed, either.

Problem 3.15 – D

Given:

```
class Twins {
    int age;
    Twins(int age) {
        this.age = age;
    }
}
```

```
class Test {
    public static void main (String[] args) {
        Twins t1 = new Twins(13);
        Twins t2 = new Twins(13);
        if (t1 == t2) {
            System.out.println("Identical");
        } else {
            System.out.println("Dissimilar");
        }
        if (t1.equals(t2)) {
            System.out.println("Identical");
        } else {
            System.out.println("Dissimilar");
        }
    }
}
```

What is the result?

A. Identical
   Dissimilar
B. Dissimilar
   Identical
C. Identical
   Identical
D. Dissimilar
   Dissimilar

This is an illustration of the fact that user-defined data types should provide their own implementation of **equals()**.

Problem 3.16 – D

   Given:

```
class Twins {
    int age;
    String gender;
    Twins(int age, String gender) {
        this.age = age;
        this.gender = gender;
    }
    public boolean equals(){
        return this.age == age & this.gender == gender;
    }
}
class Test {
    public static void main (String[] args) {
        Twins t1 = new Twins(13, "Male");
        Twins t2 = new Twins(13, "Male");
        if (t1 == t2) {
            System.out.println("Identical");
        } else {
            System.out.println("Dissimilar");
        }
        if (t1.equals(t2)) {
            System.out.println("Identical");
        } else {
            System.out.println("Dissimilar");
        }
    }
}
```

What is the result?

    A. Identical
         Dissimilar
    B. Dissimilar
         Identical
    C. Identical
         Identical
    D. Dissimilar
         Dissimilar

This problem tests your knowledge of **equals()**'s signature: the method defined by **Twins** does not override the **Object**'s **equals()** who takes an **Object** as its argument. A more proper way to override it should have been something like this (gives option B):

```
public boolean equals(Twins t){
    return this.age == t.age & this.gender == t.gender;
}
```

Problem 3.17 – E

Given:

```
class Test {
    public static void main(String[] args) {
        int x = 10;
        int y = x--;
        int z = --y;
        int a = x++;
        int b = x < y ? x < z ? x : y < z ? y : z;        // line 1
        System.out.println(b);
    }
}
```

What is the result?

    A. 16
    B. 17
    C. 18
    D. 23
    E. Compilation fails

Those assops appear overly complex, one of the vars doesn't even get used… a red herring? And just look at the ternop! It tries to hide its intentions by dropping the parentheses → the question has all the signs of being booby-trapped on line 1.

It is, of course, perfectly possible to painstakingly work out the true meaning of this ternop by writing the whole statement down and then figuring out where the parentheses should go, but there is another way, a time-saving shortcut: since each question mark in a syntactically valid nested ternop must have a matching colon, let's simply count them.

Three question marks and two colons → somewhere a term is missing → the code fails compilation. The following stat would have worked; the previously missing part is highlighted:

```
int b = x < y ? x < z ? x : y < z ? y : z : y;
```

Problem 3.18 – AC

Given the following:

As you are planning to sell your Android-based games, you need to calculate discount rates for bulk purchases using the following criteria:
-   if someone buys three or four of your apps, you are willing to offer a 20% discount;
-   buying five or more apps makes your clients eligible for a 50% discount;
-   the miserly types who refuse to spend their ill-gotten money on more than two of your amazing games, will get no discount at all.

The following **main()** method should take care of the task:

```
public static void main(String[] args) {
    double discount_rate = 0;
    int quantity = Integer.parseInt(args[0]);
    // line X;
}
```

Which two code fragments can be independently inserted at line X to meet the above criteria?

A.
```
if (quantity >= 5) { discount_rate = 0.5; }
if (quantity == 3 || quantity == 4) { discount_rate = 0.2; }
```

B.
```
discount_rate = (quantity >= 5) ? 0.5 : 0;
discount_rate = (quantity >= 3) ? 0.2 : 0;
```

C.
```
discount_rate = (quantity >= 5) ? 0.5 : (quantity >= 3)? 0.2 : 0;
```

D.
```
if (quantity >= 3 && quantity < 5) {
    discount_rate = 0.2;
} else {
    discount_rate = 0;
}
if (quantity >= 5) {
    discount_rate = 0.5;
} else {
    discount_rate = 0;
}
```

E.
```
discount_rate = (quantity > 1) ? 0.2 : (quantity >= 5) ? 0.5 : 0;
```

Option B got its logic wrong by insisting that buying three or more games means a 20% discount. Option D specifies a 0% discount for any quantity below 5. And finally, option E never provides a 50% discount for any quantity over 1.

Don't take this Problem lightly; work out exactly what's going on in it; you'll be glad you did.

Problem 3.19 – B

Given the following code fragment:

```
public static void main(String[] args) {
    int value = 22;
    if (value >= 0) {
        if (value != 0)
            System.out.print("My ");
        else System.out.print("girl ");
        if (value < 10)
            System.out.print("wove ");
        if (value > 20)
            System.out.print("six ");
        else if (value < 30)
            System.out.print("dozen ");
        else if (value < 10)
            System.out.print("plaid ");
```

```
            else
                System.out.print("jackets ");
            if (value > 10)
                System.out.print("before ");
        } else {
            System.out.print("she ");
        }
            System.out.print("quit.");
    }
```

What is the result?

    A. My plaid jackets quit.
    B. My six before quit.
    C. six before she quit.
    D. six dozen before quit.

The first `if` construct wraps up all the others, which are not even nested, so the solution is straight-forward.

Problem 3.20 – C

Given:
```
String valid = "true";
if (valid) System.out.println("valid");
else System.out.println("not valid");
```

What is the result?

    A. valid
    B. not valid
    C. Compilation fails
    D. An IllegalArgumentException is thrown

Since `if` accepts either `boolean` or a **Boolean** only, the code does not compile.

Problem 3.21 – C

Given:
```
int a = 5;

if ( !(a > 5)) {
    System.out.print("wow");
}{  System.out.print("zer"); }

System.out.print("!");
```

What is the result?

    A. wow!
    B. zer!
    C. wowzer!
    D. Compilation fails

All three printing stats fire. The first one runs because inverting `false` makes it `true`, and the second one runs simply because it doesn't even belong to the `if` stat, although is surrounded with braces.

Problem 3.22 – C

Given:

```java
public class Test {
    public static int runTest() {
        return 0;
    }
    public static void main (String[] args) {
        if (runTest()) {
            System.out.print("It works");
        }
        System.out.print("!");
    }
}
```

What is the result?

A. It works!
B. !
C. Compilation fails
D. An exception is thrown at run time

The method **runTest()** returns an int, which cannot be accepted by if.

Problem 3.23 – B

Given:

```java
class Quantity {
    private boolean flag;
    public void show() {
        int qty = flag ? 1 : 100;
        System.out.print("How many? " + qty++);
    }
    public static void main (String[] args) {
        new Quantity().show();
    }
}
```

What is the result?

A. How many? 1
B. How many? 100
C. How many? 2
D. How many? 101
E. Compilation fails

As the instance var **flag** is automatically inited to the default value, the ternary operator evaluates to 100 while the printing stat makes a feeble attempt to trip you with the postfix notation.

Problem 3.24 – A

Given the code fragment:

```
String[] numbers = {"1", "2", "1", "1"};
int counter = 0;
```

And the following decision-making construct:

```
if ("1".equals(numbers[0])) { counter++;
} else if ("1".equals(numbers[1])) { counter++;
} else if ("1".equals(numbers[2])) { counter++;
} else if ("1".equals(numbers[3])) { counter++;
}
System.out.print(counter);
```

What is the result?

A. 1
B. 3
C. Compilation fails
D. An ArrayIndexOutOfBoundsException is thrown at run time

Option D is incorrect because no index exceeds the array's length minus one. As for the `else-if` statements, the execution flow skips them altogether since `if` expression evaluates to `true`.

Problem 3.25 – B

Given the code snippet:

```
7.          boolean bool = true;
8.          switch (bool) {
9.              case true:
10.                 System.out.print("True ");
11.                 break;
12.             default:
13.                 System.out.print("False ");
14.         }
15.         System.out.println("Blue");
```

Which option will allow the code snippet print True Blue?

A. Remove the `default` section
B. Replace line 7 with `String bool = "true";` and replace line 9 with `case "true":`
C. Remove the `break;` statement at line 11
D. Replace line 7 with `boolean bool = 1;` and replace line 9 with `case 1:`

As `switch` can't work with a `boolean`, all we need is make **bool** of a proper type plus tweak the `case` value so that it's consistent with `switch`'s expression, and option B does exactly that.

Problem 3.26 – ABE

Given the code snippet:

```
class Test {
    public static void main(String[] args) {
        // line X
        switch (a) {
            case 0:
                System.out.println("Zero");
                break;
```

```
            case 1:
                System.out.println("One");
                break;
        }
    }
}
```

Which three statements can be independently inserted at line X to enable the code to print Zero?

    A.   short a = 0;
    B.   Integer a = 0;
    C.   Double a = 0;
    D.   String a = "0";
    E.   Byte a = new Byte("0");
    F.   Long a = 0;

Although the Exam Objective 2.5 tests us on **Boolean**, **Integer** and **Double** only, option F has a legitimate place here as this Problem actually checks our knowledge of `switch`. Option E is correct because all wrapper classes (except **Character** with its lonely **Character**(char value) ctor) have a constructor that accepts a **String**. Option C is incorrect since `switch` does not work with floating-point primitives and their wrappers. Everything else is just trivial.

Problem 3.27 – C

Given the code snippet:

```
class Modulo{
    public static void main(String[] args) {
        int a = 10;
        Short s = (short)(int)(long)(float) (a % 4.d);    // line 1
        switch(s) {                                        // line 2
            case 0:
                System.out.print("Divisible by 4");
                break;
            default:
                System.out.print("Not divisible by 4");
                break;
        }
    }
}
```

What is the result?

    A.   Compilation error on line 1
    B.   Compilation error on line 2
    C.   The code prints Not divisible by 4
    D.   The code prints Divisible by 4

Option B is obviously incorrect because `switch` does accept a **Short**. As for line 1, it is syntactically valid since all those casts are allowed.

Problem 3.28 – B

Given:

```
String friend = "Alice";
switch(friend) {
    case "Alice":
        System.out.println("Hi Alice!");
    case "Bob":
        System.out.println("Hi Bob!");
        break;
    case "Carol":
        System.out.println("Hi Carol!");
        break;
    default:
        System.out.println("Hello stranger!");
}
```

What is the result?

A. Hi Alice!

B. Hi Alice!
    Hi Bob!

C. Hi Alice!
    Hi Bob!
    Hi Carol!

C. Hi Alice!
    Hi Bob!
    Hi Carol!
    Hello stranger!

Option B is correct due to falling through because of a missing `break` in the `case` "Alice".

Problem 3.29 – CD

Given:

```
class Week {
    public static void main (String[] args) {
        int day = 1;
        switch (day) {
            case "6": System.out.print("Saturday");
            case "7": System.out.print("Sunday");
            case "1": System.out.print("Monday");
            case "2": System.out.print("Tuesday");
            case "3": System.out.print("Wednesday");
            case "4": System.out.print("Thursday");
            case "5": System.out.print("Friday");
        }
    }
}
```

Which two modifications, made independently, enable the code to compile and run?

A. Adding a break statement after each print statement
B. Adding a default section
C. Removing the double quotes from each case label
D. Changing the type of the variable day to String
E. Arranging the case labels in ascending order

The problem with this class in its unmodified form is that the local var **day**'s type is inconsistent with `case` labels.

Problem 3.30 – B

Given:

```
class Switcher{
    public static void main(String[] args) {
        final String str = "String ";
        switch ( str.trim() + "!" ) {              // line 1
            case "String " + "!":                  // line 2
                System.out.println("String !");
                break;
            case "String" + "!" :                  // line 3
                System.out.println("String!");
                break;
        }
    }
}
```

What is the result?

    A. String !

    B. String!

    C. Compilation fails on line 1

    D. Compilation fails on lines 2 and 3

This problem demonstrates that `switch` expression is evaluated at run time while `case` labels must be compile-time constants. Since the compiler is perfectly able to evaluate the concatenation of **Strings**, neither line 2 nor line 3 throws a comperr.

As for the `final` modifier, it doesn't do anything useful.

Problem 3.31 – C

Given:

```
class Test {
    int test;
    int a = 10;
    int run(){ return 42; }
    void switchMe(){
        switch ( run() ) {}            // line 1
        switch ( test ) {              // line 2
            case a:                    // line 3
            default:
        }
    }
}
```

Which statement about this code is true?

    A. Line 1 throws a comperr

    B. Line 2 throws a comperr

    C. Line 3 throws a comperr

    D. There is nothing wrong with the code

The problem is similar to the previous one although this time the code violates the rule about `case` labels: the var **a** isn't a constant. Declaring it `final` would have cleared the comperr.

Problem 3.32 – BE

Given:

```
class AnotherTest {
    int a, b;
    final int c = 0;
    void switchMe(){
        switch ( a = 0 ) {}          // line 1
        switch ( int d = 0 ) {}      // line 2
        switch ( 1 ) {}              // line 3
        switch ( a++ ) {             // line 4
            case a:                  // line 5
            case c:                  // line 6
        }
    }
}
```

Which two LOCs fail compilation?

    A. Line 1
    B. Line 2
    C. Line 3
    D. Line 4
    E. Line 5
    F. Line 6

The var **a** isn't a constant to be used as a `case` label, that's why line 5 throws a comperr whereas line 1 doesn't. The var **c** is `final` so line 6 is OK. Line 3 compiles since the numeric literal 1 is an `int`, and line 4 doesn't violate any rule, either. As for line 2, it attempts to declare a var right inside the `switch` expression, which is not allowed.

Problem 3.33 – C

Given:

```
class YetAnotherTest{
    final static int a1 = 0;
    final static Integer i1 = 1;
    public static void main(String[] args) {
        int x = 666;
        StringBuilder str = new StringBuilder("Java");
        switch (x) {
            case -123: str.append("S");
            case a1:   str.append("E");      // line 1
            case i1:   str.append("8");      // line 2
        }
        System.out.println(str);
    }
}
```

Which statement about the code is true?

    A. The code compiles and prints Java
    B. The code throws a comperr on line 1
    C. The code throws a comperr on line 2
    D. The code throws a RuntimeException

Line 1 compiles because the var **a1** is `final` while line 2 fails compilation as wrapper classes are not considered compile-time constants – even when they are declared `final`.

Chapter II.4

EXAM OBJECTIVES – Group Four:
Creating and Using Arrays

The 1Z0-808 objectives within this group:

4.1   Declare, instantiate, initialize and use one-dimensional arrays;

4.2   Declare, instantiate, initialize and use multi-dimensional arrays.

 CORE RULES (with some Extras):

As the 2nd objective is just an extension of the first one, we'll cover them both in a single block.

4.1 & 4.2   Declare, instantiate, initialize and use one- and multi-dimensional arrays:

- ❑   An array is an **Object**.

  Corollaries: Arrays can access any method that is available to the class **Object**;

  Unlike primitive types, changes to an array are reflected wherever the array is used.

- ❑   Arrays are used to store collections of values and are structurally immutable (in other words, once an array has been allocated, we can't change its length and the number of its dimensions).

- ❑   Java provides support for one-dimensional and multi-dimensional arrays.

- ❑   A two-dimensional array refers to a collection of one-dimensional arrays, which can be of different length (**other wording**: rows may have different number of columns in them).

- ❑   The creation of an array involves three steps:
  - ■   declaration,
  - ■   allocation, and
  - ■   initialization.

- ❑   The type of an array can be any including an abstract data type or interface.

- ❑   As arrays are **Object**s, they are allocated by using the keyword `new`.

- ❑   The number of matching square brackets specifies the number of dimensions in the array. The square brackets may follow either the data type or the variable name, or both if the array is multi-dimensional.

- ❑   A standalone declaration of an array that isn't followed by allocation creates a reference var that points to `null`.

- ❑   Because declaration does not create elements, it is illegal to specify the size of the array in the declaration part.

❑ It is permitted to declare and allocate an array without initing it:

```
int[] arr = new int[5];              // VALID
```

❑ Once allocated, all elements receive their default values according to the declared data type:

- 0 for integral numerical types such as `byte`, `short`, `int` and `long`;
- 0.0 for floating-point numerical types (`float` and `double`);
- `false` for `boolean`;
- `'\u0000'` for `char`, and
- `null` for reference types.

Corollaries: Accessing an uninited array of any reference type with a printing stat won't throw an NPE;

A properly allocated array *will* be inited even if it's a local var and there's no explicit initialization.

❑ When all the steps are combined into a single stat, defining the length of the array is not permitted because it is calculated automatically on the basis of the number of values that are assigned to the array. For example, we cannot specify the length of the array when using an initializer block at the point of declaration:

```
String[] sarr = new String[1]{"a"};     // INVALID; must be String[]{"a"};
```

❑ An initializer block without `new` is valid only in the declaration:

```
int[] a = {1};       // VALID
int[] b;
b = {1};             // INVALID; must read b = new int[]{1};
```

❑ The code throws an AIOOBE at run time if the requested index does not fall within the valid range of the number of elements.

❑ The dimension expressions are evaluated first (left to right).

❑ While counting curly braces may seem at the first glance a reliable solution to checking the consistency of dimensions, exercise extreme caution as some elements just might be arrays in themselves:

```
int[] a = {};
int[][][][] arr4D = {{{{1}, {2}, {3}, {4}, {5}, {6}}}};
```
four opening braces... aha! so the number of dimensions must be four, too; what a nifty trick!.. so the next LOC isn't valid... or is it?

```
int[][] arr2D = {a};                        // VALID      oops...
```

❑ Accessing slots in allocated arrays with undefined dimension(s) results in an NPE:

```
int[][] arr = new int[5][];              // VALID
System.out.println(arr[0][0]);           // throws NPE
```

❑ The upper-level dimension *must* be defined in the absence of initializer block:

```
int[][][][] arr1 = new int[5][ ][ ][ ];     // VALID
int[][][][] arr2 = new int[5][4][3][ ];     // VALID
int[][][][] arr3 = new int[ ][ ][ ][ ];     // INVALID
int[][][][] arr4 = new int[ ][1][ ][ ];     // INVALID
int[][][][] arr5 = new int[5][ ][1][ ];     // INVALID
int[][][][] arr6 = new int[ ][1][1][1];     // INVALID
```

- EXTRA: To see if an array is assignable to another array, check the <u>number of dimensions</u> the slots are referring to and *not* the length of the array on the right-hand side:

```
int[][] a1 = new int[5][];
int[][] a2 = new int[2][];
int a3 = 10;
int[][][][] a4 = new int [1][2][3][4];
a4[1][1] = a2;
a1[1][0] = a3;
// a4[0][1][1] = a1;                    // INVALID as a1 is 2-dim
a4[1][1][0][1] = a1[1][0];
a4[0][1] = a1;
```

- EXTRA: When accessing an array, the expression to the left of the square brackets gets evaluated before any part of the expression within the brackets. If this evaluation completes abruptly, the expression inside the brackets won't be evaluated:

```
class Test{
    int[] arr = new int[]{10, 20, 30};
    int[] getArr1() { return arr; }
    int[] getArr2() { throw new NullPointerException(); }
    public static void main(String[] args){
        int idx = 0;
        System.out.println(
            new Test().getArr1()[idx = 1] + ", idx = " + idx);
        try {
            System.out.println(new Test().getArr2()[idx++]); // 20, idx = 1
        }
        catch (NullPointerException npe){
            System.out.println("Caught NPE!");                // Caught NPE!
        }
        System.out.println("idx is still " + idx);            // idx is still 1
    }
}
```

- EXTRA: A vararg passed to a method will be used as a regular array. Say, in case of a vararg-based **main()** method invocation, the compiler internally converts **String**... into a **String[]** → the JVM doesn't have any idea about the vararg. It sees only a **String[]**.

- EXTRA: A trailing comma is acceptable: `new String[]{"Hi",}`. This is used to simplify changes in the order of elements particularly when they are written vertically.

- EXTRA: There are no true, matrix-type multi-dimensional arrays in Java, and since they are implemented as arrays of arrays, the structural immutability concerns only the first dimension:

```
int[][] array = new int[2][0];
System.out.println(array[0].length);    // prints 0
// array[0][0] = 2;                      // throws AIOOBE at index 0
array[0] = new int[2];                   // extending 2nd dim by 2 more slots
System.out.println(array[0].length);    // prints 2
array[0][1] = 2;                         // runs just fine
```

Problem 4.1 Given the class:

```
1. class Score {
2.     public static void main(String[] args) {
3.         /* INSERT CODE HERE */
4.         arr[0] = 3;
5.         arr[1] = 1;
6.         System.out.println("MU vs FCB " + arr[0] + " : " + arr[1]);
7.     }
8. }
```

Which code fragment, when inserted at line 3, lets the code print MU vs FCB 3 : 1?

   A. byte[] new arr = byte[2];
   B. short[] arr;
       arr = new short[2];
   C. int arr = new int[2];
   D. long arr[2];

Problem 4.2 Given the following main method:

```
public static void main(String[] args){
    String[] students = {"Alice", "Bob", "Carol", "Daisy", "Eric"};
    System.out.print(students.length);
    System.out.println(students[1].length());
}
```

What is the result?

   A. 53
   B. 55
   C. Compilation fails
   D. Run-time exception is thrown

Problem 4.3 Given:

```
11.  String[] arrStr = {"a", "b", "c", "d", "e", "f"};
12.  arrStr[3] = arrStr[5];
13.  arrStr[5] = "g";
```

Which option represents the contents of the array arrStr after line 13?

   A. abcdef
   B. abcfef
   C. abcfeg
   D. abcgeg

Problem 4.4 Given:

```
String arr[][] = new String[2][2];
arr[0][0] = "0";
arr[0][1] = "1";
arr[1][0] = "false";
arr[1][1] = "true";
```

Which option outputs all elements of the array referred to as arr?

A. for (int index = 1; index < 2; index++) {
        for (int idx = 1; idx < 2; idx++) {
            System.out.println(arr[index][idx]);
        }
    }

B. for (int index = 0; index < 2; ++index) {
        for (int idx = 0; idx < index; ++idx) {
            System.out.println(arr[index][idx]);
        }
    }

C. for (String c : integers) {
        for (String s : booleans) {
            System.out.println(s);
        }
    }

D. for (int index = 0; index < 2;) {
        for (int idx = 0; idx < 2;) {
            System.out.println(arr[index][idx]);
            idx++;
        }
        index++;
    }

Problem 4.5 Given:

```
int arr[][] = new int[1][3];
for (int i = 0; i < arr.length; i++) {
    for (int j = 0; j < arr[i].length; j++) {
        arr[i][j] = 10;
    }
}
```

Which option represents the state of the arr array after successful completion of the outer loop?

A. arr[0][0]=10
    arr[1][0]=10
    arr[2][0]=10

B. arr[0][0]=10
    arr[0][1]=10
    arr[0][2]=10

C. arr[0][0]=10
    arr[0][1]=10
    arr[0][2]=10
    arr[0][3]=10
    arr[1][0]=0
    arr[1][1]=0
    arr[1][2]=0
    arr[1][3]=0

D. arr[0][0]=10
    arr[0][1]=0
    arr[0][2]=0

Problem 4.6 Given:

```
int[][] arr = {{0}, {1, 2}, {3, 4, 5}, {6, 7, 8, 9}, {10, 11, 12, 13, 14}};
System.out.println(arr[4][2]);
System.out.println(arr[2][4]);
```

What is the result?

- A. 12 followed by null
- B. 2 followed by 4
- C. An IllegalArgumentException is thrown at run time
- D. 12 followed by an ArrayIndexOutOfBoundsException

Problem 4.7

Which two are valid declarations of a two-dimensional array?

- A. int[][] arr2D;
- B. int[2][2] arr2D;
- C. int arr2D[];
- D. int[][] arr2D[];
- E. int[] arr2D[];

Problem 4.8 Given:

```
int[][] arr2D = {{0, 1, 2}, {3, 4, 5, 6}};
System.out.print(arr2D[0].length + " ");
System.out.print(arr2D[1].getClass().isArray() + " ");
System.out.print(arr2D[0][1]);
```

What is the result?

- A. 3 false 1
- B. 3 true 1
- C. 2 false 1
- D. 2 true 1

Problem 4.9

Which two are valid declarations, instantiations and initializations of a multi-dimensional array?

- A. int[][] arr2D = { { 0, 1, 2, 3 } { 4, 5 } };
- B. int[][] arr2D = new int[2][2];
  arr2D[0][0] = 0;
  arr2D[0][1] = 1;
  arr2D[1][0] = 2;
  arr2D[1][1] = 3;
- C. int[][][] arr3D = { {0,1}, {2, 3}, {4, 5} };
- D. int[] arr = { (0), (1), (2), (3), (4) };
  int[][][] arr3D = new int[2][2][2];
  arr3D[0][0] = arr3D[0][1] = arr;
  arr3D[1][0] = arr3D[0][1] = arr;
- E. int[][] arr2D = { 0, 1 };

Problem 4.10

Which two are valid array declarations?

A. Object arr1[];
B. boolean arr2[3];
C. char[] arr3;
D. double[2] arr4;

Problem 4.11   Given the class:

```
class Test{
    public static void main(String[] args){
        int[][] array2D = new int[3][4];
        System.out.println("Setting:");
        for (int a = 0; a < array2D.length; a++) {
            for (int b = 0; b < array2D[0].length; b++) {

                // SETTING STATEMENT GOES IN HERE

                System.out.println("[" + a + "][" + b + "]=" + array2D[a][b]);
            }
        }

        System.out.println("Modifying:");
        for (int a = 0; a < array2D.length; a++) {
            for (int b = 0; b < array2D[0].length; b++) {

                // MODIFYING STATEMENT GOES IN HERE

                System.out.println("[" + a + "][" + b + "]=" + array2D[a][b]);
            }
        }
    }
}
```

Which pair of statements will set each element of the array to the sum of the element indices and then modify it by multiplying the value by 2?

A. Setting statement: array2D(a,b) = a + b;
   Modifying statement: array2D(a,b) = array2D(a,b) * 2;
B. Setting statement: array2D[a b] = a + y;
   Modifying statement: array2D[a b] = array2D[a b] * 2;
C. Setting statement: array2D[a,b] = a + y;
   Modifying statement: array2D[a,b] = array2D[a,b] * 2;
D. Setting statement: array2D[a][b] = a + y;
   Modifying statement: array2D[a][b] = array2D[a][b] * 2;
E. Setting statement: array2D[[a][b]] = a + y;
   Modifying statement: array2D[[a][b]] = array2D[[a][b]] * 2;

Problem 4.12

Which two statements are true for a two-dimensional array?

A. Internally, Java stores it as an array of an array of the specified data type.
B. Each row of a two-dimensional array must be of the same size.
C. The number of elements of the array in each dimension must be specified at the moment of declaration.
D. All methods defined in the class Object may be invoked on the two-dimensional array.

Problem 4.13   Given the following method:

```
void fillArr(){
    // INSERT CODE HERE                          line X
    array[0] = new int[2];
    array[0][0] = 1;
    array[0][1] = 2;

    array[1] = new int[3];
    array[1][0] = 10;
    array[1][1] = 20;
    array[1][2] = 30;
}
```

Which two statements, when inserted independently at line X, enable the code to compile and run without throwing an exception?

    A.   int[][] array = null;
    B.   int[][] array = new int[2];
    C.   int[][] array = new int[2][];
    D.   int[][] array = new int[][4];
    E.   int[][] array = new int[2][0];
    F.   int[][] array = new int[0][4];

Problem 4.14   Given the following class:

```
class ArrayTest{
    public static void main(String args[]){
        String[][][] array = new String[][][]
            {{{"a","b","c"},{"d","e","f"}}, {{"g"}, null}, {{"y"}}, {{"z","Q"}, {}}};

        // INSERT PRINTING STAT HERE            line X

    }
}
```

Which statement, when inserted at line X, will print null?

    A.   System.out.println(array[1]);
    B.   System.out.println(array[1][1]);
    C.   System.out.println(array[1][1][1]);
    D.   None of the above because the code fails compilation

Problem 4.15   Given the following graphic representation of an array:

X			X
	X		
X	X		
		X	X

And given the code fragment that was used to fill in the array as pictured above:

```
String[] starr[] = new String[][]{
    {"X","","","X"},{"","X","",""},{"X","X","",""},{"","","X","X"}
};
```

Which statement will make four crosses in a row?

    A. starr[3][3] = "X";
    B. starr[2][3] = "X";
    C. starr[2][2] = "X";
    D. starr[3][2] = "X";
    E. starr[2][4] = "X";

Problem 4.16   Given:

```
class TestArrayForNPE {
    static int spoil() throws Exception {
        throw new Exception();
    }
    public static void main(String[] args) {
        int[] a = null;
        try {
            a[spoil()]++;
        } catch (ArrayIndexOutOfBoundsException aioobe) {
            System.out.println("Caught AIOOBE");
        } catch (NullPointerException npe) {
            System.out.println("Caught NPE");
        } catch (Exception e) {
            System.out.println("Caught E"); }
    }
}
```

What is the result?

    A. Caught E
    B. Caught NPE
    C. Caught AIOOBE
    D. Compilation fails

Problem 4.1 – B

Given the class:

```
1. class Score {
2.     public static void main(String[] args) {
3.         /* INSERT CODE HERE */
4.         arr[0] = 3;
5.         arr[1] = 1;
6.     System.out.println("MU vs FCB " + arr[0] + " : " + arr[1]);
7.     }
8. }
```

Which code fragment, when inserted at line 3, lets the code print MU vs FCB 3 : 1?

  A. byte[] new arr = byte[2];
  B. short[] arr;
    arr = new short[2];
  C. int arr = new int[2];
  D. long arr[2];

Options A, C and D are syntactically invalid because A misplaces the keyword new and C specifies a non-array primitive in the left-hand part. As for option D, it violates syntax by specifying the number of elements right in the declaration part.

Option B correctly declares a one-dimensional array of shorts in its first stat, then instantiates the array.

Problem 4.2 – A

Given the following main method:

```
public static void main(String[] args){
    String[] students = {"Alice", "Bob", "Carol", "Daisy", "Eric"};
    System.out.print(students.length);
    System.out.println(students[1].length());
}
```

What is the result?

  A. 53
  B. 55
  C. Compilation fails
  D. Run-time exception is thrown

The length of an array is stored in the instance field **length** whereas getting the length of a **String** requires invoking the method **length()** on the **String** object.

Problem 4.3 – C

Given:

```
11.    String[] arrStr = {"a", "b", "c", "d", "e", "f"};
12.    arrStr[3] = arrStr[5];
13.    arrStr[5] = "g";
```

Which option represents the contents of the array arrStr after line 13?

    A. abcdef
    B. abcfef
    C. abcfeg
    D. abcgeg

The answer seems obvious – even insultingly so. And while this particular problem is indeed simple, I'd like to seize the opportunity to remind you that we always should be on guard when dealing with objects.

The problem is not booby-trapped only because the class **String** is immutable, so after line 13 each element of the array still points to a different object. Now consider what happens when the objects are not immutable:

```
 1 StringBuilder sb1 = new StringBuilder("One");
 2 StringBuilder sb2 = new StringBuilder("Two");
 3 StringBuilder[] sbar = {sb1, sb2};
 4
 5 System.out.println(sbar[0] + " " + sbar[1]);          // One Two
 6
 7 sbar[0] = sbar[1];
 8 System.out.println(sbar[0] + " " + sbar[1]);          // Two Two
 9
10 sbar[1].reverse();
11 System.out.println(sbar[0] + " " + sbar[1]);          // owT owT
```

Line 7 makes both elements point to the same object just like line 12 in Problem 4.3 did. But unlike the **String**s where a change in an object creates another object, a change in a **StringBuilder** gets reflected inside the original object, so that's why line 10 affects **sbar**[0], too.

Reminder: Here's the list of the immutable core Java 1.8 classes that are on the exam:

  – **String**
  – all **LDT**s } you *will* be tested on the immutability of **String** and at least one of the **LDT**s, guaranteed

    EXTRA: all wrapper classes
    EXTRA: *structurally*-immutable is any **List** created by **Arrays.asList(arr)**

I admit: it was tempting to use a user-defined mutable data type to lay a nice trap for you but the actual exam uses something similar to the way Problem 4.3 is presented, so in the end I voted for a better consistency. Do remember, however, that acting on a reference can lead to radically different results as compared to acting on a primitive data type.

Problem 4.4 – D

    Given:

```
String arr[][] = new String[2][2];
arr[0][0] = "0";
arr[0][1] = "1";
arr[1][0] = "false";
arr[1][1] = "true";
```

Which option outputs all elements of the array referred to as arr?

A. for (int index = 1; index < 2; index++) {
        for (int idx = 1; idx < 2; idx++) {
            System.out.println(arr[index][idx]);
        }
    }

B. for (int index = 0; index < 2; ++index) {
        for (int idx = 0; idx < index; ++idx) {
            System.out.println(arr[index][idx]);
        }
    }

C. for (String c : integers) {
        for (String s : booleans) {
            System.out.println(s);
        }
    }

D. for (int index = 0; index < 2;) {
        for (int idx = 0; idx < 2;) {
            System.out.println(arr[index][idx]);
            idx++;
        }
        index++;
    }

Indexation of arrays starts with zero so option A misses the first row entirely and the first column in the second row. Option B should have compared the loop var **idx** to **arr[index].length** while option C is simply irrelevant as the code declares neither the var **integers** nor the var **booleans**.

I met a similar question on both sittings so take all the time you need to get this Problem's logic right.

Problem 4.5 – B

Given:

```
int arr[][] = new int[1][3];
for (int i = 0; i < arr.length; i++) {
    for (int j = 0; j < arr[i].length; j++) {
        arr[i][j] = 10;
    }
}
```

Which option represents the state of the array arr after successful completion of the outer loop?

A. arr[0][0]=10
    arr[1][0]=10
    arr[2][0]=10
B. arr[0][0]=10
    arr[0][1]=10
    arr[0][2]=10

C. arr[0][0]=10
   arr[0][1]=10
   arr[0][2]=10
   arr[0][3]=10
   arr[1][0]=0
   arr[1][1]=0
   arr[1][2]=0
   arr[1][3]=0
D. arr[0][0]=10
   arr[0][1]=0
   arr[0][2]=0

The instantiation part of the array declaration stat says that the array has only one row with three slots in it, so options A and C are obviously out (A needs three rows and C, two).

Option D is also incorrect because the nested `for` loop executes successfully thus setting each element to the value of ten.

Problem 4.6 – D

Given:

```
int[][] arr = {{0}, {1, 2}, {3, 4, 5}, {6, 7, 8, 9}, {10, 11, 12, 13, 14}};
System.out.println(arr[4][2]);
System.out.println(arr[2][4]);
```

What is the result?

A. 12 followed by null
B. 2 followed by 4
C. An IllegalArgumentException is thrown at run time
D. 12 followed by an ArrayIndexOutOfBoundsException

The initialization part of the array declaration specifies that the array will contain a single row with five slots in it, each of which is an array in itself. While the element referred to as **arr**[4][2] does exist, the third one-dimensional array contains only three slots so the code tries to access an element well beyond the valid range.

Problem 4.7 – AE

Which two are valid declarations of a two-dimensional array?

A. int[][] arr2D;
B. int[2][2] arr2D;
C. int arr2D[];
D. int[][] arr2D[];
E. int[] arr2D[];

Options C and D are obviously incorrect as they specify a wrong number of dimensions (one and three, respectively), and option B is syntactically invalid as the declaration part may not contain the number of elements.

Problem 4.8 – B

Given:

```
int[][] arr2D = {{0, 1, 2}, {3, 4, 5, 6}};
System.out.print(arr2D[0].length + " ");
System.out.print(arr2D[1].getClass().isArray() + " ");
System.out.print(arr2D[0][1]);
```

What is the result?

    A. 3 false 1
    B. 3 true 1
    C. 2 false 1
    D. 2 true 1

Although the **getClass()** and **isArray()** methods are not on the exam[75], it is probably not a bad idea to remind ourselves that a multi-dimensional array in Java is actually implemented as an array of arrays who can be of different lengths and even change the number of their slots.

Problem 4.9 – BD

Which two are valid declarations, instantiations and initializations of a multi-dimensional array?

    A. int[][] arr2D = { { 0, 1, 2, 3 } { 4, 5 } };

    B. int[][] arr2D = new int[2][2];
        arr2D[0][0] = 0;
        arr2D[0][1] = 1;
        arr2D[1][0] = 2;
        arr2D[1][1] = 3;

    C. int[][][] arr3D = { {0, 1}, {2, 3}, {4, 5} };

    D. int[] arr = { (0), (1), (2), (3), (4) };
        int[][][] arr3D = new int[2][2][2];
        arr3D[0][0] = arr3D[0][1] = arr;
        arr3D[1][0] = arr3D[0][1] = arr;

    E. int[][] arr2D = { 0, 1 };

Option A is syntactically invalid as it is missing a comma between the elements. Option B is a 'straight arrow': it instantiates a two-dim array then fills it with `int`s. Option C says that **arr3D** is a three-dim array while the initialization part is suitable for a two-dim array only (observe that here the trick about counting the number of leading braces works quite well). Option E is similar to C in being inconsistent about the number of dimensions, and as for option D, it is perfectly valid although looks a bit twisted. The redundant parentheses do not affect the statement's compilability, and chained assignments of the already declared vars are also legal.

---

[75] **getClass()** is defined in **Object** and **isArray()** is defined in the class **Class**.

Problem 4.10 – AC

Which two are valid array declarations?

  A. Object arr1[];
  B. boolean arr2[3];
  C. char[] arr3;
  D. double[2] arr4;

While the square brackets can indeed be placed after the reftype or the var's name, the array declaration never accepts the number of elements.

Problem 4.11 – D

Given the class:

```
class Test{
    public static void main(String[] args){
        int[][] array2D = new int[3][4];
        System.out.println("Setting:");
        for (int a = 0; a < array2D.length; a++) {
            for (int b = 0; b < array2D[0].length; b++) {

                // SETTING STATEMENT GOES IN HERE

                System.out.println("[" + a + "][" + b + "]=" + array2D[a][b]);
            }
        }
        System.out.println("Modifying:");
        for (int a = 0; a < array2D.length; a++) {
            for (int b = 0; b < array2D[0].length; b++) {

                // MODIFYING STATEMENT GOES IN HERE

                System.out.println("[" + a + "][" + b + "]=" + array2D[a][b]);
            }
        }
    }
}
```

Which pair of statements will set each element of the array to the sum of the element indices and then modify it by multiplying the value by 2?

  A. Setting statement: array2D(a,b) = a + b;
      Modifying statement: array2D(a,b) = array2D(a,b) * 2;
  B. Setting statement: array2D[a b] = a + y;
      Modifying statement: array2D[a b] = array2D[a b] * 2;
  C. Setting statement: array2D[a,b] = a + y;
      Modifying statement: array2D[a,b] = array2D[a,b] * 2;
  D. Setting statement: array2D[a][b] = a + y;
      Modifying statement: array2D[a][b] = array2D[a][b] * 2;
  E. Setting statement: array2D[[a][b]] = a + y;
      Modifying statement: array2D[[a][b]] = array2D[[a][b]] * 2;

This one illustrates that the questions contain sometimes just too much chaff: we actually don't even need to look at the class to work out the correct answer as option D is the only one that is syntactically correct regardless of its business logic.

Problem 4.12 – AD

Which two statements are true for a two-dimensional array?

A. Internally, Java stores it as an array of an array of the specified data type.
B. Each row of a two-dimensional array must be of the same size.
C. The number of elements of the array in each dimension must be specified at the moment of declaration.
D. All methods defined in the class Object may be invoked on the two-dimensional array.

By now answering this question should present no problems whatsoever.

Problem 4.13 – CE

Given the following method:

```
void fillArr(){
    // INSERT CODE HERE              line X
    array[0] = new int[2];
    array[0][0] = 1;
    array[0][1] = 2;

    array[1] = new int[3];
    array[1][0] = 10;
    array[1][1] = 20;
    array[1][2] = 30;
}
```

Which two statements, when inserted independently at line X, enable the code to compile and run without throwing an exception?

A. int[][] array = null;
B. int[][] array = new int[2];
C. int[][] array = new int[2][];
D. int[][] array = new int[][4];
E. int[][] array = new int[2][0];
F. int[][] array = new int[0][4];

Only options B and D are syntactically incorrect as B is inconsistent about the number of dimensions while D is missing the number of elements in the very first array.

The compiler always needs to know how many slots an upper-level array should contain. So if we have a two-dim array, the code must specify the number of elements for at least the first dimension; a three-dim array will need number of slots for at least the first two dimensions, etc.

Although option A does compile, it throws an NPE because the reference points to `null`. This is hugely important subject for the exam so let's list all the NPE-throwing scenarios right away:

The Magnificent Five:
In what cases JVM throws NullPointerException?

ABSOLUTELY NEEDED

1. Calling the instance method on a `null` object.
2. Accessing or modifying the field of a `null` object.
3. Taking the length of `null` as if it were an array.
4. Accessing or modifying the slots of `null` as if it were an array. ← a popular trap!
5. Throwing `null` as if it were a **Throwable** value. ← didn't meet on the exam, though

By choosing option A, we'll be implementing the 4th scenario.

Although option C leaves out the number of elements in the second dimension, it's alright since the code then starts defining the arrays that go in each slot. Option E is similar to option C as it is immaterial how many elements we declare in the very last dimension.

And finally, option F throws an AIOOBE because the array is instantiated with zero elements in its first dimension, and the code wants to work with an element that does not even exist. Since the first dimension is structurally immutable, there isn't much we can do about fixing the problem.

Problem 4.14 – B

Given the following class:

```
class ArrayTest{
    public static void main(String args[]){
        String[][][] array = new String[][][]
            {{{"a","b","c"},{"d","e","f"}},{{"g"},null},{{"y"}},{{"z","Q"},{}}};
        // INSERT PRINTING STAT HERE            line X
    }
}
```

Which statement, when inserted at line X, will print null?

    A. System.out.println(array[1]);
    B. System.out.println(array[1][1]);
    C. System.out.println(array[1][1][1]);
    D. None of the above because the code fails compilation

The exam GUI doesn't allow code editing; on the other hand, everything is pretty-typed and you will not meet such a 'hairy' snippet on the real exam. But practice is still practice.

It is, of course, possible to work out diligently each and every element's address but I would like to show you a shortcut. The `null` element here simply holds a place of a one-dim array so we can mentally replace it with a pair of matching curly braces. It becomes apparent then that the first two closing braces indicate the end of the first row, the next two closing braces (the last one of them is imaginary) mark the end of the second row – and all the rest is simply irrelevant. By mentally restoring `null` to its lawful place, we finally get its address: [1][1].

All in all, the entire array contains four rows. More specifically, the uppermost array has four slots occupied by arrays: the first two of them contain two 3-element-long slots each, the third one stores just "y" in the third dimension, and the fourth array has two slots with the last one – that is, array[3][1] – of zero length:

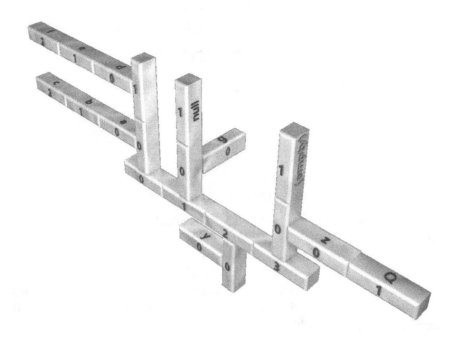

You probably should practice more until reading dimensions even in horrendous 'dendritic' arrays like this one becomes your second nature. For example – and look only at the code, not the picture – what is the address of the letter "y"? what about "Q"?[76]

Problem 4.15 – C

Given the following graphic representation of an array:

X			X
	X		
X	X		
		X	X

And given the code fragment that was used to fill in the array as pictured above:

```
String[] starr[] = new String[][]{
    {"X","","","X"},{"","X","",""},{"X","X","",""},{"","","X","X"}
};
```

Which statement will make four crosses in a row?

    A.   starr[3][3] = "X";
    B.   starr[2][3] = "X";
    C.   starr[2][2] = "X";
    D.   starr[3][2] = "X";

---

[76] [2][0][0] and [3][0][1], respectively.

The array initialization part mimics the rows in the table, so the solution is obvious – especially when you mentally re-arrange the elements vertically. Note, however, that we don't even need to consult the code fragment to see what element should be assigned the literal "X". Even if we somehow confuse rows with columns, it still will be the last element in a 3-by-3 grid (provided, of course, we start counting from the upper left corner and continue clockwise, which is only natural).

The question on the exam used separate statements to assign Xs to the appropriate cells so you may want to practice with that version, too.

And one more thing: I met a similar question on the second sitting[77] only, which may mean that it is of the 'Guinea Pigs' variety, in other words, ungraded. Who knows…

Problem 4.16 – A

Given:

```
class TestArrayForNPE {
    static int spoil() throws Exception {
        throw new Exception();
    }
    public static void main(String[] args) {
        int[] a = null;
        try {
            a[spoil()]++;
        } catch (ArrayIndexOutOfBoundsException aioobe) {
            System.out.println("Caught AIOOBE");
        } catch (NullPointerException npe) {
            System.out.println("Caught NPE");
        } catch (Exception e) {
            System.out.println("Caught E"); }
    }
}
```

What is the result?

    A. Caught E
    B. Caught NPE
    C. Caught AIOOBE
    D. Compilation fails

According to the JLS §15.10.4, *Run-Time Evaluation of Array Access Expressions*, the evaluation process starts to the left of the square brackets, then – if successful – the JVM looks at the part within the brackets. The Specification also adds that

> If the array reference expression produces null instead of a reference to an array, then a NullPointerException is thrown at run time, but only after all parts of the array access expression have been evaluated and only if these evaluations completed normally.

In our case it means that since the evaluation of the index expression **spoil()** completes abruptly due to a thrown **Exception**, an NPE never occurs because the evaluation process doesn't even reach the moment of truth where it must check whether value of the array reference expression is null.

This exercise also demonstrates that although accessing a slot of null as if it were an array does produce an NPE, we shouldn't jump to the conclusion as soon as we see that the code intends to do something to a null reference: the chances are it won't get to that point at all…

---

[77] On the first sitting there was no graphics at all…

Chapter
II.5

EXAM OBJECTIVES – Group Five:
Using Loop Constructs

The 1Z0-808 objectives within this group:

5.1 Create and use `while` loops
5.2 Create and use `for` loops including the enhanced `for` loop
5.3 Create and use `do-while` loops
5.4 Compare loop constructs
5.5 Use `break` and `continue`

As loops are arguably the most widely used constructs, it becomes indispensable to fully master them for the exam. The harder the training the better the results so we'll cover all loop-related objectives first and only then do exercises, otherwise it'll be too obvious what each particular question is asking for thus making spotting traps easier. We will also pay a close attention to labels since they are generally go with loops.

CORE RULES (with some Extras):

❑ The standard `for` loop is the most basic and versatile loop of all; it can replace any other loop construct.

❑ `do-while` executes at least once.

❑ The `break` statement breaks out of a loop 'cleanly', in other words, by fully abandoning current iteration and any other remaining iterations of the loop. Control is transferred to the first statement after the loop.

❑ When the loop `for(i = 0; i < n; i++)` terminates, the value of **i** is **n** and not **n-1**.

❑ Nested loops can appear intimidating but chances are the flow won't even enter some of those damned loops.

Reminder: The weirder the loop the higher the chances the code is booby-trapped somewhere else and, what's more, on a pretty simple aspect.

If your analysis shows that the flow does enter a loop, write down each iteration with all its steps; cracking loops mentally at home is cool but probably not a good idea on the exam. Vertical notation works better than writing the results of each iteration in rows because it's easier to correct values this way or start over from a particular point if you lose concentration for a sec:

```
int s = 5;
for(int i = 0; i < 3; i++){
    s += i;
    System.out.print(s);
}
```

```
i 0
s 5
p 5 (== "prints 5")
i 1
s 6
p 6
i 2
s 8
p 8
```

is better
than

```
i 0 1 2
s 5 6 8
p 5 6 8
```

❑ EXTRA: Any section of the `for` loop can be moved to its body; what's more, the ForInit section accepts chained assignments (the vars must be of the same type, though):

```
int i, s, count = 10;
for (i = 0, s = 0; i < count; i++) { s+=i; }
-------------------------------------------------
int i, s, count = 10;
for(i = 0, s = 0; i < count; s+=i, i++);
-------------------------------------------------
int s = 0, count = 10;
for(int i=0; i < count; s+=i++);
-------------------------------------------------
int i=0, s=0, count=10;
for(; i< count; s+=i){ i++; }
-------------------------------------------------
int i=0, s=0, count=10;
for(; i < count; ){ s+=i; i++; }
-------------------------------------------------
int i=0, s=0, count=10;
for(; ;){ s+=i++; if (i>count) break; }
```

❑ The compiler treats `for(;;)` as `for(;true;)`.

❑ An endless loop makes subsequent stat unreachable → comperr.

The rule sounds pretty obvious but endless loops are tricky: the code will throw the "unreachable statement" comperr only if 1) the boolean expression can be evaluated at compile time, and 2) there's no escape from the loop. Consider the following example:

```
 1 class Looping {
 2     public static void main(String[] args) {
 3         for(;;) {}
 4         for(;;) if (args.length > 0) break;    // unreachable
 5         try { for(;;) {} }
 6         catch(Throwable t) { System.out.println("Caught!"); }
 7         finally {}
 8         System.out.println("Out!");
 9     }
10 }
```

This code fails compilation since line 3 creates a truly endless loop and the compiler can see it → the next LOC becomes unreachable → comperr. If, however, we comment out the offending line 3, the class will compile because the other loops have an escape hatch built right in.

For example, line 4 says that we could break out of the endless `for(;;)` if such and such condition evaluates to `true` → 'Alright, I admit it's possible so have it your way', shrugs the compiler.

The TCF construct on lines 5 thru 7 is even more interesting: although the `for` loop in the `try` block doesn't have a rabbit hole and simply runs idly for eternity, the compiler trusts us when we say that there's still a theoretical possibility for an exception and, therefore, a way to transfer control out of the loop. This trick works, however, only if `catch` specifies either an RTE or, by extension, a **Throwable** or **Exception**; for example, an IOE will trip a comperr 'exception **IOException** is never thrown in body of corresponding `try` statement'.

Removing the `catch` block will make the compilation fail on line 8 because the TCF construct is treated as a single block → the compiler sees that this block contains an 'escapeless' endless loop that is followed by one more stat → which is therefore unreachable.

And if you think this stuff is too exotic, let me tell you that I did meet on the exam a `while(true)` loop wrapped up in a `try` block... Don't worry, though: we'll cover this scenario again in Chapter II.8, *Handling Exceptions*.

❑ The curly braces {} are NOT required for loops → be careful: the code's business logic can be in jeopardy.

❑ `continue` is valid only inside loops; ANY loop will do including `for-each`, `do-while` and `while`.

❑ Labels:

- ■ can be added to:
  - – a sub-block;
  - – any looping construct such as `for`, `for-each`, `while`, or `do-while`;
  - – conditional constructs such as `if` and `switch`;
  - – expressions and assignments;
  - – `return` stats;
  - – TCF constructs, and
  - – `throw` stat.
- ■ cannot be added to declarations of variables.

Although labeled `break` is commonly used with loops, it is still valid outside them (e.g., in the `if` constructs, etc.). Watch out, however, for its scope as it might lead to the 'unreachable statement' comperr.

Labeled `break` needs a block or an `if` with at least a single `break label;` stat in it:

```
class Label {
    String label(){
//        label int a = 10;                      // INVALID
        int a = 10;
//        label: if (true) break;                // INVALID
        label: if (true) break label;
        label: for (;true;) break label;
        label: switch(a) {}
        label: a = 42;
        label: a++;
        label: try{ label2: throw new NullPointerException(); }
               catch(NullPointerException npe){ break label; }
        label: return "Label!";
    }
}
```

As labels bind to either loops or blocks, outside them they are out of scope → comperr.

Corollary: If there's a labeled `continue` it must always be inside the loop the label is declared for.

❑ The `for-each` loop is routinely used to iterate over **Collection**s such as **List**s. However, it cannot be used to:

- ■ initialize or modify the elements of an array;
- ■ delete the elements of a **Collection**;
- ■ iterate over multiple collections or arrays within the same loop.

- <u>Nested loops</u> – Rules of Engagement:
    - use `break` to exit the inner loop;
    - use `continue` to abandon the current iteration of the inner loop;
    - use a labeled `break` to exit the outer loop;
    - use a labeled `continue` to skip the iteration of the outer loop.

- EXTRA: It is not possible to break out of an `if` construct when it isn't wrapped up in a loop or `switch` UNLESS the `break` stat is labeled (already demonstrated):

```
//  if(true) break;                            // INVALID
    for(;true;) if(true) break;
```

- EXTRA: `while` expression accepts assignments:

```
int a = 0;
while( (a = a + 1) > 0) {                      // VALID
    System.out.println("hello");
    break;
}
```

- EXTRA: `while` doesn't accept var declarations; can use method invocation, though.

- EXTRA: The ForUpdate section of the standard `for` loop allows only the following:
    - – an assignment expression;
    - – pre/post incr/decr op;
    - – method invocation;
    - – class instance creation;

- EXTRA: `while` and regular `for` can't have explicit `false` as their termination condition[78] but `do-while` *can*.

    What's more, `while(!true)` doesn't compile – because `!true` is a straightforward constant that can be evaluated at compile time – but `while(!(x=true))` does compile. Same goes for the standard `for`:

```
    boolean x = false;
    do {  }
       while (false);                          // VALID
//     while(false)) {  }                      // INVALID
//     while(!true) {  }                       // INVALID

    while(!(x=true)) {  }                      // VALID, doesn't enter loop
//     for (int i=0;false;i++){  }             // INVALID
//     for (int i=0;!true;i++){  }             // INVALID
    for (int i=0;!(x=true);i++){ }             // VALID, doesn't enter loop
```

    <u>Remark</u>: `if(false)` is an exception to the rule (to make if(DEBUG) possible).

- EXTRA: Can't use an existing/predefined var in the var declaration part of the enhanced `for` loop. What's interesting, this var (even of a primitive type!) can be `final`[79]. In fact, this is the only modifier that is allowed inside an enhanced `for` declaration:

```
    int[] arr = {0, 1};
    for (final int e : arr) {  }               // VALID
```

---

[78] It is not that `false` isn't allowed in principle, no; it's simply about unreacheable stats. E.g.:

```
    do { doStuff(); } while (false)   // VALID because doStuff() is reachable
```
[79] https://docs.oracle.com/javase/specs/jls/se8/html/jls-14.html#jls-14.14.2

❏ EXTRA: Labels are 'recyclable' (because they go out of scope as soon as the block or construct they bind to is over):

```java
public static void main(String[] args){          // outputs 1234
    label: {
        System.out.print("1");
        if (false) break label; System.out.print("2");
    }
    label:
        if (1 > 0) {
        System.out.print("3");
        if (false) break label; System.out.print("4");
    }
}
```

❏ EXTRA: <u>Booby-trapped patterns:</u>

■ `i = i++;` never increments.[80]

■ a `break-continue` fork in ANY loop makes subsequent stats inside the loop unreachable:

```java
for(int i = 0; i<10; i++){
    if(i == 3){ break;
    } else { continue; }
    // System.out.println("!");              // unreachable stat → comperr
}
```

■ `for(...;...;<no update>) {<no update>}` creates a valid, endless loop.

---

[80] See the discussion here: http://stackoverflow.com/questions/3831341/why-does-this-go-into-an-infinite-loop

EXERCISES (for Key Summary ref.to App.D):

Problem 5.1 Given the following class:

```
class Test {
    public static void main(String[] args) {
        int[] arr = {1, 2, 3};
        for ( *** ) { }
    }
}
```

Which option(s) can replace * so that the class will compile and run successfully? (Choose all that apply)**

    A. int e : arr
    B. int i = 0; i < 0; i++
    C. ; ;
    D. int i; i < 4; i++
    E. boolean b = true; b; b = !b

Problem 5.2 Given the following class:

```
 1 class Test{
 2     public static void main(String[] args) {
 3         short a = 5;
 4         while (isValid(a)) {
 5             System.out.print(a);
 6         }
 7     }
 8     public static boolean isValid (int a) {
 9         return a-- > 0 ? true : false;
10     }
11 }
```

Which option will enable the code to print 54321?

    A. Replace line 5 with System.out.print(--a);
    B. Replace line 5 with System.out.print(a); a--;
    C. Replace line 5 with --a; System.out.print(a);
    D. Replace line 9 with return a > 0 ? false : true;

Problem 5.3 Given:

```
int arr[] = {1, 2, 3, 4, 5};
for(***) {
    System.out.print(arr[idx]);
}
```

Which option can replace * to enable the code to print 135?**

    A. int idx = 0; idx <= 4; idx++
    B. int idx = 0; idx < 5; idx += 2
    C. int idx = 1; idx <= 5; idx += 1
    D. int idx = 1; idx < 5; idx += 2

Problem 5.4 Given the following main method:

```
public static void main(String[] args) {
    int a = 5;
    do {
        System.out.print(a-- + " ");
    } while(a == 0);
}
```

What is the result?

    A. 5

    B. 4 2 1

    C. 5 4 3 2 1

    D. 5 4 3 2 1 0

    E. Nothing is printed

Problem 5.5 Given the code fragment:

```
String[] letters = {"a", "b", "c", "d", "e", "f"};
```

Given the requirements:

    1. Process all the elements of the array in the order of entry.

    2. Process all the elements of the array in the reverse order of entry.

    3. Process alternating elements of the array in the order of entry.

Which two statements are true?

    A. All three Requirements can be successfully implemented by using the enhanced `for` loop.

    B. Requirements 1, 2 and 3 can be implemented by using the standard `for` loop.

    C. The standard `for` loop is not suitable to implement Requirements 2 and 3.

    D. The enhanced `for` loop can be used to implement Requirement 1.

    E. It is impossible to implement Requirement 3 by using either the enhanced `for` loop or the standard `for` loop.

Problem 5.6 Given the following main method:

```
public static void main(String[] args) {
    int[] age = {20, 30, 40, 50, 60};
    for (int i = 0; i < age.length; i++) {
        System.out.print(age[i] + " ");
        if (age[i] == 40) {
            continue;
        }
        System.out.println("Processed");
        break;
    }
}
```

What is the result?

    A. 20 30 40 50 60 Processed

    B. 20 30 40 50 Processed

    C. 20 Processed

    D. Compilation fails

Problem 5.7 Given the code snippet:

```
public static void main(String[] args) {
    int xx;
    int yy = 9;
    for (xx = 0; xx < yy - 1; xx += 2) {
        System.out.print(xx + "; ");
    }
}
```

What is the result?

    A.   Compilation fails
    B.   2; 4; 6;
    C.   0; 2; 4; 6;
    D.   0; 2; 4; 6; 8;

Problem 5.8 Given:

```
public static void main(String[] args) {
    String[][] arr = {{"byte", "short", "int"}, {"long", "char"}};
    for (int i = 0; i < arr.length; i++) {
        for (int j = 0; j < arr[i].length; j++) {
            System.out.print(arr[i][j] + " ");
            if (arr[i][j].equals("short")) {
                break;
            }
        }
        continue;
    }
}
```

What is the result?

    A.   byte short int
    B.   byte short long char
    C.   byte short int long char
    D.   Compilation fails

Problem 5.9 Given the following array of ints:

```
int[] intArr = {1, 2, 4, 8, 16};
```

Which two code fragments, when used independently, print all elements in the array?

    A.
```
for (int i : intArr) {
    System.out.print(intArr[i] + " "); }
```
    B.
```
for (int i : intArr) {
    System.out.print(i + " "); }
```
    C.
```
for (int i=0 : intArr) {
    System.out.print(intArr[i] + " ");
    i++; }
```
    D.
```
for (int i=0; i < intArr.length; i++) {
    System.out.print(i + " "); }
```
    E.
```
for (int i=0; i < intArr.length; i++) {
    System.out.print(intArr[i] + " "); }
```
    F.
```
for (int i; i < intArr.length; i++) {
    System.out.print(intArr[i] + " "); }
```

Problem 5.10   **Given the following code snippet:**

```
public static void main(String[] args) {
    String[] arr1 = new String[4];
    String[] arr2 = {"a", "b", "c", "d", null};
    arr1 = arr2;
    for (String e : arr1){
        System.out.print(e + " : ");
    }
}
```

What is the result?

    A. a : b : c : d : null :
    B. Compilation fails.
    C. NullPointerException is thrown at run time
    D. An ArrayIndexOutOfBoundsException is thrown at run time.

Problem 5.11   **Given:**

```
class Test{
    public static void main(String[] args) {
        int[] arr = new int[]{2013, 2014, 2015, 2016, 2015};
        int count = 0;
        for (int i = 0; i < arr.length; i++) {
            if (arr[i] != 2015) continue;
            count++;
        }
        System.out.println(count + " found!");
    }
}
```

What is the result?

    A. 0 found!
    B. 1 found!
    C. 2 found!
    D. Compilation fails
    E. An exception is thrown

Problem 5.12   **Given:**

```
class Test{
    public static void main(String[] args) {
        int i = 0;
        for(;;) i++;                          // line 1
        if (i == Integer.MAX_VALUE)           // line 2
            System.out.println("Done! " + ++i);
    }
}
```

What is the result?

    A. Done! 2147483647
    B. Done! -2147483648
    C. Compilation fails on line 1.
    D. Compilation fails on line 2.
    E. Code throws a run-time exception.

Problem 5.13   **Given the following class:**

```
class LoopyDoopy{
    public static void main(String[] args) {
        int i = 0, j = 4;
//      line X
        for (i = 0; i < x; i++) {
            do {
                int k = 0;
                while (k < z) {
                    System.out.print(k + " ");
                    k++;
                }
                System.out.println("");
                j--;
            } while (y >= j);
            System.out.println("---------");
        }
    }
}
```

Which statement, when inserted at line X, will make the code print the following table?

```
0 1 2 3 4
---------
0 1 2 3 4
---------
0 1 2 3 4
---------
```

    A. int x = 2, y = 3, z = 2;
    B. int x = 3, y = 2, z = 4;
    C. int x = 3, y = 0, z = 5;
    D. int x = 4, y = 3, z = 4;

Problem 5.14   **Given the following class:**

```
1 class LuckySeven {
2     public static void main(String[] args) {
3
4         int a = 0;
5         for ( ; i --> 0; )
6             a++;
7         System.out.println("a = " + a);
8     }
9 }
10
```

Which statement, when inserted at line 3, will make the code print a = 7?

    A. int i = 6;
    B. int i = 7;
    C. int i = 8;
    D. None of the above as the code fails compilation at line 5

Problem 5.15   **Given:**

```
public static void main(String[] args) {
    String[] moons = {"Luna", "Phobos", "Deimos"};
    byte b = 0;
    do while (b < moons.length)
        System.out.print(b++);
    while (b < moons.length);
}
```

What is the result?

    A. 0

    B. 012

    C. 012012012

    D. Compilation fails

Problem 5.16   **Given the following class:**

```
class ABC {
    public static void main(String[] args) {
        String[] arr = {"A", "B", "C"};
        int a = 0;
        for (String e: arr) {
            while (a < arr.length) {
                System.out.print(a);
                a++;
                break;
            }
        }
    }
}
```

What is the result?

    A. 0

    B. 01

    C. 012

    D. The program runs but produces no output

    E. Compilation fails

Problem 5.17   **Given:**

```
public static void main (String[] args) {
    int a = 1;
    do {
        System.out.print(a);
    }
    while (--a);
}
```

What is the result?

    A. 1

    B. 10

    C. The program enters an endless loop

    D. Compilation fails

Problem 5.18   **Given:**

```
class Test {
    public static void main(String[] args) {
        boolean b1, b2;
        int a = 0;
        while (b1 = b2 = false) { }
        while (!!true) { break; }
        while (a == 0 ? false : true) { }
        while (new Test().equals("?!")) { }
    }
}
```

How many LOCs fail compilation?

    A. None
    B. One
    C. Two
    D. Three
    E. Four

Problem 5.19   **Given:**

```
class Breaker {
    public static void main(String[] args) {
        String[] letters = {"A", "B", "C", "D"};
        for (String e : letters) {
            if (e.equals(letters[1])) {
                continue;
            }
            System.out.print(e + " ");
            if (e.equals(letters[3])) {
                break;
            }
        }
    }
}
```

What is the result?

    A. A D
    B. B D
    C. A C D
    D. B C D
    E. Compilation fails

Problem 5.20   **Given:**

```
int[] array = {0, 1, 2, 3, 4, 5};
for (int e : array) {
    if ( e < 1) {
        // LOC1
    }
    System.out.print(e + " ");
    if ( e == 2 || e == 3) {
        // LOC2
    }
}
```

What statements should replace LOC1 and LOC2, respectively, in order to print 12345?

    A. break, continue
    B. break, break
    C. continue, break
    D. continue, continue

Problem 5.21   **Given the array:**

```
String[] citrus = {
    "lemon",
    "orange",
    "grapefruit",
    "lime",
    "pomelo",
    "tangerine",
    "pompia",
    "clementine",
    "citron",
};
```

Which option prints orange pomelo pompia citron ?

A.
```
for (String e : citrus) {
    if (e.length() != 6) continue;
    System.out.print(e + " ");
}
```

B.
```
for (String e : citrus) {
    if (e.length() <= 6) continue;
    System.out.print(e + " ");
}
```

C.
```
for (String e : citrus) {
    if (e.length() >= 6) continue;
    System.out.print(e + " ");
}
```

D.
```
for (String e : citrus) {
    if (e.length() != 6) System.out.print(e + " ");
    continue;
}
```

Problem 5.22   **Given the following classes in the same package:**

```
class Counter {
    private int i;
    public void count() {
        while (i <= 1) {
            for (int i = 0; i <= 4; ) {
                System.out.print(i + " ");
                i++;
            }
            i++;
        }
    }
}

public class Caller{
    public static void main (String args[]) {
        new Counter().count();
    }
}
```

What is the result?

A. The sequence 0 1 2 3 4 is printed once
B. The sequence 0 1 2 3 4 is printed twice
C. The sequence 0 1 2 3 4 5 is printed once
D. The sequence 0 1 2 3 4 5 is printed twice

Problem 5.23   Given:

```
public class Java8 {
    public static void main(String[] args) {
        String[] starr = {"J", "a", "v", "a", "8"};

        for (int i = 0; i < starr.length; i++) {
            switch (starr[i]) {
                case "J": System.out.print("J"); continue;
                case "a": System.out.print("a"); continue;
                case "v": System.out.print("v"); continue;
                case "8": System.out.print("8"); break;
            }
        }
    }
}
```

What is the output?

    A. Jav8av8v8av88
    B. Jav8Jav8Jav8Jav8Jav8
    C. Java8
    D. Compilation fails

Problem 5.24   Given:

```
public static void main(String[] args) {
    for (int row = 3; row > 0; row--) {
        int column = row;
        while (column <= 3) {
            System.out.print(column);
            column++;
        }
        System.out.println();
    }
}
```

What is the result?

    A. 3
        23
        123

    B. 30
        230
        1230

    C. 23
        123

    D. 230
        1230

Problem 5.25   Given:

```
class Test {
    static int count = 0;
    public int count(int qty) {
        if (qty <= 0) break;
        else {
            for (int i = 0; i < qty; i++) {
                count += i;
            }
        }
        return count;
    }

public static void main(String[] args) {
        Test t = new Test();
        System.out.print(t.count(5));
        System.out.print(t.count(3));
    }
}
```

What is the result?

    A. 53

    B. 58

    C. 106

    D. 1013

    E. Compilation fails

Keys & Discussion:

Problem 5.1 – ABCE

Given the following class:

```
class Test {
    public static void main(String[] args) {
        int[] arr = {1, 2, 3};
        for ( *** ) { }
    }
}
```

Which option(s) can replace * so that the class will compile and run? (Choose all that apply)**

A. int e : arr
B. int i = 0; i < 0; i++
C. ; ;
D. int i; i < 4; i++
E. boolean b = true; b; b = !b

Option A is a plain vanilla `for-each` loop.

Option B is a `for` loop in its classic form; the execution flow won't enter this loop, though, as the termination condition evaluates to `false` right from the beginning.

Since option C is treated as `for(true)`, the loop is endless and the program never terminates. Should the code have some other stats after this LOC, they would be unreachable thus throwing a comperr.

Option D is invalid as the loop var **i** is missing initialization.

As for option E, it does look just a bit out of the ordinary but is perfectly valid, nonetheless. It executes once and then the termination condition (the value of the var **b**, to be precise) gets toggled in the update section thus stopping the loop.

Problem 5.2 – B

Given the following class:

```
 1 class Test{
 2     public static void main(String[] args) {
 3         short a = 5;
 4         while (isValid(a)) {
 5             System.out.print(a);
 6         }
 7     }
 8     public static boolean isValid (int a) {
 9         return a-- > 0 ? true : false;
10     }
11 }
```

Which option will enable the code to print 54321?

A. Replace line 5 with `System.out.print(--a);`
B. Replace line 5 with `System.out.print(a); a--;`
C. Replace line 5 with `--a; System.out.print(a);`
D. Replace line 9 with `return a > 0 ? false : true;`

The code in its unmodified form enters an endless `while` loop and prints 5 over and over again.

Option A is incorrect since its initial output is four and not five because the increment operator in the prefix notation changes the value of the variable first and only then the variable is used so the output will be 43210.

Option C is essentially the same as option A, and option D doesn't help, either, because all it does is just prevents the execution flow from entering the loop.

The correct answer, option B, can be also rewritten as `System.out.print(a--);`

Problem 5.3 – B

Given:

```
int arr[] = {1, 2, 3, 4, 5};
for(***) {
    System.out.print(arr[idx]);
}
```

Which option can replace *** to enable the code to print 135?

```
A.   int idx = 0; idx <= 4; idx++
B.   int idx = 0; idx <  5; idx += 2
C.   int idx = 1; idx <= 5; idx += 1
D.   int idx = 1; idx <  5; idx += 2
```

Since the output should start with the first element's value, options C and D are obviously incorrect. As for option A, it uses all five elements but we need only three.

Problem 5.4 – A

Given the following main method:

```
public static void main(String[] args) {
    int a = 5;
    do {
        System.out.print(a-- + " ");
    } while(a == 0);
}
```

What is the result?

```
A.   5
B.   4 2 1
C.   5 4 3 2 1
D.   5 4 3 2 1 0
E.   Nothing is printed
```

The `do-while` loop always executes at least once. As the termination condition evaluates to `false`, the loop stops running right after the first iteration.

Problem 5.5 – BD

Given the code fragment:

```
String[] letters = {"a", "b", "c", "d", "e", "f"};
```

Given the requirements:

1. Process all the elements of the array in the order of entry.
2. Process all the elements of the array in the reverse order of entry.
3. Process alternating elements of the array in the order of entry.

Which two statements are true?

A. All three Requirements can be successfully implemented by using the enhanced for loop.
B. Requirements 1, 2 and 3 can be implemented by using the standard for loop.
C. The standard for loop is not suitable to implement Requirements 2 and 3.
D. The enhanced for loop can be used to implement Requirement 1.
E. It is impossible to implement Requirement 3 by using either the enhanced for loop or the standard for loop.

Since the enhanced for loop visits each element of an array (or, say, a **Collection** such as **List, ArrayList** and so on) only in the order of entry, option A is incorrect.

The standard for loop is almighty, which makes options C and E incorrect.

Problem 5.6 – C

Given the following main method:

```
public static void main(String[] args) {
    int[] age = {20, 30, 40, 50, 60};
    for (int i = 0; i < age.length; i++) {
        System.out.print(age[i] + " ");
        if (age[i] == 40) {
            continue;
        }
        System.out.println("Processed");
        break;
    }
}
```

What is the result?

A. 20 30 40 50 60 Processed
B. 20 30 40 50 Processed
C. 20 Processed
D. Compilation fails

The code is valid because both continue and break are within a loop, so option D is incorrect.

The flow enters the loop, the first element of the array gets printed and then, as the if expression evaluates to false, the second printing stat fires and the subsequent break makes the flow jump out of the loop.

Problem 5.7 – C

Given the code snippet:

```java
public static void main(String[] args) {
    int xx;
    int yy = 9;
    for (xx = 0; xx < yy - 1; xx += 2) {
        System.out.print(xx + "; ");
    }
}
```

What is the result?

A. Compilation fails
B. 2; 4; 6;
C. 0; 2; 4; 6;
D. 0; 2; 4; 6; 8;

A straightforward loop with no traps, so option A is out. As the output begins with the very first value, which is zero, option B is also incorrect.

Finally, we should recall that with the termination condition that uses the 'less than' op such as **myVar** < **ceiling**, the value of **myVar** can never become equal to **ceiling** *inside the loop*. Since in our case the 'ceiling' is 9 - 1 = 8, we can never reach it, which eliminates option D.

Problem 5.8 – B

Given:

```java
public static void main(String[] args) {
    String[][] arr = {{"byte", "short", "int"}, {"long", "char"}};
    for (int i = 0; i < arr.length; i++) {
        for (int j = 0; j < arr[i].length; j++) {
            System.out.print(arr[i][j] + " ");
            if (arr[i][j].equals("short")) {
                break;
            }
        }
        continue;
    }
}
```

What is the result?

A. byte short int
B. byte short long char
C. byte short int long char
D. Compilation fails

Since `continue` is within a loop (the outer one, to be exact), there's no problem with compilation.

When the `if`'s expression evaluates to `true`, `break` will force the execution flow to abandon the inner loop, so "int" never gets printed, which makes option A and C incorrect.

Problem 5.9 – BE

Given the following array of ints:

```
int[] intArr = {1, 2, 4, 8, 16};
```

Which two code fragments, when used independently, print all elements in the array?

```
A.    for (int i : intArr) {
          System.out.print(intArr[i] + " "); }
B.    for (int i : intArr) {
          System.out.print(i + " "); }
C.    for (int i=0 : intArr) {
          System.out.print(intArr[i] + " ");
          i++; }
D.    for (int i=0; i < intArr.length; i++) {
          System.out.print(i + " "); }
E.    for (int i=0; i < intArr.length; i++) {
          System.out.print(intArr[i] + " "); }
F.    for (int i; i < intArr.length; i++) {
          System.out.print(intArr[i] + " "); }
```

Option A uses the `for-each` loop incorrectly because the variable **i** itself is a representation of an element of the array; this option prints 2 4 16 and then throws an AIOOBE.

Option C is invalid syntactically as the `for-each` loop doesn't allow initialization of the loop var; the only thing we can do with it is declare the var `final`.

Option D prints the loop var's values (that is, 0 1 2 3 4) rather than the array's elements.

And finally, option F fails compilation because the var **i** is local and therefore needs explicit initing before it can be used.

Problem 5.10 – A

Given the following code snippet:

```
public static void main(String[] args) {
    String[] arr1 = new String[4];
    String[] arr2 = {"a", "b", "c", "d", null};
    arr1 = arr2;
    for (String e : arr1){
        System.out.print(e + " : ");
    }
}
```

What is the result?

A. a : b : c : d : null :
B. Compilation fails
C. NullPointerException is thrown at run time
D. An ArrayIndexOutOfBoundsException is thrown at run time

The `for-each` loop never looks beyond array boundaries so option D is incorrect. The code does compile since `null` as a perfectly valid value for a reference variable. As for throwing an NPE, we already know that the method **System.out.print()** takes care of this problem by checking its argument for being `null`.

Problem 5.11 – C

Given:

```
class Test{
    public static void main(String[] args) {
        int[] arr = new int[]{2013, 2014, 2015, 2016, 2015};
        int count = 0;
        for (int i = 0; i < arr.length; i++) {
            if (arr[i] != 2015) continue;
            count++;
        }
        System.out.println(count + " found!");
    }
}
```

What is the result?

    A. 0 found!
    B. 1 found!
    C. 2 found!
    D. Compilation fails
    E. An exception is thrown

This is a classic `for` loop that simply visits each element of the array and checks if it equals 2015. If it does, the counter **count** gets incremented, otherwise the execution abandons the current iteration, and the loop looks at the next element of the array.

Problem 5.12 – D

Given:

```
class Test{
    public static void main(String[] args) {
        int i = 0;
        for(;;) i++;                        // line 1
        if (i == Integer.MAX_VALUE)         // line 2
            System.out.println("Done! " + ++i);
    }
}
```

What is the result?

    A. Done! 2147483647
    B. Done! -2147483648
    C. Compilation fails on line 1.
    D. Compilation fails on line 2.
    E. Code throws a run-time exception.

Compilation fails on line 2 not because this LOC is syntactically invalid; after all, **Integer.MAX_VALUE** is also an `int` and not a reference type. The problem is that line 2 is simply unreachable because the compiler interprets `for(;;)` as `for(;true;)`, which means that the execution enters an endless – and in our case escapeless! – loop.

Can you tell offhand what is the root cause for this comperr? – STOP READING! Think about it for a minute. – It's ***[81]. If they were enclosing both statements after for(;;), like this:

```
for(;;) { i++;                                      // endless but VALID
    if (i == Integer.MAX_VALUE)
        System.out.println("Done! " + ++i); }
```

the program would have compiled and obediently printed Done! -2147483648 over and over again.

Problem 5.13 – C

Given the following class:

```
class LoopyDoopy{
    public static void main(String[] args) {
        int i = 0, j = 4;

//      line X

        for (i = 0; i < x; i++) {
            do {
                int k = 0;
                while (k < z) {
                    System.out.print(k + " ");
                    k++;
                }
                System.out.println("");
                j--;
            } while (y >= j);
            System.out.println("---------");
        }
    }
}
```

Which statement, when inserted at line X, will make the code print the following table?

```
0 1 2 3 4
---------
0 1 2 3 4
---------
0 1 2 3 4
---------
```

A. int x = 2, y = 3, z = 2;
B. int x = 3, y = 2, z = 4;
C. int x = 3, y = 0, z = 5;
D. int x = 4, y = 3, z = 4;

The loop looks menacing but one still can hope to crack it eventually one step at a time – thus wasting five or even more minutes, which is an impossible luxury[82]. So no, we can't go that way; what we really need here is strategic thinking.

---

[81] missing curly braces: they are not mandatory for loops.

[82] In retrospect, I can assure you that no question on the exam requires more than 30 seconds. If solution takes over two minutes, you overlooked a clue – or, worse, are doing something wrong.

Please recall me saying that the weirder the code the more chances it's booby-trapped on something simple. However, by looking at the available options we can conclude that all LOCs are clean as the program both compiles and runs successfully. Alright, what to do then? Well, it's time to give you another useful hint: if code is both tough-looking *and* clean, there's always a soft spot in it. *Always.* Find it, take a poke – and the sucker will pop open in no time.

Let's see how it works.

Observe that the stat that prints a bunch of dashes isn't managed by any conditional construct, which means its execution at each iteration is *guaranteed* → the dashes are printed three times → three iterations in total → since **i** starts with 0, **x** must be 3 → options A and D are eliminated… And while we are at this point, let's repeat one more time: in a `for` loop whose termination condition is in the form of **myVar** < **ceiling**, **myVar**'s value can *never* be equal to **ceiling** inside the loop. You'll do extremely well by remembering this simple yet powerful rule; I myself applied it half a dozen times on the exam…

Alright, here's another logical chain to weed out the last incorrect option: the actual numbers that get printed are the values of the var **k** → there are five of them in total → the `while` loop ramps **k** one bit at a time → **z** must be 5. There!

Problem 5.14 – B

Given the following class:

```
1 class LuckySeven {
2     public static void main(String[] args) {
3
4         int a = 0;
5         for ( ; i --> 0; )
6             a++;
7         System.out.println("a = " + a);
8     }
9 }
10
```

Which statement, when inserted at line 3, will make the code print a = 7?

A. int i = 6;
B. int i = 7;
C. int i = 8;
D. None of the above as the code fails compilation on line 5

Naturally, it's just a little joke: line 5 should have been written as `for(;i-- > 0;)`. Besides, there's nothing illegal about combining the update section with the termination condition section.

Problem 5.15 – B

Given:

```
public static void main(String[] args) {
    String[] moons = {"Luna", "Phobos", "Deimos"};
    byte b = 0;
    do while (b < moons.length)            // line X
        System.out.print(b++);
    while (b < moons.length);
}
```

What is the result?

    A. 0

    B. 012

    C. 012012012

    D. Compilation fails

No loop mandates placing curly braces (they do affect business logic, though), so the code compiles just fine.

Now, let's see what it does. The termi... oh! wait a sec! did you get the structure right? do and while on line X belong to two different constructs; if re-written, it's

```
do {
    while (b < moons.length) System.out.print(b++);
}
while (b < moons.length);
```

Good; now, the termination conditions for both loops depend on the same expression → both loops will terminate at exactly same point → the printing stat fires **moons.length** times → options A and C are incorrect.

Problem 5.16 – C

Given the following class:

```
class ABC {
    public static void main(String[] args) {
        String[] arr = {"A", "B", "C"};
        int a = 0;
        for (String e: arr) {
            while (a < arr.length) {
                System.out.print(a);
                a++;
                break;
            }
        }
    }
}
```

What is the result?

    A. 0

    B. 01

    C. 012

    D. The program runs but produces no output

    E. Compilation fails

The while loop prints the var **a** each time it visits an element of the array → three elements → the output must contain three digits. The break statement is just chaff as it does nothing apart from sitting there trying to look important; we could remove it altogether.

Problem 5.17 – D

Given:

```java
public static void main (String[] args) {
    int a = 1;
    do {
        System.out.print(a);
    }
    while (--a);
}
```

What is the result?

- A. 1
- B. 10
- C. The program enters an endless loop
- D. Compilation fails

Any loop's termination expression must evaluate to a `boolean`.

Problem 5.18 – A

Given:

```java
class Test {
    public static void main(String[] args) {
        boolean b1, b2;
        int a = 0;
        while (b1 = b2 = false) { }
        while (!!true) { break; }
        while (a == 0 ? false : true) { }
        while (new Test().equals("?!")) { }
    }
}
```

How many LOCs fail compilation?

- A. None
- B. One
- C. Two
- D. Three
- E. Four

The first `while`'s termination expression generates a `boolean`, so this LOC is valid.

The second `while` evaluates at compile time to `while(true)`, which makes an endless loop – and that's why we need `break`, otherwise the subsequent stats become unreachable.

There's nothing special about the third `while`; the execution flow just doesn't enter it, that's all.

And finally, even though **Test** and **String** are incompatible data types, the method **equals()** accepts any **Object** and, therefore, is valid and will produce a `boolean`. The fact that **Test** and **String** are incompatible would have played crucial role in case of the 'double equals' op but this is entirely different story…

Problem 5.19 – C

Given:

```java
class Breaker {
    public static void main(String[] args) {
        String[] letters = {"A", "B", "C", "D"};
        for (String e : letters) {
            if (e.equals(letters[1])) {
                continue;
            }
            System.out.print(e + " ");
            if (e.equals(letters[3])) {
                break;
            }
        }
    }
}
```

What is the result?

A. A D
B. B D
C. A C D
D. B C D
E. Compilation fails

The `break` stat does precisely nothing because it is the last statement in the loop; in fact, we could get rid of the second `if` as it adds not a single semantically meaningful feature to the business logic.

The only keyword that does come into play is `continue`: as soon as the first `if` sees "B", the current iteration terminates, and the loop visits another element.

Problem 5.20 – D

Given:

```java
int[] array = {0, 1, 2, 3, 4, 5};
for (int e : array) {
    if ( e < 1) {
        // LOC1
    }
    System.out.print(e + " ");
    if ( e == 2 || e == 3) {
        // LOC2
    }
}
```

What statements should replace LOC1 and LOC2, respectively, in order to print 12345?

A. break, continue
B. break, break
C. continue, break
D. continue, continue

`break` makes the execution abandon the loop → there can be no `break` at LOC1 because the program will simply terminate as soon as it hits this keyword → options A and B are incorrect.

Now, we are charged with the task to print out all elements except the very first one → the execution shouldn't terminate at any other element, be it 2, 3, 4 or 5 → LOC2 can't read `break`, either, no matter what is the `if`'s expression.

Problem 5.21 – A

Given the array:

```
String[] citrus = {
    "lemon",
    "orange",
    "grapefruit",
    "lime",
    "pomelo",
    "tangerine",
    "pompia",
    "clementine",
    "citron",
};
```

Which option prints orange pomelo pompia citron ?

A.
```
for (String e : citrus) {
    if (e.length() != 6) continue;
    System.out.print(e + " ");      }
```

B.
```
for (String e : citrus) {
    if (e.length() <= 6) continue;
    System.out.print(e + " ");      }
```

C.
```
for (String e : citrus) {
    if (e.length() >= 6) continue;
    System.out.print(e + " ");      }
```

D.
```
for (String e : citrus) {
    if (e.length() != 6) System.out.print(e + " ");
    continue;      }
```

All we need here is prevent the flow from reaching the printing stat unless the element is exactly six letters long – and only option A answers this requirement.

Problem 5.22 – B

Given the following classes in the same package:

```
class Counter {
    private int i;
    public void count() {
        while (i <= 1) {
            for (int i = 0; i <= 4; ) {
                System.out.print(i + " ");
                i++;
            }
            i++;
        }
    }
}
public class Caller{
    public static void main (String args[]) {
        new Counter().count();
    }
}
```

What is the result?

A. The sequence 0 1 2 3 4 is printed once
B. The sequence 0 1 2 3 4 is printed twice
C. The sequence 0 1 2 3 4 5 is printed once
D. The sequence 0 1 2 3 4 5 is printed twice

The `for` loop iterates five times rather than six, therefore options C and D are out.

Now, since the instance variable **i** is automatically inited to the value of zero, the `while` loop executes twice → option B is the correct one.

On a final note, the loop var shadows the instance var **i**, so there's no clash.

Problem 5.23 – C

Given:

```
public class Java8 {
    public static void main(String[] args) {
        String[] starr = {"J", "a", "v", "a", "8"};
        for (int i = 0; i < starr.length; i++) {
            switch (starr[i]) {
                case "J": System.out.print("J"); continue;
                case "a": System.out.print("a"); continue;
                case "v": System.out.print("v"); continue;
                case "8": System.out.print("8"); break;
            }
        }
    }
}
```

What is the output?

    A.   Jav8av8v8av88
    B.   Jav8Jav8Jav8Jav8Jav8
    C.   Java8
    D.   Compilation fails

`continue` is valid only inside loops, and here we have exactly that as the `switch` block is enclosed by a `for` loop, hence the code compiles.

What's more, as `continue` is utterly irrelevant to `switch` and affects only loops, whenever the execution hits it, the loop immediately abandons the current iteration thus preventing the flow from falling through `switch` body → options A and B are incorrect.

Problem 5.24 – A

Given:

```
public static void main(String[] args) {
    for (int row = 3; row > 0; row--) {
        int column = row;
        while (column <= 3) {
            System.out.print(column);
            column++;
        }
        System.out.println();
    }
}
```

What is the result?

A. 3
   23
   123
B. 30
   230
   1230
C. 23
   123
D. 230
   1230

The digit-printing stat is controlled by the `while` loop → at the very beginning, the value of the var **column** is three → C and D are out → `while` executes just once during the first iteration of the `for` loop → the first printed line must contain a single digit.

Problem 5.25 – E

Given:

```
class Test {
    static int count = 0;
    public int count(int qty) {
        if (qty <= 0) break;                    // line X
        else {
            for (int i = 0; i < qty; i++) {
                count += i;
            }
        }
        return count;
    }
    public static void main(String[] args) {
        Test t = new Test();
        System.out.print(t.count(5));
        System.out.print(t.count(3));
    }
}
```

What is the result?

A. 53
B. 58
C. 106
D. 1013
E. Compilation fails

Yeah, this one is booby-trapped as only *labeled* `break`s are allowed outside a loop or, naturally, a `switch`. By re-writing line X as, say

```
magic: if(qty <= 0) break magic;
```

we could've made the code compile and print 1013.

Chapter II.6

EXAM OBJECTIVES – Group Six:
Working with Methods and Encapsulation

The 1Z0-808 objectives within this group:

6.1   Create methods with arguments and return values, including overloaded methods;
6.2   Apply the `static` keyword to methods and fields;
6.3   Create and overload constructors, including impact on default constructors;
6.4   Apply access modifiers;
6.5   Apply encapsulation principles to a class;
6.6   Determine the effect upon object references and primitive values when they are passed into methods that change the values.

CORE RULES (with some Extras):

6.1   <u>Create methods with arguments and return values, including overloaded methods</u> +

6.6   <u>Determine the effect upon object references and primitive values when they are passed into methods that change the values</u>:

- ❏   The structure of Java method declaration (left to right in the stated order unless noted otherwise):
  - ■   an optional access modifier such as `public`, `protected` or `private`;
  - ■   interface method modifier `default` (can be combined – redundantly – with `public` only)
  - ■   an optional specifier such as `abstract`, `final` or `static` (NOTE: `final` and `static` may be combined);
  - ■   optional specifier(s) may precede access modifier;
  - ■   the return type such as `void` or another valid data type[83];
  - ■   the method name, which is just another Java identifier, followed by a matching pair of parentheses to contain an optional list of the method parameters;
  - ■   if the parameter list is present, each parameter must be specified by its data type (which can be a primitive or reference type) and its name;
  - ■   unlike multiple variable declaration where we can state the data type just once if all the variables are of the same type, each method parameter must have its own data type specified explicitly;
  - ■   parameter declarations are separated by commas;
  - ■   after the closing parenthesis comes an optional list of exception types, which starts with the keyword `throws`;
  - ■   unlike the `catch` block where a narrower exception type must appear before a wider type, the exception types thrown by the method may be declared in any order;
  - ■   the body of any method must be enclosed by a pair of matching curly braces;
  - ■   EXTRA: the method body can be completely empty or contain any number of the empty statements, that is, semicolons;

---

[83] Yes, `void` is also a data type. The package **java.lang** contains the class **Void**, which, according to the javadocs, is "an uninstantiable placeholder class to hold a reference to the **Class** object representing the Java keyword `void`". Its parent is **java.lang.Object**. Naturally.

❑ Only a single vararg is permitted in the list of parameters per method declaration; more than that, the vararg, when present, must be the last variable among the declared parameters.

❑ Methods that do not return a value (`void` methods):

   ■ the body of such methods may contain an empty `return` statement, in other words, a `return` stat that is not followed immediately by a variable or literal;

❑ Methods that return a value:

   ■ their bodies must contain a `return` stat immediately followed by an appropriate value[84]...
   ■ ... which is passed back to the caller...
   ■ ... who may elect to disregard it altogether or assign it to a variable. If such is the case, the var's type must be compatible with the returned value's type.

❑ The `return` statement, when present, must be the last statement in the method body:

```
public void doStuff(){
    return;          // VALID although redundant
//    ;              // harmless but INVALID because unreachable
}
```

❑ Overloaded methods differ in their lists of parameters.

   Corollary: An attempt to define multiple methods that differ only in their access modifiers, optional specifiers, return types, or thrown exceptions will cause a comperr.

❑ *Learn by heart*:   In case of overloading, exact matches are used first, followed by wider primitives, then by autoboxing, and finally by varargs.

❑ Since Java uses pass-by-value, calling a method creates copies of its parameters – and these copies are used then as the method's arguments.

   Corollaries: When a primitive is passed to a method, its value *never* changes for the caller.

   When an object reference is passed to a method, changes in the object's state might be reflected for the caller unless the called method assigns a new object reference to the passed-in argument *before* modifying its field(s). **Other wording**: invoking a method on a passed-in object can potentially change it.

❑ Known traps on the actual exam:

   – the return type and method name are separated by an access modifier or optional specifier;
   – more then one vararg is defined in the parameter list;
   – the vararg isn't the last one in the parameter list;
   – the method body is missing a `return` stat although the method is declared as non-void;
   – `return` is followed by some other – therefore unreachable! – stats;
   – what `return` delivers is inconsistent with the method declaration (incompatible data types);
   – methods differ only in their return types and, therefore, are not overloaded → comperr.

---

[84] In other words, whose type doesn't clash with the declared return type.

EXERCISES (for Key Summary ref.to App.D):

Problem 6.1 Given:

```
1 package last.vegas;
2
3 class BankAccount {
4     int balance;
5
6     BankAccount(){
7         this.balance = new java.util.Random().nextInt(1000);
8     }
9
10     int getBalance(){
11         return this.balance;
12     }
13     void makeTransfer(int amount){
14         this.balance += amount;
15     }
16 }
17
18 public class HighRoller{
19     public static void main(String[] args) {
20         BankAccount ba = new BankAccount();
21         System.out.println("Was: $" + ba.getBalance());
22 //         this.balance = 0;
23 //         BankAccount.balance = 0;
24 //         new BankAccount(0);
25 //         ba.balance = 0;
26 //         ba.getBalance() = 0;
27 //         ba.makeTransfer(0);
28 //         ba.makeTransfer(ba.balance * -1);
29 //         ba.makeTransfer(-ba.getBalance());
30         System.out.println("Now: $" + ba.getBalance());
31     }
32 }
```

Which three lines, when uncommented independently, can empty the bank account created on line 20?

    A. Line 22
    B. Line 23
    C. Line 24
    D. Line 25
    E. Line 26
    F. Line 27
    G. Line 28
    H. Line 29

Problem 6.2 Given:

```
class SpeedBoat {
    float speed;
}
public class BoatRace {
    public void breakRecord(SpeedBoat sb, float speed) {
        speed = speed * 2;
        sb.speed = sb.speed + speed;
    }
```

```java
public static void main(String[] args) {
    SpeedBoat sb = new SpeedBoat();
    sb.speed = 200;
    float currentRecord = 400;

    BoatRace br = new BoatRace();
    br.breakRecord(sb, currentRecord);
    System.out.println(sb.speed + " vs " + currentRecord);
}
}
```

What is the result?

    A. 200.0 vs 400.0
    B. 600.0 vs 800.0
    C. 1000.0 vs 400.0
    D. Compilation fails

Problem 6.3 Given:

```java
class WhichOne {

    public static void run(int x, int y) {
        System.out.println("working with int: " + (x + y));
    }

    public static void run(Integer x, Integer y) {
        System.out.println("working with Integer: " + (x + y));
    }

    public static void run(float x, float y) {
        System.out.println("working with float: " + (x + y));
    }

    public static void run(double x, double y) {
        System.out.println("working with double: " + (x + y));
    }

    public static void main(String[] args) {
        run(1, 2);
        run(1.0, 2.0);
    }
}
```

What is the result?

    A. working with int: 3
       working with float: 3.0
    B. working with int: 3
       working with double: 3.0
    C. working with Integer: 3
       working with double: 3.0
    D. working with Integer: 3
       working with float: 3.0

Problem 6.4 Given:

```
public class Doubler {
    public static void main(String[] args) {
        int a = 100;
        System.out.print(doubleValue(a));
        System.out.print(" : " + a);
    }
    static int doubleValue(int a){
        a = a * 2;
        return a;
    }
}
```

What is the result?

A. 200 : 100
B. 100 : 100
C. 200 : 200
D. Compilation fails

Problem 6.5

Suppose, a method is declared to take two parameters but the caller passes to it only one argument. What is the result?

A. Compilation fails.
B. The missing argument is given the default value for its declared type.
C. An IllegalArgumentException is thrown at run time.
D. A NoSuchMethodException is thrown at run time.

Problem 6.6 Given:

```
class Test {
    public static void modify(int[] arr) {
        for (int idx = 0; idx < arr.length; idx++) {
            arr[idx] = arr[idx] + 1;
            System.out.print(arr[idx] + " ");
        }
    }
    public static void main (String[] args) {
        int[] arr = {10, 20, 30};
        for (int e : arr) { System.out.print(e + " "); }
        modify(arr);
        for (int e : arr) { System.out.print(e + " "); }
    }
}
```

What is the result?

A. 10 20 30 11 21 31 10 20 30
B. 10 20 30 11 21 31 11 21 31
C. Compilation fails
D. A RuntimeException is thrown

Problem 6.7 Given:

```
class PassByValue {
    private int a = 0;
    private int b = 0;
    public void run1(int a, int b) {
        a = a;
        b = b;
        System.out.println("a = " + this.a + ", b = " + this.b);
    }
    public void run2(int a, int b) {
        this.a = a;
        this.b = b;
        System.out.println("a = " + this.a + ", b = " + this.b);
    }
    public static void main(String[] args) {
        PassByValue pbv = new PassByValue();
        pbv.run1(1, 2);
        pbv.run2(3, 4);
    }
}
```

What is the result?

A. a = 0, b = 0
    a = 0, b = 0
B. a = 1, b = 2
    a = 3, b = 4
C. a = 0, b = 0
    a = 3, b = 4
D. a = 1, b = 2
    a = 0, b = 0

Problem 6.8 Given:

```
class OverloadTester {
    static double run(double a) {
        System.out.print("double: ");
        return a;
    }
    static int run(double a) {
        System.out.print("int: ");
        return (int)a;
    }
    static String run(double a) {
        System.out.print("String: ");
        return new String("" + a);
    }
    public static void main(String[] args) {
        System.out.println(run(1.0));
    }
}
```

What is the result?

A. double: 1.0
B. int: 1
C. String: 1.0
D. Compilation fails

Problem 6.9

Which two are valid in the body of a method that does not return a value?

- A. Omission of the `return` statement
- B. `return null;`
- C. `return void;`
- D. `return;`

Problem 6.10

Which is the valid declaration of a method that takes two arguments of the type int and returns the result of their division?

- A. `divide (int a, int b) { return a/b; }`
- B. `double divide (int a, b) { return a/b; }`
- C. `int divide (int a, int b) { return a/b; }`
- D. `double divide (int a, int b) { a/b; }`
- E. `void divide (int a, int b) { return a/b; }`
- F. None of the above

Problem 6.11   Given:

```
class Invalid {
    private static double value;
    public static int getValue(){ return value; };
    public static void Main(String[] args) {
        System.out.println(getValue());
    }
}
```

This class fails compilation. What is the reason?

- A. There is no corresponding **setValue()** method
- B. The method **getValue()** returns an incompatible data type
- C. A static field cannot be declared `private`
- D. The field value is uninitialized
- E. The **main()** method has wrong signature

6.2 <u>Apply the `static` keyword to methods and fields</u> +

6.4 <u>Apply access modifiers</u> +

6.5 <u>Apply encapsulation principles to a class</u>:

- The `static` modifier is valid with variables, methods and initers but cannot be applied to the top-level classes and interfaces.

- `static` fields are shared by all instances of a given class.

- Since `static` fields and methods belong to the class, they can be accessed even without instantiating it first. When referenced from outside the class, they are called by using the class name, e.g. **java.lang.Math.PI** or **Math.random()**.

- A `static` method may not call non-`static` variables or methods while the opposite is permitted. The exam tests us on at least three variants of this aspect: a `static` method accessing an instance var, a `static` method calling a non-`static` method and a non-`static` method either accessing a `static` field or invoking a `static` method.

- Java allows to import `static` members by using the keywords `import static`.[85]

- A method cannot be declared both `abstract` and `static`.

- EXTRA: The `static` methods defined in classes are inherited in Java although they do not take part in polymorphism. The `static` methods defined in interfaces aren't inherited.

- The access modifiers control the accessibility of a given class and its members from outside the class and its package:

  - the `public` keyword means that the code is accessible from anywhere;

  - the `protected` keyword means the code is accessible by the classes or interfaces inside the same package or by the derived classes from outside the package;

    Known trap on the exam: An attempt by a class instantiated outside its package to access its own `protected` member.

  - the default (a.k.a. package-`private`) access is denoted by the absence of any access modifier and means that the code is accessible only from within the same package;

    Known trap on the exam: An attempt to access a class defined using default access from outside its package.

  - the `private` keyword means the code is visible only inside the same class.

    Known trap on the exam: A subclass attempting to access a private member of its superclass.

    Combat versions: A non-`public` class can't be accessed from outside its package.

    `protected` members of a parent in a diff pack aren't accessible to the child whose reftype is Parent.

---

[85] Please note that it's not 'static import'. The easiest way to remember this is by taking the keyword `import` as a direct order (that is, an imperative: "Hey you! Wake up and `import static` things such as...").

❏ EXTRA: A `static` method invoked on a `null` object doesn't throw an NPE (because the object isn't used in any way):

```
class Test{
    static void test(){ System.out.println("Hi!"); }
    public static void main(String[] args) {
        Test t = new Test();
        t = null;
        t.test();                                   // Hi!
    }
}
```

❏ Encapsulation prevents callers from modifying the instance variables *directly*.

❏ Encapsulation is implemented by making instance vars `private` while providing `public` getters and/or setters.

❏ EXTRA: Immutability refers to preventing callers from modifying the instance variables *at all* and is implemented by omitting setters or by making defensive copies:

```
class A {
    private StringBuilder sb = new StringBuilder("Hello!");
    public StringBuilder getIt(){ return sb;}
    public StringBuilder getDefended(){
        return new StringBuilder(sb.toString()); }
}
class Test {
    public static void main(String[] args) {
        A a = new A();

//--  This is our object in its pristine state:
        System.out.println(a.getIt());             // Hello!

//--  After attempting to reverse it thru a defensive copy:
        a.getDefended().reverse();
        System.out.println(a.getIt());             // Hello!

//--  After attempting to reverse it without a defensive copy:
        a.getIt().reverse();
        System.out.println(a.getIt());             // !olleH
    }
}
```

❏ Properly encapsulated class exposes its state through methods.

Problem 6.12   Given:

```
class Test {
    static int[] a = {1, 2, 3, 4};
    int[] b = {5, 6, 7, 8};
    public static void main(String[] args) {
        Test t1 = new Test(), t2 = new Test();
        t1.a[3] = 10;
        t1.b[3] = 20;
        t2.a[3] = 30;
        t2.b[3] = 40;
        System.out.println (
            t1.a[3] + " " + t1.b[3] + " " +
            t2.a[3] + " " + t2.b[3]);
    }
}
```

What is the result?

A. 10 20 30 40
B. 30 20 30 40
C. A run-time exception is thrown
D. Compilation fails

Problem 6.13   Given two classes:

```
package pack1;

public class A {
    public int a = 1;
    protected int b = 2;
    int c = 3;
    private int d = 4;
}
```

```
1 package pack2;
2 import pack1.*;
3 public class B extends A {
4     public static void main(String[] args) {
5         A obj = new B();
6         System.out.println("a = " + obj.a);
7         System.out.println("b = " + obj.b);
8         System.out.println("c = " + obj.c);
9         System.out.println("d = " + obj.d);
10    }
11 }
```

How many LOCs in the class B fail compilation?

A. None
B. One
C. Two
D. Three
E. Four

Problem 6.14

What is the name of the Java concept that uses access modifiers to protect variables defined by a class?

A. Abstraction
B. Encapsulation
C. Inheritance
D. Instantiation
E. Polymorphism

Problem 6.15   Given:

```
class A {
    int a;
    static int b;
    A(int input) { if (b <= input) b = a = input; }
    void show() { System.out.println("a = " + a + ", b = " + b); }
}
public class Test {
    public static void main(String[] args) {
        A obj1 = new A(20);
        A obj2 = new A(60);
        A obj3 = new A(40);
        obj1.show();
        obj2.show();
        obj3.show();
    }
}
```

What is the result?

A. a = 20, b = 60
    a = 60, b = 60
    a = 40, b = 60
B. a = 20, b = 60
    a = 60, b = 60
    a = 0, b = 60
C. a = 20, b = 20
    a = 60, b = 60
    a = 40, b = 40
D. a = 20, b = 20
    a = 60, b = 60
    a = 0, b = 60

Problem 6.16   Given two classes:

```
public class WaterConsumer {
    WaterConsumer wcons = new WaterConsumer();
    public void useWater(double m3){
        wcons.updateBill(m3);
    }
}
public class UtilityAccount {
    private double m3;
    private double rate = 1.23;
    private double bill;
    //line X
}
```

Which code block, when inserted at line X, will implement the following requirements?

1. The code should successfully update the water consumption bill (represented by the variable `bill`), which is defined as the number of cubic meters of water consumed by the customer (the variable `m3`) multiplied by the cost of water per cubic meter (the variable `rate`);

2. The code should also protect the variable `bill` from tampering such as attempting to decrease its value by an instance of the class WaterConsumer.

A.
```java
public void updateBill(double m3) {
    this.m3 += m3;
    this.bill = this.m3 * this.rate;
}
```

B.
```java
public void updateBill(double m3) {
    if (m3 > 0){
        this.m3 += m3;
        this.bill = this.m3 * this.rate;
    }
}
```

C.
```java
private void updateBill(double m3) {
    if (m3 > 0) {
        this.m3 += m3;
        this.bill = this.m3 * this.rate;
    }
}
```

D.
```java
public void updateBill(double m3) {
    if(m3 > 0) {
        this.m3 += m3;
        calcBill(this.m3);
    }
}
public void calcBill(double m3) {
    bill = m3 * rate;
}
```

Problem 6.17   Given:

```java
class Production {
    static int count = 0;
    int a = 0;
    public void rampUp() {
        while (a < 10) {
            a++;
            count++;
        }
    }

    public static void main(String[] args) {
        Production p1 = new Production();
        Production p2 = new Production();
        p1.rampUp();
        p2.rampUp();
        System.out.print("p1.count = " + p1.count + ", p2.count = " + p2.count);
    }
}
```

What is the result?

    A.   p1.count = 20, p2.count = 20
    B.   p1.count = 10, p2.count = 10
    C.   p1.count = 10, p2.count = 20
    D.   Compilation fails

Problem 6.18   Given:

```
package base;
public class Base {
    public void run(){ System.out.print("No args! "); };
    protected void run(int arg){ System.out.print(arg + " "); };
    void run(double arg){ System.out.print(arg + " "); };
    private void run(String arg){ System.out.print("\"" + arg + "\""); };
}


package derived;
import base.Base;
public class Derived extends Base {
    public static void main(String[] args) {
        Base obj = new Derived();
        obj.run();                          // line 1
        obj.run(1);                         // line 2
        obj.run(1.0);                       // line 3
        obj.run("1");                       // line 4
    }
}
```

What is the result?

    A.   No args! 1 1.0 "1"
    B.   Compilation fails on line 4
    C.   Compilation fails on lines 4 and 3
    D.   Compilation fails on lines 4, 3 and 2
    E.   Compilation fails on lines 4, 3, 2 and 1

Problem 6.19   Given the following class:

```
1 public class A {
2     public double a;
3     public static void main (String[] args) {
4         A obj = new A();
5         a = 10;
6     }
7 }
```

Which two options, when used independently, will make this code compile and run?

    A.   Replace line 2 with `public int a;`
    B.   Replace line 2 with `static int a;`
    C.   Replace line 4 with `static int a;`
    D.   Replace line 4 with `static double a;`
    E.   Replace line 5 with `a = 10.0d;`
    F.   Replace line 5 with `new A().a = 10;`

Problem 6.20   **Given:**

```
1 class StaticTest {
2     static void run1() {
3         run2();
4         run3();
5         StaticTest.run2();
6     }
7     static void run2() {
8         run1();
9         StaticTest.run3();
10 }
11     void run3() {
12         run1();
13     }
14 }
```

Which two LOCs fail compilation?

    A. line 3
    B. line 4
    C. line 5
    D. line 8
    E. line 9
    F. line 12

Problem 6.21   **Given the contents of the file U.java:**

```
1. abstract class A{}
2. final class F{}
3. public class U{}
4. protected class O{}
5. private class R{}
6. static class S{}
```

Which three LOCs fail compilation?

    A. line 1
    B. line 2
    C. line 3
    D. line 4
    E. line 5
    F. line 6

Problem 6.22   **Given:**

```
class Test {
    static int a = 42;
    public static void main(String[] args) {
        Test t = new Test();
        t.a++;
        Test.a++;
        t.a--;
        System.out.println(--t.a + " " + Test.a);
    }
}
```

What is the result?

    A. 42 42
    B. 40 41
    C. 41 40
    D. 43 44

Problem 6.23   **Given the following two classes:**

```
class A {
    String str;
    A() {}
    private String run() {
        return this.str += "!";
    }
}

class B extends A {
    B(String str) {
        this.str = str;
    }
    private void doStuff() {
        System.out.println(run());
    }
    public static void main (String [] args) {
        new B("Hello").doStuff();
    }
}
```

What should be done to make the code compile?

  A. Make the class **A** public
  B. Declare the method **run()** as protected instead of private
  C. Make the **A()** constructor public
  D. Make the **A()** constructor protected
  E. Make the method **doStuff()** package-private

6.3 <u>Create and overload constructors, including impact on default constructors</u>:

❑ Unfortunately, the term "constructor" may be misleading as constructors do not 'construct' (read: 'build', 'assemble', 'manufacture', 'fabricate', 'make', or 'create') objects: they *initialize* them. The actual job of a constructor is to ensure that the freshly created object is in a valid state; it is usually done by setting object fields to certain initial values.

❑ Constructors resemble methods (e.g., they accept arguments, can be overloaded and may throw exceptions that require handling in the TCF constructs) but they don't specify a return type, not even `void`. In addition, ctors must share the same name with their class.

> **Known trap on the exam**: As soon as a would-be constructor specifies a return type, the compiler stops treating it as a constructor even though it shares the same name with the class → whenever you think you see a constructor, double check it's not a method.

❑ A default, no-arg constructor is implicitly declared in the class that doesn't define any constructor explicitly.

> **Known traps on the exam**: The default constructor is the one that is provided automatically by the compiler → even if an explicitly defined constructor specifies no arguments, it cannot be called the default constructor.
>
> Whenever superclass doesn't define a no-arg ctor in parallel to other constructors, explicit call to an appropriate parent ctor must be provided in the child's constructors whose bodies don't start with `this()`.

❑ The default constructor has the same accessibility as the class.

> **Corollary**: Since the humanware-defined no-arg constructor isn't the default one, the above rule doesn't apply to it. ← ***known trap on the exam***

> **Combat rule**: Different packages? Watch out! If **Parent** defines a package-`private` no-arg ctor, **Child** won't be able to access it:
>
> ```
> package one;
> public class One {  One(){} }          // ctor is neither public
>                                         // nor protected86
> package two;
> // class Two extends one.One { }        // GAME OVER
> ```

❑ EXTRA: Constructors are not inherited.

❑ Constructors accept access modifiers only.

> **Corollary**: Unlike regular methods, constructors may not be declared `abstract`, `static` or `final`.

❑ A matching pair of parentheses is mandatory for a constructor.

---

[86] Please note that the compiler generates a somewhat misleading error message saying that the ctor One() isn't `public` in One. Well, it doesn't have to be `public`; being `protected` is enough.

- A class can have multiple constructors. Just like regular methods, they are overloaded by using different lists of arguments.

- Overloaded constructors invoke each other by using the keyword `this()`, which should be the first stat in the caller's body.

  Corollaries: A constructor may not call another constructor by using its class name.
  An attempt by a regular method to use `this()` will cause a comperr.

- Constructors can differentiate between their arguments and instance vars by prepending the instance var's name with the keyword `this` followed by a dot.

- EXTRA: Constructors can declare local variables (whose scope is therefore limited to the constructor), which will shadow the similarly named fields.

- EXTRA: Polymorphisms extends to the constructors, too. (The subject will be discussed in more detail in the next group of Exam Objectives, *Working with Inheritance*).

- EXTRA: Constructors can throw exceptions. The exception-wise rule in ctors, however, is opposite to what we have for methods: an overriding method cannot throw a new or superclass ChE, whereas a subclass ctor cannot throw subclass ChE unless the same ChE or its superclass is declared in the subclass constructor's `throws` clause. Note that just like in the case of method overriding, this rule doesn't involve RTEs:

```
 1 class A {
 2     A() throws IOException {}
 3     A(int a) throws IOException {}
 4     A(double d) throws IndexOutOfBoundsException {}
 5 }
 6
 7 class B extends A{
 8     B() throws FileNotFoundException {
 9         super();                                    // INVALID
10     }
11     B(int b) throws Exception { super(1);}
12     B(double d) throws ArrayIndexOutOfBoundsException { super(1.0); }
13 }
14
15 class C extends A{
16     C() throws FileNotFoundException {              // INVALID
17         try {
18             super();                                // INVALID
19         }
20         catch(IOException ioe){}
21     }
22 }
```

Observe that although the subclass throws an AIOOBE, which is narrower than the IOOBE thrown by the superclass, line 12 compiles just fine because we are dealing with RTEs.

On the other hand, lines 9 and 16 throw the comperr "unreported exception IOException; must be caught or declared to be thrown" – which is actually misleading. Yes, again.

You see, we can only declare but not catch this ChE, and the comperr on line 18 explains why: "call to super must be first statement in constructor". Hence, our TCF construct won't work at all and we are left with only one option: declare the same ChE or its superclass, which is exactly what line 11 does.

- Although constructors routinely function as initializers, a class can define separate initializer blocks, which can be either `static` or non-`static`.

- An initializer block can declare local vars, access both `static` and instance fields or call `static` and non-`static` methods (the rule of non-`static` entities in `static` context still applies), define loops, conditional and TCF constructs.

- The order of precedence when instantiating a class[87]:

  - `static` initers for the *entire* inheritance chain; it is done only once;
  - instance initers for the superclass;
  - superclass constructors;
  - instance initers for the subclass;
  - subclass constructors;

  Corollaries: Instance initers run for every object that is being created.

  Constructors run after all other initers within the same class.

- EXTRA: `static` initers of a class are not executed unless you access something that belongs to this particular class.

  Corollary: Simply declaring a refvar isn't enough for `static` initers start running.

- `final` **_non-local_** vars must be inited even if they are never used:

  ```
  class Test {
      int a;
  //    final int b;              // INVALID
      void run(){
          final c;
      }
  }
  ```

  Where and how this initing is done depends on whether the var is `static` or not:

  - `final` instance vars can be inited in THREE places:

      - at the point of declaration,
      - in instance initers, and
      - in constructors.

  - `final static` vars can be inited in TWO places only:

      - at the point of declaration,
      - in static initers.

  <u>Pay attention</u>: `final static` vars can't be inited in constructors or instance initers. Which is understandable as `static` fields must be available to callers even in the absence of the instances of the class whereas instance initers and then constructors run only when an object is being created:

  ```
  class Test {
      final static String str;
      static{ str = "Hello"; }
      Test{ str = "Goodbye"; }      // INVALID
  }
  ```

---

[87] Both `static` and instance initializer blocks are executed in the order they appear.

By the way, in the preceding example the compiler complains of an attempt to modify a `final` var. It is interesting to note that if we comment out the `static` initer, the compiler produces yet another misleading error message: "variable **str** not initialized in default constructor". Well, you know, it can't be inited there in the first place[88]; compare it to the following case:

```
class Test {
    final static String str;        // becomes VALID when we add Test(){}
    Test(){}                        // ... and comperr moves to this LOC!
}
```

Here the error message on the line that defines the no-arg constructor quite correctly says that "variable **str** might not have been initialized".

Alright, putting this rule out in code:

```
class Test {
    final static int a, b;
    final int c, d;
    {
        a = 10;                     // INVALID: since a is static, it must be
                                    // available always, while instance initers
    }                               // run only when we ask to create an object;
                                    // also note that the comperr, however, is
                                    // about an attempt to change a final var
    static { b = 10; a = 10; }
    static {
        c = 10;                     // INVALID: non-static in static context
    }
    { c = 10; }
    Test(){
        b = 10;                     // INVALID: b is static while constructors
                                    // run only when we are creating objects;
                                    // comperr is again about b being final...
        d = 10;
    }
}
```

---

[88] For *two* reasons. First, the var **str** is `static`, so any constructor is out of the question. Second, the default constructor is by definition inserted automatically and contains just a single stat: `super();` (ref.to JLS8, §8.8.9: "...the default constructor simply invokes the superclass constructor with no arguments."). Whoever coded the error messages for `javac` would have failed the exam on this partucular aspect... Curious.

Problem 6.24   Given the following code fragment:

```
class ExamTaker {
    private String name;
    private int score;
    public ExamTaker(String name) {
        this();                                  //line E1
        setName(name);
    }
    public ExamTaker(String name, int score) {
        ExamTaker(name);                         //line E2
        setScore(score);
    }
    //setter and getter methods go here
    @Override
    public String toString() {
        return getName() + " " + getScore() + " ";
    }
}

class Results{
    public static void main(String[] args) {
        ExamTaker e1 = new ExamTaker("Alice");
        ExamTaker e2 = new ExamTaker("Bob",62);
        System.out.print(e1);
        System.out.println(e2);
    }
}
```

What is the result?

    A.   Alice 0 Bob 62
    B.   Compilation fails only on line E1
    C.   Compilation fails only on line E2
    D.   Compilation fails at both line E1 and line E2

Problem 6.25   Given:

```
class Greetings {
    String str = "Hello!";
    Greetings(String str) {
        this.str = str;
    }
    void greet() {
        System.out.println(str);
    }
    public static void main(String[] args) {
        new Greetings("Hi!").greet();
    }
}
```

What is the result?

    A.   Hi!
    B.   Hello!
    C.   No output
    D.   Compilation fails
    E.   A RuntimeException is thrown

Problem 6.26   **Given:**

```
class A { }
class B { B() {} }
class C { C(String str ) {} }
```

Which class has a default constructor?

     A.   Only A
     B.   Only B
     C.   Only C
     D.   A and B
     E.   B and C
     F.   A and C
     G.   All three of them

Problem 6.27   **Given the contents of four source code files:**

File E.java:

```
package packOne;
class A { }
public class E {
    private E() { }
}
```

File Parent.java:

```
package packTwo;
final class B{};
```

File D.java:

```
package packThree;
public abstract class D {
    private void D() {}
}
```

File Child.java:

```
package packFour;
import packOne.*;
import packTwo.*;
import packThree.*;
// line C1
```

Which class definition, when inserted at line C1, will enable the code to compile?

     A.   `class C extends A { }`
     B.   `class C extends B { }`
     C.   `class C extends D { }`
     D.   `class C extends E { }`
     E.   None of the above

Problem 6.28   **Given two classes:**

```
class Exams {
    String name;
    int year;
    List exams = new ArrayList();
    // line XXX
        this.name = name;
        this.year = year;
        this.exams = exams;
    }
    public String toString() {
        return name + " in " + year + ": " + exams;
    }
}

public class Scheduler {
    public static void main (String[] args) {
        List al = new ArrayList();
        al.add("1Z0-808");
        al.add("1Z0-809");
        Exams e = new Exams("Bob", 2016, al);
        System.out.println(e);
    }
}
```

Which option, when inserted at line XXX, will enable the class Scheduler to print Bob in 2016: [1Z0-808, 1Z0-809]?

    A.   private Exams(String name, int year, List exams){
    B.   public void Exams(String name, int year, List exams){
    C.   Exams(String name, int year, List exams){
    D.   Exams(String name, int year, ArrayList exams){

Problem 6.29   **Given:**

```
package parent;
public class Parent {
    Parent() { System.out.println("Hello"); }
}

package child;
import parent.Parent;
public class Child extends Parent {
    private Child() { }
    public static void main (String[] args) {
        new Child();
    }
}
```

Which modification will make the code compile and print Hello?

    A.   Remove the **Parent()** constructor
    B.   Make the **Child()** constructor public instead of private
    C.   Add the modifier protected to the **Parent()** constructor
    D.   Remove the **Child()** constructor
    E.   Remove the modifier private from the **Child()** constructor

Problem 6.30

Which statement is true about the default constructor?

    A. It can take arguments.
    B. It has implicit public access modifier in its declaration.
    C. It can be added by the programmer.
    D. The default constructor of a subclass always invokes the no-arg constructor of its superclass.

Problem 6.31 Given:

```
class Parent{
    int a;
    public Parent(int a) {
        this.a = a;
    }
}

class Child extends Parent{
    int b;
    public Child(int a, int b) {
        super(a);
        this.b = b;
    }
    // line X
}
```

Which two LOCs can be added independently at line X?

    A. `Child() {}`
    B. `Child(int a) { this.b = a; }`
    C. `Child(int b) { this.a = b; }`
    D. `Child(int b) { super(Math.PI > Math.E ? 3 : 2); }`
    E. `Child(int c) { this(c = 1, c = 2 ); }`

Problem 6.32   Given:

```
class Hamlet {
    static String word = "";
    Hamlet(String word){ this.word += word; }
    { word += "a"; }
    static { word += "i"; }
    { word += "o"; }
}

class TypingMonkey {
    public static void main(String[] args) {
        System.out.print(Hamlet.word + " ");
        new Hamlet("u");
        System.out.print(Hamlet.word + " ");
        new Hamlet("e");
        System.out.print(Hamlet.word + " ");
    }
}
```

What is the result?

    A. i iaou iaouaoe
    B. i iiaou iiaouaoe
    C. i iaou iaouiaoe
    D. i aiou aioue

Problem 6.33   Given:

```
class Test{
    static int a;
    int b;
    Test(int a, int b) {
        this.a += a;
        this.b += b;
    }
    void modify(int a, int b){
        this(a, b);
    }
     public static void main(String[] args) {
        Test t1 = new Test(10, 20);
        Test t2 = new Test(30, 40);
        t1.modify(10, 20);
        t2.modify(10, 20);
        System.out.println("a = " + Test.a + ", b = " + t2.b);
    }
}
```

What is the result?

    A.   a = 40, b = 40
    B.   a = 40, b = 60
    C.   a = 60, b = 40
    D.   Compilation fails

Problem 6.34

The *Real World Scenario* sidebar on page 208 in the *OCA Study Guide* by Jeanne Boyarsky and Scott Selikoff discusses the so-called defensive copy[89] and provides this example:

```
public Mutable(StringBuilder b) {
    builder = new StringBuilder(b); }
public StringBuilder getBuilder() {
    return new StringBuilder(builder);       // XXX
}
```

Now, the Constructor Summary for the class **StringBuilder**[90] says the class defines four constructors none of which lists a **StringBuilder** object as its argument:

Constructor Summary

Constructors

Constructor and Description
StringBuilder() Constructs a string builder with no characters in it and an initial capacity of 16 characters.
StringBuilder(CharSequence seq) Constructs a string builder that contains the same characters as the specified CharSequence.
StringBuilder(int capacity) Constructs a string builder with no characters in it and an initial capacity specified by the capacity argument.
StringBuilder(String str) Constructs a string builder initialized to the contents of the specified string.

---

[89] Which has been briefly mentioned a few pages earlier when we were looking at the rules related to Exam Objective 6.5, *Applying Encapsulation Principles to a Class.*

[90] https://docs.oracle.com/javase/8/docs/api/java/lang/StringBuilder.html

Hence the question: **Is line XXX valid?**

A. Oh yes, most definitely; after all, the authors of any study guide written to the masses should know what they are talking about…

B. Hell, no; it should've been `return new StringBuilder(builder.toString());`

Problem 6.35   Given:

```
class A {
    static { System.out.print("Hello from"); }
    static String name = " A";
}
class B extends A{
    static { System.out.print(" B"); }
}
class C extends B {
    static { System.out.print(" C"); }
}

class Test {
    public static void main(String[] args){
        System.out.println(C.name);
    }
}
```

What is the result?

A. A
B. Hello from A
C. Hello from C A
D. Hello from B C A

Problem 6.36   Given:

```
public class Test{
    public void testRefs(String str, StringBuilder sb){
        str = str + sb.toString();
        sb.append(str);
        str = null;
        sb = null;
    }
    public static void main(String[] args){
        String str = "aaa";
        StringBuilder sb = new StringBuilder("bbb");
        new Test().testRefs(str, sb);
        System.out.println("str=" + str + " sb=" + sb);
    }
}
```

What is the result?

A. str=null sb=null
B. str=aaa sb=null
C. str=aaa sb=bbb
D. str=aaa sb=aaabbb
E. str=aaa sb=bbbaaabbb
F. Compilation fails
G. A NullPointerException is thrown at runtime

 **Keys & Discussion:**

Problem 6.1 – DGH

   Given:

```
 1 package last.vegas;
 2
 3 class BankAccount {
 4     int balance;
 5
 6     BankAccount(){
 7         this.balance = new java.util.Random().nextInt(1000);
 8     }
 9
10     int getBalance(){
11         return this.balance;
12     }
13     void makeTransfer(int amount){
14         this.balance += amount;
15     }
16 }
17
18 public class HighRoller{
19     public static void main(String[] args) {
20         BankAccount ba = new BankAccount();
21         System.out.println("Was: $" + ba.getBalance());
22 //        this.balance = 0;
23 //        BankAccount.balance = 0;
24 //        new BankAccount(0);
25 //        ba.balance = 0;
26 //        ba.getBalance() = 0;
27 //        ba.makeTransfer(0);
28 //        ba.makeTransfer(ba.balance * -1);
29 //        ba.makeTransfer(-ba.getBalance());
30         System.out.println("Now: $" + ba.getBalance());
31     }
32 }
```

Which three lines, when uncommented independently, can empty the bank account created on line 20?

   A. line 22
   B. line 23
   C. line 24
   D. line 25
   E. line 26
   F. line 27
   G. line 28
   H. line 29

Line 22 doesn't compile because a) the method **main()** is `static` but `this` by definition refers to an instance, and b) the var **balance** is itself defined in the class **BankAccount** rather than **HighRoller**.

The problem with line 23 is somewhat similar to what we have on line 22: the var **balance** is an instance field and therefore can't be accessed by prepending its class name.

Line 24 is also invalid since the class **BankAccount** doesn't define a constructor that takes an `int`.

The totally outlandish line 26 attempts to assign zero to the method **getBalance()**, which itself returns an `int`.

And finally, line 27 simply adds zero to the var **balance**, thus not affecting it in the slightest.

It should be noted in passing that the class **BankAccount** is improperly encapsulated, and line 25 clearly illustrates this: instead of being able to access the var **balance** only through a `public` method like line 29 does, **HighRoller** has full direct control over **balance** because the var wasn't declared `private`.

Problem 6.2 – C

Given:

```java
class SpeedBoat {
    float speed;
}

public class BoatRace {
    public void breakRecord(SpeedBoat sb, float speed) {
        speed = speed * 2;
        sb.speed = sb.speed + speed;
    }
    public static void main(String[] args) {
        SpeedBoat sb = new SpeedBoat();              // line b1
        sb.speed = 200;
        float currentRecord = 400;

        BoatRace br = new BoatRace();
        br.breakRecord(sb, currentRecord);
        System.out.println(sb.speed + " vs " + currentRecord);
    }
}
```

What is the result?

   A.   200.0 vs 400.0
   B.   600.0 vs 800.0
   C.   1000.0 vs 400.0
   D.   Compilation fails

The method **breakRecord()** takes in two args: one is a reftype and the other is a primitive. Since Java is always pass-by-value, whatever happens to a primitive arg isn't reflected in the caller but in our case the method **breakRecord()** affects the instance field **speed** by accessing it through a copy of the reference that points to the object **sb** created on line b1. As the result, the value of **speed** becomes 200.0f + 400.0f*2 = 1000.0f.

Problem 6.3 – B

Given:

```java
class WhichOne {

    public static void run(int x, int y) {
        System.out.println("working with int: " + (x + y));
    }

    public static void run(Integer x, Integer y) {
        System.out.println("working with Integer: " + (x + y));
    }
```

```
        public static void run(float x, float y) {
            System.out.println("working with float: " + (x + y));
        }

        public static void run(double x, double y) {
            System.out.println("working with double: " + (x + y));
        }

        public static void main(String[] args) {
            run(1, 2);
            run(1.0, 2.0);
        }
    }
```

What is the result?

A. working with int: 3
   working with float: 3.0
B. working with int: 3
   working with double: 3.0
C. working with Integer: 3
   working with double: 3.0
D. working with Integer: 3
   working with float: 3.0

When it comes to executing an overloaded method (or a constructor, for that matter), Java always starts looking for the exact match. Failing that, it attempts to use a wider primitive, then autoboxing and, finally, a vararg. Here, both calls to the overloaded versions of **run()** have found their exact matches.

Problem 6.4 – A

Given:

```
    public class Doubler {
        public static void main(String[] args) {
            int a = 100;
            System.out.print(doubleValue(a));
            System.out.print(" : " + a);
        }
        static int doubleValue(int a){
            a = a * 2;
            return a;
        }
    }
```

What is the result?

A. 200 : 100
B. 100 : 100
C. 200 : 200
D. Compilation fails

Changes to a primitive arg are never reflected in the caller, which immediately limits us to only two choices – options A and B – because the second printing stat must output the unmodified value of the variable **a**.

Problem 6.5 – A

Suppose, a method is declared to take two parameters but the caller passes to it only one argument. What is the result?

  A. Compilation fails.
  B. The missing argument is given the default value for its declared type.
  C. An IllegalArgumentException is thrown at run time.
  D. A NoSuchMethodException is thrown at run time.

The answer is obvious. I included this question for one simple reason: to have an opportunity to talk a bit more about method calls. Consider it as a small print that helps to look at method invocation from another angle.

Method invocations are resolved at both compile and run time. The compiler concerns itself with overloading while the JVM deals with overriding (which we will be discussing in the next Chapter). Resolving a method name at compile time is performed in several steps:

- first, the compiler determines which class or interface is to be looked into;

- then the type determined in the previous step is scanned for member methods by using the name of the method and the argument expressions. The compiler wants methods that are both *accessible* and *applicable*; in other words, it looks for declarations that can be correctly invoked on the list of the given arguments;

- finally, the compiler decides whether the chosen method is appropriate by checking the compatibility of an argument to a method invocation with its target type.

Unlike overloading, overriding involves also the return type and `throws` clause.

So far so good; now for the fun part. This is what the JLS8 says:

> The descriptor (signature plus return type) of the most specific method is the one used at run time to perform the method dispatch[91].

And this what can be found in the JVM8 Spec:

> A method signature encodes type information about a (possibly generic) method declaration. It describes any type parameters of the method; the (possibly parameterized) types of any formal parameters; the (possibly parameterized) return type, if any; and the types of any exceptions declared in the method's throws clause.[92]

There you have it – the Big Divide between the legislative and executive branches of the Java Republic: the language specification, which defines what Java is, says the method signature excludes the return type, while the JVM thinks otherwise. I say, it's a wonder our programs run at all…

Although this stuff isn't on the 1Z0-808 exam, it is still nice to know that the Java ecosystem is full of contradictions, which means it is bound to develop further – at least if Hegel is to be believed[93].

---

[91] The Java Language Specification, Java SE8 Edition, §15.12.2, *Compile-Time Step 2: Determine Method Signature.*
[92] The Java Virtual Machine Specification, Java SE8 Edition, §4.7.9.1, *Signatures.*
[93] "…contradiction is the root of all movement and vitality", *Science of Logic* (1812), §956.

Problem 6.6 – B

Given:

```
class Test {
    public static void modify(int[] arr) {
        for (int idx = 0; idx < arr.length; idx++) {
            arr[idx] = arr[idx] + 1;
            System.out.print(arr[idx] + " ");   }
    }
    public static void main (String[] args) {
        int[] arr = {10, 20, 30};
        for (int e : arr) { System.out.print(e + " "); }
        modify(arr);
        for (int e : arr) { System.out.print(e + " "); }
    }
}
```

What is the result?

   A.   10 20 30 11 21 31 10 20 30
   B.   10 20 30 11 21 31 11 21 31
   C.   Compilation fails
   D.   A RuntimeException is thrown

An array is an **Object** and, as such, can be changed even though the method **modify()** works with a copy of the array's reference variable. We could even declare the array `final`, and its slots would be still modifiable.

Problem 6.7 – C

Given:

```
class PassByValue {
    private int a = 0;
    private int b = 0;
    public void run1(int a, int b) {
        a = a;
        b = b;
        System.out.println("a = " + this.a + ", b = " + this.b);   }
    public void run2(int a, int b) {
        this.a = a;
        this.b = b;
        System.out.println("a = " + this.a + ", b = " + this.b);   }
    public static void main(String[] args) {
        PassByValue pbv = new PassByValue();
        pbv.run1(1, 2);
        pbv.run2(3, 4);     }
}
```

What is the result?

   A.   a = 0, b = 0
        a = 0, b = 0
   B.   a = 1, b = 2
        a = 3, b = 4
   C.   a = 0, b = 0
        a = 3, b = 4
   D.   a = 1, b = 2
        a = 0, b = 0

The method **run1()** doesn't affect the fields because it assigns the passed-in values to the local vars, which cease to exist after the method terminates.

On the contrary, the method **run2()** acts on `this`, which is a reference that points to the current object. Although `this` is `final` by definition, we still can change its fields.

Problem 6.8 – D

Given:

```
class OverloadTester {
    static double run(double a) {
        System.out.print("double: ");
        return a;
    }
    static int run(double a) {
        System.out.print("int: ");
        return (int)a;
    }
    static String run(double a) {
        System.out.print("String: ");
        return new String("" + a);
    }
    public static void main(String[] args) {
        System.out.println(run(1.0));
    }
}
```

What is the result?

    A.   double: 1.0
    B.   int: 1
    C.   String: 1.0
    D.   Compilation fails

The methods are overloaded incorrectly: they all take in a single parameter of the type `double`. This is why the compiler generates the same error message twice, "method **run(double)** is already defined in class **OverloadTester**".

Problem 6.9 – AD

Which two are valid in the body of a method that does not return a value?

    A.   Omission of the `return` statement
    B.   `return null;`
    C.   `return void;`
    D.   `return;`

`return null` does return a value. As for the keyword `void`, it is used in method declarations only. And lastly, an empty `return` is allowed.

Problem 6.10 – C

Which is the valid declaration of a method that takes two arguments of the type int and returns the result of their division?

```
A.  divide (int a, int b) { return a/b; }
B.  double divide (int a, b) { return a/b; }
C.  int divide (int a, int b) { return a/b; }
D.  double divide (int a, int b) { a/b; }
E.  void divide (int a, int b) { return a/b; }
```
F. None of the above

Although returning an `int` will most likely screw up business logic, it is still valid. As for option A, it omits return type in the method's declaration. Option B specifies its arguments incorrectly, option D has no `return` statement even though the declaration does promise that the method returns something, and option E attempts to return a value while the declaration says it won't.

Problem 6.11 – B

Given:

```
class Invalid {
    private static double value;
    public static int getValue(){ return value; };
    public static void Main(String[] args) {
        System.out.println(getValue());
    }
}
```

This class fails compilation. What is the reason?

A. There is no corresponding `setValue()` method
B. The method `getValue()` returns an incompatible data type
C. A `static` field cannot be declared `private`
D. The field's value is uninitialized
E. The `main()` method has wrong signature

The variable **value** is of type `double`, which cannot be implicitly narrowed to `int` so the return type of the method **getValue()** clashes with the method's declaration. To make the code work, we could explicitly cast **value** to `int` or change the return type to `double`.

Problem 6.12 – B

Given:

```
class Test {
    static int[] a = {1, 2, 3, 4};
    int[] b = {5, 6, 7, 8};
    public static void main(String[] args) {
        Test t1 = new Test(), t2 = new Test();
        t1.a[3] = 10;
        t1.b[3] = 20;
        t2.a[3] = 30;
        t2.b[3] = 40;
```

```
System.out.println (
            t1.a[3] + " " + t1.b[3] + " " +
            t2.a[3] + " " + t2.b[3]);
    }
}
```

What is the result?

A. 10 20 30 40
B. 30 20 30 40
C. A run-time exception is thrown
D. Compilation fails

The array **a** is `static` and, therefore, all instances of the class share it. This is why the statement that assigns 30 to the fourth slot in **a** by acting on the refvar **t2**, also affects **a**[3] in the object **t1**.

Problem 6.13 – D

Given two classes:
```
package pack1;
public class A {
    public int a = 1;
    protected int b = 2;
    int c = 3;
    private int d = 4;
}
```

```
1  package pack2;
2  import pack1.*;
3  public class B extends A {
4      public static void main(String[] args) {
5          A obj = new B();
6          System.out.println("a = " + obj.a);
7          System.out.println("b = " + obj.b);
8          System.out.println("c = " + obj.c);
9          System.out.println("d = " + obj.d);
10     }
11 }
```

How many LOCs in the class B fail compilation?

A. None
B. One
C. Two
D. Three
E. Four

The `private` variable **d** is by definition accessible only inside the class that declares it. The package-`private` variable **c** is again by definition available only to the classes inside the same package.

As for the `protected` variable **b**, it cannot be accessed through **obj** because the reference type of this object is **A**. In the next chapter we will be talking in more detail about inheritance and its subtleties so right now it should be sufficient to recall that it is the reftype that says what's available to the object. Being `protected`, the variable **b** is by definition available to the classes inside the same package or to the data types derived from **A**. And since **A** is obviously not its own subclass, the object **obj** cannot see **b**. Had line 5 declared the object **obj** being of type **B**, line 7 would have compiled.

Problem 6.14 – B

What is the name of the Java concept that uses access modifiers to protect variables defined by a class?

    A. Abstraction
    B. Encapsulation
    C. Inheritance
    D. Instantiation
    E. Polymorphism

The question may seem surprisingly simple; there exists, however, much confusion about the precise nature of relation between abstraction and encapsulation. As if to complicate things even further, the terms *encapsulation* and *information hiding* are often used interchangeably, so it is theoretically possible that on the actual exam you'll encounter something about information hiding. I didn't but who knows what's going to be in your case…

Encyclopedia of Computer Science and Technology by Harry Henderson (2009) says that encapsulation "…both protects code from uncontrolled modification or access and hides information (details) that programmers who simply want to use functionality don't need to know about". It becomes apparent that encapsulation is wider than just data protection or data hiding.

If you want more, here's a good read on the subject although it was published a quarter of a century ago when Java didn't even exist: Berard, E. V. "Abstraction, Encapsulation, and Information Hiding." White paper, Berard Software Engineering, Inc., Baithersburg, MD, 1991.[94]

Problem 6.15 – B

Given:

```
class A {
    int a;
    static int b;
    A(int input) { if (b <= input) b = a = input; }
    void show() { System.out.println("a = " + a + ", b = " + b); }
}

public class Test {
    public static void main(String[] args) {
        A obj1 = new A(20);
        A obj2 = new A(60);
        A obj3 = new A(40);
        obj1.show();
        obj2.show();
        obj3.show();
    }
}
```

---

[94] At the moment of writing the article was available here: http://www.tonymarston.co.uk/php-mysql/abstraction.txt

What is the result?

    A. a = 20, b = 60
          a = 60, b = 60
          a = 40, b = 60
    B. a = 20, b = 60
          a = 60, b = 60
          a = 0, b = 60
    C. a = 20, b = 20
          a = 60, b = 60
          a = 40, b = 40
    D. a = 20, b = 20
          a = 60, b = 60
          a = 0, b = 60

This question resembles Problem 6.12 although here we are dealing with primitives. Both variables **a** and **b** get explicitly initialized in the same constructor but the var **b** is `static` and this complicates things. In addition, the printing stats run only after all the operations that affect our three objects have been executed.

When the first object is created, both fields are assigned the same value of 20 because non-`final` non-local variables are inited implicitly and `if(0<20)` evaluates to `true`. The second time the constructor is called, the value of **b** (which equals 20) is still less than **input** (which is 60) so both vars get the same values again. Since **b** is `static`, its current value, 60, is shared by both objects.

The situation changes when the constructor initializes the third object: as 40 is less than 60, the assignments are not executed. Being `static` and, therefore, common for all instances of the class, the variable **b** remains equal to 60, while the variable **a** is left without explicit initialization thus retaining its default value of zero.

Problem 6.16 – B

    Given two classes:

```
public class WaterConsumer {
    WaterConsumer wcons = new WaterConsumer();

    public void useWater(double m3){
        wcons.updateBill(m3);
    }
}

public class UtilityAccount {
    private double m3;
    private double rate = 1.23;
    private double bill;

    //line X

}
```

Which code block, when inserted at line X, will implement the following requirements?

1. The code should successfully update the water consumption bill (represented by the variable `bill`), which is defined as the number of cubic meters of water consumed by the customer (the variable `m3`) multiplied by the cost of water per cubic meter (the variable `rate`);

2. The code should also protect the variable `bill` from tampering such as an attempt to decrease its value by an instance of the class WaterConsumer.

```
A.  public void updateBill(double m3) {
        this.m3 += m3;
        this.bill = this.m3 * this.rate;
    }
B.  public void updateBill(double m3) {
        if (m3 > 0){
            this.m3 += m3;
            this.bill = this.m3 * this.rate;
        }
    }
C.  private void updateBill(double m3) {
        if (m3 > 0) {
            this.m3 += m3;
            this.bill = this.m3 * this.rate;
        }
    }
D.  public void updateBill(double m3) {
        if(m3 > 0) {
            this.m3 += m3;
            calcBill(this.m3);
        }
    }
    public void calcBill(double m3) {
        bill = m3 * rate;
    }
```

As encapsulation is best achieved by making instance fields `private` and providing `public` getters and setters, we will solve this problem by applying these principles methodically.

Option C can be eliminated at once because the method **updateBill()** is `private` and no other class will be able to call it.

Option A does not check the method arg thus making the calculation algorithm vulnerable to an attack: the object **wcons** just might pass a negative value in an attempt to lower the water bill.

And finally, although option D does make such a check in its **updateBill()** method, it still leaves the var **bill** wide open because anyone can invoke the public method **calcBill()** with a negative argument.

Problem 6.17 – A

Given:

```
class Production {
    static int count = 0;
    int a = 0;

    public void rampUp() {
        while (a < 10) {
            a++;
            count++;
        }
    }

    public static void main(String[] args) {
        Production p1 = new Production();
        Production p2 = new Production();
        p1.rampUp();
        p2.rampUp();
        System.out.print("p1.count = " + p1.count + ", p2.count = " + p2.count);
    }
}
```

What is the result?

A. p1.count = 20, p2.count = 20
B. p1.count = 10, p2.count = 10
C. p1.count = 10, p2.count = 20
D. Compilation fails

The question asks about the value of the same `static` variable, hence option C is immediately out. Calling the loop twice makes the answer obvious.

Problem 6.18 – D

Given:

```
package base;
public class Base {
    public void run(){ System.out.print("No args! "); };
    protected void run(int arg){ System.out.print(arg + " "); };
    void run(double arg){ System.out.print(arg + " "); };
    private void run(String arg){ System.out.print("\"" + arg + "\""); };
}

package derived;
import base.Base;
public class Derived extends Base {
    public static void main(String[] args) {
        Base obj = new Derived();
        obj.run();                          // line 1
        obj.run(1);                         // line 2
        obj.run(1.0);                       // line 3
        obj.run("1");                       // line 4
    }
}
```

What is the result?

    A. No args! 1 1.0 "1"
    B. Compilation fails on line 4
    C. Compilation fails on lines 4 and 3
    D. Compilation fails on lines 4, 3 and 2
    E. Compilation fails on lines 4, 3, 2 and 1

This question is to the tune of Problem 6.13 but concerns methods rather than fields. The situation is quite similar: we have two classes in different packages → `private` and package-`private` members are inaccessible → lines 3 and 4 fail compilation.

The `protected` method **run(int arg)** is also inaccessible because no type can be its own child.

Problem 6.19 – BF

Given the following class:

```
1 public class A {
2     public double a;
3     public static void main (String[] args) {
4         A obj = new A();
5         a = 10;
6     }
7 }
```

Which two options, when used independently, will make this code compile and run?

    A. Replace line 2 with `public int a;`
    B. Replace line 2 with `static int a;`
    C. Replace line 4 with `static int a;`
    D. Replace line 4 with `static double a;`
    E. Replace line 5 with `a = 10.0d;`
    F. Replace line 5 with `new A().a = 10;`

One of the most 'popular' coding blunders is asking a `static` method to access something non-`static`. The exam has at least two questions on this subject: one uses instance variables (like the current Problem) and the other instance methods.

Option A does not help because the var **a** remains non-`static`. Options C and D are simply illegal as the only modifier that is accepted inside a method is `final`. As for option E, it does not address the real problem.

Option F is perfectly valid although it makes line 4 redundant.

Problem 6.20 – BE

Given:

```
 1 class StaticTest {
 2     static void run1() {
 3           run2();
 4           run3();
 5           StaticTest.run2();
 6     }
 7     static void run2() {
 8           run1();
 9           StaticTest.run3();
10 }
11     void run3() {
12           run1();
13     }
14 }
```

Which two LOCs fail compilation?

    A. line 3
    B. line 4
    C. line 5
    D. line 8
    E. line 9
    F. line 12

Here we have the second version of the exam problem that tests us on the 'non-static in static context' compile-time error.

Since **run3()** is an instance method, **run1()** should've invoked it on an object. As for **run2()**, it calls **run3()** as if the method were indeed static, in other words, by prepending its class name.

Problem 6.21 – DEF

Given the contents of the file U.java:

```
1 abstract class A{}
2 final class F{}
3 public class U{}
4 protected class O{}
5 private class R{}
6 static class S{}
```

Which three LOCs fail compilation?

    A. line 1
    B. line 2
    C. line 3
    D. line 4
    E. line 5
    F. line 6

Only nested classes and interfaces may be declared private, protected or static.

Problem 6.22 – A

Given:

```
class Test {
    static int a = 42;
    public static void main(String[] args) {
        Test t = new Test();
        t.a++;
        Test.a++;
        t.a--;
        System.out.println(--t.a + " " + Test.a);
    }
}
```

What is the result?

A. 42 42
B. 40 41
C. 41 40
D. 43 44

As any `static` member can be accessed through an object or by its class name, the printing stat outputs the same value twice thus immediately eliminating options B, C and D. Another approach to solving this Problem is by noticing that two increments followed by two decrements bring the value of **a** back to its starting point…

Problem 6.23 – B

Given the following two classes:

```
class A {
    String str;
    A() {}
    private String run() {
        return this.str += "!";
    }
}

class B extends A {
    B(String str) {
        this.str = str;
    }
    private void doStuff() {
        System.out.println(run());
    }
    public static void main (String [] args) {
        new B("Hello").doStuff();
    }
}
```

What should be done to make the code compile?

A. Make the class **A** `public`
B. Declare the method **run()** as `protected` instead of `private`
C. Make the **A()** constructor `public`
D. Make the **A()** constructor `protected`
E. Make the method **doStuff()** package-`private`

Because both classes are in the same package, options A, C, D and E cannot help: they are missing the real target.

The true cause of the compilation failure is the `private` nature of **run()**, which doesn't let the class **B** inherit this method.

Problem 6.24 – D

Given the following code fragment:

```
class ExamTaker {
    private String name;
    private int score;

    public ExamTaker(String name) {
        this();                          //line E1
        setName(name);
    }

    public ExamTaker(String name, int score) {
        ExamTaker(name);                 //line E2
        setScore(score);
    }

    //setter and getter methods go here

    @Override
    public String toString() {
        return getName() + " " + getScore() + " ";
    }
}

class Results{
    public static void main(String[] args) {
        ExamTaker e1 = new ExamTaker("Alice");
        ExamTaker e2 = new ExamTaker("Bob",62);
        System.out.print(e1);
        System.out.println(e2);
    }
}
```

What is the result?

A. Alice 0 Bob 62
B. Compilation fails only on line E1
C. Compilation fails only on line E2
D. Compilation fails at both line E1 and line E2

This is an example of an exam question that omits definitions of certain methods and uses just a placeholder instead. If I remember correctly, I met it only once, on the second sitting, which just might mean it's ungraded…

I also can't recall if the actual exam uses the `@Override` annotation but I placed it here anyway to remind you to pay attention to the signature of the **Object**'s **toString()** method; one of the exam questions relies on it.

Now, to the task at hand. Line E1 is invalid because the class never defines an explicit no-arg constructor. The *default* constructor isn't available, either, since the compiler inserts it when the data type in question defines no constructors at all.

Line E2 also fails compilation because we may not call constructors by using the class name; the keywords `this()` and `super()` are to be used, instead.

And on a final note, the missing definitions of the accessors and mutators could be written like this:

```
public void setName(String name){ this.name = name;}
public void setScore(int score){ this.score = score; }
public String getName(){ return this.name; }
public int getScore(){ return this.score; }
```

Problem 6.25 – A

Given:

```
class Greetings {
    String str = "Hello!";
    Greetings(String str) {
        this.str = str;
    }
    void greet() {
        System.out.println(str);
    }
    public static void main(String[] args) {
        new Greetings("Hi!").greet();
    }
}
```

What is the result?

    A. Hi!
    B. Hello!
    C. No output
    D. Compilation fails
    E. A RuntimeException is thrown

This is just a simple illustration of an instance field initialization through a constructor. No traps or nasty tricks.

Problem 6.26 – A

Given:

```
class A { }
class B { B() {} }
class C { C(String str ) {} }
```

Which class has a default constructor?

    A. Only A
    B. Only B
    C. Only C
    D. A and B
    E. B and C
    F. A and C
    G. All three of them

The Java Language Specification, §8.8.9, *Default Constructor*, says that

> If a class contains no constructor declarations, then a default constructor is implicitly declared.

When studying constructors for the exam, I found out that many questions can be solved faster when I think of the default constructor as an invisible self-proclaimed Beauty Queen who just hates and fears competitors:

    −   the default constructor is invisible, ain't it?

    −   and if another constructor appears on the podium, Def Con never attends that particular beauty pageant.

So, as option A defines no constructors whatsoever, Def Con reigns uncontested inside the class **A**. By the same token, since both options B and C do define constructors, Def Con thinks she is way too smashing and noble to keep them company.

Problem 6.27 – C

Given the contents of four source code files:

File E.java:

```
package packOne;
class A { }
public class E {
    private E() { }
}
```

File Parent.java:

```
package packTwo;
final class B{};
```

File D.java:

```
package packThree;
public abstract class D {
    private void D() {}
}
```

File Child.java:

```
package packFour;
import packOne.*;
import packTwo.*;
import packThree.*;
// line C1
```

Which class definition, when inserted at line C1, will enable the code to compile?

A.   `class C extends A { }`

B.   `class C extends B { }`

C.   `class C extends D { }`

D.   `class C extends E { }`

E.   None of the above

A non-`public` class[95] in a different package is inaccessible; this is arguably one of the most important rules for the exam. Following it, we can see that option A is incorrect.

Option B doesn't work because the class **B** is `final` and cannot be extended by definition.

Now to option D; while the class **E** is `public` and hence accessible from outside its package, its no-arg constructor is `private` and therefore unavailable to the class **C**. The following class definitions would have worked, though:

```
package packOne;
class A { }
public class E {
    private E() { }
    public E(int arg){ }                        // line XXX
}

package packFour;
import packOne.*;
import packTwo.*;
import packThree.*;
class C extends E{ super(12345); }
```

Please recall that unlike the default constructor, which shares the level of access with its class, non-default constructors are exempt from this rule; that's why we had to add the `public` modifier to the constructor declaration on line XXX. The modifier `protected` would also help.

And finally, there's nothing wrong with option C because it is just natural to extend an abstract class (after all, how else one could implement its abstract methods, huh?). Although the declaration `private void D()` resembles a non-arg constructor, it defines a return type and, therefore, is still a method that just happens to share the same name with its class. What's more, because the class **D** is `public`, its default constructor is also `public` and hence accessible to the class **C**.

Problem 6.28 – C

Given two classes:

```
class Exams {
    String name;
    int year;
    List exams = new ArrayList();
    // line XXX
        this.name = name;
        this.year = year;
        this.exams = exams;
    }
    public String toString() {
        return name + " in " + year + ": " + exams;
    }
}

public class Scheduler {
    public static void main (String[] args) {
        List al = new ArrayList();
        al.add("1Z0-808");
```

---

[95] However, a non-`public` *constructor* in a `public` class is accessible if it's `protected`. Do remember this, OK?

```
        al.add("1Z0-809");
        Exams e = new Exams("Bob", 2016, al);
        System.out.println(e);
    }
}
```

Which option, when inserted at line XXX, will enable the class Scheduler to print
Bob in 2016: [1Z0-808, 1Z0-809]?

    A.   private Exams(String name, int year, List exams){
    B.   public void Exams(String name, int year, List exams){
    C.   Exams(String name, int year, List exams){
    D.   Exams(String name, int year, ArrayList exams){

Since the constructor in option A is `private`, the class **Scheduler** will not be able to access it.

Option B defines a method rather than a constructor, and option D wants an **ArrayList** while the call to the constructor provides just a **List**.

Problem 6.29 – C

    Given:

```
package parent;
public class Parent {
    Parent() { System.out.println("Hello"); }
}

package child;
import parent.Parent;
public class Child extends Parent {
    private Child() { }
    public static void main (String[] args) {
        new Child();
    }
}
```

Which modification will make the code compile and print Hello?

    A.   Remove the **Parent()** constructor
    B.   Make the **Child()** constructor `public` instead of `private`
    C.   Add the modifier `protected` to the **Parent()** constructor
    D.   Remove the **Child()** constructor
    E.   Remove the modifier `private` from the **Child()** constructor

Two classes in different packages again... This means we should be on alert for potential problems with accessibility. One of the traps on the exam is build upon the rule that says that the default constructor has the same access level as its class whereas an explicitly declared no-arg constructor loses the default accessibility associated with its class, so the following won't compile:

```
//In file A.java
package a;
public class A{
    A(){ }
}
//In file B.java
package b;
import a.*;
```

```
public class B extends A{
//   B(){ }                                // won't compile because A(){}
                                           // is neither public nor protected
    public static void main(String[] args){
        new B();                           // notice that this LOC is OK while the
                                           // comperr is on constructor line B() {}
    }
}
```

In our case, the superclass **Parent** is declared `public` but doesn't have the default constructor (which would be also `public`). Instead, the class **Parent** explicitly defines a no-arg constructor and makes it package-`private` thus effectively preventing the class **Child** from accessing it. All we need is make the explicit no-arg constructor in **Parent** accessible → all options except C are eliminated.

Naturally, we could make the **Parent()** constructor `public` instead of `protected`; it would have worked, too.

Problem 6.30 – D

Which statement is true about the default constructor?

    A. It can take arguments.
    B. It has implicit public access modifier in its declaration.
    C. It can be added by the programmer.
    D. The default constructor of a subclass always invokes the no-arg constructor of its superclass.

The default constructor is by definition a no-arg constructor so option A is out. Since it shares the same access level with the class, option B is also incorrect. And because the default constructor is added by the compiler only, we can rid of option C, as well.

Much more interesting is the correct option D as it reminds us that there's more in the code than meets the eye:

```
class A {}                                           class A {
                                                         A() { super(); }
                  The compiler transforms            }
class B extends A{}   the left-hand side into this:
                                                     class B extends A {
                                                         B() { super(); }
                                                     }
```

The superclass for **A** is the class **Object** whose javadocs description is probably the shortest of all:

Class **Object** is the root of the class hierarchy. Every class has **Object** as a superclass. All objects, including arrays, implement the methods of this class.

Problem 6.31 – DE

Given:

```
class Parent{
    int a;
    public Parent(int a) {
        this.a = a;
    }
}
class Child extends Parent{
    int b;
    public Child(int a, int b) {
        super(a);
        this.b = b;
    }
    // line X
}
```

Which two LOCs can be added independently at line X?

A. `Child() {}`
B. `Child(int a) { this.b = a; }`
C. `Child(int b) { this.a = b; }`
D. `Child(int b) { super(Math.PI > Math.E ? 3 : 2); }`
E. `Child(int c) { this(c = 1, c = 2 ); }`

Option A illustrates the trap that you will most definitely meet on the exam: the compiler always tries to stick a no-arg call to `super()` into every available constructor it sees. By being available I mean that the constructor does not have its own call to `super()` or `this()` regardless of the number of args in it.

In our case (we are still talking about option A), since the class **Parent** doesn't have a no-arg constructor, adding a no-arg ctor to the class **Child** throws a comperr.

Options B and C suffer from exactly same problem: although the compiler wants to insert a no-arg call to `super()`, the class **Parent** doesn't have a matching constructor.

The only cases when the compiler won't throw a tantrum are options D and E: their own calls to `super()` and `this()` prevent the compiler from inserting blindly a no-arg call to `super()`. After all, since a call to `super()` or `this()` must be the first statement in any constructor's body, no constructor may have *two* such calls in it.

Problem 6.32 – A

Given:

```
class Hamlet {
    static String word = "";
    Hamlet(String word){ this.word += word; }      // line h1
    { word += "a"; }                                // line h2
    static { word += "i"; }                         // line h3
    { word += "o"; }                                // line h4
}
class TypingMonkey {
    public static void main(String[] args) {
        System.out.print(Hamlet.word + " ");        // line t1
        new Hamlet("u");                            // line t2
        System.out.print(Hamlet.word + " ");        // line t3
        new Hamlet("e");                            // line t4
        System.out.print(Hamlet.word + " ");
    }
}
```

What is the result?

- A. i iaou iaouaoe
- B. i iiaou iiaouaoe
- C. i iaou iaouiaoe
- D. i aiou aioue

This problem is probably twice as hard as the actual exam's question that deals with the order of initialization – if you ever encounter it, that is; because I met such a question only once. Anyway, to crack it, we should keep in mind four simple rules:

<u>Rule 1</u>: `static` initializers start running first, and they do it only once;

<u>Rule 2</u>: they run one after another in the declared order for the entire inheritance chain;

<u>Rule 3</u>: then the instance initializers kick in for every object that is being created;

<u>Rule 4</u>: the constructors are the last to run.

Putting it out in code:

```
class Grandpa{
    static { System.out.println("static initer 1 - Grandpa"); }
    { System.out.println("instance initer 1 - Grandpa"); }
    static { System.out.println("static initer 2 - Grandpa"); }
    { System.out.println("instance initer 2 - Grandpa"); }
    Grandpa(){ System.out.println("constructor - Grandpa"); }
}

class Father extends Grandpa{
    static { System.out.println("static initer 1 - Father"); }
    { System.out.println("instance initer 1 - Father"); }
    static { System.out.println("static initer 2 - Father"); }
    { System.out.println("instance initer 2 - Father"); }
    Father(){ System.out.println("constructor - Father"); }
}

class Grandson extends Father {
    static { System.out.println("static initer 1 - Grandson"); }
    { System.out.println("instance initer 1 - Grandson"); }
    static { System.out.println("static initer 2 - Grandson"); }
    { System.out.println("instance initer 2 - Grandson"); }
    Grandson(){ System.out.println("constructor - Grandson"); }

    public static void main(String[] args) {
        System.out.println("==== Entered main, started creating objects ====");
        Grandson g1 = new Grandson();
        System.out.println("==== Finished creating the 1st object ====");
        Grandson g2 = new Grandson();
        System.out.println("==== Finished creating the 2nd object ====");
    }
}
```

The code prints:

```
static initer 1 - Grandpa
static initer 2 - Grandpa
static initer 1 - Father
static initer 2 - Father
static initer 1 - Grandson
static initer 2 - Grandson
```

```
==== Entered main, started creating objects ====
instance initer 1 - Grandpa
instance initer 2 - Grandpa
constructor - Grandpa
instance initer 1 - Father
instance initer 2 - Father
constructor - Father
instance initer 1 - Grandson
instance initer 2 - Grandson
constructor - Grandson
==== Finished creating the 1st object ====
instance initer 1 - Grandpa
instance initer 2 - Grandpa
constructor - Grandpa
instance initer 1 - Father
instance initer 2 - Father
constructor - Father
instance initer 1 - Grandson
instance initer 2 - Grandson
constructor - Grandson
==== Finished creating the 2nd object ====
```

According to Rules 1 and 2, when the JVM begins executing the code at its entry point, which is the method **main()**, the static initers for all three classes come into play, starting with **Grandpa**, followed by **Father** and finishing with **Grandson**. It does look as if the static initers run as soon as the class is accessed but, in fact, the process is more complicated. This is what the JLS says[96]:

> A class or interface type T will be initialized immediately before the first occurrence of any one of the following:
> - T is a class and an instance of T is created.
> - A static method declared by T is invoked.
> - A static field declared by T is assigned.
> - A static field declared by T is used and the field is not a constant variable.

There are a few more circumstances under which the initialization occurs but they are too advanced for our discussion. Anyway, we can see that in our case it is the second condition that causes the static initers to run: "a static method declared by T is invoked" – and **main()** is static.

The JLS adds that

> When a class is initialized, its superclasses are initialized (if they have not been previously initialized)

which explains why all *three* classes in the above example run their static initers. It also becomes clear why the following code prints "Hello from Base!" only once:

```
class Base {
    static String a;
    static {
        a = "\"I'm inited!\"";
        System.out.println("\"Hello from Base!\"");
    }
}
class Derived1 extends Base {}
class Derived2 extends Base {
    public static void main(String[] args) {
        new Derived1();                         // prints "Hello from Base!"
        System.out.println(new Derived2().a);   // prints only "I'm inited!"
    }
}
```

---

[96] §12.4.1, *When Initialization Occurs.*

Getting back to the previous example. After the static initers finish their job, the JVM moves its attention to the contents of the method **main()**, which prints a message that the program is about to start creating objects. Rules 3 and 4 dictate that any object is initialized beginning from its superclass, and this is exactly what we have: first the instance initers for the class **Grandpa** run in the declared order, then the **Grandpa**'s constructor follows – and the process is repeated for the classes **Father** and **Grandson**. The exact same thing happens when the JVM creates the second object.

All in all, the order of initialization boils down to the following chain of events:

superclass static initer(s) → subclass static initer(s) → superclass instance initer(s) → superclass constructor(s) → subclass instance initer(s) → subclass constructor(s)

Now it's time to look at our problem again. The process starts with assigning an empty string to the static field **word** just to make it non-`null`, otherwise our printing stats would output something like '`null`*followed-by-other-things*'.

Then the static initer on line h3 executes adding **i** to the still empty **word**, thus making its value equal to "i". At this point we run out of static initializers, be it simple declarations or entire blocks, and so the method **main()** executes line t1 thus printing the static var **word** followed by a white space, that is, "i ".

Next comes line t2 who wants to create a **Hamlet** object by calling a single-arg constructor and passing it a parameter of type **String**. This launches a whole new chain of events, this time involving instance initers and a constructor. Since the field **word** is `static`, it retains its previous value "i" to which the instance initers add "a" (line h2) and then "o" (line h4), after which the constructor on line h1 concatenates it with "u". At this point the value of **word** becomes equal to "iaou", so the printing stat on line t3 happily outputs it and adds a trailing white space → options B and D are eliminated.

When line t4 requests creation of a new **Hamlet** object, the process is repeated; this time, however, **word**'s value is "iaou", to which the instance initers add "ao" and the constructor finishes it up by appending "e".

Problem 6.33 – D

Given:

```
class Test{
    static int a;
    int b;
    Test(int a, int b) {
        this.a += a;
        this.b += b;
    }
    void modify(int a, int b){
        this(a, b);
    }
    public static void main(String[] args) {
        Test t1 = new Test(10, 20);
        Test t2 = new Test(30, 40);
        t1.modify(10, 20);
        t2.modify(10, 20);
        System.out.println("a = " + Test.a + ", b = " + t2.b);
    }
}
```

What is the result?

    A. a = 40, b = 40
    B. a = 40, b = 60
    C. a = 60, b = 40
    D. Compilation fails

Calls to `super()` or `this()` are allowed only from inside constructors while **modify()** is just a method… I met such a trap on both sittings; do be careful.

Problem 6.34 – B

The ***Real World Scenario*** sidebar on page 208 in the *OCA Study Guide* by Jeanne Boyarsky and Scott Selikoff discusses the so-called defensive copy[97] and provides this example:

```
public Mutable(StringBuilder b) {
    builder = new StringBuilder(b);   }
public StringBuilder getBuilder() {
    return new StringBuilder(builder);        // XXX
}
```

Now, the Constructor Summary for the class **StringBuilder**[98] says that the class defines four constructors none of which lists a **StringBuilder** object as its argument:

Constructor Summary

Constructors

Constructor and Description

`StringBuilder()`
Constructs a string builder with no characters in it and an initial capacity of 16 characters.

`StringBuilder(CharSequence seq)`
Constructs a string builder that contains the same characters as the specified CharSequence.

`StringBuilder(int capacity)`
Constructs a string builder with no characters in it and an initial capacity specified by the capacity argument.

`StringBuilder(String str)`
Constructs a string builder initialized to the contents of the specified string.

Hence the question: **Is line XXX valid?**

    A. Oh yes, most definitely; after all, the authors of any study guide written to the masses should know what they are talking about…

    B. Hell, no! it should've been `return new StringBuilder(builder.toString());`

This problem is equally appropriate for another Exam Objective, namely 9.1, *Manipulate Data Using the StringBuilder Class and Its Methods*, which belongs to the last group, *Working with Selected Classes from the Java API*. I must also add that the actual exam does not go to such depths, so please don't be alarmed. On the other hand, looking at things from different – preferably unexpected – perspectives helps understand and memorize them quicker and better…

---

[97] Which was also briefly mentioned a few pages earlier when we took a look at the rules related to Exam Objective 6.5, *Applying Encapsulation Principles to a Class*.

[98] https://docs.oracle.com/javase/8/docs/api/java/lang/StringBuilder.html

So far we were mostly passing primitives or objects of instantiable types to constructors except for Problem 6.28, which had to do with the interface type **List**. Here we meet an interface again; this time it is **CharSequence**.

The class **StringBuilder**[99] implements **CharSequence**; this is why any **StringBuilder** object is also a **CharSequence**, and since one of the **StringBuilder**'s constructors does accept a **CharSequence**, the code snippet in the ***Real World Scenario*** sidebar of the B&S Study Guide is perfectly valid.

Problem 6.35 – B

Given:

```
class A {
    static { System.out.print("Hello from"); }
    static String name = " A";
}
class B extends A{
    static { System.out.print(" B"); }
}
class C extends B {
    static { System.out.print(" C"); }
}

class Test {
    public static void main(String[] args){
        System.out.println(C.name);
    }
}
```

What is the result?

A. A
B. Hello from A
C. Hello from C A
D. Hello from B C A

We already know from the discussion to Problem 6.32 that static initers do not fire automatically when the class is accessed; they do it only under certain conditions. Here's another one of them (JLS, §12.4.1):

> A reference to a static field causes initialization of only the class or interface that actually declares it, even though it might be referred to through the name of a subclass, a subinterface, or a class that implements an interface.

This very condition is realized by the method **main()** who wants to access the var **name**, which is `static` and declared in the class **A**. On the other hand, were the var **name** an instance field and **main()**'s printing stat were accessing it through an object of type **C**, the program would have printed two more letters:

```
System.out.println(new C().name);        // Hello from B C A
```

---

[99] along with **String** and **StringBuffer**.

Problem 6.36 – E

    Given:

```
public class Test{

    public void testRefs(String str, StringBuilder sb){
        str = str + sb.toString();                    // line X
        sb.append(str);                               // XX
        str = null;                                   // XXX
        sb = null;                                    // XXXX
    }

    public static void main(String[] args){
        String str = "aaa";
        StringBuilder sb = new StringBuilder("bbb");
        new Test().testRefs(str, sb);
        System.out.println("str=" + str + " sb=" + sb);
    }
}
```

What is the result?

    A.   str=null sb=null
    B.   str=aaa sb=null
    C.   str=aaa sb=bbb
    D.   str=aaa sb=aaabbb
    E.   str=aaa sb=bbbaaabbb
    F.   Compilation fails
    G.   A NullPointerException is thrown at runtime

As Java is always pass-by-value, setting local references to whatever values (like `null` in our case) doesn't affect the caller. It's the method invocation on those pesky refs that does → lines XXX and XXXX are immaterial whereas line XX indeed comes into play. As for line X, it simply leads to the creation of a new object because of the immutability of **String**.

Chapter
II.7

EXAM OBJECTIVES – Group Seven:
Working with Inheritance

The 1Z0-808 objectives within this group:

7.1	Describe inheritance and its benefits;
7.2	Develop code that demonstrates the use of polymorphism, including overriding and object type *versus* reference type;
7.3	Determine when casting is necessary;
7.4	Use `super` and `this` to access objects and constructors;
7.5	Use abstract classes and interfaces

This Group of Exam Objectives is hugely important, as a good third of all exam questions is based on the aspects that have to do with inheritance and overriding. Moreover, given the fact that, starting from Java 1.8, interfaces may define three kinds of methods (`abstract`, `default` and `static`), mastering these Objectives becomes one of the most interesting – and toughest – tasks.

 CORE RULES (with some Extras):

7.1 <u>Describe inheritance and its benefits</u>:

❑ A Java class may inherit a single class only, with all classes eventually extending the class **java.lang.Object**, which has no parent.

❑ While Java does not allow true multiple inheritance, its limited form is emulated through interfaces because classes are allowed to implement multiple interfaces, each of which, in its own turn, may also extend multiple interfaces.

> <u>**Corollary**</u>: An interface `extends` an interface, while a class `extends` a class or `implements` an interface.

❑ Inheritance enables to reuse existing code by allowing a class to inherit the properties and behavior of another class; one of the most useful aspects of inheritance is polymorphism, which makes the code more flexible and dynamic.

❑ A `final` class cannot be extended.

❑ EXTRA: Below are some of the `final` core Java classes that are featured on the exam:

  ▪ **String**;

  ▪ **StringBuilder**[100];

---

[100] Its thread-safe cousin **StringBuffer** is `final`, as well.

- All primitive wrappers (namely, **Boolean**, **Character**, **Byte**, **Short**, **Integer**, **Long**, **Float**, and **Double**);

- All LDTs;

- **java.lang.System** is also `final`.

❑ A Java class that extends another class inherits all of its non-`private` members, although the package-`private` members can be accessed from inside the same package only[101].

  <u>**Corollary and known trap on the exam**</u>: `private` methods and `private` variables are not inherited.

❑ Be on alert for every class that defines all kinds of constructors except a no-arg one: its child will be locked out of the inheritance (we have already discussed it in more detail in Exam Objective 6.3).

❑ EXTRA: Constructors as well as `static` and instance initers aren't inherited.

---

[101] Official wording can be found in the JSL, §8.2, *Class Members*.

Problem 7.1 Given:

```
class One {
    public One(){
        System.out.print("1 "); }
}

class Two extends One{
    public Two(){                                    // line t1
        System.out.print("2 "); }
}

class Three extends Two{
    public Three(){                                  // line t2
        System.out.print("3 "); }
    public static void main(String[] args) {
        Three obj = new Three();
    }
}
```

What is the result?

A. 3
B. 1 2 3
C. 3 2 1
D. Compilation fails on line t1 and line t2

Problem 7.2

Which two are benefits of polymorphism?

A. More dynamic code at runtime
B. Faster code at runtime
C. More efficient code at runtime
D. More flexible and reusable code
E. Code that is protected from extension by other classes

Problem 7.3 Given the following classes:

```
class Ship {
    public int serviceLife;
}

class Starship extends Ship {
    public int shields;
}

class Enterprise extends Starship {
    public int warpSpeed;
}

public class ShipSpecs {
    public static void main(String[] args) {
        Ship ship = new Ship();
        Starship starship = new Starship();
        Enterprise enterprise = new Enterprise();
        // line XXX
    }
}
```

Which two LOCs fail to compile when inserted at line XXX?

    A. ship.serviceLife = 50;
    B. enterprise.serviceLife = 45;
    C. ship.shields = 10;
    D. starship.shields = 1000;
    E. starship.warpSpeed = 2;
    F. enterprise.warpSpeed = 12;

Problem 7.4 Given:

```
public abstract class Test { }
```

From which data type does the Java compiler implicitly derive the class Test?

    A. Object
    B. java.lang.Class
    C. An anonymous abstract class
    D. The interface Javable

Problem 7.5 Given:

```
class Parent{
    private boolean inherited = true;
    public boolean isInherited(){ return inherited; }
}

class Child extends Parent{
    public static void main(String[] args) {
        System.out.println(new Child().isInherited());
    }
}
```

Will the code print `true`?

    A. Yes
    B. No

7.2 <u>Develop code that demonstrates the use of polymorphism, including overriding and object type *versus* reference type</u>:

❑ An object may take on different forms, and its behavior will depend in part on the reference that points to the object. Unlike methods and variables that are hidden, overridden methods will be replaced by their overriding counterparts at the run time.

❑ Only inheritable methods can be overridden → `private` methods can be only hidden.

Different wording: Parent's `private` methods aren't polymorphic and bind at the compile time → the actype's version won't fire.

❑ EXTRA: Abstract methods can be overridden.

❑ <u>Essence of polymorphism through the exam taker's eyes</u>:

■ The version to be executed is selected according to the class of the actual object;

■ In Java, all non-`private` and non-`final` instance method calls are virtual and potentially polymorphic;

■ Polymorphism in Java is realized when child's method has the same name as in the parent class but its business logic differs from the overridden method.

❑ <u>Rules for method overriding</u>:

■ both methods must have the same signature,

■ the overriding method mustn't have a weaker access privilege,

■ the overriding method may not declare any new or wider ChE,

■ the return types must be at least covariant.

Corollary: The return type of the overriding method must match exactly the return type of the overridden method if the return type is a primitive.
If the methods return objects, the return type of the overriding method may be a subclass of the return type of the overridden method.

❑ EXTRA: `static` over non-`static` and *vice versa* ***between classes*** never compiles[102]:

```
class A {
    static void m1() {}
    void m2(){}
}
class B extends A{
    // void m1() {}            // INVALID: overridden method is static
    // static void m2(){}      // INVALID: overriding method is static
}
```

---

[102] It's about methods only; variables know no such restriction.

- <u>Actype</u>[103] *vs* <u>reftype</u>:

  - Actype – the type of the actual object at run time – determines which properties exist within the object in memory.

  - Reftype – the type of the reference to the object – specifies which methods and variables are accessible.

  Combat version: Reftype dictates what's available while actype says what runs.

  On the exam: See a new object? Assess its reftype first: it'll give you an idea what the object is capable of and what is out of its reach.

- Unlike methods, variables can't be overridden – but they can be HIDDEN[104]:

  - Which *variable* will be used depends on the reftype (RT), that is, the left-hand side of `RT obj = new AT();` where AT is a descendant of RT;

  - Which *method* will run depends on the actype (AT, right-hand side):

```
class A           { int i = 10;  int m1() { return i; } }
class B extends A { int i = 20;  int m1() { return i; } }
class C extends B { int i = 30;  int m1() { return i; } }
class Test{
    public static void main(String[] args){
        C o1 = new C();
        B o2 = o1;                      // reftype is B, actype is C
        System.out.println( o1.m1() );  // prints 30
        System.out.println( o2.i    );  // prints 20
    }
}
```

- EXTRA: When ancestor's var is not hidden and gets re-assigned in the descendant class, the var's value changes in the ancestor class, too.

  Corollary: Leads to a comperr if the var is `final`.

```
class Grandpa {
    // final String s = "Grandpa";     // won't let the code compile
    String s = "Grandpa";
}
class Parent extends Grandpa {  }
class Child extends Parent {
    void run(){
        s = "Child";                    // here s isn't hidden,
                                        // it is simply re-assigned
        System.out.println(s + " "
                + this.s + " "
                + super.s + " "
                + new Parent().s);      // Child Child Child Grandpa
    }
    public static void main(String[] args) {
        new Child().run();
    }
}
```

Were the var **s** `static`, the output would've been `Child Child Child Child`.

---

[103] For the record: the JLS has no notion of actype; this homebrew term is used throughout the book for the sake of brevity as it helps to make rules shorter and more easily memorizable.

[104] By declaring a var with the same name in a subclass.

❑ EXTRA: Polymorphism extends to constructors, as well[105]:

```
class Parent {
    Parent() { greet(); }
    void greet() {
        System.out.println(" Hello! ");   // prints null because greet() binds
                                           // to class Child and str at this
                                           // point still holds default value...
    }
}
class Child extends Parent {
    String str = " Hi! ";
    void greet() { System.out.print(str); }
    public static void main(String[] args){
        Parent obj = new Child();
        obj.greet();                       // ...and only now it prints Hi!
    }
}
```

In this example, the **Parent**'s no-arg constructor invokes the method **greet()**, which is virtual and, therefore, gets executed according to the overriding version. Since the **obj**'s actype is **Child**, the first call to **greet()** prints the default value of the var **str** and not the **String** " Hello! ", and only after the object has been fully initialized, the second call to the same method outputs " Hi! ".

Please also note that calling an overridable method from a constructor (like **Parent**'s ctor does) is bad coding practice as it invokes a method on an object that hasn't been properly constructed yet.

---

[105] Do appreciate the careful wording: the sentence doesn't say that constructors are polymorphic (after all, they aren't inherited); they do, however, let non-private and non-final instance methods exhibit their polymorphic nature.

EXERCISES (for Key Summary ref.to App.D):

Problem 7.6 Given two classes:

in the file ExamTaker.java:

```
package exam;
public class ExamTaker {
    String name;
    public ExamTaker(String name) { this.name = name; }
}
```

in the file Greeting.java:

```
package exam;
public class Greeting {
    public static void main(String[] args) {
        System.out.println("Hello " + new StringBuilder("Bob") + "!");
        System.out.println("Hello " + new ExamTaker("Bob") + "!");
    }
}
```

What is the result?

A. Hello Bob!
   Hello Bob!
B. Hello java.lang.StringBuilder@*<hashcode>*
   Hello exam.ExamTaker@*<hashcode>*
C. Hello Bob!
   Hello exam.ExamTaker@*<hashcode>*
D. Compilation fails

Problem 7.7 Given:

```
interface A {}
class B implements A {
    @Override
    public String toString() { return "Hello from B!"; }
    public static void main(String[] args) {
        C objC = new C();
        B objB = objC;
        A objA = objB;
        System.out.println(objA);
    }
}
class C extends B {
    @Override
    public String toString() { return "Hello from C!"; }
}
```

What is the reference type of objA and what is the actual type of the object this variable references?

A. Reference type is A; object type is A.
B. Reference type is C; object type is C.
C. Reference type is A; object type is C.
D. Reference type is C; object type is A.

Problem 7.8 Given:

```
abstract class Paint1 {
    abstract void m1();
    void m2() { System.out.print(" Red"); }
}
abstract class Paint2 extends Paint1 {
    public void m1() { System.out.print("Orange"); }
    protected void m2() { System.out.print(" Yellow"); }
    abstract void m3();
}
class Paint3 extends Paint2 {
    public void m1() { System.out.print("Green"); }
    protected void m2() { System.out.print(" Blue"); }
    void m3() { System.out.print(" Purple"); }
    public static void main (String[] args) {
        Paint2 p = new Paint3();
        p.m1();
        p.m2();
        p.m3();
    }
}
```

What is the result?

    A. Green Blue Purple
    B. Orange Yellow Purple
    C. Blue Red Purple
    D. Compilation fails

Problem 7.9 Given:

```
class A {
    void mA() { System.out.print("aaa"); }
}

class B extends A {
    protected void mA() { System.out.print("AAA"); }
    void mB() { System.out.print("BBB"); }
}

class Test {
    public static void main (String[] args) {
        final A ab = new B();
        B bb = (B) ab;                          // line t1
        bb.mB();
        ab.mA();                                // line t2
    }
}
```

What is the result?

    A. BBBAAA
    B. BBBaaa
    C. Compilation fails on line t1
    D. Compilation fails on line t2

Problem 7.10   Given:

```
1: public abstract class Tree {
2:     private void grow() {
3:         System.out.println("Tree is growing");
4:     }
5:     public static void main(String[] args) {
6:         Tree tree = new Oak();
7:         tree.grow();
8:     }
9: }
10: class Oak extends Tree {
11:    protected void grow() {
12:        System.out.println("Oak is growing");
13:    }
12: }
```

What is the result?

    A. Tree is growing

    B. Oak is growing

    C. Compilation fails on line 6

    D. Compilation fails on line 11

Problem 7.11   Given:

```
class Base{
//  int type = 0;                                    // line 1
    public void run(){};
}

class Derived extends Base{
    public Derived(){
//      int type = 10;                               // line 2
//      type = 10;                                   // line 3
    }
//    int type = 1;                                  // line 4

    public void run(){
        System.out.println("running type = " + this.type);
    }

    public static void main(String[] args){
        Base b = new Derived();
        b.run();
        System.out.println("type = " + b.type);
    }
}
```

The code is supposed to print

```
running type = 10
type = 0
```

Which LOC(s) should be uncommented to achieve the desired result?

    A. line 1

    B. line 2

    C. line 3

    D. line 4

7.3 Determine when casting is necessary:

❑ We use casting to make reference variable behave as a variable of another type when it becomes necessary to access certain members that are not available by default:

```
class Casting{
    public static void main(String[] args) {
        Object obj = new StringBuilder("Cast me plz... ");
//      obj.append("Done!");                           // INVALID
        ( (StringBuilder)obj ).append("Done!");
        System.out.println(obj);
    }
}
```

Let's recall a rule from the previous section: "Reftype dictates what's available while actype says what runs". Although the actual type of the object is **StringBuilder**, we cannot invoke on it the method **append()** because this particular method isn't available to **Object** → we need to cast the var **obj** from **Object** to **StringBuilder**.

❑ Rules of casting between reference types:

 ■ Widening (or upcast: subclass → superclass) doesn't need an explicit cast.

 ■ Narrowing (or downcast: subclass ← superclass) requires an explicit cast.

 Combat version: See no cast when reftype is narrower than actype? → comperr!

❑ Casting to unrelated types:

Lots and lots of study guides unconditionally insist that the compiler won't allow casts to unrelated types, period[106]. There's, however, an exception that concerns interfaces:

■ A cast between unrelated <u>class</u> types is *always* illegal... ← **important for the exam**

```
class Test1 {
    public static void main(String[] args) {
        Short sH = new Short("1");
//      Integer iN = (Integer) sH;     // class - class; INVALID
        Number nU = sH;
    }
}
```

■ EXTRA: Casting a non-final type[107] to unrelated *interface* type is *always* valid:

```
interface I1 {}
interface I2 {}
class Test2 {                          // Test ain't final otherwise comperr
    public static void main(String[] args) {
        Test2 t = new Test2();         // btw, t could be final
        I1 i1 = (I1) t;                // class - interface; throws CCE
        I2 i2 = (I2) i1;               // interface - interface; throws CCE
    }
}
```

---

[106] I admit, this will work for our OCA exam – but then you gonna be in a big trouble on 1Z0-809...

[107] In other words, non-final classes *plus* interfaces since interfaces are non-final by definition.

The class **Test1** in the preceding examples illustrates the compile-time error when we attempt to cast a **Short** to an **Integer**: although all wrapper classes extend the same parent type **Number**, they are unrelated to each other in terms of inheritance. The last statement works because **Short** is related to **Number** by being its child.

This clear and unambiguous picture cracks as soon as we cast a non-`final` type to an interface type as illustrated by the class **Test2**: despite the fact that all three data types are complete strangers to each other, both casts work. Naturally, there will be a CCE at run time, but as far as the compiler is concerned, everything is just peachy. It happens because the compiler assumes that on some sunny day either interface (or even both of them) might be implemented by a descendant of **Test2**.

Now you know what's going to happen should we declare **Test2** `final`: since the class cannot have children, the first cast immediately becomes illegal – and the second cast won't work without the first one…

Corollary: A cast between two unrelated interface types through a non-`final` class always compiles.

❏ Even after an explicit and valid cast the JVM may well throw a **CastClassException** at run time if the object being cast is not actually an instance of the target class:

```
class Parent {}
class Child extends Parent {}

class Test {
    public static void main(String[] args) {
        String s = "hello";
        Object o = s;
        StringBuilder sb = (StringBuilder) o;    // VALID but throws CCE

        Parent p = new Parent();
        Child c = (Child) p;                     // VALID but throws CCE
    }
}
```

The first cast in the above example compiles but the actype of the object **o** is **String** rather than **StringBuilder** → hence the types clash and produce a CCE at run time. Same sad story with the second cast…

On the other hand, we could make the references point to the same object, and then the downcast would run successfully:

```
class Parent{}
class Child extends Parent {
    public static void main(String[] args) {
        Parent p = new Parent();
        Child c = new Child();
        p = c;                              // if commented out, leads to CCE
        c = (Child) p;
    }
}
```

❏ EXTRA: Casting can be used not only to make certain fields or methods available to the refvar, but also to resolve an ambiguous reference:

```
interface I1{ int A = 10; }
interface I2{ int A = 20; }
```

```
class Test implements I1, I2{
    public static void main(String[] args) {
//      System.out.println( new Test().A );          // INVALID: "reference
                                                      // to A is ambiguous"
        System.out.println(  I1.A  );                 // prints 10
        System.out.println( ( (I1)new Test() ).A );   // prints 10
        System.out.println( ( (I2)new Test() ).A );   // prints 20
    }
}
```

Reminder: Another way to resolve an ambiguous reference is, of course, by specifying the fully qualified name (as illustrated by the first valid sout in the above example).

❑   EXTRA: Casting also helps to get hold of a carefully concealed member somewhere up the hierarchical chain:

```
class A {
    public String str = "Hello from A!";
}

class B extends A {
    private String str = "Hello from B!";
}

class C extends B{}

class Test{
    public static void main(String args[]){
        C c = new C();
//      System.out.println(c.str);              // INVALID
        System.out.println( ((A)c).str );       // Hello from A!
    }
}
```

Suppose, we want to access the var **str** declared in **A**. The first printing stat in this example fails miserably because the var **str** declared in **B** hides **A**'s **str**; more than that, **B**'s **str** is itself `private`. Even if it weren't `private`, we still wouldn't get the desired result due to hiding… A cast to **A** to the rescue!

In short, making a data type `final` can help protect its secrets… I suggest you play more with this example to see how – and if – it works when the classes are in different packages, and so on.

EXERCISES (for Key Summary ref.to App.D):

Problem 7.12   **Given the following method main():**

```
public static void main(String[] args) {
    Byte a1 = 100;
    Short a2 = 200;
    Long a3 = a1 + (long) a2;               // line m1
    String a4 = (String) (a3 + a2);         // line m2
    System.out.println("Result: " + a4) ;
}
```

What is the result?

A. Result: 500
B. Compilation fails on line m1
C. Compilation fails on line m2
D. Line m1 throws a ClassCastException
E. Line m2 throws a ClassCastException

Problem 7.13   **Given:**

In the file Plant.java:

```
public class Plant {
    public void run(){ System.out.println("Plant"); }
}
```

In the file Coffee.java:

```
public class Coffee extends Plant {
    public void run(){ System.out.println("Coffee"); }
}
```

In the file Java.java:

```
public class Java extends Coffee {
    public void run(){ System.out.println("Java"); }
    public static void main(String[] args) {
        Plant p1 = new Java();
        Plant p2 = new Coffee();
        Plant p3 = new Java();
        p1 = (Plant) p3;
        Plant p4 = (Coffee) p3;
        p1.run();
        p4.run();
    }
}
```

What is the result?

A. Plant
    Coffee
B. Plant
    Java
C. Java
    Java
D. Java
    Coffee
E. A ClassCastException is thrown at run time.

Problem 7.14   Given:

```
class Base {
    public static void main(String[] args) {
        Derived d = new Derived();
        Base b = new Base();

        // line X: insert code here

    }
}

class Derived extends Base { }
interface I{}
```

Which LOC, when inserted at line X, throws a ClassCastException?

A. d = b;
B. b = d;
C. d = (Object) b;
D. d = (I) d;
E. d = (Derived)(I) b;

Problem 7.15   Given:

```
1 class Jogger {
2     public static void main(String[] args) {
3
4         Jogger jogger = new Runner();
5         FitnessBuff runner = new Runner();
6
7         jogger.move();
8         (FitnessBuff)jogger.move();
9         ((FitnessBuff)jogger).move();
10        runner.move();
11        (FitnessBuff)runner.move();
12        ((FitnessBuff)runner).move();
13    }
14 }
15
16 class Runner extends Jogger implements FitnessBuff {
17     public void move() { System.out.println("Make way!"); }
18 }
19 interface FitnessBuff { public void move(); }
```

Which three LOCs compile and output Make way!?

A. Line 7
B. Line 8
C. Line 9
D. Line 10
E. Line 11
F. Line 12

Problem 7.16   Given:

```
class Parent {
    public static void main(String[] args) {
        Child c = new Child();
        Parent p = new Parent();
        p = c;
        System.out.print("p: " + p.getClass().getSimpleName() + ", ");
        System.out.println("c: " + c.getClass().getSimpleName());
    }
}

class Child extends Parent { }
```

What is the result?

    A. p: Object, c: Object
    B. p: Parent, c: Child
    C. p: Child, c: Parent
    D. p: Child, c: Child

Problem 7.17   Given:

```
interface Beverage { }
class Coffee implements Beverage { }
class Java extends Coffee { }
```

Which three statements will compile?

    A. Beverage obj = new Coffee();
    B. Beverage obj = new Beverage();
    C. Coffee obj = new Beverage();
    D. Coffee obj = new Java();
    E. Beverage obj = new Java();
    F. Java obj = new Coffee();

Problem 7.18

Suppose, the class Child extends the class Parent. Let's assume further that we have the following variable declarations:

```
Parent p = null;
Child c = null;
```

Which four LOCs compile?

    A. p = (Child) new Child();
    B. p = new Child();
    C. c = (Child) new Parent();
    D. c = new Parent();
    E. c = new Child(); p = c;
    F. p = new Parent(); c = p;

Problem 7.19   Given:

```
interface I { }

public class Parent implements I {
    public String toString() { return "P "; }
    public static void main(String[] args) {
        Child c = new Child();
        Parent p = c;
        I inter = p;
        System.out.print(p);
        System.out.print((Child)p);
        System.out.print(inter);
    }
}

class Child extends Parent {
    public String toString() { return "C "; }
}
```

What is the result?

    A. P P P
    B. P C P
    C. C C P
    D. C C C
    E. Compilation fails

Problem 7.20   Given:

```
class A { }
class B extends A { }
class Test{
    public static void main(String[] args){
        A[] a1 = {};
        A[] a2 = a1;
        B[] b = {};

        a1 = b;            // line t1
        b = (B[]) a1;      // line t2
        b = (B[]) a2;      // line t3
    }
}
```

Which two statements are true?

    A. Line t1 throws a compile-time error
    B. Line t2 throws a ClassCastException at run time
    C. Line t3 throws a ClassCastException at run time
    D. Line t2 fails compilation if the cast is removed

CORE RULES (with some Extras):

7.4 <u>Use `super` and `this` to access objects and constructors:</u>

❏ The keywords `super` and `this` are reference variables that are defined and initialized by the JVM itself for every object in its memory:

  ■ `this` always refers to the current object...

  ■ ... whereas `super` denotes the object's supertype;

  Known trap on the exam: Both `this` and `super` point to an instance → an attempt to access them from a `static` context such as `static` method, `static` initer or declaration of a `static` var throws a comperr.

❏ EXTRA: `super` and `this` point to the same object:

```
class Test{
    { if ( this.hashCode() == super.hashCode() )
        System.out.println("Same"); }            // prints Same
    public static void main(String[] args) {
        new Test();
    }
}
```

❏ `super` and `this` can be used to access variables, methods or constructors in the parent or child class, respectively (ctors require parentheses, though).

❏ EXTRA: `this` is `final` → e.g., `this = new Object();` throws a comperr.

❏ To call a constructor from another constructor, the form `this()` or `super()` is used.

  Known trap on the exam: `this()` or `super()` must be the first stat in a constructor's body → two such calls back to back throw a comperr.

❏ To access a shadowed var **x** within the same class, we use the form `this.x`, which is a typical idiom for constructors or methods that define a local var or an arg with the same name as an instance var:

```
class Test {
    private Object a, b;
    public Test(Object a, Object b) {
        this.a = b;
        this.b = b;
    }
    public void setField_a(Object a){ this.a = a; }
}
```

❏ To access a hidden var **x** in the superclass, we use `super.x`. It is also possible to invoke an overridden method by calling `super.methodName()`.

❏ <u>Reminders</u>: What is the difference between shadowing and hiding? And let's add obscuring for good measure...

JLS8, §6.4.1, *Shadowing*:

  Some declarations may be shadowed in part of their scope by another declaration of the same name, in which case a simple name cannot be used to refer to the declared entity.

Please take a good note of this bashful utterance: "some declarations". Does it mean that certain declarations cannot be shadowed in principle? Yes, it does; and first and foremost, these are local vars; even placing them into sub-blocks won't help. Consider the following example:

```
class Test {
    String str;                                 // line t1
    public static void main(String[] args) {
        String str;                             // t2
//      for (String str : args)                 // t3; INVALID
            System.out.println(str);
//      { String str; }                         // t4; INVALID
    }
}
```

While the local var **str** declared on line t2 successfully shadows the instance field with the same name declared on line t1, lines t3 and t4 throw a comperr – 'variable **str** is already defined in method **main(String[])**' – and the JLS explains why it happens:

> This restriction – a declaration of an identifier as a local variable of a method, constructor, or initializer block must not appear within the scope of a parameter or local variable of the same name – helps to detect some otherwise very obscure bugs. A similar restriction on shadowing of members by local variables was judged impractical, because the addition of a member in a superclass could cause subclasses to have to rename local variables.

The JLS continues by saying that

> Shadowing is distinct from *hiding*, which applies only to members which would otherwise be inherited but are not because of a declaration in a subclass.

Now to obscuring, which differs from shadowing and hiding:

> A simple name may occur in contexts where it may potentially be interpreted as the name of a variable, a type, or a package. In these situations, the rules of §6.5 specify that a variable will be chosen in preference to a type, and that a type will be chosen in preference to a package. Thus, it is may sometimes be impossible to refer to a visible type or package declaration via its simple name. We say that such a declaration is *obscured*.

Typical case of obscuring takes place when a type shares its same simple name with the package. We had a close encounter with obscuring while discussing Problem 1.21.

❑ EXTRA: Can a grandson **C** call his grandpa **A**'s method? Is `this.super.run()` possible? No, there is no way to go more than one level up for methods because `this` refers to an instance and not to a data type.

This problem, though, doesn't occur for instance variables because variables can never be overridden: they are hidden. So in order to access an ancestor's hidden var, we 'unhide' it by using a cast, such as `((A)c).var`, which gives us the var defined in **A** even if it is hidden by **B**.

As already mentioned, `super.methodName()` is a valid way to invoke a superclass' method from a subclass's instance method, instance initializer, constructor, or initializer of an instance var. But it works only for classes.

To invoke a superinterface's `default` method, we need to use the name of that interface, as well. This, however, is possible only when the interface is directly implemented – or extended – by the caller:

```
interface Laughable {
    default void getJoke(){ System.out.println("Ha-ha-ha!"); }
    static void makeJoke(){ System.out.println("A man walks into a bar..."); }
}

interface Coder extends Laughable {
    default void sayHello() {
//        super.getJoke();                // works for classes only
        Laughable.super.getJoke();
        Laughable.makeJoke();
    }
}

class JavaCoder implements Coder {
    public void sayHello() {
//        super.getJoke();                // JavaCoder's supertype isn't a class
        Laughable.makeJoke();
        Coder.super.sayHello();
    }
    public static void main(String[] args) {
        new JavaCoder().sayHello();
    }
}
```

Problem 7.21   Given:

```
public class Painter {
    int age = 20;
    Painter(int age) {
        this.age = age;
    }
}

public class Picasso extends Painter {
    int age;
    Picasso() {
        super();                           // line p1
        this(90);                          // line p2
    }
    Picasso(int age) { this.age = age; }   // line p3

    public String toString() {
        return super.age + " : " + this.age;
    }
    public static void main(String[] args) {

        // code fragment goes in here

    }
}
```

And given the code fragment:

```
Painter p = new Picasso();
System.out.println(p);
```

What is the result?

A. 20 : 90
B. Compilation error on line p1
C. Compilation error on line p2
D. Compilation error on line p3
E. Lines p1, p2 and p3 fail compilation

Problem 7.22   Given:

```
class OS {
    String name;
    OS(String name) {
        this.name = name;
    }
}

class Linux extends OS {
    int ver;
    Linux(String name, int ver) {

    // line L1

    }
}
```

And given the code fragment:

```
Linux os = new Linux("Ubuntu",16);
```

Which code fragment, when inserted at line L1, will instantiate the os object successfully?

A. ```
    super.name = name;
    this.ver = ver;
    ```

B.  ```
    super(name);
    this.ver = ver;
    ```

C. ```
    super(name);
    this(ver);
    ```

D.  ```
    this.ver = ver;
    super(name);
    ```

Problem 7.23   Given:

```
class Pokemon {
    String name;
    Pokemon(){
        this("Undefined");                  // line p1
    }
    Pokemon(String name) {
        this.name = name;
    }
}

class Pikachu extends Pokemon {
    String sound;
    Pikachu() {
        super("Pikachu");
        this("Squeak squeak!");             // line p2
    }
    Pikachu(String sound) {
        this.sound = sound;
    }
    public String toString() {
        return super.name + " says " + this.sound;
    }
}

class Test {
    public static void main(String[] args) {
        Pokemon p = new Pikachu();
        System.out.println(p);
    }
}
```

What is the result?

A. Pikachu says Squeak squeak!
B. Undefined says Squeak squeak!
C. Compilation fails on line p1
D. Compilation fails on line p2
E. Compilation fails on lines p1 and p2

Problem 7.24   Given:

```java
class Fish {
    public Fish() {
        System.out.println("Fish: swims");
    }
    public void getFish() {
        System.out.println("Fish: caught");
    }
}
class Marlin extends Fish {
    public Marlin() {
        super();
    }
    public Marlin(String arg) {
        System.out.println("Marlin: swims");
    }
    public void getFish() {
        super.getFish();
    }
    public void getFish(String arg) {
        System.out.println("Marlin: caught");
    }
}
class Hemingway {
    public static void main(String[] args) {
        // code goes here
    }
}
```

What code fragment, when inserted into the class Hemingway, will produce the following output?

Fish: swims
Marlin: caught
Fish: caught

A.   Marlin marlin = new Fish("Get the sucker!");
    marlin.getFish("Get the sucker!");
    marlin.getFish();

B.   Marlin marlin = new Marlin ("Get the sucker!");
    marlin.getFish();
    marlin.getFish("Get the sucker!");

C.   Marlin marlin = new Marlin();
    marlin.getFish();
    marlin.getFish("Get the sucker!");

D.   Marlin marlin = new Fish();
    marlin.getFish("Get the sucker!");
    marlin.getFish();

E.   Fish marlin = new Marlin();
    marlin.getFish();
    marlin.getFish("Get the sucker!");

F.   Marlin marlin = new Marlin();
    marlin.getFish("Get the sucker!");
    marlin.getFish();

CORE RULES (with some Extras):

7.5 Use `abstract` classes and interfaces:

❑ The keyword `abstract` is one of the non-access modifiers[108] that change the default properties of a Java class and its members.

❑ A class can be declared `abstract` even if it doesn't define any abstract methods.

❑ An abstract type cannot be instantiated and, therefore, requires a concrete subtype for the code to be used.

❑ An abstract method doesn't have a body but follows all the method overriding rules applicable to regular methods.

❑ The first concrete class that extends an abstract class must implement all the inherited abstract methods.

Corollary: Abstract classes and methods cannot be declared as `private` or `final`.

❑ An abstract class can extend a concrete class, and vice versa.

❑ An interface is an abstract type → can't be instantiated; **known trap on the exam!**

❑ In addition to abstract methods and `static final` variables (in other words, *constants*) that were allowed in interfaces prior to Java 1.8, now interfaces can also define `default` and `static` methods.

On the exam: As soon as you see a var declared in an interface, be on alert! The var is `final`!

Important Reminder: `final` reftypes behave differently from `final` primitives: it's only their references that are `final`, not the inner states.

Alternative wording: We can call methods on `final` refvars to change their fields; what's not allowed is re-assigning the reference itself:

```
import java.util.ArrayList;
import java.util.List;
class Test {
    public static void main(String[] args){
        final List<String> list = new ArrayList<>();
        list.add("Changed!");
        System.out.println(list);                    // prints [Changed!]
//        list = new ArrayList<>();                   // INVALID
    }
}
```

❑ All members of an interface are implicitly `public` ← **known trap on the exam!**

❑ Any interface method that is not explicitly marked as `default` or `static` is assumed to be `abstract`.

---

[108] Two more non-access modifiers featured on the 1Z0-808 exam are `final` and `static`.

- An interface cannot extend a class but can extend multiple interfaces.

- A subinterface inherits all the abstract and `default` methods declared in its superinterface(s).

- A class cannot extend an interface but can implement multiple interfaces thus achieving benefits of multiple inheritance.

- The `default` methods can be overridden, `abstract` method are meant to be overridden, and `static` methods cannot be overridden: they'll become hidden.

  On the exam: Overriding method can be `abstract` thus making the child class `abstract`. → It's a potential trap!

- EXTRA: `static` interface methods are useful for providing handy tools such as sorting, null checks, etc. → no need to define utility classes anymore.

- EXTRA: A `static` interface method can only be invoked by using its interface name.

  This rule – invocation of `static` interface methods through the interface name only – exists due to many reasons, and one of them is security as implementing classes cannot override these methods, otherwise the JVM would've simply run the actype's version as it does with classes.

  ```
  interface Inter { static void run(){ System.out.println("Inter"); } }

  class Test implements Inter{
      public void run(){ System.out.println("Test"); }
      public static void main(String[] args) {
          Inter t = new Test();
  //      t.run();                  // INVALID
          Inter.run();              // Inter
          ((Test)t).run();          // Test
      }
  }
  ```

  So how come we can call `static` methods declared in classes via object references and cannot do the same with interfaces? Answers Brian Goetz himself:

  > We consider the ability to invoke a static method through an instance to be a language design error, unfortunately one which we can't fix retroactively for classes[109].

- EXTRA: "Classes win over interfaces" (this one is also from Brian Goetz; covered in the discussion to Problem 7.34; just read on).

- EXTRA: Question: Are `static` methods inherited? Simple answer: "Yes" for classes and "No" for interfaces as per JLS8, §8.4.8, *Inheritance, Overriding, and Hiding*:

  - A class inherits from its direct superclass all concrete methods (both `static` and instance) of the superclass;

  - A class inherits from its direct superclass and direct superinterfaces all `abstract` and `default` methods;

---

[109] http://stackoverflow.com/questions/34709082/illegal-static-interface-method-call

Corollary: `default` methods may collide if not overridden:

```
interface I1 {
    default void run(){}
}

interface I2 {
    default void run(){}
}

// interface I3 extends I1, I2 {}      // INVALID

interface I4 extends I1, I2 {
    default void run(){}
}
```

- A class does not inherit `static` methods from its superinterfaces.

❑ **Reminder**: Just like classes, interfaces can also be inaccessible from outside their packages (it's only their members that are implicitly `public`) → so watch out if the code tries to peek into different packages:

```
package one;
interface Inter{}

1. package two;
2. import one.*;
3. class Test implements Inter{}   // INVALID: "Inter is not public in one,
                                   // cannot be accessed from outside package"
```

EXERCISES (for Key Summary ref.to App.D):

Problem 7.25   **Given the following classes:**

```
abstract class Programmer {
    protected void code() { }          // line 1
    abstract void debug();             // line 2
}

class JavaCoder extends Programmer {
    void code() { }                    // line 3
    protected void debug() { }         // line 4
}
```

Which two modifications, made independently, enable the code to compile?

    A.   Make the method on line 1 public.
    B.   Make the method on line 2 public.
    C.   Make the method on line 3 public.
    D.   Make the method on line 4 public.
    E.   Make the method on line 3 protected.

Problem 7.26   **Given:**

```
interface Flier {
    public void takeOff();
    public void land();
}

abstract class Plane implements Flier {    // line 1

                                           // line 2

    public void land() { }
}

class Boeing747 extends Plane {            // line 3

                                           // line 4

    public void land() { }
}
```

Which two modifications, made independently, enable the code to compile?

    A.   Replace line 1 with:
        `class Plane implements Flier {`
    B.   Insert at line 2:
        `public abstract void takeOff();`
    C.   Replace line 3 with:
        `abstract class Boeing747 extends Plane {`
    D.   Insert at line 4:
        `public void takeOff() { }`

Problem 7.27

Your enterprising teenage sister asked you to develop an inventory program for her tiny online shop, and after patiently listening to her incoherent, stumbled explanations you realize that the specifications boil down to this:

- The program must contain the classes **Dress**, **ReadyToWear**, and **HauteCouture**. The **Dress** class is the superclass of the other two classes.

- The `double calculatePrice(Dress d)` method should calculate the price of a dress. The `void showDress(Dress d)` method should output the full description of a dress.

Which definition of the class Dress can serve as a valid abstraction in the class hierarchy?

```
A.   public abstract class Dress{
         public abstract double calculatePrice(Dress d);
         public void showDress(Dress d) {
             // some valid code
         }
     }
B.   public abstract class Dress {
         public double calculatePrice(Dress d);
         public void showDress(Dress d);
     }
C.   public abstract class Dress {
         public double calculatePrice(Dress d);
         public final void showDress(Dress d) {
             // some valid code
         }
     }
D.   public abstract class Dress {
         public abstract double calculatePrice(Dress d) {
             // some valid code
         }
         public abstract void showDress(Dress d) {
             // some valid code
         }
     }
```

Problem 7.28   Given the following data type declarations:

```
interface SpaceCadet {}
abstract class Pilot {}
class CyberPilot extends Pilot implements SpaceCadet {}
class D2R2 extends CyberPilot {}

public class SpaceAcademy{
    public static void main(String[] args) {

        // code goes here                      // line XXX

    }
}
```

Which option(s), when inserted at line XXX, will fail compilation?

A. ArrayList<Pilot> alumni = new ArrayList<>();
   alumni.add(new D2R2());
B. ArrayList<SpaceCadet> alumni = new ArrayList<>();
   alumni.add(new CyberPilot());
C. ArrayList<SpaceCadet> alumni = new ArrayList<>();
   alumni.add(new D2R2());
D. ArrayList<D2R2> alumni = new ArrayList<>();
   alumni.add(new CyberPilot());
E. ArrayList<Pilot> alumni = new ArrayList<>();
   alumni.add(new Pilot());

Problem 7.29   Given:

```
public abstract class Test {
    private String test;
    public Test(String test) { this.test = test; }
    public void test() {}
    private void test2() {}
}
```

What is true about the class Test?

A. It fails compilation because an abstract class cannot have instance variables.
B. It fails compilation because an abstract class cannot have private members.
C. It fails compilation because an abstract class must have at least one abstract method.
D. It fails compilation because an abstract class must have an explicit no-arg constructor.
E. It compiles without error.

Problem 7.30

Which two statements are true?

A. An abstract class can implement an interface.
B. An abstract class can be extended by an interface.
C. An interface cannot be extended by another interface.
D. An interface can be extended by an abstract class.
E. An abstract class can be extended by a concrete class.
F. An abstract class cannot be extended by an abstract class.

Problem 7.31

Which one is valid?

A. public interface Diver { protected abstract void dive(); }
B. public abstract class ScubaDiver { protected void dive(); }
C. public abstract class ScubaDiver { protected final abstract void dive(); }
D. public abstract class ScubaDiver { protected abstract void dive(); }
E. public abstract class ScubaDiver { protected abstract void dive() {} }

Problem 7.32   Given:

```
interface I {
    public void doStuff();
}

abstract class A {
    public abstract void doStuff_A();
}
```

Which two options are valid?

    A.   `class B extends A implements I { public void doStuff_B() { } }`
    B.   `abstract class B extends A implements I { public void doStuff_B() { } }`
    C.   `class B extends A implements I { public void doStuff_A() { } }`
    D.   `abstract class B extends A implements I {}`
    E.   `class B extends A implements I { public void doStuff() { } }`

Problem 7.33   Given:

```
interface Money {
    int cash = 0;
    abstract void earn(int amount);
    public void spend(int amount);
}

class LocalCurrency implements Money {
    int cash = 100;
    public void earn(int amount) {
        cash = cash + amount;
    }
    public void spend(int amount) {
        cash = cash - amount;
    }
}

class UnderpaidJavaCoder {
    public static void main(String[] args) {
        Money m = new LocalCurrency();
        m.earn(5000);
        m.spend(200);
        System.out.println("What's left in his pocket: " + m.cash);
    }
}
```

How much money is left in this coder's pocket?

    A. 4900
    B. 4800
    C. 0
    D. -100
    E. -200

Problem 7.34   Given:

```
interface Inter{
    default void run(){ System.out.println("Inter");}
}

class Parent {
    public void run(){ System.out.println("Parent");}
}

class Child extends Parent implements Inter {
    public static void main(String[] args) {
        new Child().run();
    }
}
```

What is the result?

    A. Inter
    B. Parent
    C. Compilation fails
    D. Run-time error

 **Keys & Discussion:**

Problem 7.1 – B

> **Given:**
> ```
> class One {
>     public One(){
>         System.out.print("1 "); }
> }
> class Two extends One{
>     public Two(){                                  // line t1
>         System.out.print("2 "); }
> }
> class Three extends Two{
>     public Three(){                                // line t2
>         System.out.print("3 "); }
>     public static void main(String[] args) {
>         Three obj = new Three();
>     }
> }
> ```

What is the result?

> A. 3
> B. 1 2 3
> C. 3 2 1
> D. Compilation fails on line t1 and line t2

There's nothing wrong with lines t1 and t2: they simply declare public constructors for their respective classes, so option D is incorrect.

Option A is out of the question because the superclasses' constructors run before the object **obj** is initialized for the last time, and we have three constructors in total, which corresponds to three printing stats → we have to choose between options B and C.

Option C is incorrect since the constructors are called in the order of inheritance, starting from the base class.

Problem 7.2 – AD

> **Which two are benefits of polymorphism?**

> A. More dynamic code at runtime
> B. Faster code at runtime
> C. More efficient code at runtime
> D. More flexible and reusable code
> E. Code that is protected from extension by other classes

'Dynamic' here doesn't relate to the program execution progress; it's about the so-called dynamic binding, which occurs at run time in contrast to the static binding, which takes place at compile time. The dynamic binding is what makes polymorphism possible: the decision as to which version of a method should be executed is made according to the actual type of the object at run time.

As for option B, static dispatch is actually faster than virtual calls.

Option C is too broad, we don't even know what it refers to because the efficiency of code can be measured in terms of, say, memory footprint or CPU utilization ratio, etc. On a side note, I didn't meet any reference to 'code efficiency' on the real exam although all the study guides and prepware I know of mention it; so you are probably safe in this regard…

Option E is the exact opposite of what the OOP is all about.

Problem 7.3 – CE

Given the following classes:

```
class Ship {
    public int serviceLife;
}

class Starship extends Ship {
    public int shields;
}

class Enterprise extends Starship {
    public int warpSpeed;
}

public class ShipSpecs {
    public static void main(String[] args) {
        Ship ship = new Ship();
        Starship starship = new Starship();
        Enterprise enterprise = new Enterprise();
        // line XXX
    }
}
```

Which two LOCs fail to compile when inserted at line XXX?

    A.   ship.serviceLife = 50;
    B.   enterprise.serviceLife = 45;
    C.   ship.shields = 10;
    D.   starship.shields = 1000;
    E.   starship.warpSpeed = 2;
    F.   enterprise.warpSpeed = 12;

Both options that we need to tick off commit the same error: they attempt to access something that is not available to the object in question. For example, option C wants to set the value of the var **shields**, which is declared in the class **Starship** and, therefore, doesn't even exist in the superclass **Ship**. Similar story is with option E, where the code tries to set **warpSpeed**, which is declared in the last extending class only.

Problem 7.4 – A

Given:

```
public abstract class Test { }
```

From which data type does the Java compiler implicitly derive the class Test?

A. Object
B. java.lang.Class
C. An anonymous abstract class
D. The interface Javable

"Class **Object** is the root of the class hierarchy. Every class has **Object** as a superclass. All objects, including arrays, implement the methods of this class", says the documentation for the class **Object**.

Problem 7.5 – A

Given:

```
class Parent{
    private boolean in_memory = true;
    public boolean isIn_Memory(){ return in_memory; }
}

class Child extends Parent{
    public static void main(String[] args) {
        System.out.println(new Child().isIn_Memory());
    }
}
```

Will the code print true?

A. Yes
B. No

The JLS says that `private` members aren't inherited… Have you ever wondered what happens to `private` fields defined in the parent class? Will the child object contain them? or not? Common sense – and the OOP principles – dictate that those fields must be present inside the object even if they are 'non-inheritable'.

Apart from running the class **Child** and knowingly smiling at the result, another way to confirm validity of our logic is to serialize the object to a file and peek inside.

Step 1. Fill the file **Child.java** with the following code:

```
package org.xlator;
import java.io.Serializable;
import java.io.File;
import java.io.FileOutputStream;
import java.io.ObjectOutputStream;
import java.io.IOException;

class Parent implements Serializable {
    private String exam = "1Z0-808";
}
```

```
class Child extends Parent{
    public static void main(String[] args) {

// This is the object we are going to serialize:
        Child child = new Child();
// Specifying the file that'll represent our object on disk:
        String filename = "C:\\Experiments\\child.ser";
        File file = new File(filename);
// If the folder doesn't exist, create it:
        if (!file.getParentFile().exists()) file.getParentFile().mkdirs();
// Serializing now:
        try (
            FileOutputStream fos = new FileOutputStream(file);
            ObjectOutputStream out = new ObjectOutputStream(fos)
            )
        {   out.writeObject(child);
            System.out.println("Done!");
        } catch (IOException ioe) { ioe.printStackTrace(); };
    }
}
```

Comments:

1. To be serializable, the class should implement the interface **Serializable**.

2. The `try` block uses something that is not on our exam, namely the `try-with-resources` construct, which exists since Java 1.7 and is used for declaring resources that must be released back to the system when no longer needed (like file handles, sockets, etc.).

3. While the whole `import` block can be easily replaced with the `import java.io.*;` stat, you'd better stick to fully qualified names until you pass the exam.

Step 2. Execute the program and open **child.ser**:

```
Address  0  1  2  3  4  5  6  7  8  9  a  b  c  d  e  f  Dump
00000000 ac ed 00 05 73 72 00 10 6f 72 67 2e 78 6c 61 74  ¬í..sr..org.xlat
00000010 6f 72 2e 43 68 69 6c 64 4f 46 e3 cb c3 93 95 12  or.ChildOFãËÃ""•.
00000020 02 00 00 78 72 00 11 6f 72 67 2e 78 6c 61 74 6f  ...xr..org.xlato
00000030 72 2e 50 61 72 65 6e 74 cb 69 8e f2 07 ae c0 59  r.ParentËiŽò.®ÀY
00000040 02 00 01 4c 00 04 65 78 61 6d 74 00 12 4c 6a 61  ...L..examt..Lja
00000050 76 61 2f 6c 61 6e 67 2f 53 74 72 69 6e 67 3b 78  va/lang/String;x
00000060 70 74 00 07 31 5a 30 2d 38 30 38                 pt..1Z0-808
```

Our object does contain the sacred string "1Z0-808", which is only natural. The JLS specifies several conditions that must be met by a class member to be inheritable (§8.4.8, *Inheritance, Overriding, and Hiding*). As far as the exam is concerned, `private` members aren't inherited, and that's it. Think of them as being 'incorporated and encapsulated', if it helps…

Problem 7.6 – C

Given the file ExamTaker.java:

```
package exam;
public class ExamTaker {
    String name;
    public ExamTaker(String name) { this.name = name; }
}
```

Given the file Greeting.java:

```
package exam;
public class Greeting {
    public static void main(String[] args) {
        System.out.println("Hello " + new StringBuilder("Bob") + "!");
        System.out.println("Hello " + new ExamTaker("Bob") + "!");
    }
}
```

What is the result?

    A. Hello Bob!
        Hello Bob!
    B. Hello java.lang.StringBuilder@<*hashcode*>
        Hello exam.ExamTaker@<*hashcode*>
    C. Hello Bob!
        Hello exam.ExamTaker@<*hashcode*>
    D. Compilation fails

The problem is meant to remind us that although user-defined classes inherit **Object**'s method **toString()**, they should override the method to make it truly meaningful, and the following article[110] by Dustin Marx explains how it is to be done. The exam does contain such a question.

Problem 7.7 – C

Given:

```
interface A {}
class B implements A {
    @Override
    public String toString() { return "Hello from B!"; }
    public static void main(String[] args) {
        C objC = new C();
        B objB = objC;
        A objA = objB;
        System.out.println(objA);              // line b1
    }
}
class C extends B {
    @Override
    public String toString() { return "Hello from C!"; }
}
```

What is the reference type of objA and what is the actual type of the object this variable references?

    A. Reference type is A; object type is A.
    B. Reference type is C; object type is C.
    C. Reference type is A; object type is C.
    D. Reference type is C; object type is A.

The reftype denotes the type of the reference variable and, as dictated by Java syntax rules, is always on the left-hand side of the variable declaration.

---

[110] http://www.javaworld.com/article/2073619/core-java/java-tostring---considerations.html

The actype, or the actual object type, is determined by the constructor placed on the right-hand side of the declaration.

In our case, the object **objA** is none other but **objC** whose actype is **C**, which can be verified by replacing line b1 with the following stat:

```
System.out.println(objA.getClass().getSimpleName());    // prints C
```

The @Override annotation might not appear on the exam but is considered a good programming practice.

The code compiles without explicit casts because **B** is broader than **C** and **A** is broader than **B**. There's no **ClassCastException** at run time because the IS-A relationship between **C** and **B** as well as between **B** and **A** holds true. In contrast, the next code snippet needs an explicit cast for the last assop because **Object** is wider than **Short**, and throws a CCE since the IS-A test between **obj** and the data type of **sH** produces false:

```
StringBuilder sb = new StringBuilder("");
Object obj = sb;
System.out.println(obj instanceof Short);        // false
Short sH = (Short) obj;                           // VALID but throws CCE
```

And finally, the code in the current Problem 7.7 prints "Hello from C!" since the method **toString()** is non-private and non-static and, therefore, polymorphic → the class **C**'s version of the overridden **toString()** runs because it is the actype that dictates which version to call, and the actual object type is **C**.

Problem 7.8 – A

Given:

```
abstract class Paint1 {
    abstract void m1();
    void m2() { System.out.print(" Red"); }
}
abstract class Paint2 extends Paint1 {
    public void m1() { System.out.print("Orange"); }
    protected void m2() { System.out.print(" Yellow"); }
    abstract void m3();
}
class Paint3 extends Paint2 {
    public void m1() { System.out.print("Green"); }
    protected void m2() { System.out.print(" Blue"); }
    void m3() { System.out.print(" Purple"); }
    public static void main (String[] args) {
        Paint2 p = new Paint3();
        p.m1();
        p.m2();
        p.m3();
    }
}
```

What is the result?

A. Green Blue Purple
B. Orange Yellow Purple
C. Blue Red Purple
D. Compilation fails

The abstract method **m1()** is correctly overridden in **Paint2** (its access modifier is `public`) while the package-`private` **m2()** is also correctly overridden with the `protected` **m2()**. As for the `abstract` **m3()**, it is overridden in **Paint3** with a method with the same access privilege, which is valid, too. The object **p** is declared of type **Paint2** → all the methods from **m1()** through **m3()** are therefore available to the object so the code compiles successfully.

All three methods are non-`private` and non-`static`, hence polymorphic → they all are selected according to the actype, which is **Paint3** → the code prints Green Blue Purple.

If you are still confused as to what polymorphic means, look in the mirror. Or imagine that a Java object is made of flesh and blood and makes its living as a deep-cover secret agent known to ordinary citizens as humble Mr.Brown the accountant (the reftype), whereas his true self is, say, James Bond IV (the actype). If we were to ask Mr.Brown to shoot a fly in the eye while piloting an attack helicopter, he would flatly refuse saying that no accountant can be reasonably expected to know how to do such things. However, should we appeal to his true nature and order him to smite the wrongdoers in the name of Queen and Country, all hell would break loose… Same person, different social roles depending on the circumstances.

Problem 7.9 – A

Given:

```
class A {
    void mA() { System.out.print("aaa"); }
}

class B extends A {
    protected void mA() { System.out.print("AAA"); }
    void mB() { System.out.print("BBB"); }
}

class Test {
    public static void main (String[] args) {

        final A ab = new B();
        B bb = (B) ab;                          // line t1
        bb.mB();
        ab.mA();                                // line t2
    }
}
```

What is the result?

A. BBBAAA
B. BBBaaa
C. Compilation fails on line t1
D. Compilation fails on line t2

The modifier `final` does nothing useful; it sits there just to confuse you although there are plenty of cases when disregarding it can be fatal – particularly when it's implicit as in interfaces.

The cast on line t1 is needed because the object **ab** is of type **A**, and **A** is wider than **B**.

We can formulate a simple practical rule that says when an assignment works without an explicit cast:

LEFT-HAND SIDE CAN'T BE NARROWER THAN RIGHT-HAND SIDE

In practice, especially when dealing with collections, it is recommended to use interface type on the left because this way it becomes much easier to switch between different implementations of the same interface:

```
List list = new ArrayList();
```

can be readily replaced with `List list = new LinkedList();` and so on.

A narrower type on the left-hand side mandates the use of explicit cast but can throw a CCE:

```
Specialist spec = (Specialist) new Generalist();    // throws CCE at RT
```

Let's consider the following example:

```
interface HasTail {};
class Mammal {}
class Whale extends Mammal implements HasTail {
    public static void main(String[] args) {
        List<Whale> l = new ArrayList<>();         // line w1
        l.add( new Whale() );                      // line w2
        l.add( new Narwhal() );                    // line w3
        l.add( null );                             // line w4
        l.add( (Whale)new Mammal() );              // line w5
        l.add( (Narwhal)new Object() );            // line w6
//      l.add( new HasTail() );                    // line w7; INVALID
    }
}
class Narwhal extends Whale {}
```

The reftype **List** on line w1 says **l** will accept only **Whale** or its subtypes – and we feed it appropriate objects on lines w2 and w3.

`null` is added to the list on line w4 just to remind us that `null` is perfectly valid value for a reference data type.

Line w5 needs an explicit cast because **Mammal** is wider than **Whale** + it throws a **ClassCastException**; similar story with line w6. As for line w7, it shouldn't have asked for instantiation because **HasTail** is an interface, which is `abstract` by definition.

Coming back to Problem 7.9, we can see that line t1 won't throw a CCE since **bb**'s reftype and actype are both **B**. The method **mB()** is declared in the class **B** and, therefore, is available to **bb**. **mA()** is declared in **A**, which means it's available to **ab**; what's more, this method gets overridden in **B**, and since **ab**'s actype is also **B**, line t2 outputs AAA... Are you still with me?

Problem 7.10 – A

Given:

```
1: public abstract class Tree {
2:     private void grow() {
3:         System.out.println("Tree is growing");
4:     }
5:     public static void main(String[] args) {
6:         Tree tree = new Oak();
7:         tree.grow();
8:     }
9: }
```

```
10: class Oak extends Tree {
11:    protected void grow() {
12:        System.out.println("Oak is growing");
13:    }
12: }
```

What is the result?

    A. Tree is growing
    B. Oak is growing
    C. Compilation fails on line 6
    D. Compilation fails on line 11

Line 6 is valid because the data type **Tree** is wider than **Oak**, so no cast is needed.

Line 11 doesn't throw a comperr, either, since the `protected` access privilege is much less restrictive than the `private` one, so the method **grow()** is overridden correctly… Right? am I right or what? hello-o?..

Hopefully, you caught me red-handed even before I started dropping hints right and left: the rules of method overriding aren't even applicable here because the method **grow()** in **Tree** is `private`, hence not inherited → from which follows it doesn't participate in polymorphism → the reftype's version of **grow()** runs regardless of the actype.

Problem 7.11 – ACD

    Given:

```
class Base{
//     int type = 0;                                   // line 1
    public void run(){};
}

class Derived extends Base{
    public Derived(){
//     int type = 10;                                  // line 2
//     type = 10;                                      // line 3
    }
//     int type = 1;                                   // line 4

    public void run(){
        System.out.println("running type = " + this.type);
    }
    public static void main(String[] args){
        Base b = new Derived();
        b.run();
        System.out.println("type = " + b.type);
    }
}
```

The code is supposed to print

    running type = 10
    type = 0

Which LOC(s) should be uncommented to achieve the desired result?

    A. line 1
    B. line 2
    C. line 3
    D. line 4

The printing stats want to access the variable named **type** but all its declarations are commented out so the code doesn't even compile → first of all, we need to declare the var properly. But where?

We have three choices: declare **type** in **Base** or in **Derived** or do it in both places, in which case **Derived**'s **type** will hide its namesake in **Base**. So, which one is appropriate? That's a tough call.

Alright, now it's probably a good idea to recall how inheritance treats variables: they are not overridden but hidden.

It's because variables are not polymorphic. When the compiler maps virtual method calls, it doesn't know neither cares what's inside those methods leaving it to the JVM to sort them out, so when the JVM starts executing a method that makes use of a field, it grabs the field that exists inside the *actual* object at the execution time, which is, in our parlance, `this`.**someField**. Note, however, that access to this very field via reference that is *not* wrapped up in a virtual method is always performed regardless of the run-time type of the object.

All the **type**-related declarations in **Derived** mention values other than zero, while the last printing stat must output exactly zero → the declaration in the class **Base** must be uncommented → option A is in; this definitely makes the code compile but it prints zeroes in both cases.

Now let's take a careful look at **Derived**. What will happen if we uncomment line 2? This line declares a local var whose scope is limited to the constructor → whatever we do with it won't affect the output → by the same token, uncommenting line 2 and 3 together is also useless → option B is definitely out.

So far so good; what's going to happen if we uncomment line 3? The constructor will assign 10 to it and... oh no! since the var isn't hidden, its value will propagate to **Base** thus making the code print 10 in both cases...

Let's uncomment line 4 instead of line 3, then. The var gets hidden, so **run()** prints the value that exists in `this` – namely, 1 – whereas the printing stat in **main()** outputs the value according to the reftype, that is zero... Damn! missed again.

Grasping at the last straw, we uncomment both line 3 *and* 4. Let's see: the var is shadowed, the constructor inits it to ten, **run()** prints it out and... There! Feeling dizzy yet?

Problem 7.12 – C

> **Given the following method main():**
>
> ```
> public static void main(String[] args) {
>     Byte a1 = 100;
>     Short a2 = 200;
>     Long a3 = a1 + (long) a2;          // line m1
>     String a4 = (String) (a3 + a2);    // line m2
>     System.out.println("Result: " + a4) ;
> }
> ```
>
> **What is the result?**
>
> A. Result: 500
> B. Compilation fails on line m1
> C. Compilation fails on line m2
> D. Line m1 throws a ClassCastException
> E. Line m2 throws a ClassCastException

Line m1 unboxes a **Short** and casts it to a primitive `long`; then there's a rule (JLS §5.6.2) that says that "if either operand is of type `long`, the other is converted to `long`", after which the resulting primitive is converted to **Long**. All in all, this LOC is perfectly valid.

On the other hand, line m2 performs unboxing of a **Short** and a **Long**, converts the primitive `short` to `long` and then attempts to cast the resulting `long` to **String**, which is illegal as `long` is incompatible with **String** → a comperr on line m2.

Problem 7.13 – C

Given:

In the file **Plant.java**:

```
public class Plant {
    public void run(){ System.out.println("Plant"); }
}
```

In the file **Coffee.java**:

```
public class Coffee extends Plant {
    public void run(){ System.out.println("Coffee"); }
}
```

In the file **Java.java**:

```
public class Java extends Coffee {
    public void run(){ System.out.println("Java"); }
    public static void main(String[] args) {
        Plant p1 = new Java();
        Plant p2 = new Coffee();
        Plant p3 = new Java();
        p1 = (Plant) p3;               // line j1
        Plant p4 = (Coffee) p3;        // line j2
        p1.run();
        p4.run();
    }
}
```

What is the result?

A. Plant
   Coffee
B. Plant
   Java
C. Java
   Java
D. Java
   Coffee
E. A ClassCastException is thrown at run time.

By looking at the available options, we can see immediately that the code compiles, which means the method **run()** is properly overridden and accessible in all cases. What's left is to figure out what it prints or, possibly, throws.

The object **p1**'s reftype is **Plant**, **p3** is a **Plant**, too → the cast on line j1 is actually redundant. More than that, the LOC doesn't throw a CCE because either object's actype is **Java**.

Line j2 explicitly casts **p3** whose reftype is **Plant** to a narrower **Coffee**, which is valid, and after that the 'narrowed' object gets assigned back to a wider **Plant** → no comperr. But does it throw a CCE? The answer is "No" since **p3**'s actype is **Java** and **Java** IS-A **Plant**.

Now we apply the rule that says that polymorphic methods are selected at run time according to the actype of the object on which the method is invoked → both **p1**'s and **p4**'s actype is **Java** → the same method defined in **Java** gets called in either case.

Problem 7.14 – E

Given:

```
class Base {
    public static void main(String[] args) {
        Derived d = new Derived();
        Base b = new Base();

        // line X: insert code here


    }
}

class Derived extends Base { }
interface I{}
```

Which LOC, when inserted at line X, throws a ClassCastException?

    A. d = b;
    B. b = d;
    C. d = (Object) b;
    D. d = (I) d;
    E. d = (Derived)(I) b;

What follows, borders on heresy and is not endorsed by any study guide or tutorial – least of all by the JLS – but I found out that this homebrew approach helps see if a LOC generates a CCE.

Let's start by introducing a new notion of the so-called 'castype'. We know what the reftype and actype mean, but what on earth is a castype? It's the 'casting' data type, the one we write inside the parentheses when asking the compiler to perform a cast, e.g.:

    Son = (Father) Grandfather   // INVALID, though, as Father is wider than Son...

In the above example **Father** is the castype[111]. Now we can formulate a new combat-grade rule:

Any explicit cast throws a CCE unless actype IS-A castype (working out R to L)

Sounds cryptic; we need to see how it works.

Suppose, we have three classes along a single inheritance chain: the base type is **A**; **B** extends **A**, and **C** is the subtype of **B**. I suggest we write it down this way: **A ← B ← C**. Yes, the widest type goes to the left thus reflecting a generic comperr-free casting scenario.

---

[111] One more time and for the record: this 'castype' thingy does NOT exist in Java; it's just a handy trick to solve exam questions both reliably and quickly, that's all.

So, $\mathbf{A} \leftarrow \mathbf{B} \leftarrow \mathbf{C} \wedge$ C c = new C(); $\Rightarrow$ [112]

```
A a = c;         // VALID as A is wider than C
B b = (B) a;     // VALID + won't throw CCE since a's actype is now C and C IS-A B
```

Once again: in the above example the actype of **a** is **C**, which IS-A castype **B** $\rightarrow$ no CCE. The rule holds.

Let's make life more interesting by adding an interface; most likely, you won't have a problem deciphering the following shorthand notation:

$$\langle I \rangle \leftarrow \mathbf{A} \leftarrow \mathbf{B} \leftarrow \mathbf{C}$$

It says that the class **A** implements the interface **I**, then class **B** extends **A** and class **C** extends **B**. The angle brackets (a.k.a. chevrons) denote an interface: this way we won't forget that the data type **I** cannot be instantiated, while **A**, **B** and **C** can. By the way, **A**, **B** and **C** are concrete classes; for abstract classes I use the caret, e.g.:

$$\langle I \rangle \leftarrow \hat{\mathbf{S}} \leftarrow \hat{\mathbf{W}} \leftarrow \hat{\mathbf{Y}}$$

Fine; so $\langle I \rangle \leftarrow \mathbf{A} \leftarrow \mathbf{B} \leftarrow \mathbf{C} \wedge$ A a = new A(); B b = new B(); $\Rightarrow$

```
a = (A)(I) b;       // B is-a I, is-a A, hence no CCE
a = (B)(I) b;       // B is-a I, is-a B, hence no CCE
b = (B)(A)(I) c;    // C is-a I, is-a A, is-a B, hence no CCE
```

However, these are problematic:

```
b = (B) (I) a;      // A is-a I but not is-a B, hence CCE
// a = (I) b;       // INVALID: A is narrower than I
I i = (C) a;        // A ain't is-a C, hence CCE
```

And how about the following one?

```
A huh = (B)(I)(B)(A)(C)(B)(A)(I) b;
```

Diligently working it out R to L (right to left), we get **B** is-a **I** is-a **A** is *per se* **B** is-a… wait a sec! no way **B** is-a **C**! $\rightarrow$ CCE at the point of casting to **C**.

After the offending cast is removed, our weirdish code runs without as much as a peep:

```
interface I{}
class A implements I{}
class B extends A{}
class C extends B{}

class Casting{
    public static void main(String[] args) {
        A a = new A();
        B b = new B();
        C c = new C();

// *** these are CCE-free ****
        a = (A)(I) b;
        a = (B)(I) b;
        b = (B)(A)(I) c;
// ***************************

// uncomment these LOCs in turns after
// commenting out the previous section
```

---

[112] *"If* **A** $\leftarrow$ **B** $\leftarrow$ **C** *and* **C** c = new **C**(); *then"*

```
//          b = (B)(I) a;        // CCE @ A -> B
//          a = (I) b;           // INVALID
//          I i = (C) a;         // CCE @ A -> C

//          A huh = (B)(I)(B)(A)(C)(B)(A)(I) b;   // CCE @ B -> C
//          A huh = (B)(I)(B)(A)   (B)(A)(I) b;    // this time no CCE
    }
}
```

Now it should be fairly easy to solve our little Problem 7.14:

Option A assigns wider **Base** to a narrowed **Derived** → comperr.

Option B does the opposite → no comperr and no CCE since **Derived** IS-A **Base**.

Option C casts **Base** to even wider **Object** and then assigns it to the much narrower **Derived** → comperr.

Option D casts **Derived** to a completely unrelated **I** but this is allowed since the compiler assumes that some descendant of **Derived** might implement **I** in the future, so the cast is valid. However, **I** – which is now being treated as a provisional supertype and is, therefore, pretty wide, – then gets assigned to the narrower **Derived** → comperr.

And finally, since option E additionally downcasts **I** to **Derived** and then assigns the result again to **Derived**, there's no comperr but a CCE at the point when **Base** gets converted to **I**.

Problem 7.15 – CDF

> **Given:**
>
> ```
> 1 class Jogger {
> 2     public static void main(String[] args) {
> 3
> 4         Jogger jogger = new Runner();
> 5         FitnessBuff runner = new Runner();
> 6
> 7         jogger.move();
> 8         (FitnessBuff)jogger.move();
> 9         ((FitnessBuff)jogger).move();
> 10        runner.move();
> 11        (FitnessBuff)runner.move();
> 12        ((FitnessBuff)runner).move();
> 13    }
> 14 }
> 15
> 16 class Runner extends Jogger implements FitnessBuff {
> 17     public void move() { System.out.println("Make way!"); }
> 18 }
> 19 interface FitnessBuff { public void move(); }
> ```
>
> **Which three LOCs compile and output** Make way!?
>
>   A. Line 7
>   B. Line 8
>   C. Line 9
>   D. Line 10
>   E. Line 11
>   F. Line 12

This problem builds on the previous one, wherein we met an interface that was completely unrelated to class types. This time, however, one of the classes does implement an interface.

Let's start by taking a brief look at a somewhat simpler example that doesn't employ casts:

```
interface Flyer{ }

class Bird implements Flyer { }
class Eagle extends Bird { }

class Insect { }
class Dragonfly extends Insect implements Flyer {}

class Test {
    public static void main(String[] args) {
        Flyer fe = new Eagle();
        Eagle ee = new Eagle();
        Insect id = new Dragonfly();
        Insect ii = new Insect();

        if(fe instanceof Flyer) System.out.println("fe is a Flyer");   // line t1
        if(ee instanceof Bird) System.out.println("ee is a Bird");     // line t2
//       if(id instanceof Bird) System.out.println("id is a Bird");    // line t3
        if(id instanceof Flyer) System.out.println("id is a Flyer");   // line t4
        if(ii instanceof Flyer) System.out.println("ii is a Flyer");   // line t5
    }
}
```

The operator `instanceof` isn't on our exam but is quite helpful when studying casting and CCE-throwing scenarios. Here's a number of more or less compact rules that govern the use of `instanceof`:

- `instanceof` works with reference types only; using it with a primitive throws a comperr;
- `instanceof` throws a comperr if the left-hand operand cannot be converted to the right-hand one;
- unless the class is `final`, neither cast to nor `instanceof` an interface type throws a comperr;
- `instanceof` always produces `false` unless the left-hand side[113] isn't `null` and could be cast to the right-hand side (a.k.a. ReferenceType) without raising a CCE.

Please also note the convention used to name the objects: the first letter denotes the reftype and the second one, the actype (e.g., **fe** means RT==Flyer and AT==Eagle). This way it is easier to recall which is which when looking at the output.

Our example uses a 'dendritic' inheritance structure to which the simple shorthand notation from the previous problem cannot be applied; nothing to do but resort to drawing:

```
    <Flyer>
     / \
 Bird  \  Insect
   |    \   |
 Eagle   Dragonfly
```

Line t1 tests if the object **fe** is an instance of **Flyer**; our diagram shows that it is, so there's no comperr and no CCE → this LOC prints `fe is a Flyer`.

Line t2 looks at **ee** – while we look at our diagram: yes, this object IS-A **Bird**, so we get `ee is a Bird` printed.

By continuing checking the other tests against the diagram, we arrive at the conclusion that line t3 must throw a comperr since **Insect** cannot be converted to **Bird**; as for line t4, it is not only valid as **Dragonfly** IS-A **Flyer** but also doesn't throw a CCE for exactly same reason.

There's no comperr on line t5 because **Insect** isn't `final` and the compiler knows that any non-`final` class can theoretically have a descendant that will implement any interface in the future. But since casting **Insect** to **Flyer** does produce a CCE, the `if` stat evaluates to `false` and this LOC outputs nothing.

Getting back to our Problem 7.15. Line 7 attempts to invoke the method **move()** on the object **jogger** whose reftype is **Jogger** – and fails miserably because this method is available only to the class that either defines it or at least implements the interface **FitnessBuff**, in other words the class **Runner**, and **Jogger** ain't **Runner** → option A is out.

Line 8 does have a cast, but this cast is misplaced and doesn't help rectify the problem we encountered on line 7 thus leading to a comperr → option B is out, too.

On the contrary, option C correctly widens **jogger** to the interface type thus making **run()** available to the object, and since this cast doesn't throw a CCE (for **jogger**'s actype is **Runner**, which does implement **FitnessBuff**), we see the LOC output "Make move!".

Line 10 is trivial: it invokes a method that is available to the reftype **Runner** on the object whose actype is also **Runner** → neither comperr nor CCE, and the LOC prints what it's supposed to.

Option E resembles line 8 in its misguided attempt to cast to **FitnessBuff** whatever the method **move()** returns, so this LOC fails: it wouldn't be a syntactically correct statement even if the method weren't `void` in the first place.

As for option F, it doesn't differ much from line 10; it just casts a **Runner** object to the interface type, and then runs the same method → option F is correct.

Problem 7.16 – D

> **Given:**
>
> ```
> class Parent {
>     public static void main(String[] args) {
>         Child c = new Child();
>         Parent p = new Parent();
>         p = c;
>         System.out.print("p: " + p.getClass().getSimpleName() + ", ");
>         System.out.println("c: " + c.getClass().getSimpleName());
>     }
> }
> class Child extends Parent { }
> ```
>
> **What is the result?**
>
> A. p: Object, c: Object
> B. p: Parent, c: Child
> C. p: Child, c: Parent
> D. p: Child, c: Child

---

[113] To be exact, its full name is *RelationalExpression* operand.

After what we have been through on the previous pages, this problem can be solved in a snap. I included it here mostly to remind you that **java.lang** contains the class **Class**, which might be useful when learning inheritance with all its quirks (for example, it contains **getFields()** and **getMethods()**, which can give you all the `public` methods and variables accessible to the data type in question; there's also **getClasses()**, which returns an array with all the interfaces and `public` classes that are members of the object represented by `this`, and so forth).

As for the answer to Problem 7.16, it is option D because both objects' actype is **Child**.

Problem 7.17 – ADE

Given:

```
interface Beverage { }
class Coffee implements Beverage { }
class Java extends Coffee { }
```

Which three statements will compile?

    A.   Beverage obj = new Coffee();
    B.   Beverage obj = new Beverage();
    C.   Coffee obj = new Beverage();
    D.   Coffee obj = new Java();
    E.   Beverage obj = new Java();
    F.   Java obj = new Coffee();

Since we see no casts, all we have to do is apply the rule that says that a comperr-free assignment LOC should have a valid and wider left-hand side.

Now, why mention 'wider' while, in fact, a valid data type of the *same* width would be perfectly legal, too?

Let's ask ourselves: what is exactly the 'valid data type of the same width'? Since we are dealing with reference types, any attempt to assign an incompatible type throws a comperr → the only *valid* type of the *same* width is the very same type we have on the right-hand side; so why memorize rules that pedantically proclaim that something as trivial as A = A always compiles? Waste of time and mental resources…

By the way, the popular term 'covariant types', strictly speaking, is not applicable here because the JLS speaks only of covariant *return* types, which are "the specialization of the return type to a subtype".

Alright, alright; let's just state for the record that the right-hand type should be assignable to the left-hand one.

Now to 'valid'; this one seems redundant… unless we take into account our ultimate goal: passing the exam. Which means we should be always on alert for potential traps, and 1Z0-808 features at least one question that wants to instantiate an interface. It is awfully easy to miss an invalid stat inside a list of similarly structured and harmlessly-looking, even naive LOCs…

So what we have here is this:

    Beverage is wider than **Coffee** → option A is correct;
    Options B and C are out because **Beverage** is an interface and cannot be instantiated;
    Coffee is narrower that **Beverage** → this LOC needs an explicit cast;
    Coffee is wider than **Java** → option D is correct;
    Beverage is wider than **Java** → option E is also correct;
    Java is narrower than **Coffee** → an explicit cast is missing.

Problem 7.18 – ABCE

Suppose, the class Child extends the class Parent. Let's assume further that we have the following variable declarations:

```
Parent p = null;
Child c = null;
```

Which four LOCs compile?

    A.   p = (Child) new Child();
    B.   p = new Child();
    C.   c = (Child) new Parent();
    D.   c = new Parent();
    E.   c = new Child(); p = c;
    F.   p = new Parent(); c = p;

Hm… What's the story with those `nulls`? are they important? do they affect compilation?

Recalling the list of NPE-throwing scenarios[114], we can see that none of The Magnificent Five is at work here – which means we need to be careful about assignments and *implicit* casts only since the question doesn't even mention CCE. As for potential problems with instantiation, we are safe because interfaces are not involved.

Very well then; option A creates an instance of **Child**, redundantly casts it to **Child** again and then assigns the object to a wider type → the LOC compiles.

Option B does the same thing but without the cast.

Option C creates a **Parent** object and assigns it to the narrower **Child**; this is valid because of the explicit cast although there will be a CCE at RT. The 'castless' option D doesn't work.

Option E assigns a completely new **Child** object to **c** then re-assigns it to the wider **Parent** represented by the object **p**. There's also no CCE at RT.

The similarly constructed option F is illegal because its second stat tries to assign a wider **Parent** object to the var that is of the narrower type **Child**.

Problem 7.19 – D

Given:

```
interface I { }
public class Parent implements I {
    public String toString() { return "P "; }
    public static void main(String[] args) {
        Child c = new Child();                 // line p1
        Parent p = c;                          // line p2
        I inter = p;                           // line p3
        System.out.print(p);                   // line p4
        System.out.print((Child)p);            // line p5
        System.out.print(inter);               // line p6
    }
}
```

---

[114] Can you name them right now? We covered this in the discussion to Problem 4.13.

```
class Child extends Parent {
    public String toString() { return "C "; }
}
```

What is the result?

- A. P P P
- B. P C P
- C. C C P
- D. C C C
- E. Compilation fails

The method **toString()** is overridden correctly in both cases (it is `public` and returns a **String** in the class **Object**).

Line p1 is trivial. Line p2 assigns a narrower **Child** object to the wider type **Parent** → the LOC is valid.

Although **I** and **Parent** are unrelated, we already know that the compiler allows such assignments and casts to the interface types as long as the class type on the right-hand side is non-`final`.

Line p4 needs a **toString()** to output anything meaningful for **p**, and the class **Parent** obliges by providing its own version of the method but since the actype of **p** is **Child**, line p4 prints "C ".

Line p5 calls **Parent** a **Child**, which is not illegal, and because **p**'s actype is also **Child**, there's no CCE at RT and the LOC outputs "C ", too.

And finally... Whoa! **inter** is an interface! is **toString()** available to it at all? And if so, does it make an interface a class?! what a novel idea! Very well then, let's look into it.

Same question in disguise: Do interfaces inherit from the class **Object**?

According to the official Oracle tutorial[115], the answer is resounding and sonorous Yes:

> Reference types all inherit from **java.lang.Object**. Classes, enums, arrays, and interfaces are all reference types.

"Oh bother" said Pooh as the tripwire clicked...

On the surface it does appear as if interfaces inherit from **Object**; say, the next example compiles:

```
interface Inter {
    default void run(){
        Inter entity = null;
        entity.toString();
    }
}
```

But wait! what's this?! the following LOCs are invalid when we insert them into **Inter**:

```
//       entity.clone();      // error: cannot find symbol
                              //     symbol: method clone()
                              //     location: variable entity of type Inter
//       entity.finalize();   // similar story
```

---

http://docs.oracle.com/javase/tutorial/reflect/class/index.html

The JSL8 (§9.2, *Interface Members*) explains why it is so:

> If an interface has no direct superinterfaces, then **the interface implicitly declares a public abstract member method m with signature s, return type r, and throws clause t corresponding to each public instance method m with signature s, return type r, and throws clause t declared in Object**, unless a method with the same signature, same return type, and a compatible throws clause is explicitly declared by the interface.

Do you see it? '…corresponding to each *public* instance method[…] declared in **Object**'. Now it becomes clear why we can invoke neither **clone()** nor **finalize()** on the object **entity** although all three methods – **toString()**, **clone()** and **finalize()** – are defined by **Object**: the methods **clone()** and **finalize()** are `protected` rather than `public` → if a `protected` member defined in the class **T** is not available to an object, the data type represented by this object is not a subtype of **T** → interfaces do not inherit from **Object** and simply have their own abstract versions of **Object**'s `public` methods[116].

Alright; armed with this mind-blowing wisdom, we realize that line p6 does compile; as for the actype, it remains unchanged → there's no CCE, and the LOC cheerfully prints "C " again.

Problem 7.20 – CD

> Given:
> ```
> class A { }
> class B extends A { }
> class Test{
>     public static void main(String[] args){
>         A[] a1 = {};
>         A[] a2 = a1;        // XXX
>         B[] b = {};
>
>         a1 = b;             // line t1
>         b = (B[]) a1;       // line t2
>         b = (B[]) a2;       // line t3
>     }
> }
> ```

> Which two statements are true?
>
> A. Line t1 throws a compile-time error
> B. Line t2 throws a ClassCastException at run time
> C. Line t3 throws a ClassCastException at run time
> D. Line t2 fails compilation if the cast is removed

Since **B** is a subtype of **A**, line t1 is valid.

Line t2 explicitly downcasts a wider **a1** object to the refvar of a narrower type, which is OK and also makes option D correct along the way. Incidentally, since **a1** actually points back to **b**, we have here the so-called 'circular reference'. Anyway, this line doesn't throw a CCE as there's no conflict between the reference and run-time types.

As for line t3, it does throw CCE because **a2** still points to the same object that **a1** used to point to (ref.to line XXX) so the array **a2**'s type is **A**, and **A** ain't IS-A **B**.

---

[116] To hear the JLS saying it in the open ('[…] consider that while an interface does not have **Object** as a supertype[…]'), refer to §9.6.4.4, *@Override*, where you can also learn why the @Override annotation for, say, **toString()** works in interfaces.

Problem 7.21 – E

Given:

```
public class Painter {
    int age = 20;
    Painter(int age) {
        this.age = age; }
}
public class Picasso extends Painter {
    int age;
    Picasso() {
        super();                            // line p1
        this(90);                           // line p2
    }
    Picasso(int age) { this.age = age; }    // line p3

    public String toString() {
        return super.age + " : " + this.age;
    }
    public static void main(String[] args) {
    // code fragment goes in here
    }
}
```

And given the code fragment:

```
Painter p = new Picasso();
System.out.println(p);
```

What is the result?

A. 20 : 90
B. Compilation error on line p1
C. Compilation error on line p2
D. Compilation error on line p3
E. Lines p1, p2 and p3 fail compilation

Smack in the middle of our code sits the problematic spot: `super()` and `this()` back to back, which is not allowed as a call to another constructor, if present, must be the first one in any constructor's body → line p2 definitely fails compilation.

What about line p1? is it OK? No, because it tries to invoke a no-arg constructor in the supertype – and **Painter** doesn't have it.

Now for the tough one: which option mentions both p1 and p2?

Oh! almost forgot. Asking out of sheer curiosity, why exactly line p3 fails compilation?[117]

---

[117] For the same reason as line p1 does: since p3 has no explicit call to another constructor, the compiler tries to insert into it a call to a no-arg super() – which is not available in **Painter**. So watch out; you *will* have to dodge this trap on the exam.

Problem 7.22 – B

Given:

```
class OS {
    String name;
    OS(String name) {
        this.name = name;
    }
}

class Linux extends OS {
    int ver;
    Linux(String name, int ver) {

    // line L1

    }
}
```

And given the code fragment:

```
Linux os = new Linux("Ubuntu",16);
```

Which code fragment, when inserted at line L1, will instantiate the os object successfully?

    A.   `super.name = name;`
          `this.ver = ver;`

    B.   `super(name);`
          `this.ver = ver;`

    C.   `super(name);`
          `this(ver);`

    D.   `this.ver = ver;`
          `super(name);`

Can we use option A? No, because its first line is not a call to another constructor, which means that the compiler will try to insert at this point a call to a no-arg **super()**, and the supertype (the class **OS**) doesn't have it.

Same goes for option D, which also has another reason to fail compilation. Can you name it?[118]

Option C is out, as well, since it contains two constructor calls back to back.

---

[118] The call to **super(name)** is not the first stat in the body of this constructor.

Problem 7.23 – D

Given:

```java
class Pokemon {
    String name;
    Pokemon(){
        this("Undefined");                      // line p1
    }
    Pokemon(String name) {
        this.name = name;
    }
}

class Pikachu extends Pokemon {
    String sound;
    Pikachu() {
        super("Pikachu");
        this("Squeak squeak!");                 // line p2
    }
    Pikachu(String sound) {
        this.sound = sound;
    }
    public String toString() {
        return super.name + " says " + this.sound;
    }
}

class Test {
    public static void main(String[] args) {
        Pokemon p = new Pikachu();
        System.out.println(p);
    }
}
```

What is the result?

- A. Pikachu says Squeak squeak!
- B. Undefined says Squeak squeak!
- C. Compilation fails on line p1
- D. Compilation fails on line p2
- E. Compilation fails on lines p1 and p2

As always, the first thing we do is check the code for validity by testing the 'compilation fails' options one at a time. Line p1 seems OK because the class **Pokemon** does have a constructor that accepts a single **String** arg → options C and, therefore, E are out.

Line p2, however, is definitely illegal: it contains two constructor invocations inside the same constructor body.

Problem 7.24 – F

Given:

```java
class Fish {
    public Fish() {
        System.out.println("Fish: swims");
    }
    public void getFish() {
        System.out.println("Fish: caught");
    }
}

class Marlin extends Fish {
    public Marlin() {
        super();
    }
    public Marlin(String arg) {
        System.out.println("Marlin: swims");
    }
    public void getFish() {
        super.getFish();
    }
    public void getFish(String arg) {
        System.out.println("Marlin: caught");
    }
}

class Hemingway {
    public static void main(String[] args) {

        // code goes here

    }
}
```

What code fragment, when inserted into the class Hemingway, will produce the following output?

Fish: swims
Marlin: caught
Fish: caught

A. Marlin marlin = new Fish("Get the sucker!");
    marlin.getFish("Get the sucker!");
    marlin.getFish();

B. Marlin marlin = new Marlin ("Get the sucker!");
    marlin.getFish();
    marlin.getFish("Get the sucker!");

C. Marlin marlin = new Marlin();
    marlin.getFish();
    marlin.getFish("Get the sucker!");

    D.   Marlin marlin = new Fish();
            marlin.getFish("Get the sucker!");
            marlin.getFish();

    E.   Fish marlin = new Marlin();
            marlin.getFish();
            marlin.getFish("Get the sucker!");

    F.   Marlin marlin = new Marlin();
            marlin.getFish("Get the sucker!");
            marlin.getFish();

The good news is that the code apparently compiles so we don't have to check all those LOCs apart from the provided options... but there are so many of them (*sigh*)... I wonder if it's possible to... oh no! the problem doesn't specify an interface or an abstract class, otherwise we probably could eliminate some of the choices in a snap...[119]

Alright guys, we'll do it the old-fashioned, caveman way, pedantically cracking one skull at a time.

Option A needs a **Fish** constructor that would accept a single **String** arg → but does **Fish** have it? nope → a comperr.

Option B uses a **Marlin** single-**String** constructor → but regardless of what else happens after the code calls this constructor, it will always print Marlin: swims, which is not mentioned in the provided output.

Option C invokes the no-arg **Marlin** constructor, which calls the no-arg **Fish** constructor, which prints Fish: swims → so far so good. Now, we invoke the no-arg **marlin.getFish()**, which in its own turn calls the no-arg **super.getFish()** → Fish: caught gets printed, which is not what we need: it should've been Marlin: caught.

Option D fails compilation as it attempts to assign the wider **Fish** to the narrower **Marlin**.

Option E is invalid since **marlin** is now of type **Fish** and **Fish** doesn't define the method **getFish**(String).

And that's it; what's the point of checking if option F is correct when it is the only one that is left? So postpone it for the Review...

No sooner said than done: the no-arg **Marlin** ctor[120] calls the no-arg **super()**, which prints Fish: swims, then the overloaded-for-**String getFish()** prints Marlin: caught, and, finally, the no-arg **getFish()** calls **super.getFish()**, which outputs Fish: caught.

Gosh, it must be hard to be a fisherman...

---

[119] And yes, take it as a hint for the exam: an immediate hunt for 'un-instantiable' types will let you not only avoid potential pitfalls but also cross out incorrect options right away.

[120] By the way, ctor is a truly vintage term; as to how it should be pronounced, listen to Bjarne Stroustrup himself saying it: http://www.cpptips.com/ctor_ct.

Problem 7.25 – CE

Given the following classes:

```
abstract class Programmer {
    protected void code() { }        // line 1
    abstract void debug();           // line 2
}

class JavaCoder extends Programmer {
    void code() { }                  // line 3
    protected void debug() { }       // line 4
}
```

Which two modifications, made independently, enable the code to compile?

A. Make the method on line 1 public.
B. Make the method on line 2 public.
C. Make the method on line 3 public.
D. Make the method on line 4 public.
E. Make the method on line 3 protected.

Yikes! small but nasty… Or is it?

Starting with option A. The method **code()** on line 1 is `protected` → but the overriding version must have at least the same access privilege → the default access specified on line 3 is more restrictive → options C and E are the answer since only they mention line 3.

Hm… not that nasty, after all.

Problem 7.26 – CD

Given:

```
interface Flier {
    public void takeOff();
    public void land();
}

abstract class Plane implements Flier {    // line 1

                                           // line 2

    public void land() { }
}

class Boeing747 extends Plane {            // line 3

                                           // line 4

    public void land() { }
}
```

Which two modifications, made independently, enable the code to compile?

A. Replace line 1 with:
```
class Plane implements Flier {
```
B. Insert at line 2:
```
public abstract void takeOff();
```
C. Replace line 3 with:
```
abstract class Boeing747 extends Plane {
```
D. Insert at line 4:
```
public void takeOff() { }
```

This one should be easy. Since the class **Plane** is `abstract`, it doesn't need to implement all the `abstract` methods inherited from the superinterface **Flier**; as for the method **land()**, it is properly overridden (same access privilege + void + no extra ChE) → we can forget about options A and B as they concern the class **Plane** only → done.

On the Review, however, we'll have to confirm that it is indeed the class **Boeing747** that needs some fiddling. One option is to declare it `abstract` as the class in its current form doesn't implement the `abstract` method **takeOff()** defined in the interface **Flier**. As for option D, it eliminates the root cause of this evil problem.

Problem 7.27 – A

Your enterprising teenage sister asked you to develop an inventory program for her tiny online shop, and after patiently listening to her incoherent, stumbled explanations you realize that the specifications boil down to this:

*   The program must contain the classes **Dress**, **ReadyToWear**, and **HauteCouture**. The **Dress** class is the superclass of the other two classes.
*   The `double calculatePrice(Dress d)` method should calculate the price of a dress. The `void showDress(Dress d)` method should output the full description of a dress.

Which definition of the class Dress can serve as a valid abstraction in the class hierarchy?

```
A.  public abstract class Dress{
        public abstract double calculatePrice(Dress d);
        public void showDress(Dress d) {
            // some valid code
        }
    }
B.  public abstract class Dress {
        public double calculatePrice(Dress d);
        public void showDress(Dress d);
    }
C.  public abstract class Dress {
        public double calculatePrice(Dress d);
        public final void showDress(Dress d) {
            // some valid code
        }
    }
D.  public abstract class Dress {
        public abstract double calculatePrice(Dress d) {
            // some valid code
        }
        public abstract void showDress(Dress d) {
            // some valid code
        }
    }
```

Option B is faulty as it defines two methods with no bodies, which means the methods must be `abstract` – but the modifier `abstract` is missing in both cases.

Option C has the same problem with the method **calculatePrice()**.

Both methods in option D are declared `abstract` and, as such, shouldn't have bodies at all.

As for option A, it defines just a single `abstract` method while the other method is concrete, which is perfectly acceptable. In fact, an `abstract` class may be completely void of `abstract` methods.

Problem 7.28 – DE

Given the following data type declarations:

```
interface SpaceCadet {}
abstract class Pilot {}
class CyberPilot extends Pilot implements SpaceCadet {}
class D2R2 extends CyberPilot {}

public class SpaceAcademy{
    public static void main(String[] args) {
        // code goes here                          // line XXX
    }
}
```

Which option(s), when inserted at line XXX, will fail compilation?

A. ArrayList<Pilot> alumni = new ArrayList<>();
   alumni.add(new D2R2());
B. ArrayList<SpaceCadet> alumni = new ArrayList<>();
   alumni.add(new CyberPilot());
C. ArrayList<SpaceCadet> alumni = new ArrayList<>();
   alumni.add(new D2R2());
D. ArrayList<D2R2> alumni = new ArrayList<>();
   alumni.add(new CyberPilot());
E. ArrayList<Pilot> alumni = new ArrayList<>();
   alumni.add(new Pilot());

Option A wants to add a new **D2R2** object into an **ArrayList** generified to **Pilot** → **D2R2** IS-A **CyberPilot**, which IS-A **Pilot** → **D2R2** is narrower than **Pilot** and can easily fit into the provided place → option A compiles.

Option B works with a **CyberPilot** object, which is also a **SpaceCadet** → this option does compile.

Option C is also valid because **D2R2** extends **CyberPilot**, which implements **SpaceCadet** → compiles.

Option D attempts to stick a wider **CyberPilot** object into a place suitable for the objects of the type **D2R2** only → comperr.

As for option E, it wants to instantiate an abstract class.

Problem 7.29 – E

Given:

```
public abstract class Test {
    private String test;
    public Test(String test) { this.test = test; }
    public void test() {}
    private void test2() {}
}
```

What is true about the class Test?

    A. It fails compilation because an abstract class cannot have instance variables.
    B. It fails compilation because an abstract class cannot have private members.
    C. It fails compilation because an abstract class must have at least one abstract method.
    D. It fails compilation because an abstract class must have an explicit no-arg constructor.
    E. It compiles without error.

The only restriction that should concern us for the OCA exam is that an `abstract` class cannot be instantiated, so every option except E is incorrect.

Problem 7.30 – AE

Which two statements are true?

    A. An abstract class can implement an interface.
    B. An abstract class can be extended by an interface.
    C. An interface cannot be extended by another interface.
    D. An interface can be extended by an abstract class.
    E. An abstract class can be extended by a concrete class.
    F. An abstract class cannot be extended by an abstract class.

An interface cannot extend a class while a class cannot extend an interface → options B and D are immediately eliminated.

Classes implement interfaces, and `abstract` classes are not an exception; they don't even have to implement `abstract` methods declared by the interface → option A is true.

Option C is incorrect as interface can extend an interface (or even several of them).

As for option F, there's no such restriction.

Problem 7.31 – D

Which one is valid?

    A. public interface Diver { protected abstract void dive(); }
    B. public abstract class ScubaDiver { protected void dive(); }
    C. public abstract class ScubaDiver { protected final abstract void dive(); }
    D. public abstract class ScubaDiver { protected abstract void dive(); }
    E. public abstract class ScubaDiver { protected abstract void dive() {} }

The access modifier `public` in option A is redundant and the same goes for the modifier `abstract` but this is allowed; what's not allowed is the modifier `protected` because all the members of an interface are `public` by definition.

Option B violates the rule that says that an `abstract` method in a class must be explicitly declared `abstract` – and we can see that the method **dive()** is `abstract` because it doesn't have a body.

Option C is also faulty because an `abstract` method cannot be `final` as it would be impossible to make it concrete in a subclass.

Option E is invalid as it defines a method with a body but declares it `abstract`.

Problem 7.32 – BD

   Given:

```
interface I {
    public void doStuff();
}

abstract class A {
    public abstract void doStuff_A();
}
```
   Which two options are valid?

   A. `class B extends A implements I { public void doStuff_B() { } }`
   B. `abstract class B extends A implements I { public void doStuff_B() { } }`
   C. `class B extends A implements I { public void doStuff_A() { } }`
   D. `abstract class B extends A implements I {}`
   E. `class B extends A implements I { public void doStuff() { } }`

All the provided options implement the interface **I**, which means that if the class **B** is concrete it must at the very least implement the `abstract` method **doStuff()** → options A and C are immediately eliminated.

Option E does implement **doStuff()** but fails to override **doStuff_A()** although the concrete class **B** inherit the said method from the `abstract` class **A** → option E is out, too. And since the Problem asks for two valid options, we stop looking any further.

On the Review: **B** defines a completely new method **doStuff_B()** and does nothing to implement both **doStuff()** and **doStuff_A()** but it's OK: **B** is `abstract`, after all. Same goes for option D as the class **B** doesn't have to do anything whatsoever.

Problem 7.33 – C

Given:

```
interface Money {
    int cash = 0;
    abstract void earn(int amount);
    public void spend(int amount);
}

class LocalCurrency implements Money {
    int cash = 100;
    public void earn(int amount) {
        cash = cash + amount;
    }
    public void spend(int amount) {
        cash = cash - amount;
    }
}

class UnderpaidJavaCoder {
    public static void main(String[] args) {
        Money m = new LocalCurrency();
        m.earn(5000);
        m.spend(200);
        System.out.println("What's left in his pocket: " + m.cash);
    }
}
```

How much money is left in this coder's pocket?

A. 4900
B. 4800
C. 0
D. -100
E. -200

Fields are not polymorphic, so one of the most important rules that relate to inheritance, namely

> The reftype says what's available to the object while actype determines what runs

is not fully applicable here; we'll be using only the first half of the rule; the second half concerns virtual methods.

Alright, here's the entire logical chain: the object **m**'s reftype is **Money** → does **Money** define the variable **cash**? yes → which **cash** are we accessing through **m**: the one in **Money** or the one that is declared in **LocalCurrency** and which actually hides **Money**'s **cash**? → applying the rule: "the reftype says what's available..." → the vars declared in an interface are `public`, `static` and `final` by definition → their values cannot be changed → done.

By the way, what should this poor Java coder do in order to finally make some money – I mean, apart from passing the OCA exam?[121]

---

[121] He should better stick to **LocalCurrency**, i.e., `LocalCurrency m = new LocalCurrency()`. *That* would put a bewildered smile on his unshaven face along with 4,900 local currency units into his pocket.

Problem 7.34 – B

Given:

```java
interface Inter{
    default void run(){ System.out.println("Inter");}
}

class Parent {
    public void run(){ System.out.println("Parent");}
}

class Child extends Parent implements Inter {
    public static void main(String[] args) {
        new Child().run();
    }
}
```

What is the result?

    A. Inter
    B. Parent
    C. Compilation fails
    D. Run-time error

This one is probably too advanced for our exam and the chances of meeting something similar to it must be fairly low; nevertheless, the problem is quite interesting as it allows to peek a little deeper into interfaces.

It does appear that there's a clash between the two versions of **run()**; well, this is what Brian Goetz wrote more than six years ago for the Open JDK Mailing List[122]:

> **Rule #1: Classes win over interfaces. If a class in the superclass chain has a declaration for the method (concrete or abstract), you're done, and defaults are irrelevant.**

The rule makes perfect sense if we recall that `default` methods serve as a backup in case when a class doesn't provide an implementation for such methods and neither inherits them from its superclasses.

So the **Parent**'s **run()** wins over **Inter**'s version → the code prints Parent.

---

[122] http://mail.openjdk.java.net/pipermail/lambda-dev/2013-March/008435.html

As the inheritance-related questions are notoriously tough, let's take another look at the most important rules that just might save your day on the exam.

Rules of Inheritance Revisited*
(be especially attentive when overriding involves a `static` method)

1. A **static** method attempting to **override a non-static** one is **ALWAYS** a comperr, which includes **ALL** cases: interface-interface, class-class or interface-class **AND** throughout the entire inheritance chain (see Remark below).

2. When it comes to overriding between classes, `static` and `non-static` methods are **NEVER** compatible.

   Reminder: On the other hand, a `non-static` interface method may "override" a superinterface's `static` method. (It's just an appearance because `static` interface methods aren't inherited.)

3. **ANY** other override is valid **EXCEPT** the 'abstract static' combos which are illegal in the first place.

   *leaving out the stuff related to return types and exceptions

Note that Rule 1 holds true even in case of an implementation via inheritance:

```
interface I{
//     static void run(){ System.out.println("Inter static");  }
//     default void run(){ System.out.println("Inter default");  }
    void run();
}

class Parent {                            // *********************************
    public static void run(){             // *   the real culprit lives here   *
        System.out.println("Parent");     // *********************************
    }
}

class Child extends Parent implements I { // INVALID: 'overriding method is static'

//    public void run(){                  // even commented out so that Child wouldn't
//        System.out.println("Child");    // have its own run()... yet the inherited
//    }                                   // run() clashes with I's run()

    public static void main(String[] args) {
        new Child().run();
    }
}
```

Simple Corollaries:

- A subinterface can re-declare a `default` method and also make it `abstract`.
- A subinterface can re-declare a `static` method but it won't be overriding.
- A `static` method can't override an `abstract` method between interfaces but the opposite is permitted (again, it merely looks like overriding; @Override will flag a comperr here).

When it comes to vars, `static` may hide `non-static`, and vice versa.

AGAIN, from a different angle:

Fields and `static` methods are not overridden, therefore access to fields and `static` methods is determined at compile time based on the type of the variable (while instance methods will run according to the actual type of the object referred to by the variable).

A class cannot inherit two interfaces that both define `default` methods with the same signature, unless the class implementing the interfaces overrides those two competing methods with an `abstract` or concrete method.

More on difference between `static` and `default`/`abstract` methods in interfaces:

Interfaces define behavior, and this behavior is inherited only through non-`static` methods (**shorter wording**: interface `static` methods aren't inherited).

```
interface Inter{
    static void method1(){}
    default void method2(){}
    void method3();
}
abstract class Parent implements Inter{
    public void method3(){}
}
class Child extends Parent{
    public static void main(String[] args) {
//       method1();                        // won't compile but Inter.method1() will
         new Child().method2();     // VALID
         new Child().method3();     // VALID
    }
}
```

`static` methods defined in the **Parent** class run when the reftype is **Parent**:

```
class Parent {
  void one() { System.out.println("parent: one"); }
  static void two() { System.out.println("parent: two"); }
  public static void main(String[] args) {

    Parent p1 = new Parent();
    p1.one();                      // parent: one
    p1.two();                      // parent: two
//    p1.three();                  //<-- can't see it

    Parent c1 = new Child();
    c1.one();                      // child: one
    c1.two();                      // parent: two
//    c1.three();                  //<-- can't see it

//    Child p2 = new Parent();     // needs cast
//    p2.one();
//    p2.two();

    Child c2 = new Child();
    c2.one();                      // child: one
    c2.two();                      // child: two
    c2.three();                    // child: three
  }
}
class Child extends Parent {
  void one() { System.out.println("child: one"); }
  static void two() { System.out.println("child: two");}
  void three() {System.out.println("child: three");}
}
```

SAME STORY WITH INTERFACES:

```
interface Parent {
    void zero();
    default void one() { System.out.println("parent: one"); }
    static void two() { System.out.println("parent: two"); }
}

class Child implements Parent {
  public void zero(){System.out.println("child: zero");}
  public void one() { System.out.println("child: one"); }
  static void two() { System.out.println("child: two"); }

  public static void main(String[] args) {
    Parent c1 = new Child();
    c1.zero();                      // child: zero
    c1.one();                       // child: one
//    c1.two();                     // won't compile but next one does
    Parent.two();                   // parent: two
    Child c2 = new Child();
    c1.zero();                      // child: zero
    c2.one();                       // child: one
    c2.two();                       // child: two
  }
}
```

FOR THE LAST TIME: the reftype determines which methods and fields are available to the object while actype chooses concrete version EXCEPT fields: the fields are ALWAYS of the reftype.

Corollary:

When a var that has been declared in an interface IS NOT HIDDEN by the implementing class, we can't change its value (simply because it's implicitly `final` → comperr)

Suppose:

  1) class **Parent** declares   `int a = 0;`
  2) class **Child** declares   `int a = 100;`

Then:

```
Parent p = new Child();
System.out.println(p.a);            // 0
System.out.println(((Child)p).a);   // 100

Child c = new Child();
System.out.println(c.a);            // 100
System.out.println(((Parent)p).a);  // 0

Parent obj = new Parent();
System.out.println(obj.a);          // 0
System.out.println(((Child)obj).a); // CCE at RT
```

Same goes for interfaces except interfaces cannot be instantiated.

Chapter

II.8

EXAM OBJECTIVES – Group Eight:
Handling Exceptions

The 1Z0-808 objectives within this group:

8.1   Differentiate among checked exceptions, unchecked exceptions, and errors
8.2   Create a `try-catch` block and determine how exceptions alter normal program flow
8.3   Describe the advantages of exception handling
8.4   Create and invoke a method that throws an exception
8.5   Recognize common exception classes (such as **NullPointerException**, **ArithmeticException**, **ArrayIndexOutOfBoundsException**, **ClassCastException**)

 CORE RULES (with some Extras):

Covering everything in one common block:

❑   Checked exceptions represent expected exceptional conditions that might affect the execution of the program → the compiler forces the coder to deal with such conditions programmatically.

   Bottomline: If an API client code can reasonably be expected to recover from an exception, make it a ChE. If the client cannot do anything to recover from the exception, make it an unchecked exception.

❑   What must be handled in a `catch` or `finally` block or declared:

   ■ **Throwable**   ← *never met on the exam*
   ■ **Exception**   ← *met on the exam*
   ■ Any subclass of **Exception** other than **RuntimeException**, such as:

      – **IOException**   ← *met on the exam*
         └── **FileNotFoundException**   ← *met on the exam*

❑   The unchecked exception classes, which are exempted from compile-time checking:

   ■ **Error** + its subclasses   ← *not on the exam*
   ■ **RuntimeException**   ← *met on the exam*
   ■ **RuntimeException**'s subclasses, such as:

      – **NullPointerException**
      – **ClassCastException**
      – **ArrayIndexOutOfBoundsException**   ← *met on the exam*
      – **NumberFormatException**
      – **DateTimeException**

      – **ArithmeticException**
      – **StringIndexOutOfBoundsException** ← *never met on the exam*
      – **IllegalArgumentException**

❑ The exam does check for the proper use of the keywords `throw` and `throws`:

- `throws` is used in method declarations to indicate that an exception *might* be thrown;
- `throw` is used when the programmer wants to throw an exception; needs `new`.

❑ <u>Advantages of exceptions</u>[123]:

- Separating error-handling code from 'regular' code;
- Propagating errors up the call stack;
- Grouping and differentiating error types.

❑ ***Most Important for the Exam***:   If a method invokes another method that might throw a checked exception, the caller must either declare this ChE in its signature OR enclose the call within a TCF construct (a.k.a. 'Catch-or-Declare Requirement').

Corollary: It's OK if a method declares a ChE while not actually throwing it + it may throw any RTE without warning.

❑ A `try` block must be followed by either a `catch` or a `finally`, or both.

Corollary: Neither `catch` nor `finally` may precede `try` or exist without it.

❑ Multiple `catch` blocks are allowed, but Java runs the first one that matches.

Corollary: A wider exception may not precede its subclass in the list of `catch`es.

❑ At most one `catch` block can run.

Corollary: Nested ChEs thrown in `catch` or `finally` also require handling:

```
public class Test {
    void run(){
        try{
            System.out.println("in try");
            throw new NullPointerException();
        }
        catch(NullPointerException npe) {
            System.out.println("caught NPE");
            throw new RuntimeException();        // causes RTE
        }
        catch(RuntimeException rte) {            // won't catch the above RTE
            System.out.println("caught RTE");
        }
    }
    public static void main(String[] args) {
        Test t = new Test();
        t.run();                                 // throws RuntimeException
    }
}
```

❑ `finally` runs last and **<u>always</u>** UNLESS a `try` or `catch` is '**System.exit()ed**'.

Corollary: It runs even if `try` or `catch` has `return` (beware of unreachable stats, though! see below).

---

[123] https://docs.oracle.com/javase/tutorial/essential/exceptions/advantages.html

- The execution continues after the successfully completed TCF construct.

- If both `catch` and `finally` throw an exception, `finally` 'outshouts' `catch` (in other words, the exception thrown by `finally` supresses the exception thrown by `catch`).

- Unchecked exceptions do not affect method overriding.

- Overriding method may not throw a wider or unrelated checked exception.

- **Combat Rule:** Reftype governs checked exception handling:

```
public abstract class Pet {
    /* other abstract methods */
    public abstract void voice() throws Exception;
}
public class TalkingDog extends Pet {
    public void voice(){
        System.out.println("Yeah?..");          // you may want watch this[124]
    }
}
class UltimateTease {
    public static void main(String[] args) {
        Pet myPet = new TalkingDog();
//      myPet.voice();                           // line XXX; INVALID
    }
}
```

Line XXX fails compilation because the compiler doesn't even suspect that the actype can never produce a checked exception; it sees only the reftype, which does throw a ChE → the invocation must be wrapped up in a TCF construct or the caller – which in our case is **main()** itself – must declare a throw.

- EXTRA: An exception is an **Object** and, as such, can be `null`.

   Corollary: An NPE occurs if the `throw` stat's expression results in a `null` pointer.

- EXTRA: Exception-wise, the method overriding rule is opposite in case of constructors (ref.to Chapter II.6, *Working with Methods and Encapsulation*, for more details).

- EXTRA: `finally` executes first and only then a `catch`'s E (if any) is thrown UNLESS `finally` itself `returns` or throws an E in which case `finally`'s E/`return` suppresses the `catch`'s E/`return`.

- EXTRA: *Antipattern*: If `catch` or `finally` is followed by statements, those stats will be executed UNLESS a `catch` or `finally` `returns` or deliberately throws an exception in which case those stats become <u>unreachable</u> thus leading to a comperr.

   Corollary: When a stat follows `finally` or `catch` while BOTH the happy and unhappy paths[125] have `returns` in them → the stat becomes unreachable:

---

[124] https://www.youtube.com/watch?v=nGeKSiCQkPw

[125] Visit https://twitter.com/ronjeffries/status/586902281125232640 for other variants.

```
class Test {
    public float parseFloat(String s){
        float f = 0.0f;
        try{
            f = Float.valueOf(s).floatValue();
            return f ;
        }
        catch(NumberFormatException nfe){
            System.out.println("Invalid input " + s);
            f = Float.NaN ;
            return f;
        }
        finally {
            System.out.println("finally " + f);
        }
//      return f ;                                    // UNREACHABLE
    }

    public static void main(String[] args) {
        Test t = new Test();
// ---- happy path ------
        t.parseFloat("1.1");                          // prints 'finally 1.1'
// ---- unhappy path ------
        t.parseFloat("one-point-one");                // 'Invalid input one-point-one'
                                                      // 'finally NaN'
    }
}
```

❑ **EXTRA:** If both `catch` and `finally` have a `return` stat, the `finally`'s `return` overrides the `catch`'s return[126]. The value returned by `catch` is formed BEFORE `finally` executes:

```
public class Test {
    String testRef(){
        String str = "trying: ";
        try{ throw new NullPointerException(); }
        catch(NullPointerException npe){ return str + "caught";}
        finally{
            str += "finalized";        // doesn't affect the output...
//              return str;            // ...but this one will change it to
                                       // 'trying: finalized'
        }
    }

    int testPrim(){
        try{ throw new NullPointerException(); }
        catch(NullPointerException npe){ return 10;}
        finally { return 20; }         // primitives can also be changed
    }

    public static void main(String[] args) {
        Test t = new Test();
        System.out.println(t.testRef());   // prints 'trying: caught'
        System.out.println(t.testPrim());  // prints 20
    }
}
```

---

[126] The 1Z0-803 Study Guide by Mala Gupta mentions (p.389) that "If a `catch` block returns a primitive data type, a `finally` block can't modify the value being returned by it". The example below, however, proves otherwise.

❑ EXTRA: When a class implements multiple interfaces, its overriding method must conform to the overriding rules for each overridden method[127]:

```
interface I1 {void run() throws IOException, IllegalArgumentException;}

interface I2 {void run() throws FileNotFoundException, InterruptedException;}

class C implements I1, I2{
// the following stat is INVALID because C tries to override I2's run(),
// which throws FNFE, and IOE is wider than FNFE:

    public void run() throws IOException {}                      // INVALID

// this one is INVALID because I1's run() doesn't throw IE:
//    public void run() throws InterruptedException {}          // INVALID
}
```

❑ EXTRA: It's a comperr if a method contains some ChE catches – except for **Throwable** and **Exception** (because an RTE or **Error** might be thrown) – although `try` block doesn't even throw a ChE (since the ChE-related `catch` becomes unreachable; RTEs and **Errors** are OK, though):

```
class Test {
    public static void main(String[] args) {
        try { }

    //  catch (IOException e){}  // comperr: 'exception IOException is never
                                  // thrown in body of corresponding try stat'

        catch (RuntimeException rte){}      // these compile just fine
        catch (Error err){}                 // although silencing exceptions
        catch (Exception e){}               // with empty catch blocks is
        catch (Throwable t){}               // considered a bad idea[128]
    }
}
```

---

[127] FYI: **InterruptedException** is a ChE.

[128] "Item 65: …An empty `catch` block defeats the purpose of exceptions" (*Effective Java* by Joshua Bloch).

EXERCISES (for Key Summary ref.to App.D):

Problem 8.1 Given the following two classes:

```
class MyException extends RuntimeException { }

class Test {
    static void run() {                                    // line XXX
        try {
            throw Math.random()>0.5 ? new MyException() : new RuntimeException();
        }
        catch (RuntimeException rte) { System.out.print("B"); }
    }
    public static void main(String[] args) {
        try { run(); }
        catch (MyException me) { System.out.print("A"); }
    }
}
```

What is the result?

    A. A
    B. B
    C. Either A or B
    D. AB
    E. Line XXX fails compilation

Problem 8.2   Given:

```
import java.io.IOException;

class C {
    public static void main(String[] args) {
        try { doStuff(); }
        catch (RuntimeException e){ System.out.println(e); }
    }
    static void doStuff() {
        if (Math.random() > 0.5) throw new IOException();
        throw new RuntimeException();
    }
}
```

Which two modifications, made independently, will permit the code to compile?

    A. Adding `throws IOException` to the **main()** method signature
    B. Adding `throws IOException` to the **doStuff()** method signature
    C. Adding `throws IOException` to the **main()** method signature and to the **doStuff()** method signature
    D. Adding `throws IOException` to the **doStuff()** method signature and changing the `catch` argument to **IOException**
    E. Adding `throws IOException` to the **main()** method signature and changing the `catch` argument to **IOException**

Problem 8.3   **Given the following class:**

```
class DoNotFollowMyExample {
    public static void main(String[] args) {
        List list = new ArrayList();
        try {
            for(;;) list.add("New item");              // could be while(true)
        }
        catch (RuntimeException rte) {
            System.out.print("Caught an RTE");
        }
        catch (OutOfMemoryError oome) {                // line XXX
            System.out.print("Out of memory... ");
        }
        System.out.println("Total success!");
    }
}
```

What is the result?

    A.   Caught an RTE

    B.   Out of memory...

    C.   Out of memory... Total success!

    D.   Compilation fails because `for(;;)` is endless, which makes `catch` unreachable

    E.   Compilation fails on line XXX because catching **Error**s is not allowed

Problem 8.4   **Given:**

```
class Test {
    public static void main(String[] args) throws Exception {
        doStuff();
        System.out.println("Done!");
    }
    private static void doStuff() throws Exception {
        System.out.println("Starting... ");
        if (Math.random() > 0.5) throw new Exception();
        System.out.print ("Finishing... ");
    }
}
```

Which two are possible outcomes?

    A.   Starting...

    B.   Starting... Finishing...

    C.   Starting... Finishing... Done!

    D.   Starting... and Exception in thread "main" java.lang.Exception

Problem 8.5

Which three are advantages of the Java exception mechanism?

    A.   Improves the program structure because the error handling code is separated from the normal program function

    B.   Provides a set of standard exceptions that covers all the possible errors

    C.   Improves the program structure because the programmer can choose where to handle exceptions

    D.   Improves the program structure because exceptions must be handled in the method in which they occurred

    E.   Allows the creation of new exceptions that are tailored to the particular program being created

Problem 8.6   **Given the following two classes:**

```
1 import java.io.IOException;
2
3 class PrintingDaemon {
4     private boolean checkContents(String file){
5         boolean wrongFile = true;
6         // valid file-checking code
7         return wrongFile;
8     }
9     public void printFile(String file) {
10        if (checkContents(file)) throw new IOException();
11        else { /* valid file-printing code */ }
12    }
13 }
14 public class SimplestPrinter {
15    public static void main(String[] args) {
16        PrintingDaemon pd = new PrintingDaemon();
17        pd.printFile(args[0]);
18    }
19 }
```

Which two modifications, when used together, will make the code compile?

A. Add `throws Exception` to the **main()** method's signature on line 15

B. Replace line 17 with:
```
try {
    pd.printFile(args[0]);
}
catch(Exception e) { }
catch(IOException ioe) { }
```

C. Add `throws IOException` to the **printFile()** method's signature on line 9

D. Replace line 10 with
```
if (checkContents(file)) throw new IOException("Exception raised");
```

E. Replace line 18 with
```
throw new IOException(); }
```

Problem 8.7   **Given the following interface definition:**

```
interface Implementable {
    void runMe() throws java.io.IOException;
}
```

Which three implementations are valid?

A.
```
class Implementer implements Implementable {
    public void runMe() throws java.io.IOException {}
}
```

B.
```
class Implementer implements Implementable {
    public void runMe() throws Exception {}
}
```

C.
```
class Implementer implements Implementable {
    public void runMe() throws java.io.FileNotFoundException {}
}
```

D.
```
class Implementer implements Implementable {
    public void runMe() {}
}
```

Problem 8.8

The catch clause argument is always of type:

A. Exception
B. Exception but NOT including RuntimeException
C. Throwable
D. RuntimeException
E. CheckedException
F. Error

Problem 8.9

Suppose, the method doStuff() might throw an unchecked exception. Which of the following is true?

A. This exception must be caught inside **doStuff()**
B. This exception must be declared by **doStuff()** in its signature
C. The call to **doStuff()** must be wrapped up in a `try-catch` block
D. No action is necessary

Problem 8.10   Given:

```
public class BruisedKnee {
    private static void run() { tripOverCat(); }
    private static void tripOverCat() { throw new Exception(); }
    public static void main (String[] args) {
        run();
    }
}
```

What modification will make the code compile and run successfully?

A. Wrap up the `throw new Exception()` statement in a `try-catch` block that catches a **Throwable**
B. Wrap up the call to **tripOverCat()** in a `try-catch` block that catches an **Exception**
C. Add `throws Exception` to the signature of **run()**
D. Add `throws Exception` to the signature of **run()** and wrap up the call to **tripOverCat()** in a `try-catch` block that catches an **Exception**

Problem 8.11   Given:

```
public class Test {
    public static void main (String[] args){
        String str = "Hi!";
        System.out.println(str.charAt(3));
    }
}
```

What is the result?

A. !
B. A StringIndexOutOfBoundsException is thrown at runtime
C. A NullPointException is thrown at runtime
D. An IllegalArgumentException is thrown at runtime

Problem 8.12

Which three statements are true?

A. In multicatch blocks, the subclass exception handler may be placed after the superclass exception handler.
B. A `try` block must be followed by either a `catch` or `finally` block.
C. The class **Exception** is the superclass of all errors and exceptions in Java.
D. A checked exception must be handled explicitly by either catching or declaring it.
E. A single `catch` block can handle more than one type of exception.

Problem 8.13   Given:

```
class Miller { String contents; }

class TGIF {
    public static void main(String[] args) {
        try { enjoyQuietEvening(); }
            catch (IOException e) {
                System.out.println(e.getMessage());
            }
            catch (RuntimeException rte) {
                System.out.println(rte.getMessage());
            }
    }
    static void enjoyQuietEvening() throws IOException {
        Miller[] sixPack = new Miller[6];
        for (Miller coldOne : sixPack)
            if (coldOne.contents == null)
                throw new IOException("WHAT?! No more beer?");
            else drink(coldOne);
    }
    static void drink(Miller mmm) {
        throw new RuntimeException("Excellent!");
    }
}
```

What is the result?

A. WHAT?! No more beer?
B. Excellent!
C. null
D. Total bliss and serenity of being

Problem 8.14   Given the following classes:

```
class Cargo { /* valid, customs-cleared code */ }

class CargoPlane{
    void load(Cargo cargo) throws RuntimeException {      // line c1
        System.out.print("Cargo loaded - ");      }
    void fly(){ /* valid, ICAO-cleared code */ }
    void unload(Cargo cargo) throws Exception {
        System.out.println("Cargo unloaded");      }
    public static void main(String[] args) {
        Cargo cargo = new Cargo();
        CargoPlane plane = new CargoPlane();
        plane.load(cargo);                                // line c2
        plane.fly();
        plane.unload(cargo);                              // line c3
    }
}
```

What is the result?

    A.   Cargo loaded - Cargo unloaded
    B.   Compilation fails only on line c1.
    C.   Compilation fails only on line c2.
    D.   Compilation fails only on line c3.
    E.   Compilation fails at both line c2 and line c3.

Problem 8.15

Which two statements correctly describe checked exceptions?

    A.   These are exceptional conditions that a well-written application should anticipate and recover from.
    B.   These are exceptional conditions that are internal to the application, and that the application usually cannot anticipate or recover from.
    C.   Every class that is a subclass of RuntimeException and Error is categorized as checked exception.
    D.   Every class that is a subclass of Exception, excluding RuntimeException and its subclasses, is categorized as checked exception.

Problem 8.16   Given the following classes:

```
IndexOutOfBoundsException
FileNotFoundException
StackOverflowException
IllegalFormatException
ArrayOutOfBoundsException
ClassCastException
IOException
IllegalArgumentException
```

How many of them are defined in the java.lang package?

    A.   One
    B.   Two
    C.   Three
    D.   Four
    E.   Five
    F.   Six
    G.   Seven
    H.   All of them

Problem 8.17   Given:

```
class Thrower {
    public static void main(String[] args) {
        try {
            doStuff();
            System.out.print("A");
        }
        catch(RuntimeException rte) { System.out.print("B"); }
        finally { System.out.print("C"); }
    }
```

```
public static void doStuff() {
    if (Math.random() > 0.5) throw new RuntimeException();
    doMoreStuff();
    System.out.print("D");
}

public static void doMoreStuff() {
    System.out.print("E");
}
}
```

What is the maximum number of letters the code can print?

    A. One
    B. Two
    C. Three
    D. Four
    E. All five
    F. The code prints nothing because compilation fails

Problem 8.18   **Given the following two files:**

```
class WeightOutOfBoundsException extends Exception {
    @Override
    public String toString(){ return "Oh no... "; }
}

class GoodMorning {
    private int weight;

    void standOnScale(GoodMorning gm) throws Exception {
        gm.weight = (int)(Math.random()*21 + 90);        // generates random
                                                         // integer numbers
                                                         // from 90 to 110 (kg)
        if (weight > 100)
            throw new WeightOutOfBoundsException();
        else {
            System.out.print("I'm ordering pizza tonight! ");
        }
    }

    public static void main(String[] args) {
        GoodMorning gm = new GoodMorning();
        try {
            gm.standOnScale(gm);
        } catch (WeightOutOfBoundsException woobe) {
            System.out.print(woobe);
        }
        finally { System.out.println("Finally!"); }
    }
}
```

What is the result?

    A. Oh no…
    B. Oh no… Finally!
    C. I'm ordering pizza tonight!
    D. I'm ordering pizza tonight! Finally!
    E. Compilations fails

Problem 8.19   Given:

```
interface Prince {
    default void marryHeroine(String girl ) throws java.io.IOException {
        System.out.println("Lemme think...");
    }
}

class Charming implements Prince{
    static String prospectiveMate = "Green Fiona";
    public void marryHeroine(String girl) {
        System.out.println("Marry her?! You gotta be kidding me!");
    }
    public static void main (String[] args) {
        Prince prince = new Charming();
        prince.marryHeroine(prospectiveMate = null);
    }
}
```

What is the result?

    A.   Lemme think…
    B.   Marry her?! You gotta be kidding me!
    C.   Compilation fails
    D.   NullPointerException at run time

Problem 8.20   Given:

```
public class ManyHappyReturns {
    static int run(){
        int a = Math.random() > 0.5 ? 1 : 0;
        try {
            return 1/a ;                          // line X
        }
        catch(ArithmeticException ae){
            return 666;                           // line XX
        }
        finally {
            return 42;                            // line XXX
        }
         return 123;                              // line XXXX
    }
    public static void main(String[] args) {
        System.out.println(run());
    }
}
```

Which four are true?

    A.   If lines X and XX are commented out, the code prints 42
    B.   If line XXX is commented out, the code prints either 1 or 666
    C.   If lines X and XXX are commented out, the code prints 123
    D.   If line XX is commented out, the code prints 123
    E.   If lines XX and XXX are commented out, the code prints either 1 or 123
    F.   If line XXXX is commented out, the code prints 42
    G.   If lines XXX and XXXX are commented out, the code prints either 1 or 666

Problem 8.21   Given:

```
public class Test{
    public double test(double d){
        if(d > 0.5) return 1;
        try{
            if(d < 0.1) throw new Exception("Too small!");      // line t1
        }
        catch(Exception e) {
            return 666;                                          // line t2
        }
        finally {
            return 42;                                           // line t3
        }
    }
    public static void main(String args[]){
        System.out.println(new Test().test(Math.random()));
    }
}
```

Which one is true?

    A.   The code always prints 42

    B.   The code will fail compilation if either of lines t1 and t3 is commented out

    C.   The code compiles if both t1 and t2 are commented out

    D.   None of the above

Problem 8.22   Given:

```
1 import java.io.IOException;
2
3 public class StayAlert {
4     public static void main(String args[]) throws IOException {
5         IOException ioe = null;
6         try {
7             throw null;
8         }
9         catch(NullPointerException npe){ System.out.print("Caught NPE ");}
10        try {
11            throw ioe;
12        }
13        catch(IOException ioe){System.out.print("+ Caught IOE");}
14    }
15 }
```

Which two are true?

    A.   The keyword `throws` on line 4 is redundant

    B.   The `try-catch` statement on lines 6 through 9 is redundant

    C.   The code prints Caught NPE + Caught IOE

    D.   A **RuntimeException** is thrown at run time

    E.   Compilation fails

Keys & Discussion:

Problem 8.1 – B

Given the following two classes:

```
class MyException extends RuntimeException { }
class Test {
    static void run() {                                          // line XXX
        try {
            throw Math.random()>0.5 ? new MyException() : new RuntimeException();
        }
        catch (RuntimeException rte) { System.out.print("B"); }     // line t1
    }
    public static void main(String[] args) {
        try { run(); }
        catch (MyException me) { System.out.print("A"); }          // line t2
    }
}
```

What is the result?

A. A
B. B
C. Either A or B
D. AB
E. Line XXX fails compilation

As **MyException** IS-A **RuntimeException**, either of them gets caught on line t1, so **run()** never throws an exception to the outside → the printing stat on line t2 has no chance to fire.

Option C would have been correct if before line t1 there were another handler that catches **MyException** and prints **A**.

Problem 8.2 – CD

Given:

```
import java.io.IOException;
class C {
    public static void main(String[] args) {                 // line c1
        try { doStuff(); }                                    // line c2
        catch (RuntimeException e){ System.out.println(e); }  // line c3
    }
    static void doStuff() {                                    // line c4
        if (Math.random() > 0.5) throw new IOException();      // line c5
        throw new RuntimeException();                          // line c6
    }
}
```

Which two modifications, made independently, will permit the code to compile?

A. Adding `throws IOException` to the **main()** method signature
B. Adding `throws IOException` to the **doStuff()** method signature
C. Adding `throws IOException` to the **main()** method signature and to the **doStuff()** method signature
D. Adding `throws IOException` to the **doStuff()** method signature and changing the `catch` argument to **IOException**
E. Adding `throws IOException` to the **main()** method signature and changing the `catch` argument to **IOException**

To solve this one, we need to see what's wrong with the code in the first place.

The available options tell us that the error must be caused by an unhanded exception, and the only kind of exceptions the compiler cares about is checked exceptions.

The so-called Catch-or-Specify Requirement[129] that governs the handling of checked exceptions says that the code that might throw a ChE must be placed inside an appropriate `try-catch` block or the caller itself must declare this exception (or its superclass).

The source of trouble, namely line c5, lives inside the method **doStuff()**, which does nothing to prevent an **IOException** from escaping. Now let's ask ourselves how can **doStuff()** fulfill the Catch-or-Specify Requirement? The CSR offers two ways to do this but only one of them is available to us because the list of options doesn't mention wrapping up the offending code in a TCF construct → we have no choice but modify **doStuff()**'s signature → any option that fails to do so is out → options A and E are eliminated.

What about option B? By confessing that it can't handle the exception, **doStuff()** washes its hands of all responsibility for whatever might happen at run time and transfers it to the caller instead. Alas, the caller – the method **main()** – is armed with the butterfly net that is suitable for catching RTEs but not IOEs because there's no IS-A relationship between **IOException** and **RuntimeException**. This means, in turn, that **main()**, too, must warn its caller, Lady Jay V. Emme, by chanting "By the pricking of my thumbs, something wicked your way comes!". The method **main()**, however, is ominously silent, its signature says nothing about the nasty surprise brewing inside **doStuff()**'s bowels → the compiler can't and won't let the unspeakable thing happen.

On the other hand, option C forms an appropriate chain of warnings – from **doStuff()** to **main()** and beyond – while option D equips **main()** with an upgraded net that won't let IOEs through this time.

Problem 8.3 – C

Given the following class:

```
class DoNotFollowMyExample {
    public static void main(String[] args) {
        List list = new ArrayList();
        try {
            for(;;) list.add("New item");
        }
        catch (RuntimeException rte) {
            System.out.print("Caught an RTE");
        }
        catch (OutOfMemoryError oome) {            // line XXX
            System.out.print("Out of memory... ");
        }
        System.out.println("Total success!");
    }
}
```

What is the result?

   A. Caught an RTE
   B. Out of memory...
   C. Out of memory... Total success!
   D. Compilation fails because `for(;;)` is endless, which makes `catch` unreachable
   E. Compilation fails on line XXX because catching **Error**s is not allowed

---

[129] https://docs.oracle.com/javase/tutorial/essential/exceptions/catchOrDeclare.html

The API documentation for the class **java.lang.Error** says that

> An Error is a subclass of **Throwable** that indicates serious problems that a reasonable application should not try to catch. Most such errors are abnormal conditions.

Catching errors is considered bad programming practice. A better way to react to such problems is to print a stack trace and exit → option E is incorrect since Java does not explicitly forbid catching **Error**s.

Now let's consider option D. While it is true that an endless `for` well might bring about a comperr because of a potentially unreachable statement after the loop, wrapping it up in a `try` block[130] provides a non-zero chance of escape → option D is out.

However, what does happen in our code? `for(;;)` is indeed endless[131], and the **add()** method will be happily adding new elements one after another until… until… Wait a sec! just how long can be **ArrayList**?!

The documentation for **ArrayList** says that the method `size()` returns an `int`; we also know that **Integer.MAX_VALUE** is two in the power of 31 (for an `int` holds a signed 32-bit integral value, and a half of this space is used to represent negative numbers). Can we take it as an indication that after our **list** reaches this limit, something must give in throwing an exception along the way? Sounds logical but we aren't out of hot water yet for it is still necessary to figure out what kind of exception it's going to be: an RTE or an Error.

The description for **ArrayList**'s **size()** is tight-lipped: all it says is that the method "returns the number of elements in this list". On the other hand, **ArrayList** implements **List**, and **List**'s documentation is more accommodating:

```
int size()
```

> Returns the number of elements in this list. If this list contains more than Integer.MAX_VALUE elements, returns Integer.MAX_VALUE.

There you have it: **ArrayList** may contain more than 2^{31} elements, it's only its reported size that cannot exceed this limit → our initial chain of reasoning wasn't entirely correct for the code is going to gobble up all available heap space → and only then the JVM will throw **OutOfMemoryError** → which gets caught → the execution will terminate normally (it'll take a few seconds, though).

My gentle readers might object: we are not allowed to consult the API docs on the exam. That much is true but none of the actual questions run that deep. Consider this problem to be a sort of a bridge to the next Chapter, which deals with a number of core Java classes including **ArrayList**. Besides, it is probably not entirely a bad idea to remember that sometimes there's more than meets the eye.

On a final note please also observe that the listing does not mention an import for either **java.util.List** or **java.util.ArrayList**. This is in line with the assumptions that we are told to make for the exam (ref.to *Missing package and import statements* in Chapter II.0, *Opening Remarks*).

---

[130] We discussed this scenario in Chapter II.5, *Using Loop Constructs*.

[131] In its place we could have, for example, `while(true)` or `do-while(true)`, as well.

Problem 8.4 – CD

   Given:

```
class Test {
    public static void main(String[] args) throws Exception {
        doStuff();
        System.out.println("Done!");
    }
    private static void doStuff() throws Exception {
        System.out.println("Starting... ");
        if (Math.random() > 0.5) throw new Exception();      // line t1
        System.out.print ("Finishing... ");
    }
}
```

   Which two are possible outcomes?

   A. Starting...
   B. Starting... Finishing...
   C. Starting... Finishing... Done!
   D. Starting... and Exception in thread "main" java.lang.Exception

When line t1 doesn't throw an exception, nothing prevents the last printing stat from firing, while the alternative case makes the uncaught exception propagate up the call stack.

Problem 8.5 – ACE

   Which three are advantages of the Java exception mechanism?

   A. Improves the program structure because the error handling code is separated from the normal program function
   B. Provides a set of standard exceptions that covers all the possible errors
   C. Improves the program structure because the programmer can choose where to handle exceptions
   D. Improves the program structure because exceptions must be handled in the method in which they occurred
   E. Allows the creation of new exceptions that are tailored to the particular program being created

The official Oracle tutorial lists "separation, propagation and differentiation" as the three advantages. In all probability, the actual wording will be different so you'll be needing to think for a moment what these three concepts might imply.

A question to this tune *is* on the exam in the 'Core' section for I personally met it both times.

Problem 8.6 – AC

   Given the following two classes:

```
1 import java.io.IOException;
2
3 class PrintingDaemon {
4     private boolean checkContents(String file){
5         boolean wrongFile = true;
6         // valid file-checking code
7         return wrongFile;
8     }
```

```
 9     public void printFile(String file) {
10         if (checkContents(file)) throw new IOException();
11         else { /* valid file-printing code */ }
12     }
13  }
14 public class SimplestPrinter {
15     public static void main(String[] args) {
16         PrintingDaemon pd = new PrintingDaemon();
17         pd.printFile(args[0]);
18     }
19 }
```

Which two modifications, when used together, will make the code compile?

A. Add `throws Exception` to the **main()** method's signature on line 15

B. Replace line 17 with:
```
try {
    pd.printFile(args[0]);
}
catch(Exception e) { }
catch(IOException ioe) { }
```

C. Add `throws IOException` to the **printFile()** method's signature on line 9

D. Replace line 10 with
```
if (checkContents(file)) throw new IOException("Exception raised");
```

E. Replace line 18 with
```
throw new IOException(); }
```

"Catch or Declare", a.k.a. Catch-or-Specify Req: this is the rule we'll be applying in every single case when dealing with ChEs on the exam. Let's see what we've got here; the culprit lives on line 10, and the code provides no handler for it → following the CSR, we need either to put a TCF construct here or change **printFile()**'s signature → available options do not list a `try-catch` block that would successfully handle the ChE-throwing LOC → we are left with no choice but declare `throws IOException` on line 9 → option C is in.

Now that the caller, namely the method **main()**, is informed of the impending attack and must take appropriate countermeasures, it's time to set the defensive perimeter ('`catch`') or, failing that, dispatch a warning to the GHQ ('`throws`').

Option B offers something promising, something that appears suitable for catching ChEs but a closer look reveals that this particular block of code is faulty: the clause `catch(Exception e)` makes the next `catch` unreachable because **Exception** is wider than **IOException** → option B is out.

Since the options don't give us an appropriate TCF construct to protect **main()** from the inside, we must declare → the only choice that has anything to do with **main()**'s signature is A. And we stop here immediately without even checking if this option is indeed correct because it is better to leave the validity analysis for the Review; the first pass is about saving time…

Out of curiosity, what else can be done to the code to satisfy the CSR? Now it should be rather obvious that we might wrap up lines 10 or 17 in `try-catch` blocks whose `catch` clauses can have **IOException**, **Exception** or even **Throwable** in them; swapping the `catch` clauses in option B would also help.

Problem 8.7 – ACD

Given the following interface definition:

```
interface Implementable {
    void runMe() throws java.io.IOException;
}
```

Which three implementations are valid?

A. ```
class Implementer implements Implementable {
    public void runMe() throws java.io.IOException {}
}
```

B. ```
class Implementer implements Implementable {
    public void runMe() throws Exception {}
}
```

C. ```
class Implementer implements Implementable {
    public void runMe() throws java.io.FileNotFoundException {}
}
```

D. ```
class Implementer implements Implementable {
    public void runMe() {}
}
```

One of the rules that govern method overriding says that the version defined in a subtype may not throw a new ChE. Fine; so what exactly would be a "new checked exception" in this particular case?

Obviously, it must be something that fails IS-A test. Let's methodically run through the options to see what we can find.

Option A throws **IOException** → the option does not violate the rule of method overriding and, therefore, is in.

Option B throws **Exception**, which is a supertype for **IOException** → we can't say that **Exception** IS-A **IOException**, although the opposite is true → option B is out.

As for the next two options, they are all correct for **FileNotFoundException** IS-A **IOException** because **IOException** is its parent, and option D is so timid that it does not throw any exception at all, not even an RTE.

Problem 8.8 – C

The catch clause argument is always of type:

A. Exception
B. Exception but NOT including RuntimeException
C. Throwable
D. RuntimeException
E. CheckedException
F. Error

An exception is represented by an instance of the class **Throwable** (a direct subclass of **Object**) or one of its subclasses, says the Java Lang Spec in its §11.1.1, *The Kinds of Exceptions*.

Problem 8.9 – D

Suppose, the method **doStuff()** might throw an unchecked exception. Which of the following is true?

    A.   This exception must be caught inside **doStuff()**
    B.   This exception must be declared by **doStuff()** in its signature
    C.   The call to **doStuff()** must be wrapped up in a `try-catch` block
    D.   No action is necessary

The unchecked exception classes, says the JLS, are the run-time exception classes and the error classes; what's more, the unchecked exception classes are exempted from compile-time checking (ref.to §11.2, *Compile-Time Checking of Exceptions*) → options A through C are out.

Problem 8.10 – A

Given:

```
public class BruisedKnee {
    private static void run() { tripOverCat(); }
    private static void tripOverCat() { throw new Exception(); }
    public static void main (String[] args) {
        run();
    }
}
```

What modification will make the code compile and run successfully?

    A.   Wrap up the `throw new Exception()` statement in a `try-catch` block that catches a **Throwable**
    B.   Wrap up the call to **tripOverCat()** in a `try-catch` block that catches an **Exception**
    C.   Add `throws Exception` to the signature of **run()**
    D.   Add `throws Exception` to the signature of **run()** and wrap up the call to **tripOverCat()** in a `try-catch` block that catches an **Exception**

"Catch or Declare" all over again. Remember: we always start from the point of origin going up the call stack.

Has **tripOverCat()** a `try-catch` handler? nope → does the list of options provide a suitable handler? yeap. Done.

Problem 8.11 – B

Given:

```
public class Test {
    public static void main (String[] args){
        String str = "Hi!";
        System.out.println(str.charAt(3));            // line t1
    }
}
```

What is the result?

    A. !

    B. A StringIndexOutOfBoundsException is thrown at runtime

    C. A NullPointException is thrown at runtime

    D. An IllegalArgumentException is thrown at runtime

Although we are going to look into the class **String** in detail in the next Chapter, *Working with selected classes from the Java API*, the method invocation on line t1 is self-explanatory: the code wants to know what character occupies the 4th slot in the string known as **str**. Besides, the Exam Objective we are discussing right now prescribes knowledge of the most 'popular' exceptions thrown by **String**, **StringBuilder**, **ArrayList**, and a number of other core Java classes…

Do you remember the strange-but-true example from our talk on the constructors? the one that deals with a single-arg **StringBuilder** constructor that accepts a **StringBuilder** object as its argument?[132] simply because one of the constructors accepts a **CharSequence** object, and **StringBuilder** does implement the interface **CharSequence**?

Well, here we have a similar situation, in the sense that **String** implements **CharSequence**, too[133]. The method **charAt()** is specified by **CharSequence** and, according to the API documentation, throws an **IndexOutOfBoundsException** (removing option D along the way). We don't have this choice in out list of options but a **StringIndexOutOfBoundsException**, which is a subtype of IOOBE, does get mentioned → this is the correct answer because, after all, SIOOBE IS-A IOOBE. What's more, the javadocs for IOOBE says that "Applications can subclass this class to indicate similar exceptions", and this is exactly what happens in practice with the **charAt()** refined by the class **String**… *at least in its current implementation* although it is unlikely that Oracle is indeed going to change **String** some day. On the other hand, Java 9 is going to have something called Compact Strings[134], which just might declare throwing a certain BrandNewException that is a subtype of IOOBE without breaking the documented contract.

Fortunately for us, the options do not mention **ArrayIndexOutOfBoundsException** although this exception does extend IOOBE and is SIOOBE's sibling. Given the fact that **String** is backed by an array of characters it would be rather hard to decide between these two exceptions without consulting documentation.

And finally, I would like to call your attention to option C. Can you tell why an NPE isn't applicable here?[135]

---

[132] Problem 6.34.

[133] There are only three more **CharSequence**-implementing classes in the core Java API – **CharBuffer**, **Segment** and **StringBuffer** – but they are not on the exam.

[134] https://blogs.oracle.com/java/strings-in-java-9

[135] This is about remembering those NPE-throwing scenarios; yes, again; because it's so important for the exam… Alright, the reason why option C is out is that none of those five scenarios can be realized in our example: the code doesn't throw a `null` and as for the object itself, it has been properly inited and is not `null`.

Problem 8.12 – BDE

Which three statements are true?

   A. In multicatch blocks, the subclass exception handler may be placed after the superclass exception handler.
   B. A `try` block must be followed by either a `catch` or `finally` block.
   C. The class **Exception** is the superclass of all errors and exceptions in Java.
   D. A checked exception must be handled explicitly by either catching or declaring it.
   E. A single `catch` block can handle more than one type of exception.

Option A is obviously incorrect because a wider exception type will intercept all its subtypes thus making the next `catch` unreachable.

Option B is in line with the JLS requirements while option C is an arrogant impostor who is trying to pass itself for the class **Throwable**.

Option D is another wording for the Catch-or-Specify Requirement, and option E is correct, too, because the JLS does provide for multi-`catch` clauses[136], like this:

```
try {
    if (flag) { throw new ClassNotFoundException();
    } else { throw new NoSuchMethodException(); }
}
catch (ClassNotFoundException | NoSuchMethodException e) {
    e.printStackTrace();
}
```

Although it seems that the multi-`catch` clauses are not on the 1Z0-808, they are interesting animals in themselves and offer a lot of opportunities to place and arm some nice traps. For instance, the exception parameter in a uni-`catch` is `final` effectively whereas in a multi-`catch` clause it is `final` implicitly, which could blow off a finger or two. Or consider the following example:

```
try{
    if (Math.random() > 0.5) throw new FileNotFoundException();
    else throw new Exception();
}
catch(IOException | Exception e){}    // INVALID
```

Even though the above `catch` clause resembles a correctly coded multi-`catch` block (the narrower **IOException** comes before **Exception**, which is wider), this snippet won't work because alternatives in a multi-`catch` clause cannot be related by inheritance. Just so you know.

---

[136] A single `catch` clause that handles only one type of exceptions is called a uni-`catch`.

Problem 8.13 – C

> **Given:**

```
class Miller { String contents; }

class TGIF {
    public static void main(String[] args) {
        try { enjoyQuietEvening(); }
        catch (IOException e) {
            System.out.println(e.getMessage());
        }
        catch (RuntimeException rte) {
            System.out.println(rte.getMessage());
        }
    }
    static void enjoyQuietEvening() throws IOException {
        Miller[] sixPack = new Miller[6];              // XXX
        for (Miller coldOne : sixPack)
            if (coldOne.contents == null)
                throw new IOException("WHAT?! No more beer?");
            else drink(coldOne);
    }
    static void drink(Miller mmm) {
        throw new RuntimeException("Excellent!");
    }
}
```

> **What is the result?**
>
> A. WHAT?! No more beer?
> B. Excellent!
> C. null
> D. Total bliss and serenity of being

Apparently, the class **TGIF** compiles so we need only to figure out what exception type the `try` block throws and what happens next. Since all three potential exceptions get thrown inside the enhanced `for` loop, let's take a closer look at it.

Our `for-each` loop iterates over a **String** array that is referenced by a local var → from the previous chapters we know that local vars offer two popular spots to place mines: 1) the vars must be explicitly inited before being used, and 2) their scope is limited to the method / block they are declared in.

Has been **sixpack** inited? Oh yes; because it's a reference var[137]. But what about the slots of this array? what values do they hold? The answer is, of course, the default values – which are `null` → **coldOne.contents** attempts to access a field on a `null` object → NPE.

As NPE IS-A **RuntimeException**, the second `catch` intercepts it and prints out the message that the exception object contains. Since the code didn't specify the message for an NPE-throwing scenario, the JVM constructs a new **Throwable** with `null` as its detail message, which gets passed to **toString()**; so this is why the correct answer is option C.

---

[137] We covered this already when discussing Problem 2.1.

If **coldOne.contents** were replaced with just **coldOne**, the result would have been option A... not to mention that filling[138] the bottles after LOC XXX with something like

```
for (int i = 0; i < sixPack.length; i++) {
    sixPack[i] = new Miller();
    sixPack[i].contents = "Genuine Draft Beer";   }
```

would have yielded option B... and then – as a bonus – ;D.

Problem 8.14 – D

Given the following classes:

```
class Cargo { /* valid, customs-cleared code */ }
class CargoPlane{
    void load(Cargo cargo) throws RuntimeException {    // line c1
        System.out.print("Cargo loaded - ");
    }
    void fly(){ /* valid, ICAO-cleared code */ }
    void unload(Cargo cargo) throws Exception {
        System.out.println("Cargo unloaded");
    }
    public static void main(String[] args) {
        Cargo cargo = new Cargo();
        CargoPlane plane = new CargoPlane();
        plane.load(cargo);                              // line c2
        plane.fly();
        plane.unload(cargo);                            // line c3
    }
}
```

What is the result?

A. Cargo loaded - Cargo unloaded
B. Compilation fails only on line c1.
C. Compilation fails only on line c2.
D. Compilation fails only on line c3.
E. Compilation fails at both line c2 and line c3.

So many options hinting at an imminent compilation failure... → in all probability, the code doesn't compile. Very well, let's see if it is indeed the case.

Line c1 looks fine, it just throws a **RuntimeException**, which is not a checked exception so the compiler can't care less if the method declares an RTE or not. Since line c1 doesn't do anything illegal, option B is out.

As the method **load()** throws a **RuntimeException**, the caller doesn't have to do anything → option C is also incorrect → since option E needs a comperr on line c2, it gets automatically eliminated → now we have to choose only between A and D.

Line c3 calls the method **unload()**, which throws an **Exception**, which – being unhandled – goes up the call stack meaning that the caller, namely the method **main()**, must do something about it. Since **main()** didn't declare a thrown exception in its signature, it should have wrapped up line c3 in a `try-catch` block, which is missing → compilation does fail on line c3.

---

[138] We can't use the enhanced `for` loop here because it is a sort of 'read-only' operation: its equivalent form written as a regular `for` stat uses the method **next()** defined by the interface **Iterator** (JLS, §14.14.2, *The enhanced `for` statement*).

Problem 8.15 – AD

Which two statements correctly describe checked exceptions?

    A. These are exceptional conditions that a well-written application should anticipate and recover from.

    B. These are exceptional conditions that are internal to the application, and that the application usually cannot anticipate or recover from.

    C. Every class that is a subclass of RuntimeException and Error is categorized as checked exception.

    D. Every class that is a subclass of Exception, excluding RuntimeException and its subclasses, is categorized as checked exception.

The wording of this Problem comes straight from the official Oracle tutorial[139]:

> The first kind of exception is the checked exception. These are exceptional conditions that a well-written application should anticipate and recover from...

> The second kind of exception is the error. These are exceptional conditions that are external to the application, and that the application usually cannot anticipate or recover from...

> The third kind of exception is the runtime exception. These are exceptional conditions that are internal to the application, and that the application usually cannot anticipate or recover from.

And this is what the JLS has to say on the matter (§11.1.1, *The Kinds of Exceptions*):

> Exception is the superclass of all the exceptions from which ordinary programs may wish to recover.

> The class RuntimeException is a direct subclass of Exception. RuntimeException is the superclass of all the exceptions which may be thrown for many reasons during expression evaluation, but from which recovery may still be possible.

> The unchecked exception classes are the run-time exception classes and the error classes.

> The checked exception classes are all exception classes other than the unchecked exception classes.

Options B and C are eliminated based on the above definitions.

Problem 8.16 – C

Given the following classes:

      IndexOutOfBoundsException
      FileNotFoundException
      StackOverflowException
      IllegalFormatException
      ArrayOutOfBoundsException
      ClassCastException
      IOException
      IllegalArgumentException

---

[139] https://docs.oracle.com/javase/tutorial/essential/exceptions/catchOrDeclare.html

How many of them are defined in the java.lang package?

    A. One
    B. Two
    C. Three
    D. Four
    E. Five
    F. Six
    G. Seven
    H. All of them

As far as I remember, no exception-related question on the exam was missing imports because most of the **Throwable**s were from the **java.lang** package. Two notable exceptions (no pun intended) were **IOException** (defined in **java.io**) and its subclass **FileNotFoundException**.

The following exceptions, which the options mention, are defined in **java.lang**:

```
IndexOutOfBoundsException
    ├── ArrayIndexOutOfBoundsException
    └── StringIndexOutOfBoundsException

ClassCastException
IllegalArgumentException
```

So far so good. Now, can you guess which package **FileNotFoundException** is defined in? Let's do it together: since **IOException** lives in **java.io**, it is only reasonable that FNFE would be camping there, too. And, in fact, it does. Outstanding. Our logic is impeccable.

But the architects of the core Java classes are not linear beings; or, at the very least, they seem to follow a more convoluted path to Ultimate Truth: although **IllegalArgumentException** does reside in **java.lang**, its child **IllegalFormatException** is at home in **java.util**…

As for StackOverflowException and ArrayOutOfBoundsException, these are not amongst the core Java classes, to put it mildly.

Problem 8.17 – D

    Given:

```
class Thrower {
    public static void main(String[] args) {
        try {
            doStuff();
            System.out.print("A");
        }
        catch(RuntimeException rte) { System.out.print("B"); }
        finally { System.out.print("C"); }
    }
    public static void doStuff() {
        if (Math.random() > 0.5) throw new RuntimeException();
        doMoreStuff();
        System.out.print("D");
    }

    public static void doMoreStuff() {
        System.out.print("E");
    }
}
```

What is the maximum number of letters the code can print?

A. One
B. Two
C. Three
D. Four
E. All five
F. The code prints nothing because compilation fails

Let's consider the happy path first: **main()** calls **doStuff()** → **doStuff()** calls **doMoreStuff()** → **doMoreStuff()** prints E and terminates → **doStuff()** then prints D and terminates → `try` prints A → `finally` prints C → FULL STOP → 'EDAC' => four letters in total. As the class contains only four printing stats and no loops, we can conclude our analysis at this point.

On the Review, however, we should also consider the unhappy path: **main()** calls **doStuff()** → **Math.random()** throws an RTE → we jump out of `try` and the exception gets caught → `catch` prints B → then `finally` prints C → 'BC' => two letters only.

Problem 8.18 – E

Given the following two files:

```
class WeightOutOfBoundsException extends Exception {
    @Override
    public String toString(){ return "Oh no... "; }
}

class GoodMorning {
    private int weight;

    void standOnScale(GoodMorning gm) throws Exception {
        gm.weight = (int)(Math.random()*21 + 90);      // generates random
                                                        // integer numbers
                                                        // from 90 to 110 (kg)
        if (weight > 100)
            throw new WeightOutOfBoundsException();
        else {
            System.out.print("I'm ordering pizza tonight! ");
        }
    }

    public static void main(String[] args) {
        GoodMorning gm = new GoodMorning();
        try {
            gm.standOnScale(gm);
        } catch (WeightOutOfBoundsException woobe) {
            System.out.print(woobe);
        }
        finally { System.out.println("Finally!"); }
    }
}
```

What is the result?

A. Oh no…
B. Oh no… Finally!
C. I'm ordering pizza tonight!
D. I'm ordering pizza tonight! Finally!
E. Compilations fails

When `if` throws a **WeightOutOfBoundsException**, this object goes up the call stack (after all, the method **standOnScale()** doesn't have a `try-catch` block but declares that it might throw an **Exception**, and WOOBE IS-A **Exception** → this exception gets caught because the `catch` stat is specifically tailored to WOOBE → since this particular exception class overrides **toString()**, the code outputs 'Oh no...' → then `finally` adds its own two cents... Right?

Wrong. Because **Exception**, which is declared by **standOnScale()**, is wider than its user-defined child; the code needs another handler, something along these lines:

```
catch (Exception e) {
    System.out.println("Gotta loosen my belt more... again :(");
}
```

to get rid of the comperr although we would never see this particular 'butterfly net' engaged: the catch intercepts the *run-time* object whose type is WOOBE rather than **Exception**.

Replacing **Exception** with **WeightOutOfBoundsException** in **standOnScale()**'s signature would have yielded randomly alternating options B and D.

By the way, an attempt to arrive at the correct answer by elimination (like: since the code forks at `if`, there should be *two* possible outputs → the question uses singular case implying that only one option is valid → therefore, it must be E) is faulty because, speculating purely theoretically, both branches of a conditional construct may lead to exact same end result, that's why we need to analyze the code itself.

Problem 8.19 – C

> **Given:**
>
> ```
> interface Prince {
>     default void marryHeroine(String girl ) throws java.io.IOException {
>         System.out.println("Lemme think...");
>     }
> }
>
> class Charming implements Prince{
>     static String prospectiveMate = "Green Fiona";
>     public void marryHeroine(String girl) {
>         System.out.println("Marry her?! You gotta be kidding me!");
>     }
>     public static void main (String[] args) {
>         Prince prince = new Charming();
>         prince.marryHeroine(prospectiveMate = null);
>     }
> }
> ```

What is the result?

- A. Lemme think...
- B. Marry her?! You gotta be kidding me!
- C. Compilation fails
- D. NullPointerException at runtime

What can be the reasons for the compilation to fail? Let's check: interface members are implicitly `public` + **marryHeroine()** in **Prince** isn't `static` and, therefore, can be inherited → the overriding method in the implementing class must be both `public` and non-`static` → which is exactly what **Charming** does. Good.

Another landmine: the overriding method may not throw a new ChE → well, it doesn't → if the compilation fails, it isn't because of invalid overriding. Hm-m...

Alright, it's time to apply the Catch-or-Declare rule: **main()** invokes **marryHeroine()** on the object **prince** and... Aha! Since the compiler cannot know what will be the actual type of the object at run time (it's the JVM's prerogative, after all), it just looks at the reftype → and the reftype does threaten to throw a ChE → the invocation must be either enclosed in a `try-catch` or **main()** itself must declare in its signature that it might throw an IOE...

This simple rule

Reftype Governs Exception Handling

will surely come in handy on the exam. Let's play with it and see how it works one more time. Consider the following class definitions:

```
class Parent {
    void doStuff() throws Exception{
        throw new Exception();
    }
}
class Child extends Parent {
    public void doStuff(){ }
    public static void main(String[] args) {
        _____ obj = new _____();
        obj.doStuff();
    }
}
```

Now the question: how can we fill in the blanks so that the code compiles?

'Reftype governs exception handling' → does **Parent**'s version of **doStuff()** throw a ChE? yes → neither the invocation is wrapped up in a `try-catch` nor **main()** declares → the reftype cannot be **Parent** for it would violate the CSR otherwise → the reftype must be **Child** → the only compilable combination of types is **Child – Child** because **Child – Parent** won't work without an explicit cast, which is absent.

And since we mentioned casting, let's add that one more way to make code compile is cast the object to a subtype that doesn't throw an unhandled ChE, and then invoke a method on this object:

```
((Child)obj).doStuff();
```

Now we can even refine our rule:

> When a reftype throws a ChE outside, the caller MUST handle it somehow UNLESS the reference is explicitly cast to a silent actype.

Or maybe it's just too long; maybe the four-word version works better... It's up to you.

Problem 8.20 – CEFG

Given:

```java
public class ManyHappyReturns {
    static int run(){
        int a = Math.random() > 0.5 ? 1 : 0;
        try {
            return 1/a ;                       // line X
        }
        catch(ArithmeticException ae){
            return 666;                        // line XX
        }
        finally {
            return 42;                         // line XXX
        }
         return 123;                           // line XXXX
    }
    public static void main(String[] args) {
        System.out.println(run());
    }
}
```

Which four are true?

A. If lines X and XX are commented out, the code prints 42
B. If line XXX is commented out, the code prints either 1 or 666
C. If lines X and XXX are commented out, the code prints 123
D. If line XX is commented out, the code prints 123
E. If lines XX and XXX are commented out, the code prints either 1 or 123
F. If line XXXX is commented out, the code prints 42
G. If lines XXX and XXXX are commented out, the code prints either 1 or 666

The most important thing[140] to remember about `finally` is that it always runs unless there's `System.exit()` somewhere in `try-catch`. Moreover, `finally`'s `return` always suppresses `return` in `catch` or `try`. And here's another practical guideline to crack questions on the exam:

> The post-exception-handling stats are unreachable if there's an unconditional `return` in ether `finally` or in _both_ try _and_ catch.

Apparently, we have both scenarios, which means line XXXX must be definitely unreachable. Duly noted; now, is there other reasons to suspect an imminent compilation failure? for example, what about the exception itself? what if the code is missing some handlers?

Nope, the worst thing the `try` block can do is divide by zero, and this generates **ArithmeticException**, which is a **RuntimeException**, and the compiler doesn't care about RTEs; besides, this exception does get caught.

We can conclude, therefore, that all that commenting out is about getting rid of the 'unreachable statement' comperr. Fine; now we may start analyzing our options.

If line X is removed, `catch` won't even run but `finally` will → line XXXX remains unreachable → option A is incorrect.

---

[140] Exam-wise, that is.

If line XXX is commented out, the 'happy' `try` returns unconditionally whereas 'unhappy' `try` hands the execution flow over to `catch`, which also returns unconditionally → line XXXX is still out of reach → option B is incorrect.

When we remove lines X and XXX, `try` doesn't throw anything → `catch` won't run → and since `finally` is 'returnless', line XXXX runs freely → option C is correct.

Option D cannot work because even though `catch` is now 'returnless', both `try` and `finally` still return some values unconditionally → line XXXX becomes again unreachable.

Commenting out both XX and XXX lets 'happy' `try` output 1 while the unhappy path leads to printing 123 → option E is correct.

Since our code doesn't have `System.exit()` in it, `finally` always runs, and uncommenting the unreachable line XXXX makes compilation succeed → option F is correct, as well.

Lastly, as soon as we comment out line XXXX, the code becomes compilable, and removing overriding `return` in `finally` gives green light to whatever `catch` has to say whenever `try` is unhappy → option G is in, too.

Let's conclude this twisted example by stating firmly that putting `return` in `finally` is unadvisable.

Problem 8.21 – D

Given:

```
public class Test{
    public double test(double d){
        if(d > 0.5) return 1;
        try{
            if(d < 0.1) throw new Exception("Too small!");      // line t1
        }
        catch(Exception e) {
            return 666;                                         // line t2
        }
        finally {
            return 42;                                          // line t3
        }
    }
    public static void main(String args[]){
        System.out.println(new Test().test(Math.random()));
    }
}
```

Which one is true?

A. The code always prints 42
B. The code will fail compilation if line t1 is commented out
C. The code compiles if both t1 and t2 are commented out
D. None of the above

Removing line t1 could have led to a comperr if the exception argument in `catch` clause were of any subtype of **Exception** other than an RTE: the compiler would have objected saying that such and such exception 'is never thrown in body of corresponding `try` statement'.

Making both t1 and t2 disappear won't affect compilation, either, because `finally` guarantees a returning value. By the same token, commenting out line t3 is suicidal as the happy path will be left without `return`.

There's one more side to the story. The *'unless-system.exited-finally-runs-always'* rule holds true ONLY IF the code enters the `try-catch-finally`. Do not automatically assume that if there's a 'returning' `finally` somewhere in the code you can instantly grab this `return` and use it; check first if the flow indeed enters the TCF block (for example, in our case there is a fifty-fifty chance that it doesn't → strictly speaking, the rule should read: "Once the execution enters the TCF block, `finally` always runs unless there is a `System.exit()` in `try` or `catch`".

Problem 8.22 – AE

Given:

```
1  import java.io.IOException;
2
3  public class StayAlert {
4      public static void main(String args[]) {
5          IOException ioe = null;
6          try {
7              throw null;
8          }
9          catch(NullPointerException npe){ System.out.print("Caught NPE ");}
10         try {
11             throw ioe;
12         }
13         catch(IOException ioe){System.out.print("+ Caught IOE");}
14     }
15 }
```

Which two are true?

- A. The `try-catch` statement on lines 10 through 13 is needed
- B. The `try-catch` statement on lines 6 through 9 is redundant
- C. The code prints Caught NPE + Caught IOE
- D. A **RuntimeException** is thrown at run time
- E. Compilation fails

IOException is a checked exception, so the code must fulfill the CSR, which it does by enclosing line 11 in a `try-catch` stat → option A is correct.

Now let's consider option B. Line 7 throws `null`, which is the last scenario among the Magnificent Five → line 7 results in a NPE → since NPE is a **RuntimeException**, the code doesn't have to handle it at all → it seems that the `try-catch` stat on lines 6 thru 9 is not needed... Unfortunately, this is not the case.

What will happen if we comment out the first `try-catch` on lines 6–9? Line 7 will throw an NPE – which is now unhandled – and the JVM will abort the execution so the `try` on line 10 becomes unreachable. In other words, the `try-catch` on lines 6 thru 9 is needed *not* because of exception handling requirements but because it makes the subsequent stats reachable.

What about option C? It contains two sub-outputs, which imply that both catches run with the first `catch` printing Caught NPE. Now, line 11 actually throws `null` since **ioe** is `null` (ref.to line 5) but the fact is `catch` on line 13 handles only IOE or its subtypes → this `catch` can't even run.

So, may we conclude that option D is the correct one? that the code will first print 'Caught NPE' and then throw an NPE?

The answer is No. Because the compilation fails.

So far our job was somewhat easier than on the actual exam since we could make an educated guess what the problem was about; say, the questions to a loop-discussing chapter must be testing us on loops, the questions in a chapter that relates to exception handling must be about the CSR, and so on. The actual exam isn't like that: the problems come in randomly, so we have no idea what they can be asking for... Alright, so why does the compilation fail? It's because the exception argument declared in the `catch` clause on line 13 clashes with the variable **ioe** declared earlier on line 5... Scope of variables; yes, it's that simple...

That's why we have to be on our guard all the time – especially when there's a 'Compilation fails' option (although it does seem to be a mere place holder in our problem).

EXAM OBJECTIVES – Group Nine:
Working with Selected Classes from Java API

The 1Z0-808 objectives within this group:

9.1 Manipulate data using the **StringBuilder** class and its methods

9.2 Creating and manipulating **String**s

9.3 Create and manipulate calendar data using classes from **java.time.LocalDateTime**, **java.time.LocalDate, java.time.LocalTime, java.time.format.DateTimeFormatter, java.time.Period**

9.4 Declare and use an **ArrayList** of a given type

9.5 Write a simple lambda expression that consumes a lambda **Predicate** expression

CORE RULES (with some Extras):

9.1 Manipulate data using the **StringBuilder** class and its methods +

9.2 Creating and manipulating **String**s:

❏ Both **String** and **StringBuilder** implement the interface **CharSequence** and use a `char` array to store their characters but, unlike **StringBuilder** objects, **String** objects are immutable.

Most important corollary: *None* of the methods defined in the class **String** can modify original **String** object's value.

(other wording) If a **String** method returns a modified **String**, this object is new.

❏ In practice, **String**s can be created in two ways: by forming a string literal (a sequence of characters enclosed by double quotes) or by using the keyword `new`.

❏ In Java, a string literal is itself an object, which gets interned in a common string pool[141] (as per JLS, §3.10.5, *String Literals*: "A string literal is a reference to an instance of class **String**. Moreover, a string literal always refers to the same instance of class **String**"). Whenever the code requests creation of a string literal, the pool is scanned and, if a **String** object with the same value already exists in the pool, the reference to this object is returned. **String** objects created using the keyword `new` are never placed in the pool of **String** objects; same goes for the **String**s that are products of methods and, therefore, computed at run time:

---

[141] Do not confuse "string pool" with "constant pool", which is allocated at run time and "…contains several kinds of constants, ranging from numeric literals known at compile-time to method and field references that must be resolved at run-time" (JVM Spec, Java SE8 Ed., §2.5.5, *Run-Time Constant Pool*).

```
String str1 = "Hello";
String str2 = new String("Hello");
String str3 = new String(new StringBuilder("Hello"));

System.out.println("Hello" == str1);              // true → same object
System.out.println(str1 == str2);                 // false
System.out.println(str2 == str3);                 // false
System.out.println(str1 == "Hello!".substring(0,5)); // false
```

❑ Not only all string literals but the string-valued constant expressions (such as `"Hello " + "world!"`) are interned, too.

Corollary: **String**s computed by concatenation *at run time* are created anew, hence distinct:

```
class Test{
    static String gimme(){ return "world!"; }
    public static void main(String[] args) {
        String str1 = "Hello world!";
        String str2 = "Hello " + "world!";   // Constant expressions are computed
                                             // at compile time and then treated
                                             // as if they were literals
        String str3 = "Hello " + gimme();    // This one is computed at run time
                                             // and doesn't get interned
        System.out.println(str1 == str2);    // true
        System.out.println(str1 == str3);    // false
    }
}
```

❑ EXTRA: String pool is common for all the classes from all the packages that are being used by the running application.

❑ **String** constructors likely to appear on the exam (*italics*: didn't meet personally):

`String(String str)`
String(StringBuilder sb)

EXTRA: Although a no-arg constructor **String()** does exist, it isn't used in practice because **String** objects are immutable in the first place.

❑ **StringBuilder** constructors likely to appear on the exam (*italics*: didn't meet):

`StringBuilder(String str)`
StringBuilder()   ←   Constructs an empty **sb** with initial capacity of 16 characters.
StringBuilder(int capacity)

❑ **String** and **StringBuilder** methods likely to appear on the exam:

Method	args	str	sb	Note
`substring()`	(int start) *or* (int start, int end)	✓	✓	NB: returns String rather than SB
`length()`	()	✓	✓	
`replace()`	str: (CS trgt, CS replcmnt) *or* (oldCh, newCh) sb: (int start, int end, String str)	✓	✓	NB: diff params for str and sb no change? → current object
`equals()`	(Object obj)	✓	✓	SB doesn't override equals()
`concat()`	(String str)	✓	✗	no change? → current object
`toLowerCase()`	()	✓	✗	no change? → current object
`toUpperCase()`	()	✓	✗	no change? → current object
`trim()`	()	✓	✗	no change? → current object
`equalsIgnoreCase()`	(String anotherString)	✓	✗	
`append()`	(all kinds of types including String)	✗	✓	
`insert()`	(int offset, all kinds of types including String)	✗	✓	
`delete()`	(int start, int end)	✗	✓	

REMARK: The table is not exhaustive; it only means that I personally met those methods on the exam. To be on the safe side, learn the following methods, as well:

- concat(), endsWith, startsWith()   **String only**
- reverse(), capacity(), ensureCapacity()   **StringBuilder only**
- charAt(), indexOf()   **String & StringBuilder**

❑ <u>**Known traps on the exam**</u>:

- **str[sb].substring(int start, int end)**[142] excludes the character at the `end` position:

```
System.out.println("Hello".substring(0,4));        // Hell
```

- although **str.replace()**, **str.trim()** and **str.concat()** *seem* to modify the value of a **String**, they actually return a completely new **String** object UNLESS there has been no change:

```
String str = "Hello";
System.out.println(str == str.replace("Z","z"));   // true
System.out.println(str == str.trim());             // true
System.out.println(str == str.substring(0));       // true
```

- since == tests for 'physical' equality, the equality of contents should be tested with the method **equals()**;

- whereas **String** and **ArrayList** override **Object**'s **equals()**, **StringBuilder** does not → use a workaround: **sb1.toString().equals(sb2.toString())**;

❑ Easily confused methods (**list** refers to **ArrayList**):

Method	str	sb	list	Note
insert()	✗	✓	✗	inserts at any position up to **length()**; returns current SB
append()	✗	✓	✗	attaches to the tail; returns current **StringBuilder**
add()	✗	✗	✓	returns `boolean` except `void` **add**(int index, E element)
replace()	✓	✓	✗	str: replaces each occurrence; sb: replaces a substring
replaceAll()	✓	✗	✓	String uses regexing; List replaces a **Collection**
set()	✗	✗	✓	returns the element previously at the specified position
setCharAt()	✗	✓	✗	void
delete()	✗	✓	✗	returns current SB; if start == end → no changes ≡ same object
deleteCharAt()	✗	✓	✗	returns **StringBuilder**
clear()	✗	✗	✓	void; removes all the elements
remove()	✗	✗	✓	returns the element previously at the specified position
removeAll()	✗	✗	✓	returns `true` if the list changed as a result of the call
charAt()	✓	✓	✗	returns the char value at the specified index
get()	✗	✗	✓	returns the element at the specified position
contains()	✓	✗	✓	`true` if obj contains specified CharSeq / or Object (**List**)
isEmpty()	✓	✗	✓	`true` if String's length is 0 / if **List** contains no elements
size()	✗	✗	✓	returns the # of elements (stops at Integer.MAX_VALUE)
length()	✓	✓	✗	returns the length of this String / char count in case of SB
setLength()	✗	✓	✗	appends `null`(s) '\u0000' if newLength > oldLength
ensureCapacity()	✗	✓	✗	void
trim()	✓	✗	✗	removes leading and trailing whitespace; same obj if no change
trimToSize()	✗	✓	✗	resizes the buffer if it is larger than currently necessary
reverse()	✗	✓	✗	NB: surrogate pairs are treated as single characters

---

[142] Means either **str.substring()** or **sb.substring()**.

❏ **Other possible traps**:

  – **str.trim()** doesn't remove whitespace[143] inside the string;

  – **sb.substring()** returns a newly created **String** without affecting the current **sb** object whereas **sb.append()**, **sb.delete()** and **sb.insert()** do change it;

  – **str[sb].substring()** throws SIOOBE if the `end` arg exceeds **str[sb].length()**:

```
System.out.println(new StringBuilder("Hi").substring(1,3)); // SIOOBE
```

  – chained methods are to be evaluated left to right;

  – only two **StringBuilder** methods return a **String**: **substring()** and **toString()**;

  – while **substring()** can be invoked in similar ways for both **StringBuilder** and **String** – the method is overloaded for (int start) and (int start, int end) in either class – calls to **replace()** lead to different results: **sb.replace()** substitutes a string between two positions and **str.replace()** substitutes *all* occurrences of a `char` or a **CharSequence**.

❏ EXTRA: **str[sb].indexOf()** returns -1 if no match was found.

❏ EXTRA: **sb.insert()** doesn't throw a SIOOBE when inserting at the index i = **sb.length()**; the result simply mimics **sb.append()**.

❏ The + op is overloaded for **String**, so if either operand of a + expression is a **String**, concatenation is used; otherwise, addition is used.

  Corollary: + accepts anything when assigning to a **String**:

```
String a = "";

a = 1 + 10 + a;     // 11

// all of the following compile since each means a = a + smth
a += 2;             // 112
a += 'a';           // 112a
a += true;          // 112atrue
```

❏ The principal operations on a **StringBuilder** object are the **append()** and **insert()** methods, which are overloaded so as to accept data of *any* type. Each effectively converts a given datum to a string.

  Corollaries: **append()**ing and **insert()**ing a `null` object won't throw an NPE.

  EXTRA: When a `null` object (such as **String**, etc.) is passed in as a parameter to these two methods, it will be converted to the four characters 'null'.

  EXTRA: However, **append(null)** and **insert(null)** won't compile as the reference is ambiguous: `null` can refer to either `char[]` or **CharSequence**

---

[143] space (0x20), horizontal tab (0x09), form feed (0x0C) and line terminators LF (0x0A), CR (0x0D) and CRLF.

❑ <u>Useful reminders:</u>

■ **charAt()**, **indexOf()**, **substring()**, and **length()** work in the same way both in **String** and **StringBuilder**.

■ **append()** adds only to the end of the current **StringBuilder** object whereas **insert()** allows to put in one or multiple characters at a specified position

→ **sb.insert(sb.length(),"***")** behaves as **sb.append("***")**;

■ **StringBuilder** uses a char array and throws a SIOOBE rather than AIOOBE.

■ **StringBuilder** doesn't have **remove()**; it's **delete()**.

Problem 9.1 Given:

```
class Hello {
    public static void main(String[] args) {
        String str = "Hello";
        StringBuilder sb = new StringBuilder(str);
        str.replace("o", "");
        System.out.print(str + " ");
        System.out.print(str.replace("o","") + " ");
        System.out.print(sb.append("?").equals(sb.append("!")) + " ");
        System.out.println(str.replace("o","").equals(str.replace("o","")));
    }
}
```

What is the result?

A. Hell Hell false false
B. Hell Hell true true
C. Hello Hell false false
D. Hello Hell true true
E. Hello Hell false true
F. Hello Hell true false

Problem 9.2 Given:

```
class OurPets {
    static String checkPets(StringBuilder myPet, StringBuilder yourPet){
        return myPet == yourPet ? "same" : "different";
    }
    static String checkNames(StringBuilder myPet, StringBuilder yourPet){
        return myPet.equals(yourPet) ? "same" : "different";
    }
    public static void main(String[] args) {
        StringBuilder myPet = new StringBuilder("Fluffy");
        StringBuilder yourPet = new StringBuilder("Fluffy");
        System.out.print(checkPets(myPet, yourPet) + " pets, ");
        System.out.println(checkNames(myPet, yourPet) + " names");
    }
}
```

What is the result?

A. same pets, same names
B. different pets, same names
C. same pets, different names
D. different pets, different names
E. Compilation fails

Problem 9.3 Given:

```
class TheFifthElement {
    public static void main(String[] args) {
        StringBuilder sb = new StringBuilder("1");    // earth
        sb.append("2");                               // water
        sb.append("3");                               // air
        sb.append("4");                               // fire
        sb.replace(4,4,"Leeloo");
        System.out.println(sb);
    }
}
```

What is the result?

    A. 1234Leeloo

    B. Compilation fails

    C. The code throws a run-time exception

Problem 9.4 Given the following class:

```
class Test {
    public static void main(String[] args) {
        int[] arr = {1,2,3,4,5};
        String str = null;
        for(int e : arr){ str += e; }
        System.out.println(str);
    }
}
```

What is the result:

    A. _12345 (*where _ denotes an empty space*)

    B. 12345

    C. null12345

    D. Compilation fails

    E. A **NullPointerException** is thrown

Problem 9.5

Hoping to land a job as a junior programmer at a local bank, you came to a Java interview and were asked to complete the following class that masks 20-digit account numbers so that only the last five digits will be visible to the user while each of the first 15 digits is replaced with an asterisk:

```
public class AccountMasker {
    public static String maskAccount(String accNum) {
        String lead = "***************";     // contains 15 asterisks in a row

        // your code goes here

    }

    public static void main(String[] args) {
        String accNum = args[0];
        System.out.println(maskAccount(accNum.replace(" ","")));
    }
}
```

Specifically, your task is to finish up the method **maskAccount(String accNum)** so that the class **AccountMasker** will output ***************67541 when run with the following command:

    java AccountMasker "34296 01853 49820 67541"

Which two LOCs, when used independently, will achieve this requirement?

    A. `return (new StringBuilder(accNum)).substring(15, 20).toString();`

    B. `return lead + accNum.substring(15, 20);`

    C. `return new StringBuilder(accNum).append(lead, 15, 20).toString();`

    D. `return new StringBuilder(accNum).insert(0, lead).toString();`

    E. `return new StringBuilder(lead).append(accNum, 15, 20).toString();`

Problem 9.6

Which statement initializes a StringBuilder to a capacity of 256?

A. StringBuilder sb = new StringBuilder(new String(256));
B. StringBuilder sb = StringBuilder.setCapacity(256);
C. StringBuilder sb = StringBuilder.setLength(256);
D. StringBuilder sb = new StringBuilder(256);

Problem 9.7 Given the code fragment:

```
StringBuilder sb = new StringBuilder();
String exam = "1Z0";
int code = 808;
```

Which two options will output the following:

I'll pass 1Z0-808

A. System.out.println(sb.append("I'll pass " + exam + "-" + code));
B. System.out.println(sb.insert("I'll pass ").append(exam + "-" + code));
C. System.out.println(sb.insert("I'll pass ").insert(exam).insert("-").insert(code));
D. System.out.println(sb.append("I'll pass ").append(exam).append("-").append(code));

Problem 9.8 Given:

```
public static void main(String[] args) {
    String a = "B ";
    a = a.concat("U ");
    String b = "L ";
    a = a.concat(b);
    a.replace('U', 'A');
    a = a.concat(b);
    System.out.println(a);
}
```

What is the result?

A. B A L L
B. B L A
C. B U L L
D. B U A
E. B U A L

Problem 9.9 Given:

```
public class Simple{
    public static void main (String[] args){
        char c = 6;
        System.out.println("Hello".charAt(c));
    }
}
```

What is the result?

A. There is no output
B. Compilation fails
C. The code throws an **IndexOutOfBoundsException**
D. The code throws a **NullPointException**

Problem 9.10   Given:

```
StringBuilder bucket = new StringBuilder("Empty me!");
```

Which statement(s) will empty the contents of the bucket object?

    A. bucket.empty();
    B. bucket.clear();
    C. bucket.delete(0, bucket.size());
    D. bucket.delete(0, bucket.length());
    E. bucket.deleteAll();
    F. bucket.remove(0, bucket.length());
    G. bucket.removeAll();

Problem 9.11   Given:

```
class PoorGirl {
    public static void main(String[] args) {
        String name = "Javeline";
        System.out.println("Hi! I'm " + name.replace("e", "a"));
    }
}
```

What is the result?

    A. Hi! I'm Javaline
    B. Hi! I'm Javalina
    C. Hi! I'm Jevaline
    D. Hi! I'm Jeveline

Problem 9.12   Given the following main() method:

```
public static void main(String[] args) {
    String str = " ";
    str.trim();
    System.out.println(str.equals("") + " " + str.isEmpty());
}
```

What is the result?

    A. true true
    B. true false
    C. false true
    D. false false

Problem 9.13   Given:

```
StringBuilder sb = new StringBuilder();
sb.append("Duke");
```

And the following LOCs:

```
System.out.println(sb.insert(0, "Hello "));
System.out.println(sb.append(0, "Hello "));
System.out.println(sb.add(0, "Hello "));
System.out.println(sb.set(0, "Hello "));
```

How many of them print Hello Duke?

    A. None
    B. One
    C. Two
    D. Three

Problem 9.14   **Given the following code fragment:**

```
String str1 = "null";
String str2 = new String("NULL");
System.out.println(str1.equalsIgnoreCase(str2.toLowerCase()));
System.out.println(str2 == str2.replace('L','l').toLowerCase());
System.out.println(str1 == str1.replace('L','l').toLowerCase());
```

How many times the code prints true?

    A. Not a single time
    B. Once
    C. Twice
    D. Three times

Problem 9.15   **Given:**

```
public class TheMatrix {
    public static void main(String[] args) {
        String movie = "The";
        movie.concat(" ").concat("MATRIX".toLowerCase());
        System.out.print(movie.substring(5,6));
    }
}
```

What is the result?

    A. a
    B. at
    C. Compilations fails
    D. An exception is thrown at run time

Problem 9.16   **Given:**

```
public class TheMatrixReloaded {
    static void reload(StringBuilder sb) {
        sb.append(" Matrix");
        sb.insert(" Reloaded", sb.length());
    }
    public static void main (String[] args) {
        StringBuilder sb = new StringBuilder("The");
        reload(sb);
        System.out.println(sb);
    }
}
```

What is the result?

    A. The
    B. The Matrix Reloaded
    C. Compilation fails
    D. An exception is thrown at run time

Problem 9.17   **Given the code fragment:**

```
public static void main (String[] args) {
    String[] str = new String[2];
    int i = 0;
    for (String e : str)
        System.out.print(e.concat(" " + i++).trim());
}
```

What is the result?

    A.   01
    B.   0 1
    C.   0 1
    D.   Compilation fails.
    E.   An exception is thrown at run time.

Problem 9.18   **Given:**

```
public class Exam {
    String str = "";
    static void pass(String str) {
        str.concat("Passed");
    }
    public static void main(String[] args) {
        String str = "Failed ";
        pass(str);
        System.out.println(str);
    }
}
```

What is the result?

    A.   Passed
    B.   Failed
    C.   Failed Passed
    D.   Compilation fails
    E.   An exception is thrown at runtime

Problem 9.19   **Given:**

```
public class AnotherExam {
    public static void main (String[] args) {
        StringBuilder sb = new StringBuilder("Passed");
        System.out.print(sb + ": ");
        System.out.println(sb.replace(0,4,"Fail") ==
                        sb.delete(0,666).insert(0,"Failed"));
    }
}
```

What is the result?

    A.   Passed: false
    B.   Passed: true
    C.   Failed: false
    D.   Failed: true
    E.   Compilation fails
    F.   The code throws IndexOutOfBoundsException

Problem 9.20   Given:

```java
public class Capricchio {
    public static void main (String[] args) {
        Object obj = null;
        StringBuilder sb = new StringBuilder();
        sb.append(obj);
        System.out.println(sb.length());
    }
}
```

What is the result?

    A. 1
    B. 4
    C. 16
    D. Compilations fails
    E. A **NullPointerException** is thrown at run time

Problem 9.21   Given:

```java
public class HowAboutThisOne {
    public static void main (String[] args) {
        String str = null;
        StringBuilder sb = new StringBuilder(str += str);
        sb.delete(0,sb.length());
        System.out.println(sb.capacity());
    }
}
```

What is the result?

    A. 8
    B. 16
    C. 24
    D. Compilations fails
    E. A **NullPointerException** is thrown at run time

Problem 9.22   Given:

```java
class Slogan {
    public static void main(String[] args) {
        String str = "String Beans Forever!";
        // line XXX: only a single LOC goes in here!
    }
}
```

And the following LOCs:

```java
System.out.println(str.delete(6,11));
str = str.delete(6,11); System.out.println(str);
str.replace(" Bean",""); System.out.println(str);
System.out.println(new StringBuilder(str).remove(" Bean").toString());
```

How many LOCs, when inserted independently at line XXX, will make the code print Strings Forever!?

    A. None
    B. One
    C. Two
    D. Three

Problem 9.23   Given:

```
final String str = "";
while(str.equals("")) System.out.print(str+1);
```

What is the result?

A. 1
B. No visible output at all
C. Code compiles but enters endless loop at run time
D. Compilation fails because of an unreachable statement
E. Compilation fails because str+1 attempts to create a new object but str is final
F. Compilation fails because the expression str+1 is illegal

Problem 9.24   Given:

```
"a".replace("a","b");
"a".replace('a','b');
"a".replace(0,"a".length(),"b");
"a".replace(new StringBuilder('a'),"");
"a".replace(new StringBuilder('a'), new StringBuilder("b"));
new StringBuilder("a").replace("","b");
new StringBuilder("a").replace('a','b');
new StringBuilder("a").replace(0,1,"b");
```

How many LOCs fail compilation?

A. Two
B. Three
C. Four
D. Five

Problem 9.25   Given:

```
public class Dissonance{
    public static void main(String[] args) {
        Object obj = "Quartet No. 19 in C Major, K. 465";
        System.out.println(obj.getClass().getSimpleName() + " " + obj);
    }
}
```

Is it true that the code prints String Quartet No. 19 in C Major, K. 465?

A. true
B. false

CORE RULES (with some Extras):

9.3 Create and manipulate calendar data using classes from **java.time.LocalDateTime,
java.time.LocalDate, java.time.LocalTime, java.time.format.DateTimeFormatter,
java.time.Period**

- ❏ *All* of the LDT-related classes are immutable.

- ❏ *None* of the LDT-related classes (incl. DTF and **Period**) have `public` constructors.

  Corollary: All three primary classes are instantiated with **now()** or **of()**, e.g.:

  ```
  LocalTime.now();                      // 09:10:11.123 @ 9:10:11.123 a.m.
  LocalDateTime.now();                  // 2016-06-13T09:10:18.429
  LocalDate.of(2016, Month.JUNE, 13);   // 2016-06-13
  LocalDateTime.of(2016,6,13,23,59);    // 2016-06-13T23:59
  ```

  NB: Months can be specified in two ways (see above).
                   Months start with 1 rather than zero (January is 01).

  EXTRA: The overloaded **of()** that accepts months as words rather than numbers, uses the enum **Month** defined in **java.time** together with most of the other LDT-related classes.

  EXTRA: The class **DateTimeFormatter** is defined in **java.time.format**.

- ❏ **LocalDate** doesn't contain time-related fields whereas **LocalTime** doesn't contain date-related fields.

  Known trap on the exam: A missing or unexpected field → comperr or RTE

  ```
  LocalDate.of(2016,6,13,23,59);        // INVALID: unexpected time
  LocalDateTime.of(2016,6,13);          // INVALID: missing time
  LocalDateTime.parse("2016-06-13");    // DTPE: missing time
  LocalTime.parse("2016-06-13T10:12");  // DTPE: unexpected date
  ```

- ❏ The methods likely to appear on the exam:

Class	Methods	
LocalTime	minusHours(long hoursToSubtract)	plusHours(long hoursToAdd)
	minusMinutes(long minutesToSubtract)	plusMinutes(long minutesToAdd)
LocalDate	minusDays(long daysToSubtract)	plusDays(long daysToAdd)
	minusMonths(long monthsToSubtract)	plusMonths(long monthsToAdd)
	minusWeeks(long weeksToSubtract)	plusWeeks(long weeksToAdd)
	minusYears(long yearsToSubtract)	plusYears(long yearsToAdd)
LocalDateTime	*all of the above*	
Methods common to all 3 classes	**now()** accesses the system clock in the default time-zone	
	of() **LocalDateTime** also has **of(LocalDate, LocalTime)**	
	parse(CharSeq) / parse(CharSeq, DateTimeFormatter) same args for all three classes	
	format(DateTimeFormatter)	
	equals() only LT overrides **Object**'s **equals()** directly; other two implement interfaces	
	toString() Generates string in ISO-8601 format (e.g., 2016-06-13T23:29:50)	

  Known trap on the exam: Since the classes are immutable, adding or subtracting time units becomes meaningless unless the code uses the values returned by these methods (similarly to the methods invoked on **String** objects).

  ```
  LocalDate ld = LocalDate.of(2016, Month.JUNE, 13);
  ld.plusDays(2);
  System.out.println(ld);   // still 2016-06-13...
  ```

- ❑ **plusXXX()** or **minusXXX()** methods are used to manipulate date and time values.

  EXTRA: Method chaining for **minusXXX()** and **plusXXX()** works properly:

  ```
  LocalDate date = LocalDate.of(2016, Month.SEPTEMBER, 30)
                      .plusMonths(-3)
                      .plusYears(20);        // 2036-06-30
  ```

- ❑ **parse(CharSequence)** and **parse(CharSequence, DataFormatter)** methods are used to obtain a date & time object from a text string.

  Known trap on the exam: **parse()** needs appropriate number of components in the text string (both date & time for **LocalDateTime**, time only for **LocalTime**, date only for **LocalDate**), otherwise a **DateTimeParseException** is thrown:

  ```
  LocalTime lt = LocalTime.parse("10:12");
  System.out.println(lt);                             // 10:12
  LocalDateTime ldt = LocalDateTime.parse("2016-06-13T10:12");
  System.out.println(ldt);                            // 2016-06-13T10:12
  LocalDate ld = LocalDate.parse("2016-06-13T10:12"); // DTPE: unexp time
  ```

  NB: Days, months, hours and minutes should be specified with *TWO* digits, otherwise a **DateTimeParseException** is thrown; this rule isn't applicable to the method **of()**.

  ```
  LocalDate ld = LocalDate.parse("2016-6-13");         // throws DTPE
  System.out.println(LocalDate.parse("2016-06-13"));   // 2016-06-13
  LocalTime lt = LocalTime.parse("1:2");               // throws DTPE
  System.out.println(LocalDateTime.of(2017,1,1,1,1));  // 2017-01-01T01:01
  ```

- ❑ The class **Period** represents a number of days, months, weeks, or years, which can be added to or subtracted from a **LocalDate** or a **LocalDateTime** object:

  ```
  LocalDate someDate = LocalDate.of(2001, Month.JANUARY, 1)
                          .plus(Period.ofMonths(-3))
                          .minus(Period.ofYears(5));   // 1995-10-01
  ```

- ❑ EXTRA: Chaining for **Period**'s **ofXXX()** methods doesn't work properly[144]:

  ```
  LocalDate ld1 = LocalDate.of(2000, Month.JANUARY, 1);
  ld1 = ld1.minus(Period.ofDays(1)
                  .ofMonths(2)
                  .ofYears(3));                        // 1997-01-01
  ```

  → instead of **Period.ofDays(1).ofMonths(2).ofYears(3)** use **Period.of(3, 2, 1)**:

  ```
  LocalDate ld2 = LocalDate.of(2000, Month.JANUARY, 1);
  ld2 = ld2.minus(Period.of(3,2,1));                   // 1996-10-31
  ```

- ❑ EXTRA: **Period.parse("P1Y2M3D")** is the same as **Period.of(1, 2, 3)**.

- ❑ **DateTimeFormatter** is used to output dates and times in the desired format.

  Potential trap: All DTF formatters that are likely to appear on the exam, start with ISO, e.g.: ISO_DATE, ISO_TIME, ISO_LOCAL_DATE, ISO_LOCAL_DATE_TIME, and so on → any other form[145] leads to a comperr:

  ```
  String today = LocalDate.parse("2016-09-20")
                    .format(DateTimeFormatter.LOCAL_DATE);  // INVALID
  ```

  EXTRA: Difference between ISO_**** and ISO_LOCAL_**** is the offset (e.g., ISO_DATE can output either '2011-12-03' or '2011-12-03+01:00' if the offset is available while ISO_LOCAL_DATE outputs only '2011-12-03').

---

[144] Because **Period**'s **ofXXX()** methods are static; all they do is just return a newly created **Period** object.

[145] Something like **ofLocalizedTime(timeStyle)** or RFC_1123_DATE_TIME is obviously out of scope for 1Z0-808.

EXERCISES (for Key Summary ref.to App.D):

Problem 9.26   Given the following code fragment:

```
LocalDate today = LocalDate.of(2016, Month.JUNE, 13);
today.plusHours(24);
System.out.println(today);
```

What is the result?

  A. 2016-06-14
  B. 2016-06-13
  C. Compilation fails
  D. An exception is thrown at run time

Problem 9.27   Given:

```
public static void main(String[] args) {
    String date = LocalDate.parse("2016-07-13")
                            .plusDays(31)
                            .format(DateTimeFormatter.ISO_DATE_TIME);
    System.out.println(date);
}
```

What is the result?

  A. 2016-07-13
  B. 2016-07-14
  C. 2016-07-15
  D. Compilation fails
  E. An exception is thrown at run time

Problem 9.28   Given:

```
LocalDate ld = LocalDate.of(2016, 6, 13);
ld.plusMonths(6).format(DateTimeFormatter.ISO_LOCAL_DATE);
System.out.println(ld);
```

What is the result?

  A. December 13, 2016
  B. June 13, 2015
  C. 2016-12-13
  D. 2016-06-13

Problem 9.29

Which two LOCs fail compilation?

  A. LocalDateTime.of(2016,6,13);
  B. LocalDate.of(2016, Month.JUNE, 50);
  C. LocalDateTime.of(2016,06,13,14,15);
  D. LocalDate ld = new LocalDate(2016,6,13);
  E. LocalTime.now().format(DateTimeFormatter.ISO_DATE);

Problem 9.30   Given:

```
System.out.println(LocalDate.now().plus(Period.of(0,0,0)));
System.out.println(LocalDate.of(2016, Month.JUNE, 13)
                        .format(DateTimeFormatter.ISO_LOCAL_DATE));
System.out.println(LocalDate.parse("2016-06-13", DateTimeFormatter.ISO_DATE));
```

What is the result if the system date is June 13, 2016?

     A.   2016-06-13
          2016-06-13
          2016-06-13
     B.   Compilation fails.
     C.   A DateParseException is thrown at runtime.

Problem 9.31   **Given the full contents of the file JavaBirthday.java:**

```
1 package birthday;
2 import java.time.LocalDate;
3 import java.time.format.DateTimeFormatter;
4
5 public class JavaBirthday {
6     public static void main(String[] args) {
7         LocalDate birthday = LocalDate.of(1995, Month.MAY, 23);
8         DateTimeFormatter formatter =
9                       DateTimeFormatter.ofPattern("MMM dd, YYYY");
10        System.out.println("Java was born on " + birthday.format(formatter));
11    }
12 }
```

One of the LOCs fails compilation. Which two modifications, used independently, will make the code print Java was born on May 23, 1995?

     A.   Replace line 2 with import java.time.*;
     B.   Replace line 3 with import java.time.format.*;
     C.   Replace Month.MAY on line 7 with Month.May
     D.   Replace Month.MAY on line 7 with 05

CORE RULES (with some Extras):

9.4 <u>Declare and use an **ArrayList** of a given type:</u>

❑   **ArrayList** implements **List**, which extends **Collection** and **Iterable** → that's why:

■ **ArrayList** works with reference types only:
  – can accept a mixture of types when used without generics;
  – primitives get autoboxed and unboxed as needed;
  <u>Corollary</u>:   `for-each` with a primitive loop var throws an NPE at `null` element.

■ is structurally mutable and resembles a resizable array:
  – **ArrayList**s are zero-based like ordinary arrays;
  – unlike arrays, initial size of an **ArrayList** cannot be specified;
  – internally, the elements are stored in an **Object[]** array → throws AIOOBE

■ is ordered and iterable:
  – allows positional (indexed) access to the elements;
  – enhanced `for` loop returns the elements in the order they were added;
  EXTRA: `for-each` cannot remove elements; use **Iterator** or **ListIterator**;

■ allows duplicates;

■ allows `nulls`;

■ can be made type-safe by using generics, for example, if **Vehicle** ← **SUV**:

```
List<Vehicle> al = new ArrayList<>();
SUV s = al.get(0);      // INVALID because SUV is narrower than Vehicle
SUV s = (SUV)al.get(0); // OK but throws AIOOBE 'cause al isn't populated
```

<u>NB:</u>   Empty diamond on the left is not allowed.

<u>NB:</u>   **contains()** is comperr-proof even if the **List** is generified:

```
List<String> list = new ArrayList<>();
list.add("hello");
System.out.println(list.contains(666));     // prints false
```

❑   <u>**ArrayList** constructor likely to appear on the exam:</u>

`ArrayList()`   →   constructs an empty list with an initial capacity of ten

❑   <u>Methods likely to appear on the exam:</u>

Method	Function
`add()`	**add**(E element) appends; returns `true` if successful
	add(int index, E element) inserts at the specified position; `void`
`get()`	**get**(int index) returns the element at the specified position
`set()`	**set**(int index, E e) modifies the elem at the spec'd position; returns what was before
`remove()`	**remove**(int indx) deletes the elem at the specified position (returns the deleted elem)
	remove(Object obj) deletes 1st occurrence of **obj** (returns `true` if **obj** was present)
`clear()`	Empties the list by setting its size to zero and each element to `null`
`isEmpty()`	Returns `true` if the list contains no elements
`contains()`	**contains**(Object obj) returns `true` if the list contains at least one **obj**
`indexOf()`	**indexOf**(Object obj) returns the index of the 1st occurrence of **obj** (-1 if not found)
`size()`	Returns the number of elements in this list (up to **Integer.MAX_VALUE**)
`equals()`	Returns `true` if both lists contain the same elements in the same order
`toString()`	Returns smth like '[elem1, elem2, elem3]' (note square brackets and spaces after commas)

Possible trap on the exam: Easily confused methods

StringBuilder	ArrayList
length()	size()
insert()	add()
delete()	remove()
replace()	set()
capacity()	–

❑   One more way to create a **List** is with the method **Arrays.asList()**:

```
List<String> list = java.util.Arrays.asList("one",
                                            "two",
                                            "three");
```

Remarks:

1. The reftype *must* be **List** rather than **ArrayList**.

2. Unlike the lists created with a constructor defined in a **List**-implementing class, this particular list is structurally immutable (i.e., it cannot change its size[146]).

3. I met this idiom on both sittings but only in the question that was related to lambdas so the first two points are probably not terribly important for our exam…

❑   EXTRA: **List** and **ArrayList** don't have a simple **sort()** method; their **sort()** needs a comparator → to sort an **ArrayList**, use **java.util.Collections.sort(al)**[147]:

```
List<String> myList = new ArrayList();
myList.add("Hi");
myList.add("G'bye");
java.util.Collections.sort(myList);
System.out.println(myList);                    // [G'bye, Hi]
```

<u>(Just a reminder:)</u>   To sort a regular array, use **java.util.Arrays.sort(arr)**:

```
Integer[] arrInt = {1,3,4,2};
java.util.Arrays.sort(arrInt);
for(Integer E : arrInt) System.out.print(E);   // 1234
```

---

[146] Citing the **Arrays** API docs: "static <T> **List**<T> **asList**(T... a) returns a fixed-size list backed by the specified array".

[147] Being a utility class, **Collections** is made up entirely of static methods; same goes for **java.util.Arrays**.

EXERCISES (for Key Summary ref.to App.D):

Problem 9.32   **Given the following class definition:**

```
class LangsToLearn {
    public static void main(String[] args) {
        List<String> langs = new ArrayList<>();
        langs.add("Ruby");
        langs.add("Perl");
        langs.add("Perl");
        langs.add("Closure");
        if (langs.remove("Perl")) langs.add("Emacs Lisp");
        System.out.println(langs);          }
}
```

What is the result?

- A.   [Ruby, Perl, Closure, Emacs Lisp]
- B.   [Ruby, Closure, Emacs Lisp, Emacs Lisp]
- C.   [Ruby, Closure, Emacs Lisp]
- D.   Compilation fails

Problem 9.33   **Given:**

```
ArrayList<String> someTypes = new ArrayList<>();
someTypes.add("byte");
someTypes.add("long");
someTypes.add("int");
```

Which two expressions evaluate to 3?

- A.   someTypes.size();
- B.   someTypes.capacity();
- C.   someTypes.length();
- D.   someTypes.get(2).size;
- E.   someTypes.get(2).length;
- F.   someTypes.get(2).length();

Problem 9.34   **Given the following code fragment:**

```
ArrayList<Integer> list = new ArrayList();      // a1
list.add(1);                                     // a2
System.out.println(list.get(list.size()));       // a3
```

What is the result?

- A.   1
- B.   Compilation fails on line a1
- C.   Compilation fails on line a2
- D.   Compilation fails on line a3
- E.   An IndexOutOfBoundsException is thrown at run time

Problem 9.35   Given:

```
class TestingArrayList {
    public static void main (String[] args) {
        List<String> list = new ArrayList<>();
        for (int i = 0; i < 5; i++) list.add("" + i);
        System.out.println(list.remove(list.indexOf("4")));
    }
}
```

What is the result?

    A. true
    B. 4
    C. [0, 1, 2, 3, 4]
    D. Compilation fails

Problem 9.36   Given:

```
public class MutatisMutandis {
    public static void main(String[] args) {
        List list = new ArrayList();
        list.add(new StringBuilder(""));
        list.add("");
        for (Object e : list )
            if (e instanceof StringBuilder) ((StringBuilder)e).append("OK");
            else ((String)e).concat("OK");
        System.out.println(list);
    }
}
```

What is the result?

    A. [OK, OK]
    B. [OK,]
    C. Compilations fails
    D. A RuntimeException is thrown

Problem 9.37   Given:

```
class Birdies{
    public static void main(String[] args) {
        List aviary = new ArrayList<>();          // line b1
        aviary.add("kinglet");
        aviary.add("finch");
        aviary.add("titmouse");
        aviary.add(aviary.set(0,"jay"));          // line b2
        System.out.println(aviary);
    }
}
```

What is the result?

    A. [jay, finch, titmouse, kinglet]
    B. [jay, finch, titmouse, true]
    C. Compilation fails on line b1
    D. Compilation fails on line b2

Problem 9.38   Given:

```
class Sweet16 {
    public static void main(String[] args) {
        List<Integer> ages = new ArrayList<>();
        ages.add(16);
        ages.add(null);
        for (int i = 0; i < ages.size(); i++) System.out.print(ages.get(i));
        for (int i : ages) System.out.println(i);
    }
}
```

What is the result?

A. 16null16
B. 16null16null
C. 16null16 and a NullPointerException
D. Compilation fails

CORE RULES (with some Extras):

9.5 <u>Write a simple lambda expression that consumes a lambda **Predicate** expression:</u>

❑ The abstract method **test()** declared in the interface **Predicate** returns a `boolean` and takes an argument of type **Object**.

❑ Since there's only one formal parameter (which corresponds to **test()**'s arg), its type and enclosing parentheses are optional.

❑ If the method body contains a single `boolean`-returning stat, the braces can be omitted UNLESS the stat uses an explicit `return` – in which case we must apply the Semirebra[148] Rule.

❑ **The Semirebra Rule:**

> Semicolon, return and braces in lambda method body always go together.

<u>Traps!</u> – empty parameter list, or
– `return` without semicolon and braces, or
– semicolon without `return` and braces, or
– the method body does not return a `boolean`.

Typical invalid patterns likely to appear on the exam:

```
( )    -> whatever              // param list is empty
(x,y)  -> whatever              // too many params
 (x)   -> System.out.print(x)   // System.out.print() is void
  x    -> { return "" + x; }    // String instead of a boolean
 str   -> return str.isEmpty(); // return and ; need {}
 str   -> { return str.isEmpty() }  // return and {} need ;
 str   -> str.isEmpty();        // ; needs both return and {}
whtvr  -> return true           // missing both ; and {}
```

❑ What **Predicate** is typed to must be consistent with the parameter's type.

Consider the following:

```
static String check(List list, Predicate p){
    return p.test(list)? "Empty" : "Not empty"; }
public static void main(String[] args) {
   ArrayList list = new ArrayList();
   System.out.println(check(list, al -> al.isEmpty()));  // INVALID
}
```

The above example fails to compile because **p** isn't generified → its type is therefore **Object** → and **Object** doesn't have the method **isEmpty()**. On the other hand, the code would have compiled if **al.isEmpty()** were replaced, say, with **al.equals("")**. Better yet, cast the formal param to **List** or **ArrayList** (e.g., ((List)al).isEmpty()) as this wouldn't break the logic behind the code, which happens with **equals("")**.

---

[148] Just an acronym: 'semi' for 'semicolon', 're' for 'return', and 'bra' for 'braces'. As the Semirebra Rule is specifically tailored to **java.util.function.Predicate**, it is meant to be used on the 1Z0-808 exam only.

Let's have another example that doesn't compile:

```
static String check(List list, Predicate<ArrayList> p){
    return p.test(list)? "Empty" : "Not empty";          // INVALID
}
public static void main(String[] args) {
    List list = new ArrayList();
    System.out.println(check(list, al -> al.isEmpty()));
}
```

Here, **Predicate** is typed to **ArrayList** while the object it must work with is of type **List**. In other words, the method **test()** was promised that its argument is going to have everything that is typical for an **ArrayList**; instead, **test()** gets just a **List**, which is not sufficient.

Alright, let's flip the types in the **check()** method's signature:

```
static String check(ArrayList list, Predicate<List> p){
    return p.test(list)? "Empty" : "Not empty";
}

public static void main(String[] args) {
    List list = new ArrayList();
    System.out.println(check(list, al -> al.isEmpty()));  // INVALID
}
```

Did it help? Nope, the comperr just moved to the printing stat's line: although **test()** is perfectly happy now because it expected a toy of type **List** while what it's gonna get will be even more sophisticated and amusing, the actual call to **check()** provides the same unrefined, boring **List**. If the available options prevent us from touching the **check()** method's signature, we could change **list**'s reftype:

```
ArrayList list = new ArrayList();
```

Another way to deal with this problem involves casting **list** to **ArrayList**:

```
System.out.println(check((ArrayList)list, al -> al.isEmpty()));
```

After all, the actual type of the object at run time is **ArrayList**, so this quick'n'dirty hack will even work…

❑ EXTRA: Watch out for already declared vars in lambdas: while the parameter list does declare new vars to be used in the body part of the lambda expression, these variables won't get new scope and, therefore, cannot shadow the previously declared vars:

```
List al = new ArrayList();
System.out.println(check(al, al -> al.isEmpty()));     // INVALID
```

Problem 9.39   Given the following class definitions:

```
class Examinee {
    private String name;
    private int score;
    public Examinee(String name, int score) {
        this.name = name;
        this.score = score;
    }
    public String getName() { return name; }
    public int getScore() { return score; }
}
class ReleasingResults{
    public static void checkScore(List<Examinee> list, Predicate<Examinee> p){
        for (Examinee e : list) {
            if (p.test(e)) {
                System.out.print(e.getName() + ", ");
            }
        }
    }
    public static void main(String[] args) {
        List<Examinee> list = Arrays.asList(new Examinee("Alice", 98),
                                    new Examinee("Bob", 48),
                                    new Examinee("Charlie", 62),
                                    new Examinee("Doug", 88));
        System.out.print("Passed: ");
//  line r1
    }
}
```

Which LOC, when inserted at line r1, enables the code to print Passed: Alice, Doug, ?

    A.   checkScore(list, () -> e.getScore() > 65);

    B.   checkScore(list, Examinee e -> e.getScore() > 65);

    C.   checkScore(list, e -> e.getScore() > 65);

    D.   checkScore(list, (Examinee e) -> { e.getScore() > 65; });

Problem 9.40

Let sb refer to a StringBuilder object. Which of the following fail(s) compilation?

    A.   sb -> sb.toString()

    B.   StringBuilder sb -> sb.toString()

    C.   (StringBuilder sb) -> return sb.length();

    D.   (StringBuilder sb) -> { return sb.length(); }

Problem 9.41   Given:

```
class Test {
    String check(List list, Predicate p){              // line t1
        return p.test(list)? "Empty" : "Populated";
    }
    void run() {
        ArrayList list = new ArrayList();               // line t2
        System.out.println(
            check(list, list -> list.isEmpty()));       // line t3
    }
    public static void main(String[] args) {
        new Test().run();
    }
}
```

Which two options can make the code compile and run successfully?

A. Replace line t3 with `check(list, myList -> list.isEmpty()));`
B. Replace line t2 with `List list = new ArrayList();`
    and replace line t3 with `check(list, myList -> myList.isEmpty()));`
C. Replace line t1 with `String check(List list, Predicate<ArrayList> p){`
    and line t3 with `check(list, myList -> myList.isEmpty()));`
D. Replace line t1 with `String check(ArrayList list, Predicate<ArrayList> p){`
    line t2 with `List mist = new ArrayList();`
    and line t3 with `check(mist, list -> list.isEmpty()));`
E. Replace line t1 with `String check(List list, Predicate<List> p){`
    and line t3 with `check(list, myList -> myList.isEmpty()));`

Problem 9.42   Given:

```
class Suspect {
    private String name;
    private boolean statement;

    public Suspect (String name) {
        this.name = name;
        this.statement = Math.random() < 0.5 ? false : true;
    }

    public boolean getStatement() { return statement; }
    public String  getName()      { return name;      }
}

class Interrogation {
    private static void interrogate(List<Suspect> perps){
        for(Suspect e : perps)
            if (e.getStatement() != true)
                System.out.println(e.getName() + " is lying!");
    }

    public static void main(String[] args) {
        List<Suspect> roundUp = new ArrayList();
        roundUp.add(new Suspect("Alice"));
        roundUp.add(new Suspect("Bob"));
        roundUp.add(new Suspect("Charlie"));
        roundUp.add(new Suspect("Doug"));
        roundUp.add(new Suspect("Eugine"));
        roundUp.add(new Suspect("Frances"));

        interrogate(roundUp);
    }
}
```

Which modification will achieve the same result?

A. Overload the method **interrogate()** with the following code fragment:

```
private static void interrogate(List<Suspect> perps, Predicate p){
    for(Suspect s : perps)
        if(!p.test(s))
            System.out.println(s.getName() + " is lying");
}
```

and replace the call to **interrogate()** with the following LOC:

```
interrogate(roundUp, perps -> perps.getStatement());
```

B. Overload the method **interrogate()** with the following code fragment:

```
private static void interrogate(List perps, Predicate<Suspect> p){
    for(Suspect s : perps)
        if(!p.test(s))
            System.out.println(s.getName() + " is lying");
}
```

and replace the call to **interrogate()** with the following LOC:

```
interrogate(roundUp, perps -> perps.getStatement());
```

C. Add the following interface:

```
interface LieDetector {
    default boolean test(Suspect s){ return s.getStatement(); }
}
```

then overload the method **interrogate()** with the following code fragment:

```
private static void interrogate(List<Suspect> perps, LieDetector ld){
    for(Suspect s : perps)
        if(!ld.test(s))
            System.out.println(s.getName() + " is lying");
}
```

and replace the call to **interrogate()** with the following LOC:

```
interrogate(roundUp, perps -> perps.getStatement());
```

D. Add the following interface:

```
interface LieDetector { boolean analyze(Suspect s); }
```

then overload the method **interrogate()** with the following code fragment:

```
private static void interrogate(List<Suspect> perps, LieDetector ld){
    for(Suspect s : perps)
        if(!ld.analyze(s))
            System.out.println(s.getName() + " is lying");
}
```

and replace the call to **interrogate()** with the following LOC:

```
interrogate(roundUp, perps -> perps.getStatement());
```

Problem 9.43

Which one is true?

A. Functional interface may not contain more than one method.
B. Any interface that has a single abstract method is therefore functional.
C. Functional interface cannot have superinterfaces.
D. Functional interface cannot be extended.
E. None of the above.

 **Keys & Discussion:**

Problem 9.1 – D

Given:

```
class Hello {
    public static void main(String[] args) {
        String str = "Hello";
        StringBuilder sb = new StringBuilder(str);
        str.replace("o", "");                                          // h1
        System.out.print(str + " ");                                   // h2
        System.out.print(str.replace("o","") + " ");                   // h3
        System.out.print(sb.append("?").equals(sb.append("!")) + " "); // h4
        System.out.println(str.replace("o","").equals(str.replace("o",""))); // h5
    }
}
```

What is the result?

A. Hell Hell false false
B. Hell Hell true true
C. Hello Hell false false
D. Hello Hell true true
E. Hello Hell false true
F. Hello Hell true false

The first thing coming to your mind whenever you see a **String** object on the exam should be something like "Ah! This animal is immutable, so I'd better be careful…" Naturally, there are also some quirky methods to watch out for but, basically, this is it.

Now please list the immutable classes that are on our exam; we mentioned them when discussing the solution to Problem 4.3… Did you get them all[149]? Good.

Back to **String**. Since **str** is immutable, line h1 doesn't change the original object; instead, a new object is created – and wasted because the reference to it isn't used in any way, so line h2 prints the same old 'Hello'. With a trailing space, of course. On the other hand, line h3 outputs 'Hell ' because the printing stat acts on the object that was returned by **replace()**.

As for line h4, **StringBuilder** doesn't override **Object**'s **equals()** → hence the method simply compares two identical references and returns `true`. We should always keep in mind that methods act on objects *through a reference*, so that's why when the second **append()** completes its job, both operands will contain the same sequence of characters, namely 'Hello?!'. Let's have a simple illustration of this principle, this time with a class that does override **equals()**:

```
class General{
    int stars = 1;
    General bePromoted(int stars){
        this.stars += stars;
        return this;
    }
    @Override
    public String toString(){ return "" + stars; }
}
```

---

[149] **String** + all **LDT**s + all Wrappers such as **Byte**, etc. + *structurally*-immutable **List** created by **Arrays.asList()**.

```
class ChiefOfStaff {
    public static void main(String[] args) {
        General g = new General();
        System.out.println(g.bePromoted(1).equals(g.bePromoted(2)));   // true
        System.out.println(g);                                          // 4
    }
}
```

In the above example, the object is always the same, and any change made to it through a reference gets reflected on both sides of **equals()**.

Next step (we are getting back to the current Problem 9.1, by the way); what happens when we have a mirror situation: the class **String** that, unlike **StringBuilder**, is not only immutable but also overrides **equals()**? Line h5 answers that by printing `true`, but why? Specifically, is it because **String** is immutable or for some other reason?

Alright, the first operand, namely **str.replace("o","")**, creates an identical twin to **str**, changes its contents, delivers this freshly baked object to **equals()**, who grabs it, peeks inside and sees… hmm… it sees Hell.

The second operand in its own turn takes the reference to the original and immutable **str**, which still reads "Hello", does its thing and returns another new object that again contains "Hell". So on both palms of **equals()** lie pointers to two different objects, which just happen to be made of the same hellish stuff. Compare it to the situation with the mutable **StringBuilder** where **append()** each time acts on and returns reference to the same object…

And what about an immutable object in a class that does not overrides **equals()**? Here we go:

```
class General{
    int stars = 1;
    General bePromoted(int stars){      // 'stars' denotes rank itself
        if (stars - this.stars != 0) {  // so bePromoted(2) means
            General g = new General();  // promotion to two-star general
            g.stars += stars;           // rather than three-star
            return g;
        }
        else return this;               // returns same obj if no change in rank
    }
    General beDemoted(int stars){
        if (this.stars - stars != 0) {
            General g = new General();
            g.stars -= stars;
            return g;
        }
        else return this;
    }

//      @Override
//      public String toString(){ return "" + stars; }
}

class ChiefOfStaff {
    public static void main(String[] args) {
        General g = new General();
        System.out.println(g.bePromoted(2).equals(g.bePromoted(2)));   // false
        System.out.println(g.stars);                                    // 1
        System.out.println(g.beDemoted(1).equals(g.beDemoted(1)));     // true
        System.out.println(g.stars);                                    // 1
    }
}
```

Our brave general became unsinkable although unpromotable!

Problem 9.2 – D

Given:

```
class OurPets {
    static String checkPets(StringBuilder myPet, StringBuilder yourPet){
        return myPet == yourPet ? "same" : "different";
    }
    static String checkNames(StringBuilder myPet, StringBuilder yourPet){
        return myPet.equals(yourPet) ? "same" : "different";
    }
    public static void main(String[] args) {
        StringBuilder myPet = new StringBuilder("Fluffy");
        StringBuilder yourPet = new StringBuilder("Fluffy");
        System.out.print(checkPets(myPet, yourPet) + " pets, ");
        System.out.println(checkNames(myPet, yourPet) + " names");
    }
}
```

What is the result?

- A. same pets, same names
- B. different pets, same names
- C. same pets, different names
- D. different pets, different names
- E. Compilation fails

Since **StringBuilder** doesn't override **equals()**, **checkNames()** is virtually identical to **checkPets()**: it simply compares references.

Problem 9.3 – A

Given:

```
class TheFifthElement {
    public static void main(String[] args) {
        StringBuilder sb = new StringBuilder("1");     // earth
        sb.append("2");                                // water
        sb.append("3");                                // air
        sb.append("4");                                // fire
        sb.replace(4,4,"Leeloo");                      // line t1
        System.out.println(sb);
    }
}
```

What is the result?

- A. 1234Leeloo
- B. Compilation fails
- C. The code throws a run-time exception

StringBuilder does have a constructor that accepts a **String**, and its **append()** is overloaded for all imaginable types.

Now, unlike the class **String**, **StringBuilder**'s **replace()** isn't overloaded: its only version takes three args, namely (int start, int end, String replacementString). In short, the code is perfectly valid.

As with all the other methods in **String** and **StringBuilder** that accept two indices to limit a specific part of the character sequence (such as **str.substring**(int beginIndex, int endIndex), **sb.append**(CharSequence s, int start, int end), etc.), the first index is inclusive while the second one is exclusive → the substring on line t1 starts with the 5th element and ends with the element number 4. Looks mighty suspicious.

The code, however, doesn't throw a **RuntimeException** (a SIOOBE, to be exact) because – according to the **StringBuilder** API docs – the exception is generated "if start is negative, greater than **length()**, or greater than end".

And what **replace()** does, then? It

> ...replaces the characters in a substring of this sequence with characters in the specified String. The substring begins at the specified start and extends to the character at index end - 1 or to the end of the sequence if no such character exists. First the characters in the substring are removed and then the specified String is inserted at start. (This sequence will be lengthened to accommodate the specified String if necessary.)[150]

Problem 9.4 – C

Given the following class:

```
class Test {
    public static void main(String[] args) {
        int[] arr = {1,2,3,4,5};
        String str = null;                    // line t1
        for(int e : arr){ str += e; }
        System.out.println(str);
    }
}
```

What is the result:

- A. _12345 (*where _ denotes an empty space*)
- B. 12345
- C. null12345
- D. Compilation fails
- E. A **NullPointerException** is thrown

String is a reference type and, as such, can be null, so the assop on line t1 is valid.

What about the next LOC? Let's run the entire logical chain:

Step 1.   str += e actually means str = str + e;

Step 2.   JLS, §15.18, *Additive Operators*: "If the type of either operand of a + operator is **String**, then the operation is string concatenation".

Step 3.   JLS, §5.1.11, *String Conversion*: "If the reference is null, it is converted to the string "null" (four ASCII characters n, u, l, l)".

→ so there's neither a comperr nor RTE → this is why the first iteration results in 'null1' – and everything after that is trivial.

---

[150] Quoting from the **StringBuilder** API docs.

Hoping to land a job as a junior programmer at a local bank, you came to a Java interview and were asked to complete the following class that masks 20-digit account numbers so that only the last five digits will be visible to the user while each of the first 15 digits is replaced with an asterisk:

```java
public class AccountMasker {
    public static String maskAccount(String accNum) {
        String lead = "***************";   // contains 15 asterisks in a row

        // your code goes in here

    }
    public static void main(String[] args) {
        String accNum = args[0];
        System.out.println(maskAccount(accNum.replace(" ","")));
    }
}
```

Specifically, your task is to finish up the method **maskAccount**(String accNum) so that the class **AccountMasker** will output ***************67541 when run with the following command:

java AccountMasker "34296 01853 49820 67541"

Which two LOCs, when used independently, will achieve this requirement?

A. `return (new StringBuilder(accNum)).substring(15, 20).toString();`
B. `return lead + accNum.substring(15, 20);`
C. `return new StringBuilder(accNum).append(lead, 15, 20).toString();`
D. `return new StringBuilder(accNum).insert(0, lead).toString();`
E. `return new StringBuilder(lead).append(accNum, 15, 20).toString();`

As usual, we start our analysis by looking at the available options: what if some of them can be eliminated right away? It happens a lot on the exam, and this time is not an exception.

The output must contain asterisks (disguised as the var **lead**) → option A doesn't even mention that var → A is immediately out.

What about B? **substring()** works in the same way for both **String** and **StringBuilder**: it returns a **String** and is overloaded for (int start) and (int start, int end) → we have the second version, which returns whatever sits between index 15 inclusive and index 20 exclusive → what does this method receive? → it receives the object returned by **replace**(" ", "") → to wit, a 20-digit sequence now void of spaces because **String**'s **replace()** acts on *each* occurrence of the target char or **CharSequence** → substring contains 67541 → it gets prepended with **lead** → bingo.

Now to option C. **maskAccount()**'s arg, represented by the local var **accNum**, contains 20 digits without spaces → a new **StringBuilder** object gets created → it contains **accNum** → then **append()** attempts to add to it five characters taken from **lead** → but in doing so it goes too far, beyond the last available value since **lead** contains only 15 characters → an IOOBE.

Option D: **insert()** places **lead** at the first position in the **StringBuilder** object thus shifting to the right entire bunch of whatever the object used to contain, namely a 20-digit string → the result is way too long.

And since what's left is just option E, we accept it without even analyzing its logic → but at the Review stage we must do it → **append()** adds to **lead** a five-digit string extracted from **accNum**'s tail → then converts the whole works to **String** and returns it → yeap, looks fine.

Problem 9.6 – D

Which statement initializes a StringBuilder to a capacity of 256?

    A.   StringBuilder sb = new StringBuilder(new String(256));
    B.   StringBuilder sb = StringBuilder.setCapacity(256);
    C.   StringBuilder sb = StringBuilder.setLength(256);
    D.   StringBuilder sb = new StringBuilder(256);

Since the answer to the problem is obvious, we can afford to spend a minute to take a look at the bigger picture.

Only two classes on our exam have something that relates – either directly or indirectly – to this particular creature called **capacity**, namely **StringBuilder** and **ArrayList**:

	ArrayList	StringBuilder
Constructors	`ArrayList()` Constructs an empty list with an initial capacity of ten.	`StringBuilder()` Constructs a string builder with no characters in it and an initial capacity of 16 characters.
	`ArrayList(int initialCapacity)` Constructs an empty list with the specified initial capacity.	`StringBuilder(int capacity)` Constructs a string builder with no characters in it and an initial capacity specified by the capacity argument.
Methods	`void ensureCapacity(int minCapacity)` Increases the capacity of this ArrayList instance, if necessary, to ensure that it can hold at least the number of elements specified by the minimum capacity argument.	`void ensureCapacity(int minimumCapacity)` Ensures that the capacity is at least equal to the specified minimum.
	`void trimToSize()` Trims the capacity of this ArrayList instance to be the list's current size.	`void trimToSize()` Attempts to reduce storage used for the character sequence.
		`int capacity()` Returns the current capacity.

Although it may sound so, capacity is not an upper limit of how much we can put into the **StringBuilder** or **ArrayList**; it's a value defining a boundary beyond which the internal array must be reallocated to accommodate the necessary number of elements (in case of **ArrayList**) or the **CharSequence**'s length (in case of **StringBuilder**). Whereas **StringBuilder** lets both get and set its capacity, **ArrayList** does not provide a direct read access.

Back to our problem; option A doesn't compile because **String** defines no constructor that would take an `int` as its only arg; now please list the **String** constructors that are likely to appear on the exam[151].

As for options B and C, they are just plain wrong. First of all, **StringBuilder** doesn't have static methods so the name of the class cannot be used in any invocation. Secondly, **setCapacity()** doesn't even exist in **StringBuilder**; lastly, either method would have to return a **StringBuilder** object, and setters in a mutable class are usually `void` – just as **setLength()** is…

---

[151] **String**(String str) and **String**(StringBuilder sb) + **String**(), which is virtually useless because the object is immutable.

Problem 9.7 – AD

> **Given the code fragment:**
>
> ```
> StringBuilder sb = new StringBuilder();
> String exam = "1Z0";
> int code = 808;
> ```
>
> **Which two options will output the following:**
>
> > I'll pass 1Z0-808
>
> A. System.out.println(sb.append("I'll pass " + exam + "-" + code));
> B. System.out.println(sb.insert("I'll pass ").append(exam + "-" + code));
> C. System.out.println(sb.insert("I'll pass ").insert(exam).insert("-").insert(code));
> D. System.out.println(sb.append("I'll pass ").append(exam).append("-").append(code));

Of all the core Java classes we are supposed to learn for the exam only **StringBuilder** defines **insert()** – which is indeed our case. However, this **insert()** in all its overloaded versions requires at least two args (we need to specify *what* is to be inserted and *where*) → options B and C are immediately eliminated.

Problem 9.8 – C

> **Given:**
>
> ```
> public static void main(String[] args) {
>     String a = "B ";
>     a = a.concat("U ");            // line X
>     String b = "L ";
>     a = a.concat(b);               // line XX
>     a.replace('U', 'A');           // line XXX
>     a = a.concat(b);               // line XXXX
>     System.out.println(a);
> }
> ```
>
> **What is the result?**
>
> A. B A L L
> B. B L A
> C. B U L L
> D. B U A
> E. B U A L

We are dealing with **String**, which is immutable → the LOC on line XXX is immaterial as it doesn't assign the newly created object back to the var **a**. What is left for us is imitate the work of lines X, XX and XXXX on paper → line X results in B U → then line XX appends 'L' to what **a** holds → and line XXXX does the same.

Problem 9.9 – C

> **Given:**
>
> ```
> public class Simple{
>     public static void main (String[] args){
>         char c = 6;
>         System.out.println("Hello".charAt(c));
>     }
> }
> ```

What is the result?

    A. There is no output
    B. Compilation fails
    C. The code throws an **IndexOutOfBoundsException**
    D. The code throws a **NullPointException**

String's **charAt()** takes an `int`, and Java treats `char` as an integral type representing values from 0 to 65535 inclusive → there is no comperr.

As for what happens at run time, since 'Hello' contains only five characters, the code attempts to access something that doesn't exist → IOOBE (or, to be more precise, a SIOOBE).

Problem 9.10 – D

    Given:

```
StringBuilder bucket = new StringBuilder("Empty me!");
```

Which statement(s) will empty the contents of the bucket **object?**

    A. bucket.empty();
    B. bucket.clear();
    C. bucket.delete(0, bucket.size());
    D. bucket.delete(0, bucket.length());
    E. bucket.deleteAll();
    F. bucket.remove(0, bucket.length());
    G. bucket.removeAll();

This problem is obviously about one of the easily confused methods. Consult the table among the rules that relate to Exam Objectives 9.1 & 9.2 to refresh your memory, when in doubt.

Neither **String** nor **StringBuilder** nor **ArrayList** has an **empty()** method. The method **clear()** belongs to **ArrayList**, and same goes for **remove()** and **removeAll()** → we are left to choose among the three versions of **delete()**.

deleteAll() is there to confuse you; there's no such method, it simply bears a resemblance to **ArrayList**'s **removeAll()**.

Finally, as **size()** is defined in **ArrayList** while **StringBuilder** – together with **String** – uses **length()**, we arrive at the correct conclusion that the answer to our Problem 9.10 is option D.

Problem 9.11 – B

    Given:

```
class PoorGirl {
    public static void main(String[] args) {
        String name = "Javeline";
        System.out.println("Hi! I'm " + name.replace("e", "a"));
    }
}
```

What is the result?

    A. Hi! I'm Javaline
    B. Hi! I'm Javalina
    C. Hi! I'm Jevaline
    D. Hi! I'm Jeveline

The method **replace()** is defined in both **String** (where it is overloaded and takes *two* args – target followed by replacement – in both cases) and **StringBuilder** (where it is not overloaded and accepts *three* args). One of the most remarkable features of **replace()** in **String** is that it substitutes *each* occurrence of the target → every 'e' in Javeline gets replaced with an 'a'.

Problem 9.12 – D

Given the following main() method:

```
public static void main(String[] args) {
    String str = " ";
    str.trim();
    System.out.println(str.equals("") + " " + str.isEmpty());
}
```

What is the result?

    A.   true true
    B.   true false
    C.   false true
    D.   false false

The **String**s created with double quotes are placed into a common string pool; everything else – such as **String**s instantiated with the `new` keyword or computed at run time – isn't…

The above sentence is just a reminder; it's not directly relevant to our Problem because **str.trim()** returns a completely new object (but only if there were changes, that is), which in our case doesn't get used at all → **str** still points to the same object.

Now, it is immaterial whether or not the **String**s " " and "" live in a common pool: they are definitely distinct → and since **equals()** is overridden in **String**, it compares different contents.

Problem 9.13 – B

Given:

```
StringBuilder sb = new StringBuilder();
sb.append("Duke");
```

And the following LOCs:

```
System.out.println(sb.insert(0, "Hello "));
System.out.println(sb.append(0, "Hello "));
System.out.println(sb.add(0, "Hello "));
System.out.println(sb.set(0, "Hello "));
```

How many of them print Hello Duke?

    A. None
    B. One
    C. Two
    D. Three

The first printing stat appears quite natural. As for **append()**, it works with the tail only, so even its args look suspicious.

add() gets used so often that by now we should remember that it is a dweller of the **ArrayList** realm.

The method **set()** is a rarer bird but its logic dictates that it would simply replace the very first element with Hello – and the very first element in our **StringBuilder** is just 'D'. Still, it would have worked if only it were invoked on a proper object because **set()** also belongs to **ArrayList**…

Problem 9.14 – C

    Given the following code fragment:

```
String str1 = "null";
String str2 = new String("NULL");
System.out.println(str1.equalsIgnoreCase(str2.toLowerCase()));   // line 1
System.out.println(str2 == str2.replace('L','l').toLowerCase());  // line 2
System.out.println(str1 == str1.replace('L','l').toLowerCase());  // line 3
```

    How many times the code prints true?

    A. Not a single time
    B. Once
    C. Twice
    D. Three times

Alright, as we start reading the code, here comes immediate realization that both objects are immutable and that **str1** is a member of a common string pool whereas **str2** isn't. But is it important? We don't know yet; need to analyze further.

Next step: **str2.toLowerCase()** on line 1 returns 'null' and **equalsIgnoreCase()** compares it with **str1**'s 'null'.

Line 2 uses ==, which compares references only → **str2.replace**('L', 'l') returns a completely new object on which **toLowerCase()** is then invoked resulting in yet another object. All in all, on both sides of == sit different objects so it's no wonder that line 2 outputs false.

Line 3 resembles line 2 so damn much that it's tempting to assume both LOCs lead to identical results, which would be a disaster. As **str1** is made up of letters in lowercase from the very beginning, **replace()** – finding not a single match – returns reference to the same object. Then **toLowerCase()** follows its steps → in the end, on either palm of == sits the same object.

When reviewing you answers, pay close attention so something like option A, which might mean that the code doesn't compile. In our case, the only point of concern is probably the invocation of **replace()** that uses chars as the method's args.

You'll do mighty well remembering that **String** overloads **replace()** and that this method indeed can take `chars` as its args. The overloaded version accepts **CharSequence**... What about **StringBuilder**? and **ArrayList**?[152]

Problem 9.15 – D

Given:

```
public class TheMatrix {
    public static void main(String[] args) {
        String movie = "The";
        movie.concat(" ").concat("MATRIX".toLowerCase());
        System.out.print(movie.substring(5,6));
    }
}
```

What is the result?

    A. a
    B. at
    C. Compilations fails
    D. An exception is thrown at run time

A **String**? and the reference to it doesn't get reassigned? → same object all along.

And whoever wrote that **substring()** invocation was obviously half asleep for the method wants to grab the 6th character while **movie** still has only three.

Problem 9.16 – C

Given:

```
public class TheMatrixReloaded {
    static void reload(StringBuilder sb) {
        sb.append(" Matrix");
        sb.insert(" Reloaded", sb.length());
    }
    public static void main (String[] args) {
        StringBuilder sb = new StringBuilder("The");
        reload(sb);
        System.out.println(sb);
    }
}
```

What is the result?

    A. The
    B. The Matrix Reloaded
    C. Compilation fails
    D. An exception is thrown at run time

---

[152] **ArrayList** has no **replace()**: it uses **set**(int index, E element) instead. **StringBuilder** defines **replace**(int start, int end, String str) and doesn't overload it.

Many people prefer to read code starting from the **main()** method and then just following the program's business logic. The questions on our exam aren't long (with a possible exception of lambda-related problems – soon you'll see what I mean) so it is also possible to start on the top and then work your way to the bottom. Either way, you should notice that the invocation of **insert()** is wrong: its args switched places.

Otherwise the answer would have been option B because **StringBuilder** is mutable, and we do remember that Java is pass-by-value.

Problem 9.17 – E

Given the code fragment:

```
public static void main (String[] args) {
    String[] str = new String[2];
    int i = 0;
    for (String e : str)
        System.out.print(e.concat(" " + i++).trim());
}
```

What is the result?

A.   01
B.   0 1
C.   0 1
D.   Compilation fails
E.   An exception is thrown at run time

str is an array, and arrays, when allocated, always get inited with default values in their slots. In our case, the slots are of type **String**, which is a reference type, hence the default value is `null`.

Invoking a method on a `null` object is one of the most typical NPE-throwing scenarios on the exam.

Problem 9.18 – B

Given:

```
public class Exam {
    String str = "";                           // line e1
    static void pass(String str) {
        str.concat("Passed");
    }
    public static void main(String[] args) {
        String str = "Failed ";
        pass(str);
        System.out.println(str);
    }
}
```

What is the result?

A.   Passed
B.   Failed
C.   Failed Passed
D.   Compilation fails
E.   An exception is thrown at runtime

The var **str** declared in the method **main()** is local and, therefore, shadows the instance var **str** on line e1, which is a good thing because **pass()** is `static` → the code doesn't throw a comperr.

The method **concat()** is invoked correctly: it is overloaded for any data type so accepting a **String** isn't a problem, and the object itself isn't `null`.

If the class **String** were mutable, the method **pass()** would have returned 'Failed Passed' – but it isn't, so **str.concat()** dutifully creates a new object, which is then simply wasted.

Problem 9.19 – B

Given:

```
public class AnotherExam {
    public static void main (String[] args) {
        StringBuilder sb = new StringBuilder("Passed");
        System.out.print(sb + ": ");
        System.out.println(sb.replace(0,4,"Fail") ==
                            sb.delete(0,666).insert(0,"Failed"));
    }
}
```

What is the result?

A. Passed: false
B. Passed: true
C. Failed: false
D. Failed: true
E. Compilation fails
F. The code throws IndexOutOfBoundsException

StringBuilder's **replace()** is not overloaded, takes three args (int start, int end, String str) and returns the reference to the current object, so the left-hand side of == is valid → the object contains now 'Failed'.

Now to the right-hand side: **StringBuilder**'s **delete()** isn't overloaded, either, and takes two args, namely (int start, int end). A question arises: is it OK if the `end` index is way beyond the object's boundary? won't the code throw an IOOBE?

No, says the API documentation: "[the method] throws **StringIndexOutOfBoundsException** if `start` is negative, greater than **length()**, or greater than `end`" → the method successfully deletes the entire string → and then **insert()** – which is overloaded, by the way – slips in 'Failed' at the first position.

Whatever the object contains is, however, immaterial as == compares references and we are dealing here with a mutable data type → the last printing stat outputs true.

Problem 9.20 – B

Given:

```
public class Capricchio {
    public static void main (String[] args) {
        Object obj = null;
        StringBuilder sb = new StringBuilder();     // line c1
        sb.append(obj);
        System.out.println(sb.length());
    }
}
```

What is the result?

    A. 1
    B. 4
    C. 16
    D. Compilations fails
    E. A **NullPointerException** is thrown at run time

Line c1 creates a **StringBuilder** object with no characters in it and an initial capacity of 16. As for the method **append()**, it is overloaded for all imaginable types → its operation is therefore successful.

But what exactly does it append? The mike goes to the API documentation:

> **append(**Object obj**)** appends the string representation of the Object argument.

Next question: how this 'string representation' thingy is obtained? In a traditional way, that is, by calling **toString()** on **obj**? If so, this will surely throw an NPE... Option E, then?

Not at all; let's listen further to the API docs for **StringBuilder**'s **append(**Object obj**)**:

> The overall effect is exactly as if the argument were converted to a string by the method **String.valueOf(**Object**)**, and the characters of that string were then appended to this character sequence.

And **String.valueOf(**Object**)** pipes in with this:

> If the argument is null, then a string equal to "null"; otherwise, the value of **obj.toString()** is returned.

In short, our **StringBuilder** contains now the string 'null' – which is four characters long.

Problem 9.21 – C

    Given:

```
public class HowAboutThisOne {
    public static void main (String[] args) {
        String str = null;
        StringBuilder sb = new StringBuilder(str += str);
        sb.delete(0,sb.length());
        System.out.println(sb.capacity());
    }
}
```

What is the result?

    A. 8
    B. 16
    C. 24
    D. Compilations fails
    E. A **NullPointerException** is thrown at run time

Every LOC is valid so there's no comperr:

- **str** is a refvar and can be assigned `null`;
- `str += str` means `str = str + str`, and the + op is overloaded for **String** resulting in 'nullnull';
- **StringBuilder** indeed have an overloaded constructor that accepts a **String**;
- **delete()** is invoked correctly → no RTE, and
- **StringBuilder** class does define an instance field named **capacity**.

Now we only have to choose among options A, B and C. The **StringBuilder** API documentation defines capacity in this way: "The capacity is the amount of storage available for newly inserted characters, beyond which an allocation will occur". As for length, it's a character count.

Unfortunately, this information is not enough to arrive at the correct answer; we really need to look at the definition of the **StringBuilder** constructor that accepts a **String**:

Constructs a string builder initialized to the contents of the specified string. The initial capacity of the string builder is 16 plus the length of the string argument.

QED.

Problem 9.22 – A

Given:

```
class Slogan {
    public static void main(String[] args) {
        String str = "String Beans Forever!";
        // line XXX: only a single LOC goes in here!
    }
}
```

And the following LOCs:

```
System.out.println(str.delete(6,11));
str = str.delete(6,11); System.out.println(str);
str.replace(" Bean",""); System.out.println(str);
System.out.println(new StringBuilder(str).remove(" Bean").toString());
```

How many LOCs, when inserted independently at line XXX, will make the code print Strings Forever!?

- A. None
- B. One
- C. Two
- D. Three

First and foremost – please do pay attention, this one is important – **String** has neither **delete()** nor **insert()**; they belong to **StringBuilder**. The only methods that *appear* to change a **String** structurally are **concat()**, **replace()** and **trim()** → the first two LOCs are definitely out.

LOC number three, while valid, isn't what we need: it does remove the string " Bean" but the computed result gets wasted because the hasty slogan writer forgot to assign it back to **str**.

Now, I don't know about you, but in my eyes the last line of code looks entirely logical: it first constructs an SB by passing a **String** object to the correctly chosen constructor, then **remove()** gets rid of an extra " Bean" after which **toString()** converts the result to a **String**, which then gets printed → this one should apparently work… only it doesn't because **StringBuilder** has no **remove()** → the last LOC is invalid.

Rather confusing, if you ask me. So, when preparing for the exam, I tried to come up with a single logical rule:

> No **delete()** or **insert()** in **String** → they are defined in **StringBuilder** only → **remove()** would be totally redundant in SB because the class already has **delete()** that takes care of the task.

Or on a lighter note,

> *Rules for **String** are mean 'n tough,*
> *Learn by heart this bloody stuff:*
> *No **delete()** and no **insert()** –*
> *That's the way to Java cert.*
> ***add()** to **List** to feel no pain,*
> *Use **remove()** – or **clear()** its brain.*
> *And remember that **replace()***
> *Can explode right in your face:*
> *While in **String** it overloads,*
> ***SB** follows other roads.*

HTH.

Problem 9.23 – C

Given:

```
final String str = "";
while(str.equals("")) System.out.print(str+1);
```

What is the result?

- A. 1
- B. No visible output at all
- C. Code compiles but enters endless loop at run time
- D. Compilation fails because of an unreachable statement
- E. Compilation fails because str+1 creates a new object but str is final
- F. Compilation fails because the expression str+1 is illegal

Although it is a fact that something like `while(true)` may lead to a comperr if the loop is followed by other statements, which become therefore unreachable, it doesn't happen in our case because the evaluation of **equals()** happens at run time.

The expression `str+1` is also valid since the + op is overloaded for **String**; it simply appends 1 to the already existing string at each iteration, creating another **String** object – every time anew:

```
final String str = "";
int a = 0;
while(str.equals("")) {
    System.out.println((str+1).hashCode());    // same number over and over again
    a++;
    if (a > 4) break;
}
```

As for the `final` keyword, it is actually irrelevant since the new object never gets assigned to the original reference – unlike, for example, the following code snippet, which throws a comperr because **str** was declared `final`:

```
final String str = "";
// System.out.print(str+=1);    // INVALID: 'cannot assign a value to final variable str'
```

One more word of caution: Java doesn't require braces around loop bodies, which not only might break business logic if the coder isn't attentive but also can create endless loops when a semicolon is placed behind, for example, `while(`*smth_that_evaluates_to_true*`)` out of habit:

```
final String str = "";
while(str.equals(""));
    System.out.println(str+1);
```

Similarly to our Problem 9.23, this code fragment also compiles and runs indefinitely although without any visible output. What a nasty, well hidden trap… Fortunately, the exam seems not to abuse semicolons but you should be on your guard just the same.

Problem 9.24 – B

　　Given:

```
"a".replace("a","b");                                        // line 1
"a".replace('a','b');                                        // line 2
"a".replace(0,"a".length(),"b");                             // line 3
"a".replace(new StringBuilder('a'),"");                      // line 4
"a".replace(new StringBuilder('a'), new StringBuilder("b")); // line 5
new StringBuilder("a").replace("","b");                      // line 6
new StringBuilder("a").replace('a','b');                     // line 7
new StringBuilder("a").replace(0,1,"b");                     // line 8
```

　　How many LOCs fail compilation?

　　　　A.　Two
　　　　B.　Three
　　　　C.　Four
　　　　D.　Five

The literal "a" is a full-fledged **String** object → does **String** have the method **replace()**? → yes, it does but there are only two overloaded versions, either of which takes *two* args → line 3 is definitely invalid. It would have been fine, though, if it were invoked on a **StringBuilder** object because **StringBuilder** does have **replace()** that accepts three args: two `int`s – start and end – and a **String**.

What about line 4? It looks mighty odd: the args are of different – and even incompatible types… Will it compile? To find out what's going to happen, we need to test our knowledge of the **replace()** method in **String**. Please answer: what are the arguments for **replace()** in **String**?

By looking at our code (lines 1 and 2), it is tempting to say: "two **String**s and two `char`s". Close, very close – but no cigar… because the API actually defines **replace**(char oldChar, char newChar) and **replace**(CharSequence target, CharSequence replacement).

String and **StringBuilder** both implement the interface **CharSequence** (we have already met this when discussing Problem 6.34); this is precisely why we can use **String**s as arguments in **str.replace()** – and same goes for **StringBuilder** objects. What's more, **StringBuilder** does define a constructor that accepts a **CharSequence** → line 4 is valid. By the same token, line 5 also compiles.

Alright, what can be said about line 6? Ah, but this one should be easy by now: **StringBuilder** has no **replace()** that would take two args → line 6 is invalid → line 7 fails compilation, as well.

As for the last LOC, it looks clean: three args of correct types in correct places…

One more thing about **replace()** that you might find useful on the exam is that the method returns a reference to the same object if there was no change:

```
String str = "h";
System.out.println(str == str.replace('Z','a'));                        // true
System.out.println(str);                                                // h
System.out.println(
    str == str.replace(new StringBuilder("Z"), new StringBuilder("a"))); // true
System.out.println(str);                                                // h
```

Boring, eh? Getting on your nerves already… Alright, let's play with **replace()** for the very last time. Please riddle me this:

Given:

```
String str = "_";
str = str.replace(new StringBuilder('Z'), new StringBuilder("^"));
System.out.println(str);
```

What is the result?

Do run this code; it may brighten up your day[153]…

Problem 9.25 – A

Given:

```
public class Dissonance{
    public static void main(String[] args) {
        Object obj = "Quartet No. 19 in C Major, K. 465";      // line D1
        System.out.println(obj.getClass().getSimpleName() + " " + obj); }
}
```

Is it true that the code prints String Quartet No. 19 in C Major, K. 465?

A. true
B. false

The question strongly hints on the most famous string quartet by Mozart so answering it should be easy. A bit harder is figuring out why the code compiles and works as intended because we get used to the idea that employing double quotes as the way to create objects is reserved for **String**s only, from which sort of follows that the reftype must be also **String** – and this is not so.

As soon as we realize that the double-quoted literal "String" is just a handy replacement[154] for

```
char string[] = {'S', 't', 'r', 'i', 'n', 'g'};
String str = new String(string);
```

it becomes clear as day that there's nothing wrong with line D1.

---

[153] As there's no **StringBuilder** constructor that would take a char *per se*, 'Z' gets widened to int, so new **StringBuilder**('Z') creates just an empty **StringBuilder** with capacity of 90. Effectively, the **replace()** invocation reads **replace**("","^") – and "" matches boundaries of "_" because of the way the regex engine works…

[154] Ref.to the API javadoc's preambule for the class **String**.

Problem 9.26 – C

Given the following code fragment:

```
LocalDate today = LocalDate.of(2016, Month.JUNE, 13);
today.plusHours(24);
System.out.println(today);
```

What is the result?

    A.   2016-06-14
    B.   2016-06-13
    C.   Compilation fails
    D.   An exception is thrown at run time

LocalDate contains only date → the second stat is invalid.

Problem 9.27 – E

Given:

```
public static void main(String[] args) {
    String date = LocalDate.parse("2016-07-13")
                        .plusDays(31)
                        .format(DateTimeFormatter.ISO_DATE_TIME);
    System.out.println(date); }
```

What is the result?

    A.   2016-07-13
    B.   2016-07-14
    C.   2016-07-15
    D.   Compilation fails
    E.   An exception is thrown at run time

Once again: **LocalDate** cannot contain time but formatter wants to extract time out of that object, so the code should apparently misbehave, that much is clear. What's not so clear is what it's gonna throw: a comperr or an RTE?

As a rule of thumb for the exam: improperly applied **format()** throws an RTE whereas incorrect invocations of **parse()** and **plus/minusXXX()** usually lead to a comperr.

Problem 9.28 – D

Given:

```
LocalDate ld = LocalDate.of(2016, 6, 13);
ld.plusMonths(6).format(DateTimeFormatter.ISO_LOCAL_DATE);
System.out.println(ld);
```

What is the result?

    A.   December 13, 2016
    B.   June 13, 2015
    C.   2016-12-13
    D.   2016-06-13

Now all the LOCs are clean, and the code does output the date contained in the object **ld** – which is, of course, immutable but we already know that. The only question is what form this date will be printed in: after all, the code compiles as can be easily deduced from the list of options.

Alright, the API documentation defines the class **LocalDate** in the following way:

> A date without a time-zone in the ISO-8601 calendar system, such as 2007-12-03.

This is it; by default, the date is output as YYYY-MM-DD; notice two mandatory digits for both months and days. To get something like option A or B, we'd need to call on our **LocalDate** object the method **format()** with an appropriate **DateTimeFormatter** as its argument…

I wonder what you will make out of this little gem:

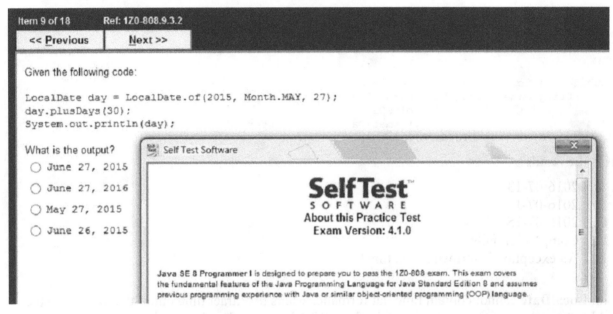

This is oh-so-praised Kaplan: the software *officially* endorsed by both Oracle and Pearson Vue. That's how those guys propose – quoting – "to prepare you to pass the 1Z0-808 exam". Well then, be prepared…

Problem 9.29 – AD

Which two LOCs fail compilation?

    A.   LocalDateTime.of(2016,6,13);
    B.   LocalDate.of(2016, Month.JUNE, 50);
    C.   LocalDateTime.of(2016,06,13,14,15);
    D.   LocalDate ld = new LocalDate(2016,6,13);
    E.   LocalTime.now().format(DateTimeFormatter.ISO_DATE);

Option A needs time (no pun intended) but gets none.

Option B is fine as far as the compiler is concerned although the LOC throws

> java.time.DateTimeException: Invalid value for DayOfMonth (valid values 1 - 28/31): 50

Option C is also valid because it provides both components (14 denotes hours and 15, minutes).

As for option D, it's a trap. We are so used to calling constructors that this LOC appears totally innocent. But please do remember:

LDTs don't have `public` **constructors. None of 'em has.**

The LDT objects are usually created by invoking `static` methods such as **of()**, **now()** or **parse()**.

And finally, option E. It does nothing illegal although its desire to format the **LocalTime** object with something that also concerns date will be frowned upon by the JVM:

java.time.temporal.UnsupportedTemporalTypeException: Unsupported field: Year

Problem 9.30 – A

Given:

```
System.out.println(LocalDate.now().plus(Period.of(0,0,0)));
System.out.println(LocalDate.of(2016, Month.JUNE, 13)
                        .format(DateTimeFormatter.ISO_LOCAL_DATE));
System.out.println(LocalDate.parse("2016-06-13", DateTimeFormatter.ISO_DATE));
```

What is the result if the system date is June 13, 2016?

    A.   2016-06-13
          2016-06-13
          2016-06-13
    B.   Compilation fails.
    C.   A DateParseException is thrown at runtime.

All three LOCs correctly create their corresponding **LocalDate** objects. Yes, it is that simple. And even a simpler version of this question you are going to meet on the exam. Congrats.

Problem 9.31 – AD

Given the full contents of the file JavaBirthday.java:

```
1 package birthday;
2 import java.time.LocalDate;
3 import java.time.format.DateTimeFormatter;
4
5 public class JavaBirthday {
6     public static void main(String[] args) {
7         LocalDate birthday = LocalDate.of(1995, Month.MAY, 23);
8         DateTimeFormatter formatter =
9                         DateTimeFormatter.ofPattern("MMM dd, YYYY");
10        System.out.println("Java was born on " + birthday.format(formatter));
11    }
12 }
```

One of the LOCs fails compilation. Which two modifications, used independently, will make the code print Java was born on May 23, 1995?

    A.   Replace line 2 with import java.time.*;
    B.   Replace line 3 with import java.time.format.*;
    C.   Replace Month.MAY on line 7 with Month.May
    D.   Replace Month.MAY on line 7 with 05

The LDT classes often borrow things from other classes and even different packages, such as **DateTimeFormatter**, which is defined in **java.time.format**. By using fully qualified names rather than wildcards in imports, the code can create a situation when something is amiss.

That's exactly what's happening here: line 7 invokes the method **of()**, which takes as its second arg a constant that is defined in the enum **Month**, which belongs to **java.time**. Using a 'wildcarded' import stat restores the compilability of the class.

Another way to get rid of the comperr is to use a two-digit int for the desired month instead of the enum constant.

Problem 9.32 – A

> Given the following class definition:

```
class LangsToLearn {
    public static void main(String[] args) {
        List<String> langs = new ArrayList<>();
        langs.add("Ruby");
        langs.add("Perl");
        langs.add("Perl");
        langs.add("Closure");
        if (langs.remove("Perl")) langs.add("Emacs Lisp");
        System.out.println(langs);
    }
}
```

> What is the result?

> A. [Ruby, Perl, Closure, Emacs Lisp]
> B. [Ruby, Closure, Emacs Lisp, Emacs Lisp]
> C. [Ruby, Closure, Emacs Lisp]
> D. Compilation fails

There is no reason for the compilation to fail since all methods are invoked correctly and the object itself is also created in a valid way. Note, however, that it can contain only **Strings**. And don't forget that unlike **StringBuilder**, **ArrayList** defines **remove()** rather than **delete()**.

Another important thing to keep in mind is that **remove()** acts on the first match only (compare it to **replace()** in **String**).

This useful functionality is possible because **List** is an ordered collection. Which can also be sorted. By the way, what's the difference between 'ordered' and 'sorted'? This is what the **List** API documentation says:

> public interface List<E> extends Collection<E>
>
> An ordered collection (also known as a sequence). The user of this interface has precise control over where in the list each element is inserted. The user can access elements by their integer index (position in the list), and search for elements in the list.

In other words, 'ordered' means in practice 'addressable' while 'sorted' implies that the elements are physically placed in a certain order, which is imposed by the interface **Comparable** and is referred to as 'natural ordering'. The natural ordering of elements is specific for each class that implements **Comparable**. For example, **Strings** are sorted lexicographically:

```
List<String> list = new ArrayList<>();
list.add("1");  list.add("03");
list.add("20"); list.add("123");
list.add("ah"); list.add("Zed");
Collections.sort(list);
System.out.println(list);              // [03, 1, 123, 20, Zed, ah]
```

Back to our Problem 9.32; **ArrayList**'s **remove(**Object obj**)** returns `true` if the list contained the specified object → "Emacs Lisp" gets added to the list.

Problem 9.33 – AF

Given:

```
ArrayList<String> someTypes = new ArrayList<>();
someTypes.add("byte");
someTypes.add("long");
someTypes.add("int");
```

Which two expressions evaluate to 3?

  A. someTypes.size();
  B. someTypes.capacity();
  C. someTypes.length();
  D. someTypes.get(2).size;
  E. someTypes.get(2).length;
  F. someTypes.get(2).length();

ArrayList doesn't have the method **capacity()** (which is **StringBuilder**'s member) although it defines **ensureCapacity()**; **length()** belongs to both **String** and **StringBuilder**.

As for the method **get()**, it returns the element at the specified position, and we then invoke **length()** on it because, after all, our **ArrayList** is generified to **String**.

Let's note in passing that option D wouldn't have compiled even if **someTypes** were generified to **List** and contained three three-element-long **List**s because the number of elements in **someTypes** must be computed by calling a method rather than by accessing a field.

As for option E, it would have worked, for example, in the following case:

```
ArrayList someTypes = new ArrayList();
Object obj = new Object();
int[] arrInt = new int[0];
String[] arrStr = {"","",""};
someTypes.add(obj);
someTypes.add(arrInt);
someTypes.add(arrStr);
System.out.println(   ((String[])someTypes.get(2)).length   );     // 3
```

Problem 9.34 – E

Given the following code fragment:

```
ArrayList<Integer> list = new ArrayList();       // a1
list.add(1);                                      // a2
System.out.println(list.get(list.size()));        // a3
```

What is the result?

A. 1
B. Compilation fails on line a1
C. Compilation fails on line a2
D. Compilation fails on line a3
E. An IndexOutOfBoundsException is thrown at run time

Even though the right-hand side of the **list**-creating LOC is missing angle brackets, it's OK because the compiler can infer our intentions.

As type safety via generics is provided at compile time, the compiler looks at the reftype only and disregards the diamond op on the right:

```
List list1 = new ArrayList();              // accepts anything
List list2 = new ArrayList<>();            // ditto
List list3 = new ArrayList<String>();      // ditto
```

On the other hand, the diamond on the left may not be empty → otherwise a comperr:

```
// List<> list4 = new ArrayList();            // INVALID
// List<> list5 = new ArrayList<>();          // INVALID
// List<> list6 = new ArrayList<String>();    // INVALID

List<String> list7 = new ArrayList();         // accepts Strings only
// list7.add(new Object());                   // INVALID
// list7.add(1);                              // INVALID
list7.add("");
list7.add(null);
List<String> list8 = new ArrayList<>();       // accepts Strings only
List<String> list9 = new ArrayList<String>(); // ditto
```

All in all, option B is incorrect as line a1 is valid.

Line a2 is also fine as primitives get autoboxed because **List** works with reference types only. (Reminder: using something like `list.add((byte)1);` at line a2 would have thrown a comperr since the compiler would have autoboxed byte to **Byte**, and then what? **Byte** can't be converted to **Integer** implicitly…)

Now to option D; both methods are invoked correctly but `list.get(1)` will definitely throw an RTE as it wants to look at the second element while **list** has only one.

Problem 9.35 – B

Given:

```
class TestingArrayList {
    public static void main (String[] args) {
        List<String> list = new ArrayList<>();
        for (int i = 0; i < 5; i++) list.add("" + i);
        System.out.println(list.remove(list.indexOf("4")));
    }
}
```

What is the result?

A. true
B. 4
C. [0, 1, 2, 3, 4]
D. Compilation fails

The invocation `list.add("" + i)` works correctly because our **list** is generified to **String** and the op + is overloaded for **String**s. The methods **indexOf()** and **remove()** are also called in valid ways → option D is out.

remove() receives an `int` whose value is 4 (since elements are enumerated starting with zero) → **remove(int index)** strips **list** of the element at the specified position and returns it (the element, that is) → the code prints 4.

In short, it is important to remember that **remove(int index)** returns what was taken out from the **List** and not, for example, a `boolean` as if to say 'Alright boss, I successfully did what you have requested'. Because it doesn't need to: it either removes an element or reports a failure by throwing an IOOBE, that's all. On the contrary, the overloaded version of the method, namely **remove(Object obj)**, does return a `boolean`...

Please also note what kind of loop was used to populate the **list**. It may be tempting to employ an enhanced `for`, like this:

```
List<String> list = new ArrayList<>();
int i = 0;
while(i<5)
    for (String e : list) list.add("" + i++);
System.out.println(list.remove(list.indexOf("4")));
```

but it won't work: **list** is still empty, there's no elements to iterate over → `for` won't run, and the code will enter an endless loop because the loop var **i** has no chance to increment...

Problem 9.36 – B

Given:

```
public class MutatisMutandis {
    public static void main(String[] args) {
        List list = new ArrayList();
        list.add(new StringBuilder(""));
        list.add("");
        for (Object e : list )
            if (e instanceof StringBuilder) ((StringBuilder)e).append("OK");
            else ((String)e).concat("OK");
        System.out.println(list);
    }
}
```

What is the result?

    A.   [OK, OK]
    B.   [OK,]
    C.   Compilations fails
    D.   A RuntimeException is thrown

As **list** isn't generified, it accepts any object. Casts ensure that the code may call methods specific for either **StringBuilder** or **String**. And finally, since **String** is immutable, invoking the method **concat()** doesn't affect the original **String** object, which remains empty.

Problem 9.37 – A

Given:

```
class Birdies{
    public static void main(String[] args) {
        List aviary = new ArrayList<>();          // line b1
        aviary.add("kinglet");
        aviary.add("finch");
        aviary.add("titmouse");
        aviary.add(aviary.set(0,"jay"));          // line b2
        System.out.println(aviary);
    }
}
```

What is the result?

A. [jay, finch, titmouse, kinglet]
B. [jay, finch, titmouse, true]
C. Compilation fails on line b1
D. Compilation fails on line b2

Using an empty diamond in the right-hand side of the stat on line b1 doesn't affect code's compilability, so **aviary** gets successfully populated with virtual birds whose reftype is **Object** and the actype **String**. Line b2 is valid, as well; it replaces the first element with **String** "jay", and since the method **set()** returns what was replaced, **add()** appends "kinglet" to the list.

Problem 9.38 – C

Given:

```
class Sweet16 {
    public static void main(String[] args) {
        List<Integer> ages = new ArrayList<>();
        ages.add(16);                                   // line s1
        ages.add(null);
        for (int i = 0; i < ages.size(); i++) System.out.print(ages.get(i));
        for (int i : ages) System.out.println(i);
    }
}
```

What is the result?

A. 16null16
B. 16null16null
C. 16null16 and a NullPointerException
D. Compilation fails

List autoboxes primitive args, so line s1 actually appends an **Integer**. Adding `null` to **ages** isn't problematic, either. What happens next, however, is: the first `for` loop behaves itself but the enhanced `for` throws an NPE. Let's see why.

As `get(i)` returns an **Integer**, the printing stat receives what **Integer**'s **toString()** returns → the first `for` outputs 16null. The enhanced `for` successfully unboxes the first element and assigns it to a primitive, but a similar attempt with `null` fails. Replacing `int` with a compatible reference type would have cleared up the problem.

Conclusion: using a primitive loop var in an enhanced `for` can lead to an NPE when iterating over a **List** → always make sure that the loop var is suitable for the task.

Problem 9.39 – C

Given the following class definitions:

```java
class Examinee {
    private String name;
    private int score;

    public Examinee(String name, int score) {
        this.name = name;
        this.score = score;
    }
    public String getName() { return name; }
    public int getScore() { return score; }
}

class ReleasingResults{
    public static void checkScore(List<Examinee> list, Predicate<Examinee> p){
        for (Examinee e : list) {
            if (p.test(e)) {
                System.out.print(e.getName() + ", ");
            }
        }
    }
    public static void main(String[] args) {
        List<Examinee> list = Arrays.asList(new Examinee("Alice", 98),
                                            new Examinee("Bob", 48),
                                            new Examinee("Charlie", 62),
                                            new Examinee("Doug", 88));
        System.out.print("Passed: ");
//  line r1
    }
}
```

Which LOC, when inserted at line r1, enables the code to print Passed: Alice, Doug,?

A. checkScore(list, () -> e.getScore() > 65);
B. checkScore(list, Examinee e -> e.getScore() > 65);
C. checkScore(list, e -> e.getScore() > 65);
D. checkScore(list, (Examinee e) -> { e.getScore() > 65; });

The Problem looks rather demanding but, in fact, lambda-related questions are arguably among the easiest ones on the exam. As always, we start our analysis by glancing at the list of available options, and a bunch of lambda expressions immediately indicates what the question is about.

The exam requires us to work with predicative lambdas; we just need to make sure if this is the case; the **checkScore()** method's signature confirms it.

Since the interface **Predicate**'s **test()** method takes a single arg, option A is out. Option B is also invalid because the explicit use of the parameter type requires parentheses.

Option D fails compilation because semicolon, braces and `return` should be used together[155] – but `return` is missing.

---

[155] One more time: please keep in mind that this rule is applicable only on our exam where we are supposed to deal with predicative lambdas. The interface **Predicate**'s **test()** returns a `boolean` → hence `return` is mandatory when the LE uses braces and a semicolon → but whenever the functional method is `void`, the Semirebra rule stops working.

Problem 9.40 – BC

Let sb refer to a StringBuilder object. Which of the following fail(s) compilation?

    A.   sb -> sb.toString()
    B.   StringBuilder sb -> sb.toString()
    C.   (StringBuilder sb) -> return sb.length();
    D.   (StringBuilder sb) -> { return sb.length(); }

The question hints that the list of options may contain more than one invalid LOC so we'll be needing to check every option. All four cases indicate that the lambda method takes a single arg of type **StringBuilder** and returns either a **String** or an `int` – and this info is enough to start the analysis.

Option A: the formal parameter has no explicit data type but this is OK; the method body contains a single **String**-returning stat so braces, semicolon and `return` aren't necessary → option A looks perfectly compilable.

What about option B? While the method body appears to be correct, the parameter list is missing parentheses, which are now mandatory because of the explicitly stated data type.

Option C is also invalid since it is omitting braces; option D, on the other hand, dutifully follows all the rules: the parentheses around the paramlist are in place, and the method body is written in its full form, with braces, `return` and semicolon → only options B and C fail compilation.

Let's see if our conclusion is indeed correct:

```
interface Lambdable1{ String run(StringBuilder sb); }
interface Lambdable2{ int run(StringBuilder sb); }
class Test{
    static void test1(Lambdable1 l){
        System.out.println(l.run(new StringBuilder("lambda")));
    }
    static void test2(Lambdable2 l){
        System.out.println(l.run(new StringBuilder("lambda")));
    }
    public static void main(String[] args) {
        test1(  sb -> sb.toString()  );                              // lambda
//      test1(  StringBuilder sb -> sb.toString()  );                // INVALID
//      test2(  (StringBuilder sb) -> return sb.length()  );         // INVALID
        test2(  (StringBuilder sb) -> { return sb.length(); }  );    // 6
    }
}
```

Problem 9.41 – AE

Given:

```
class Test {
    String check(List list, Predicate p){                    // line t1
        return p.test(list)? "Empty" : "Populated";
    }
    void run() {
        ArrayList list = new ArrayList();                    // line t2
        System.out.println(
            check(list, list -> list.isEmpty()));            // line t3
    }
    public static void main(String[] args) {
        new Test().run();
    }
}
```

Which two options can make the code compile and run successfully?

A. Replace line t3 with `check(list, myList -> list.isEmpty()));`

B. Replace line t2 with `List list = new ArrayList();`
and replace line t3 with `check(list, myList -> myList.isEmpty()));`

C. Replace line t1 with `String check(List list, Predicate<ArrayList> p){`
and line t3 with `check(list, myList -> myList.isEmpty()));`

D. Replace line t1 with `String check(ArrayList list, Predicate<ArrayList> p){`
line t2 with `List mist = new ArrayList();`
and line t3 with `check(mist, list -> list.isEmpty()));`

E. Replace line t1 with `String check(List list, Predicate<List> p){`
and line t3 with `check(list, myList -> myList.isEmpty()));`

First of all, we need to see why the original code doesn't compile. All options mention line t3; is this LOC problematic? Indeed, it is: its paramlist clashes with the already declared variable **list**. Renaming the parameter saves the day → option A (incidentally, it completely disregards the functional method's argument and accesses **list** directly, then prints Empty) is in.

What about option B? It changes the object's reftype to a wider one but how can this help when **myList** is passed to **test()** that sees it as an **Object** only? After all, **Object** has no **isEmpty()** method...

All the other options hint that there may be something wrong with the compatibility of the data types in the signature of the **check()** method and its invocation.

Why? Because line t1 specifies ungenerified **List** and **Predicate** → they will accept any object → expect illegal implicit downcasts and CCEs at run time.

We can use the following rule of thumb:

> A predicative lambda? Check its type first! Object, Predicate and the formal parameter are ideally should be of the same type; no sub/superclasses combos for Predicate and the parameter.

Let's see how the rule works in practice; we'll start with something simpler: will this print `true`?

```
class Test{
   public static boolean checkList(List list, Predicate<List> p){
      return p.test(list);                                      // line X
   }
   public static void main(String[] args) {
      boolean boo = checkList(new ArrayList(), (ArrayList al) -> al.isEmpty());
      System.out.println(boo);
   }
}
```

The answer is 'No' because the code fails compilation. Reason: **Predicate** is generified to **List** → **Predicate**'s **test()** expects **List** → but **checkList()** offers **ArrayList al** → won't work; after all, lambda expression's ultimate *raison d'être* is to override the functional method...

Very well; what if we change **Predicate**<List> to **Predicate**<ArrayList>? Now lambda's body does override the method **test()** but the code still won't compile since the invocation `p.test(list)` specifies an arg of type **List** → we have an implicit downcast from **List** to **ArrayList** on line X, which is illegal. On the other hand, an explicit cast such as `p.test(<ArrayList>list)` works, and the code prints `true`.

Recapping: **Predicate<T>** and paramlist (T param) must be of the same type T and the object must be assignable to that type (or use a cast).

Please also note that removing <> from **Predicate<>** means that we will have to remove type from the paramlist, too – and *that* automatically makes **Predicate** of **Object** – which doesn't have **isEmpty()** method, so we'll be needing something that returns a `boolean`; for example:

```
class Test{
    public static boolean checkList(List list, Predicate p){
        return p.test(list);
    }
    public static void main(String[] args) {
        boolean boo = checkList(new ArrayList(), al -> al instanceof List ); //true
        System.out.println(boo);
    }
}
```

Now we can get back to our Problem 9.41; option C makes **test()** expect an **ArrayList** but delivers a **List** → which cannot be converted to **ArrayList** implicitly → a comperr. Doing the same thing with a cast in a strategic place would have helped, though:

```
String check(List list, Predicate<ArrayList> p){
    return p.test((ArrayList)list)? "Empty" : "Populated";  }
```

Option D resolves the conflict of types between the **check()** method's signature and the **test()** method's invocation; however, the fact that this option also changes the object's reftype on line t2 to **List** leads to the same problem: an illegal implicit downcast in the **check()** method's invocation. Casting **mist** would have cleared the problem:

```
check((ArrayList)mist, list -> list.isEmpty()));
```

Option E finally restores balance: the signature of **check()** specifies a **List** for both its args, and the object created on line t2 is of type **ArrayList**, which IS-A **List**…

Problem 9.42 – D

>   **Given:**

```
    class Suspect {
        private String name;
        private boolean statement;

        public Suspect (String name) {
            this.name = name;
            this.statement = Math.random() < 0.5 ? false : true;
        }

        public boolean getStatement() { return statement; }
        public String  getName()      { return name;      }
    }

    class Interrogation {
        private static void interrogate(List<Suspect> perps){
            for(Suspect e : perps)
                if (e.getStatement() != true)
                    System.out.println(e.getName() + " is lying!");
            }
```

```
    public static void main(String[] args) {
        List<Suspect> roundUp = new ArrayList();
        roundUp.add(new Suspect("Alice"));
        roundUp.add(new Suspect("Bob"));
        roundUp.add(new Suspect("Charlie"));
        roundUp.add(new Suspect("Doug"));
        roundUp.add(new Suspect("Eugine"));
        roundUp.add(new Suspect("Frances"));

        interrogate(roundUp);
    }
}
```

Which modification will achieve the same result?

A. Overload the method **interrogate()** with the following code fragment:

```
private static void interrogate(List<Suspect> perps, Predicate p){
    for(Suspect s : perps)
        if(!p.test(s))
            System.out.println(s.getName() + " is lying");
}
```

and replace the call to **interrogate()** with the following LOC:

```
interrogate(roundUp, perps -> perps.getStatement());
```

B. Overload the method **interrogate()** with the following code fragment:

```
private static void interrogate(List perps, Predicate<Suspect> p){
    for(Suspect s : perps)
        if(!p.test(s))
            System.out.println(s.getName() + " is lying");
}
```

and replace the call to **interrogate()** with the following LOC:

```
interrogate(roundUp, perps -> perps.getStatement());
```

C. Add the following interface:

```
interface LieDetector {
    default boolean test(Suspect s){ return s.getStatement(); }
}
```

then overload the method **interrogate()** with the following code fragment:

```
private static void interrogate(List<Suspect> perps, LieDetector ld){
    for(Suspect s : perps)
        if(!ld.test(s))
            System.out.println(s.getName() + " is lying");
}
```

and replace the call to **interrogate()** with the following LOC:

```
interrogate(roundUp, perps -> perps.getStatement());
```

D. Add the following interface:

```
interface LieDetector { boolean analyze(Suspect s); }
```

then overload the method **interrogate()** with the following code fragment:

```
private static void interrogate(List<Suspect> perps, LieDetector ld){
    for(Suspect s : perps)
        if(!ld.analyze(s))
            System.out.println(s.getName() + " is lying");
}
```

and replace the call to **interrogate()** with the following LOC:

```
interrogate(roundUp, perps -> perps.getStatement());
```

As the available options make use of not only predicative lambdas but also lambdas in general, you will not meet such a question on the exam; practicing with fundamental principles, however, can be beneficial, so let's do it unhurriedly and methodically.

To have a lambda, we'll be needing a functional interface, in other words, an interface with a single abstract method. Although this handy definition isn't entirely correct – as you'll see in the very next Problem 9.43 – it's good enough in practice.

What else do we need? Obviously, a properly written lambda expression (LE). An LE is made up of three basic components:

① <u>A comma-separated list of formal parameters enclosed in parentheses...</u>
   Reminder: We can omit the LE params' data types – and also get rid of the parentheses altogether if there is only one param.

② <u>... the arrow token, -></u>

③ <u>... and a body, which can consist of a single expression or a statement block.</u>
   Reminder: Single expression doesn't require braces REGARDLESS of whether the method is `void` or not.

Also let's not forget that `return` in a lambda expression can't live without its pals Semicolon and the Braces brothers.

In short, all of the following can work if the functional method is `void`, and the last LOC is also valid for a functional method that returns a **String**:

```
m1(arg, s -> { System.out.println(s); } );
m2(arg, s -> System.out.println(s)      );
m3(arg, s -> s += 1                     );
```

Example 1:

```
interface Lambdable{
    void doStuff(String str);
}
interface AnotherLambdable{
    String doStuff(String str);
}
class Test {
    static String str = "hello";
    static void run1(String str, Lambdable l){
        l.doStuff(str);
    }
    static String run2(String str, AnotherLambdable al){
        return al.doStuff(str);
    }
    public static void main(String[] args) {
        run1(str, p ->   System.out.println(p)              );    // hello
        run1(str, p -> { System.out.println(p); }           );    // hello
        run1(str, p -> { p += 1; System.out.println(p); }   );    // hello1
//        run1(str, p -> {return p;});                              // INVALID
        run1(str, p -> {return;});
        System.out.println(run2(str, p -> { return p + "2"; } ));    // hello2
        System.out.println(run2(str, p ->    p + "2"          ));    // hello2
    }
}
```

In Example 1 we defined our own functional interfaces; one of them, **Lambdable**, has a `void` method →
no invocation of **run1()** may mention `return` that actually returns something; the fourth, invalid
invocation would have worked if **run1()** were replaced with **run2()**.

Time to play with the interface **Predicate**. Coming from the field of linguistics, I couldn't at first get the
whole notion through my skull because to me a predicate meant either a verb or a verb phrase. For
example, in the sentence 'It doesn't compute' the predicate is 'doesn't compute', and in 'Lambdas are
weird' the predicate is 'are weird'. And how exactly can it help to conquer those LEs? As for the attempt
to get enlightened by asking Wiki, it only made my head spin…

The real breakthrough came after I had found a short, workable definition of predicate in the *Dictionary of
Logic* by Nikolay Kondakov[156]; basically it says that "…a predicate is an utterance that affirms or negates
something about an object… It reflects presence or absence of a certain feature… In mathematical logic,
the predicate is a logical function that is defined for a specific task and whose value can be either `true` or
`false`".

And that was it. From this definition it immediately follows that 1) predicate needs an object, and 2) it
returns a boolean. Exactly as it is with the method `boolean test(T t)` defined in the interface
java.util.function.Predicate… Everything fell into place.

Example 2 (with Predicate):

```
class Panda {
    int age;
    public static void main(String[] args) {
        Panda pa = new Panda();
        pa.age = 1;
        check(pa, p -> p.age < 5);                    // simplified form
        check(pa, (Panda p) -> {return p.age < 5;});  // full form
//      check(pa, p -> {p.age < 5});                  // missing ; and return
//      check(pa, p -> {p.age < 5;});                 // missing return
    }
    static void check(Panda panda, java.util.function.Predicate<Panda> pred) {
        String result = pred.test(panda) ? "younger" : "older";
        System.out.println(result);
    }
}
```

Getting back to our Problem. Option A suggests to overload the method **interrogate()** with:

```
private static void interrogate(List<Suspect> perps, Predicate p){
    for(Suspect s : perps)
        if(!p.test(s))
            System.out.println(s.getName() + " is lying");
    }
```

and replace the call to **interrogate()** with:

```
interrogate(roundUp, perps -> perps.getStatement());
```

The code compilability analysis on the exam should start with the verification of the lambda method body
followed by signature check. Yes, in this order because the exam question will most likely test you on the
correctness of the lambda expression rather than the compatibility of the involved objects.

---

[156] Not available in English; there's a German translation, though: *Wörterbuch der Logik* von N.I.Kondakow. The book is awesome, it helped
me untold number of times…

Verifying the lambda expression:

Step 1. Since we are overriding **test()** in **Predicate**, a single formal parameter is mandatory:
  – is it in place?
  – does it have its type specified?
    if 'yes', the paramlist must be enclosed in parentheses;
    if 'no', parentheses are optional;
  – what about the param's name? does it clash with any of the previously declared vars that are still in scope?

Step 2. Is the lambda token in place?

Step 3. **test()** in **Predicate** is supposed to return a `boolean`, therefore:
  – does the method body specify a single statement?
    if 'yes', does it use `return`?
      if 'yes', it must end with a semicolon and be enclosed in braces;
      if 'no', the body must be 'naked' (neither braces nor semicolon);
    if 'no', the body must be written in a full form, with braces and semicolons.
  – does it indeed return a `boolean`?

Step 4. See if the same lambda expression is used in other options. For example, in our current case (Problem 9.42) it is → since the expression is valid, we don't have to bother ourselves with validating it anymore.

Verifying the signature:

Use this rule: If the object, predicate and formal parameter are of the same data type → OK

If they aren't... (*sigh*) well, expect all kinds of trouble.

Let's see what we've got:

```
private static void interrogate(List<Suspect> perps, Predicate p){
```

The signature specifies an ungenerified **Predicate** → as the result, the method **test()** sees only an **Object** instead of the promised **Suspect** → **Object** has no **getStatement()** method → a comperr.

Now to option B; it wants us to overload the method **interrogate()** with the following:

```
private static void interrogate(List perps, Predicate<Suspect> p){
    for(Suspect s : perps)
        if(!p.test(s))
            System.out.println(s.getName() + " is lying");
    }
```

and use the same method invocation as in option A (which we have already ascertained as being valid) → skipping the lambda expression verification → applying signature verification rule → **Predicate** is generified to **Suspect** whereas the object **perps**' reftype is an ungenerified **List** → but the enhanced `for` will want to use **perps**' elements as **Suspect**s rather than **Object**s → a comperr because of an implicit downcast from **Object** to **Suspect**, which is illegal.

If we only had a *carte blanche*, we still could, theoretically speaking, save the day by making the enhanced `for` to iterate over **Object**s rather than **Suspect**s and then apply a couple of casts in strategic places, like this:

```
    private static void interrogate(List perps, Predicate<Suspect> p){
        for(Object s : perps)                                       // line X
            if(!p.test((Suspect)s))                                 // XX
                System.out.println(((Suspect)s).getName() + " is lying"); // XXX
            }
```

Line X gets rid of the comperr that reads 'incompatible types: Object cannot be converted to Suspect'; the cast on line XX gives the method **test()** what it wants; and the cast on line XXX allows to invoke **getName()**. Option B, however, isn't that flexible so we mark it as incorrect.

Now, option C. Ah, but this is fun! We get to create our own interface that should mimic **Predicate** in **java.util.function**:

```
interface LieDetector {
    default boolean test(Suspect s){ return s.getStatement(); }
}
```

Wait a minute... How come the method **test()** in **LieDetector** is declared as `default`?! it must be `abstract`! No, this won't do: our brand new interface isn't functional → option C isn't what we need, either...

During the initial pass, we stop our analysis at this point because we have arrived at the correct answer by the process of elimination. The Review stage, however, is different: we will have to verify our conclusion by checking option D, too.

Alright, so we add a new interface:

```
interface LieDetector { boolean analyze(Suspect s); }
```

then overload the method **interrogate()** with the following:

```
    private static void interrogate(List<Suspect> perps, LieDetector ld){
        for(Suspect s : perps)
            if(!ld.analyze(s))
                System.out.println(s.getName() + " is lying");
            }
```

and replace the call to **interrogate()** with this:

```
        interrogate(roundUp, perps -> perps.getStatement());
```

As we saw when analyzing option A, the invocation is valid. The interface is indeed functional: it declares a single abstract method. The signature, however, looks suspicious because **LieDetector** isn't generified... Hmm... what could that mean?.. Ah! unlike **test()** in **Predicate**, the method **analyze()** declares that it will accept only objects of type **Suspect** → this is a perfect match with **List**<Suspect> → the enhanced `for` is valid → this option is indeed correct.

Now, what's the story with **Predicate**'s **test()** and how it differs from our **analyze()**? Compare the definitions:

```
interface Predicate<T> { boolean test(T t);    /* plus four other non-abstract methods */ }

interface LieDetector  { boolean analyze(Suspect s); }
```

In its current form, our **LieDetector** cannot be generified because <T> is missing; that's why the method **analyze()** was specifically tailored to **Suspect**. After making **LieDetector** generifiable, we could use the already familiar idiom with the generified **List** and **LieDetector** in the method's signature :

```
interface LieDetector<T> { boolean analyze(T t); }

class Interrogation {

    // other necessary LOCs

    private static void interrogate(List<Suspect> perps, LieDetector<Suspect> ld){
        // enhanced for, printing stat, etc.
    }
```

Problem 9.43 – E

Which one is true?

    A. Functional interface may not contain more than one method.
    B. Any interface that has a single abstract method is therefore functional.
    C. Functional interface cannot have superinterfaces.
    D. Functional interface cannot be extended.
    E. None of the above.

The following code answers the question by illustrating how available options work:

```
interface Inter{}
interface Interable extends Inter{
    void walk();
    int run(StringBuilder sb);
}

@FunctionalInterface
interface Lambdable extends Interable{
    default void walk(){};      // must override super's walk to make it non-abstract;
//    int run();                // when uncommented, makes Lambdable non-functional
    boolean equals(Object obj);
}

@FunctionalInterface
interface Omegable extends Lambdable{}

class Test{
    static void test(Lambdable l){
        System.out.println(l.run(new StringBuilder("lambda")));
    }
    static void protest(Omegable o){
        System.out.println(o.run(new StringBuilder("omega")));
    }
    public static void main(String[] args) {
        test(sb -> sb.length());                        // prints 6
        protest(sb -> { sb.delete(0, sb.length());      // 5
                    return sb.append("alpha").length();
                });
    }
}
```

The program has two functional interfaces, namely **Lambdable** and its child, **Omegable** → options C and D are incorrect.

Option A is obviously incorrect as **Lambdable** (and, therefore, **Omegable**) has three methods (`default` **walk()** plus `abstract` **equals()** plus inherited `abstract` **run(StringBuilder sb)**), yet it works as intended (just look at the `@FunctionalInterface` annotations to which the compiler doesn't object) → options A and B are also incorrect…

We were taught that

> Conceptually, a functional interface has exactly one abstract method[157]

which is a bit disconcerting as **Lambdable** has *two* abstract methods. As usual, to understand what the heck is going on, we have to turn to the JLS (§9.8, *Functional Interfaces*):

> The definition of *functional interface* excludes methods in an interface that are also public methods in Object. This is to allow functional treatment of an interface like java.util.Comparator<T> that declares multiple abstract methods of which only one is really "new" - int compare(T,T). The other method - boolean equals(Object) - is an explicit declaration of an abstract method that would otherwise be implicitly declared, and will be automatically implemented by every class that implements the interface.

So for an interface to define an `abstract` method that has its `public` namesake in **Object** doesn't count toward being functional.

Well, basically this is it for lambdas. Since our book is also at its end, how about adding a couple of extra touches to the discussion? and then we'll call it quits…

Consider the following program, which tests certain animal species for their ability to swim, hop or fly[158]:

```
1  package org.xlator;
2  import java.util.ArrayList;
3  import java.util.List;
4  import java.util.function.Predicate;
5
6  class Animal{
7      private String species;
8      private boolean canHop;
9      private boolean canSwim;
10     private boolean canFly;
11     boolean getHop() { return canHop;  }
12     boolean getSwim(){ return canSwim; }
13     boolean getFly() { return canFly;  }
14
15     public Animal(String species, boolean canHop, boolean canSwim, boolean canFly){
16         this.species = species;
17         this.canHop  = canHop;
18         this.canSwim = canSwim;
19         this.canFly  = canFly; }
20
21     @Override
22     public String toString(){ return species; }
23 }
24
25 @FunctionalInterface
26 interface CheckTrait{ boolean test(Animal a); }
27
28 class TestHopper implements CheckTrait{
29     public boolean test(Animal a){ return a.getHop(); }
30 }
31
```

---

[157] https://docs.oracle.com/javase/8/docs/api/java/lang/FunctionalInterface.html
[158] You can find its listing without line numbers in Appendix C.

```
32 public class Filter {
33
34     public static void main(String[] args) {
35         List<Animal> animals = new ArrayList<>();
36  //                                    swimmer hopper flier
37         animals.add(new Animal("fish",     false, true,  true  ));
38         animals.add(new Animal("kangaroo", true,  false, false ));
39         animals.add(new Animal("cat",      true,  false, false ));
40         animals.add(new Animal("dog",      true,  true,  false ));
41         animals.add(new Animal("bird",     true,  true,  true  ));
42         animals.add(new Animal("turtle",   false, true,  false ));
43         animals.add(new Animal("rabbit",   true,  false, false ));
44         animals.add(new Animal("ladybug",  false, false, true  ));
45
46         Predicate<Animal> hop  = a -> a.getHop();
47         Predicate<Animal> swim = a -> a.getSwim();
48         Predicate<Animal> fly  = a -> a.getFly();
49
50         System.out.println("Can hop (old school):\n--------");
51         filterOldWay(animals, new TestHopper());
52
53         System.out.println("\nCan swim (with lambdas):\n--------");
54         filterNewWay(animals, a -> a.getSwim());
55  //        filterNewWay(animals, swim);                              // more compact
56
57         System.out.println("\nCan fly (with .stream):\n--------");
58         animals.stream().filter(fly).forEach(a -> System.out.println(a));
59
60         System.out.println("\nCan both hop and fly (complex filter):\n--------");
61         animals.stream().filter(a -> hop.and(fly).test(a))
62                         .forEach(a -> System.out.println(a));
63     }
64
65     static void filterOldWay(List<Animal> animals, CheckTrait checker){
66         for (Animal a : animals){
67             if(checker.test(a))
68                 System.out.println(a); }
69     }
70
71     static void filterNewWay(List<Animal> animals, Predicate<Animal> checker){
72         animals.stream().filter(a -> checker.test(a))
73                         .forEach(a -> System.out.println(a)); }
74 }
```

And this is what the code outputs:

```
Can hop (old school):
--------
kangaroo
cat
dog
bird
rabbit

Can swim (with lambdas):
--------
fish
dog
bird
turtle

Can fly (with .stream):
--------
fish
bird
ladybug

Can both hop and fly (complex filter):
--------
bird
```

Several approaches are being used to check the traits: the ability to hop is tested in the old-school fashion, so to speak, by explicitly creating an object that has a getter method that returns a `boolean`; then we use a lambda expression to check animals for their ability to swim; note that it can take two forms: we either write the LE directly on the LOC with the method invocation (line 54), or use the **Predicate**<Animal> var that holds the appropriate LE (the commented-out line 55). The two last checks (for the ability to fly and, after that, the ability to both fly and hop) demonstrate the use of streams and complex, multi-stage filters, which are possible thanks to the additional methods that the interface **Predicate** defines.

For example, replacing line 61 with the following:

```
animals.stream().filter(a -> hop.or(fly).test(a))
```

would have selected only those animals that can either hop or fly (i.e., fish, kangaroo, cat, dog, bird, rabbit, and ladybug), while this LOC

```
animals.stream().filter(a -> hop.and(fly.negate()).test(a))
```

would have chosen those who can hop but are unable to fly (namely, kangaroo, cat, dog, and rabbit). This is where our decision to assign the LEs to separately declared **Predicate** variables comes in handy as the code becomes less cluttered and, therefore, more readable and maintainable…

★ ★ ★ ★ ★

The book is practically over, and under any other circumstances I would be saying goodbye and wishing you good luck on the exam. Instead, I've chosen to lay a finishing touch by quoting Mark Twain:

It ain't what you don't know that gets you into trouble. It's what you know for sure that just ain't so.

And here's the steam hammer to drive the point home:

Given full contents of the file Daddy.java **located in** C:\Try_Java\tempa **folder:**

```
1 package tempa;
2 public class Daddy {
3     protected void kiss() {
4         System.out.println("Sweet dreams!");
5     }
6 }
```

Given full contents of the file Twin_1.java **located in** C:\Try_Java\org\xlator **folder:**

```
1 package org.xlator;
2 import tempa.*;
3 public class Twin_1 extends Daddy{
4     public static void main(String[] args) {
5         new Twin_1().kiss();
6         new Twin_2().kiss();
7     }
8 }
```

Given full contents of the file Twin_2.java **located in** C:\Try_Java\org\xlator **folder:**

```
1 package org.xlator;
2 import tempa.*;
3 public class Twin_2 extends Daddy{
4     public static void main(String[] args) {
5         new Twin_1().kiss();
6         new Twin_2().kiss();
7     }
8 }
```

What is the result when we try to compile and run Twin_1.java?

A. Daddy says "Sweet dreams!" twice and both twins get their goodnight kisses
B. Compilation fails in the class Twin_1 but not in the class Twin_2
C. Compilation fails in the class Twin_2 but not in the class Twin_1
D. Both classes fail compilation

The correct answer is option D:

Guys, this is hilarious. The method **kiss()** is indeed `protected` but, after all, both descendants extend **Daddy**. So how come we get two errors as if neither of the child classes may access a lawfully inherited method? And if you think the failure to get a loving goodnight kiss has something to do with the fact that Daddy and his twin children live under different roofs, I can give you another, even more bizarre example that uses classes within the same package.

Look here: any class we create extends **Object**, therefore all the non-private methods defined in **Object**[159] are available to each and every class; this is Java's ABC. Yet the following code throws a similar comperr, "**clone()** has protected access in **Object**":

```
1 package org.xlator;
2 class A {}
3 class B {
4     public static void main(String[] args) throws Exception {
5         new A().clone();    // INVALID
6         new B().clone();    // VALID but throws a CloneNotSupportedException
7     }
8 }
```

What happens at run time isn't our immediate concern; right now the question is why line 5 fails compilation.

This entire brain-wracking conundrum is only possible due to an immensely popular yet hopelessly wrong view of what `protected` access means in Java. When asked about it, most people would dutifully mumble something close to the following quote from the official Oracle Java tutorial[160]:

> The `protected` modifier specifies that the member can only be accessed within its own package (as with package-private) and, in addition, by a subclass of its class in another package.

So what of it? irritatingly asks my gentle reader. The definition is true, ain't it? Oh yes, most definitely. My point is that lots of people don't realize clearly that it contains *two* fundamental conditions rather than one that concerns *where* the classes are located. The second condition to be taken into account is *who* attempts to access the `protected` member.

You'll get what I mean as soon as you answer this question: who wants to invoke **clone()** on the object created on line 5? is it class **A** or class **B**?

See? **clone()** is defined in **java.lang.Object** → it may be accessed outside the **java.lang** package only by **Object**'s subclasses along a direct inheritance line → **A** and **B** are on parallel but distinct inheritance lines → yet **B** wants to invoke a method that belongs to a different data type → 'No mister, says the compiler, although **A** is your brother, he inherited his own stuff from Daddy-O, and you've got no right to touch something that ain't yours. So mind your own business and keep your hands off other people's property. Now scram!'

Or look at it this way: the compiler maintains ethical cloning standards: 'Thou shalt not clone other people. Clone only thyself'. On the other hand, you can override **clone()** to make it `public` in your class.

---

[159] **java.lang.Object** has no default-access methods and only one `private` method (`private static native void registerNatives()`).
[160] https://docs.oracle.com/javase/tutorial/java/javaOO/accesscontrol.html

The following example illustrates how **B** could use **A** as a proxy; now the code compiles because **B** actually calls its own **clone()**, the one that it inherited itself:

```
class A { B proxify(){ return new B(); } }
class B {
    public static void main(String[] args) {
        try {
            (new A().proxify()).clone();
        }
        catch(CloneNotSupportedException cnse){
            System.out.println("Darn it! Another useless inheritance...");}
    }
}
```

Poor, poor **B**: it is still pretty much unhappy because it forgot to support the **Cloneable** interface and doesn't know how to reproduce, but this is another story.

Anyway, what should be remembered from our brief excursion into the wiles and woes of inheritance is this (JLS, §6.6.2, *Details on* `protected` *Access*):

> A `protected` member or constructor of an object may be accessed from outside the package in which it is declared only by code that is responsible for the implementation of that object.

An illustration:

```
package one;
public class One {
    protected One(){};         // line 1
    protected One(int a){};    // line 2
}

package test;
import one.One;
class Test extends One {
    public static void main(String[] args) {
        new One(1);            // INVALID: 'One(int) has protected access in One'
    }
}
```

So, while `protected` on line 1 lets the class **Test** properly extend **One**, the very same modifier on line 2 kills compilation...

Now go and break a leg. Rock the test.

Appendix

A Registering for the Exam

Step 1. If you don't have an Oracle account, go to https://www.oracle.com/index.html to create one; you'll need it anyway to access your exam score. It is also possible to register your Oracle account *post factum*.

Step 2. Next go to http://www.pearsonvue.com/. Select For test takes → Test taker home:

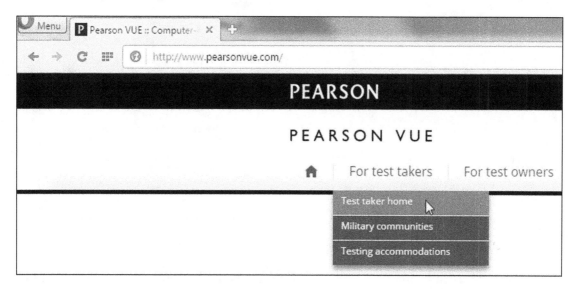

Step 3. Select vendor (obviously, in our case it's Oracle):

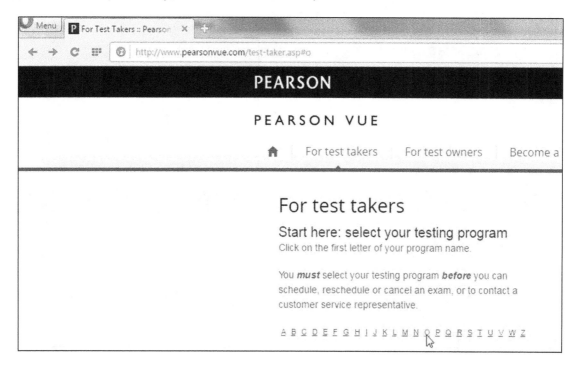

Step 4. In the section **Schedule An Exam** click on and read the **Oracle Certification Program Candidate Agreement**, because the page warns that

BY SELECTING THE "START" BUTTON BELOW YOU ARE AGREEING TO THE TERMS AND CONDITIONS OF THE ORACLE CERTIFICATION PROGRAM CANDIDATE AGREEMENT

Moreover, you'll have to sign this document on paper when you come to the test center to take the exam.

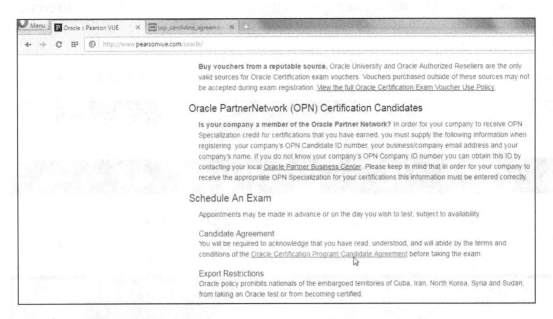

Please also note that Agreement contains certain restrictions that concern minors, etc.

Step 5. Click **Schedule An Exam** and create you own account with **Pearson Vue** (unless, of course, you already have one):

Step 6. Agree to the Pearson Vue's **Privacy and Cookies Policy**, then fill in your personal data, contact info, etc., and finally press **Finish**:

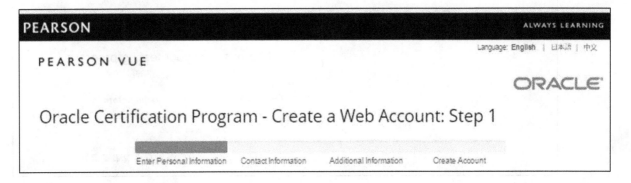

Step 7. On successful creation of your web account, you'll be taken to an exam selection page, where you click **Proctored Exams**…

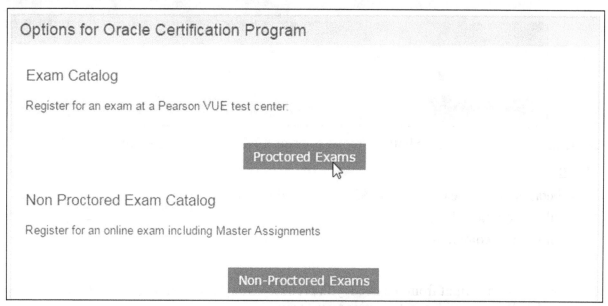

… which offers three choices: order a bundle, a beta exam or just a regular certification exam:

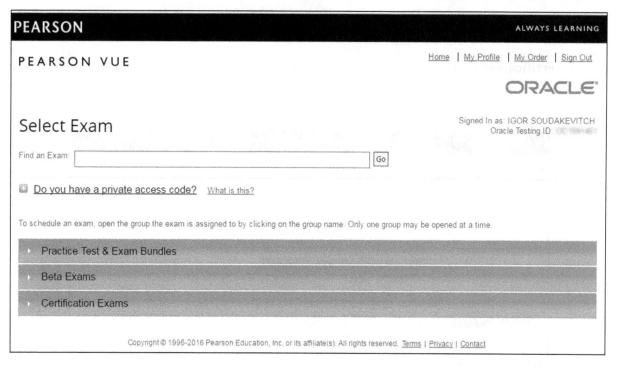

Exam Bundles let you buy a desired exam together with Kaplan's practice tests for it:

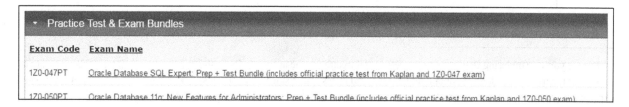

Beta Exams are those freshly created exams that Oracle tests on us, exam takers:

Oracle uses betas to determine both correctness of questions and passing score threshold.

Pros:

- betas are a lot cheaper (around $50-90 depending on the exam);
- allocated time is longer;
- entire Java community benefits from your feedback.

Cons:

- as the exam is right from the oven, you probably won't find comprehensive (or at least recently updated) study guides and practice tests for it;
- you'll be waiting for your score for months while Oracle collects enough statistical data.

Since betas are available for a limited time only and 1Z0-808 is now in its mature state, our next chance to sit a beta OCAJSE will come after Oracle releases Java 1.9.

As for **Certification Exams**, there are so many of them it's easier to type the desired code right into the search field; it'll give you two options: standard 1Z0-808 and 1Z0-808-JPN, which is available only in Japan[161]:

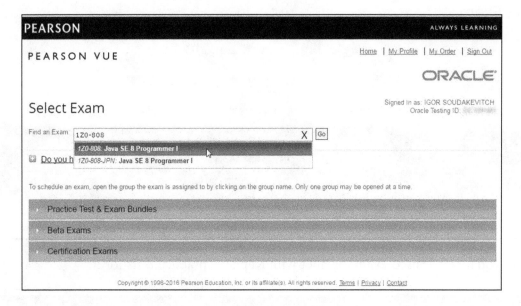

---

[161] In case you're wondering if Japanese get preferential treatment, the answer is 'No': the allocated time and passing score are exactly the same, and the translation doesn't contain hints. Yes, I did check – and since I am a professional Japanese-Russian translator with 20+ years of experience, you'd better take my word for it.

Clicking **Go** will take you to the exam scheduling page:

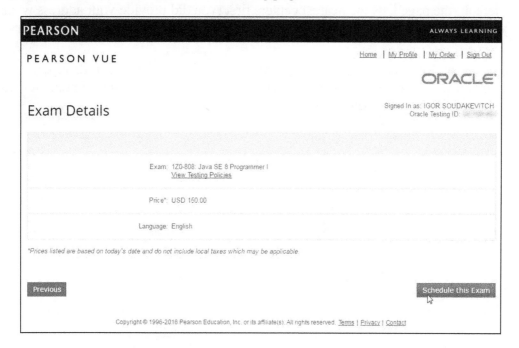

Make sure you read **Testing Policies** before clicking the **Schedule this Exam** button.

Step 8. Click [**Schedule this Exam**] to confirm that you indeed want to register for this particular exam (note that you can also schedule more exams to be taken on the same day) and then click **Proceed to Scheduling**:

Step 9. Now you have to choose a test center and indicate the date & time when you want to sit the exam there; by default, the page lists the nearest centers first (you did provide your address when creating your Pearson Vue profile, right?); if needed, click the **Display more test centers...** link.

You'll get to select three centers to check their availability on that particular date; some of them will accept exam takers only once a week, others are more accommodating; if none of them provide what you want, click **Change Test Centers**:

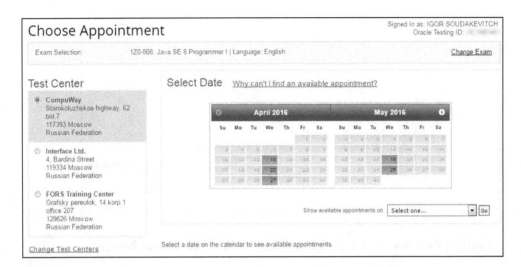

After finding a convenient combination, select the start time:

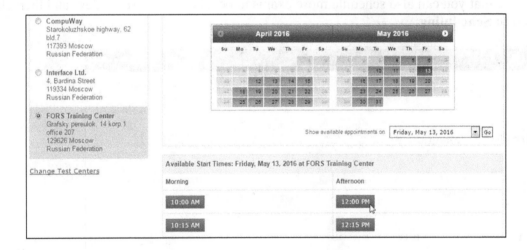

On having made sure that the appointment info is correct, **Proceed to Checkout**:

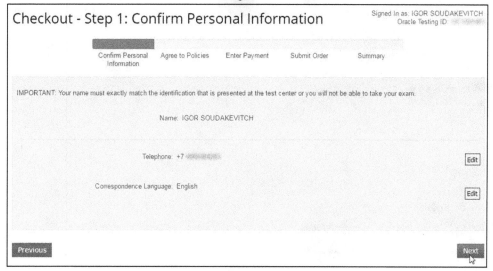

My Order

Signed In as: IGOR SOUDAKEVITCH
Oracle Testing ID:

Description	Details	Price	Actions
Exam 1Z0-808: Java SE 8 Programmer I Language: English Exam Length: 150 minutes	**Appointment** Friday, May 13, 2016 Start Time: 12:00 PM MSK Change Appointment **Location** FORS Training Center Grafsky pereulok, 14 korp.1 office 207 129626 Moscow Russian Federation Change Test Center	150.00	Remove

Subtotal: 150.00
Estimated Tax: 0.00
ESTIMATED TOTAL DUE: USD 150.00

Add Another Exam or **Proceed to Checkout**

You can enter voucher/promotion codes on the payment screen.

Checkout - Step 1: Confirm Personal Information

Signed In as: IGOR SOUDAKEVITCH
Oracle Testing ID:

Confirm Personal Information | Agree to Policies | Enter Payment | Submit Order | Summary

IMPORTANT: Your name must exactly match the identification that is presented at the test center or you will not be able to take your exam.

Name: IGOR SOUDAKEVITCH

Telephone: +7   [Edit]

Correspondence Language: English   [Edit]

Previous   Next

Checkout - Step 2: Agree to Policies

Signed In as: IGOR SOUDAKEVITCH
Oracle Testing ID:

Confirm Personal Information | Agree to Policies | Enter Payment | Submit Order | Summary

Oracle Certification Program Policies

Admission Policy
We ask that you arrive at the test center 15 minutes before your scheduled appointment time. This will give you adequate time to complete the necessary sign-in procedures. If you arrive more than 15 minutes late for an exam and are refused admission, payments are due for the exam and

☑ I have read and agree to the Oracle Certification Program policies listed above.

Previous   Next

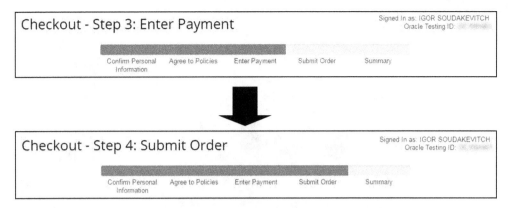

After the payment is processed, you get your confirmed order summary:

On clicking **Return Home** you'll see that your appointment was successfully registered with Pearson Vue:

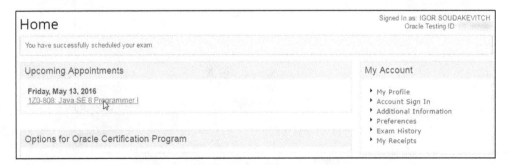

Also check your email box, which should already contain the official exam purchase invoice. *Voilà!* Done and done.

Step 10. Now contact your test center to see if they got notified by Pearson Vue and that they will be waiting for you on that particular day and time. Also check if they'll accept those two IDs you're planning to take with you. Ask if they allow bringing water to the test room. Tissue paper or handkerchiefs to wipe off your blood, sweat and tears. Ask about eye drops, too.

Apparently, Oracle firmly believes we are going to use our paper money, candy wrappers, bottle labels and whatnots to make crib notes and cheat sheets. Truly desperate souls may want to follow Michael Scofield's example although I've no idea about Oracle's policy on tattoos – including shedding all of your cloths and bending backwards to cast a glance at that last rule on method overriding. So ask.

As the last resort consider printing your own T-shirt – and not upside down if you want to look particularly enigmatic on CCTV monitors – so use your social engineering skills to figure out if those proctors can read Klingon or the Easter Island's script…

On a more serious note you may want to 'case the joint', so to speak, by running a brief recon mission a couple of weeks in advance to see if the facility does provide a separate test room, which should be sufficiently quiet, and so on.

Upon finishing the exam you'll get a piece of paper attesting to the fact, and then – most likely, within the next two hours – your score will be made available. Follow the link in the notification email from Oracle to logon to the CertView using your Oracle account user name and password.

It really shouldn't take more than a couple of hours to get your score processed, so if there's no email and you have been waiting long enough, go directly to Oracle University[162], sign in, click on **Certification** then on **CertView**…

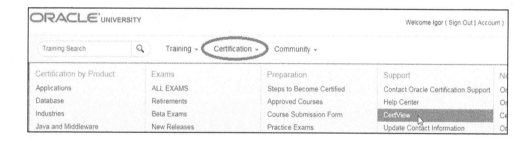

… and then on **Exam Results**…

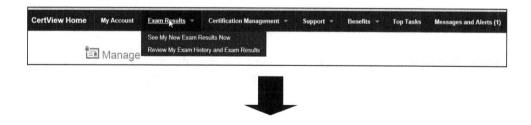

---

[162] https://education.oracle.com/pls/eval-eddap-dcd/ocp_interface.ocp_candidate_login?p_include=Y

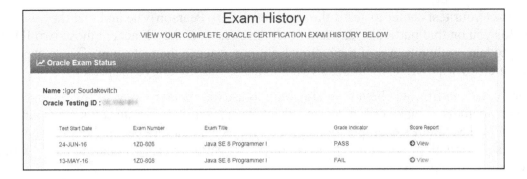

...upon which you should see something close to this:

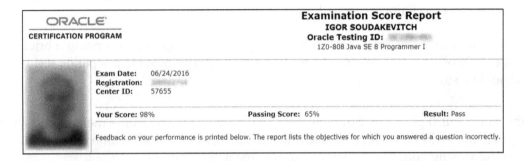

If you did pass, soon a new email will arrive to take you to Acclaim site, which provides virtual badges you could use in your correspondence and CVs; also you'll get a link to your electronic certificate:

... with a validation code in the bottom right corner that you could use to order your free Oracle Certification T-shirt to show off:

As for printed certificate, you'll need to explicitly ask for one through a CertView request form or by following a link in the notification email; the delivery can take up to ten weeks.

B   RWJ.bat (or ref.to External Resources)

```
echo off
rem ********************************************************************************
rem *                RWJ.bat: Compiles Java classes and launches JVM               *
rem *                   Coded by Igor Soudakevitch; www.igor.host                   *
rem *              Distributed under the terms and conditions of the GPL            *
rem ********************************************************************************
rem ver.0.18 / Jan.24, 2016 /

rem ---------------- Just a reminder: javac & JVM invocation ----------------------
rem        javac -encoding UTF-8 -d C:\Garbage\classes org\xlator\_main_class_.java
rem       java -cp C:\Garbage\classes org.xlator._main_class_

rem Resulting cp dir structure: C:\Garbage\classes\org\xlator

rem Suppose we've got RunMe.java with a reference to ClassA, which is defined in
rem ClassA.java located in the same dir. Both classes belong to the same package
rem org.xlator, and are located in the _whatever_dir_\org\xlator.
rem In this case run from _whatever_dir_:
rem            javac .\org\xlator\RunMe.java     where .\ is actually redundant
rem            java org.xlator.RunMe

rem Source files should be UTF-8 encoded to correctly support Unicode output
rem ----------------- End of introductory comments ---------------------------------


rem     This is THE ONLY place to mutate settings; refer to 'RULES' below

          set args=1234 1Z0-808 5678
          set packaged=ON
          set javac_d_switch_cp=C:\Garbage\classes
          set package_name=org.xlator
          set pack_root_dir=C:\Try_Java
          set dos_pack_path=org\xlator
          set added_path1=tempa
          set added_path2=tempb
          set all_added=.\%added_path1%;.\%added_path2%

          set enc=-encoding UTF-8
rem          set enc=
          set enc_type=UTF-8
rem          set enc_type=
rem          set Xlint=
          set Xlint=-Xlint:unchecked
          set warn=
rem          set warn=-nowarn
rem          set Xdiags=
          set Xdiags=-Xdiags:verbose
          set add_cp=;%CLASSPATH%
rem          set add_cp=
          set removal=ON
rem          set removal=NO


rem                              RULES:
rem     Added paths must be present BELOW %pack_root_dir%, e.g.:
rem     C:\
rem      |--- ..........
rem      |--- Try_Java
rem      |        |
rem      |        |--- org
rem      |        |      |--- xlator
rem      |        |
rem      |        |--- tempa
rem      |        |--- tempb
rem      |--- ..........

rem --- 'packaged' var defines whether the source files contain the package statements

rem --- If packaged==NO then classes will be compiled and run according to
rem --- the 'simple_process' section (i.e., within the current dir)

rem --- If packaged==YES then the compiled classes will be placed inside
rem --- the javac_d_switch_cp dir that is to be used with -d switch (ref.to javac -help)
```

```
if "%enc%" == "" (
    set enc_flag=OFF
    ) ELSE (
    set enc_flag=ON
    )
if "%add_cp%" == "" (
    set add_cp_flag=OFF
    ) ELSE (
    set add_cp_flag=ON
    )
if "%warn%" == "" (
    set warn_flag=ON
    ) ELSE (
    set warn_flag=OFF
    )
if "%Xlint%" == "" (
    set Xlint_flag=OFF
    ) ELSE (
    set Xlint_flag=ON
    )
if "%Xdiags%" == "" (
    set Xdiags_flag=OFF
    ) ELSE (
    set Xdiags_flag=ON
    )
if "%packaged%" == "ON" (
    goto packaged_process
    ) ELSE (
    goto simple_process
    )


:simple_process
echo.
echo.
echo ---------------------------- FYI ------------------------------------
echo.
echo    args                       : %args%
echo    main class package         : void
echo    package path               : void
echo    referenced class package(s) : void
echo    javac -d switch classpath  : void
echo    appended CLASSPATH env var : void
echo    forced encoding            : %enc_flag% (%enc_type%)
echo    -Xlint:unchecked           : %Xlint_flag%
echo    -Xdiags:verbose            : %Xdiags_flag%
echo    warnings                   : %warn_flag%
echo    *.class removal            : %removal%
echo.
echo -------------------- End of batch file messages ----------------------
echo.
echo.
echo.
javac %enc% %Xlint% %Xdiags% %1
java -cp . %~n1
echo.
echo ************************************************************************
echo *    all classes in the current dir(s) will be removed now; hit ^^C to abort    *
echo ************************************************************************
echo.
if "%removal%" == "ON" del *.class
pause
exit

:packaged_process
cls

rem    The following 'if' checks whether the specified dir exists
rem    because a special file named 'nul' is present in every dir.
rem    And one more thing: the 'exist' test only checks for *files*;
rem    that's precisely why we have to use \nul

if exist %javac_d_switch_cp%\nul goto get_to_it
    echo *
    echo *
    echo ****************************************************
    echo *            Packaged mode is ON but
    echo *            %javac_d_switch_cp% dir doesn't exist
    echo ****************************************************
    echo *
    echo *
    set /p answer=Do you want to create it now (Y/N)?
    if /i "%answer:~,1%" EQU "Y" goto create_dir
    if /i "%answer:~,1%" EQU "N" goto exiting
```

```
:create_dir
md %javac_d_switch_cp%
echo.
echo.
if not errorlevel 1 (
    echo %javac_d_switch_cp% dir created successfully.
    ) ELSE (
    echo Uh-huh! Couldn't create %javac_d_switch_cp% dir!
    echo.
    echo.
    pause
    exit
)
goto get_to_it

:exiting
echo.
echo.
echo I ain't got nothing to do then. Bye.
echo.
echo.
pause
rem   to set errorlevel, use '\b' switch on exit, like this:    exit \b
exit


:get_to_it
echo.
echo.
echo ----------------------------- FYI -----------------------------------
echo.
echo     args                        :   %args%
echo     main class package          :   %package_name%
echo     package path                :   %pack_root_dir%\%dos_pack_path%
echo     referenced class package(s) :   %pack_root_dir%\%added_path1%;%pack_root_dir%\%added_path2%
echo     javac -d switch classpath    :   %javac_d_switch_cp%\%dos_pack_path%
echo     appended CLASSPATH env var  :   %add_cp_flag%
echo     forced encoding             :   %enc_flag% (%enc_type%)
echo     -Xlint:unchecked            :   %Xlint_flag%
echo     -Xdiags:verbose             :   %Xdiags_flag%
echo     warnings                    :   %warn_flag%
echo     *.class removal             :   %removal%
echo.
echo -------------------- End of batch file messages ----------------------
echo.
echo.
echo.
cd %pack_root_dir%
javac %enc% -cp %all_added%%add_cp% -d %javac_d_switch_cp% %Xlint% %Xdiags% %1
java -cp %javac_d_switch_cp%%add_cp% %package_name%.%~n1 %args%
echo.
echo ***************************** CLEANING UP ****************************
echo *   all classes in -d cp dir(s) will be removed now; hit ^^C to abort   *
echo *********************************************************************
echo.
pause
if "%removal%" == "ON" (
    del %javac_d_switch_cp%\%dos_pack_path%\*.class
    if exist %javac_d_switch_cp%\%added_path1%\*.class del %javac_d_switch_cp%\%added_path1%\*.class
    if exist %javac_d_switch_cp%\%added_path2%\*.class del %javac_d_switch_cp%\%added_path2%\*.class
    )
```

```java
package org.xlator;
import java.util.ArrayList;
import java.util.List;
import java.util.function.Predicate;

class Animal{
    private String species;
    private boolean canHop;
    private boolean canSwim;
    private boolean canFly;
    boolean getHop() { return canHop;  }
    boolean getSwim(){ return canSwim; }
    boolean getFly() { return canFly;  }

    public Animal(String species, boolean canHop, boolean canSwim, boolean canFly){
        this.species = species;
        this.canHop  = canHop;
        this.canSwim = canSwim;
        this.canFly  = canFly; }

    @Override
    public String toString(){ return species; }
}

@FunctionalInterface
interface CheckTrait{ boolean test(Animal a); }

class TestHopper implements CheckTrait{
    public boolean test(Animal a){ return a.getHop(); }
}

class Filter {
    public static void main(String[] args) {
        List<Animal> animals = new ArrayList<>();
        //                                  swimmer hopper flier
        animals.add(new Animal("fish",     false, true,  true ));
        animals.add(new Animal("kangaroo", true,  false, false ));
        animals.add(new Animal("cat",      true,  false, false ));
        animals.add(new Animal("dog",      true,  true,  false ));
        animals.add(new Animal("bird",     true,  true,  true ));
        animals.add(new Animal("turtle",   false, true,  false ));
        animals.add(new Animal("rabbit",   true,  false, false ));
        animals.add(new Animal("ladybug",  false, false, true ));

        Predicate<Animal> hop  = a -> a.getHop();
        Predicate<Animal> swim = a -> a.getSwim();
        Predicate<Animal> fly  = a -> a.getFly();

        System.out.println("Can hop (old school):\n--------");
        filterOldWay(animals, new TestHopper());

        System.out.println("\nCan swim (with lambdas):\n--------");
        filterNewWay(animals, a -> a.getSwim());
        //    filterNewWay(animals, swim);                        // more compact

        System.out.println("\nCan fly (with .stream):\n--------");
        animals.stream().filter(fly).forEach(a -> System.out.println(a));

        System.out.println("\nCan both hop and fly (complex filter):\n--------");
        animals.stream().filter(a -> hop.and(fly).test(a))
                        .forEach(a -> System.out.println(a));
    }
    static void filterOldWay(List<Animal> animals, CheckTrait checker){
        for (Animal a : animals){
            if(checker.test(a))
                System.out.println(a); }
    }
    static void filterNewWay(List<Animal> animals, Predicate<Animal> checker){
        animals.stream().filter(a -> checker.test(a))
                        .forEach(a -> System.out.println(a)); }
}
```

Appendix
D

Key Summary

Problem 1.1 – C
Problem 1.2 – A
Problem 1.3 – C
Problem 1.4 – E
Problem 1.5 – C
Problem 1.6 – B
Problem 1.7 – E
Problem 1.8 – BCE
Problem 1.9 – A
Problem 1.10 – C
Problem 1.11 – ADE
Problem 1.12 – B
Problem 1.13 – B
Problem 1.14 – AB
Problem 1.15 – CD
Problem 1.16 – B
Problem 1.17 – A
Problem 1.18 – ABD
Problem 1.19 – A
Problem 1.20 – D
Problem 1.21 – BCF
Problem 1.22 – C
Problem 1.23 – D

Problem 2.1 – A
Problem 2.2 – C
Problem 2.3 – C
Problem 2.4 – AD
Problem 2.5 – AD
Problem 2.6 – C
Problem 2.7 – E
Problem 2.8 – E
Problem 2.9 – E
Problem 2.10 – E
Problem 2.11 – A
Problem 2.12 – D
Problem 2.13 – B
Problem 2.14 – C
Problem 2.15 – D
Problem 2.16 – D
Problem 2.17 – C
Problem 2.18 – C
Problem 2.19 – C
Problem 2.20 – C
Problem 2.21 – A
Problem 2.22 – C
Problem 2.23 – C
Problem 2.24 – B
Problem 2.25 – B
Problem 2.26 – D
Problem 2.27 – A
Problem 2.28 – C
Problem 2.29 – C
Problem 2.30 – D
Problem 2.31 – AC
Problem 2.32 – B
Problem 2.33 – E

Problem 3.1 – B
Problem 3.2 – D
Problem 3.3 – C
Problem 3.4 – A
Problem 3.5 – A
Problem 3.6 – A
Problem 3.7 – A
Problem 3.8 – A
Problem 3.9 – A
Problem 3.10 – B
Problem 3.11 – A
Problem 3.12 – B
Problem 3.13 – B
Problem 3.14 – D
Problem 3.15 – D
Problem 3.16 – D
Problem 3.17 – E
Problem 3.18 – AC
Problem 3.19 – B
Problem 3.20 – C
Problem 3.21 – C
Problem 3.22 – C
Problem 3.23 – B
Problem 3.24 – A
Problem 3.25 – B
Problem 3.26 – ABE
Problem 3.27 – C
Problem 3.28 – B
Problem 3.29 – CD
Problem 3.30 – B
Problem 3.31 – C
Problem 3.32 – BE
Problem 3.33 – C

Problem 4.1 – B

Problem 4.2 – A

Problem 4.3 – C

Problem 4.4 – D

Problem 4.5 – B

Problem 4.6 – D

Problem 4.7 – AE

Problem 4.8 – B

Problem 4.9 – BD

Problem 4.10 – AC

Problem 4.11 – D

Problem 4.12 – AD

Problem 4.13 – CE

Problem 4.14 – B

Problem 4.15 – C

Problem 4.16 – A

Problem 5.1 – ABCE

Problem 5.2 – B

Problem 5.3 – B

Problem 5.4 – A

Problem 5.5 – BD

Problem 5.6 – C

Problem 5.7 – C

Problem 5.8 – B

Problem 5.9 – BE

Problem 5.10 – A

Problem 5.11 – C

Problem 5.12 – D

Problem 5.13 – C

Problem 5.14 – B

Problem 5.15 – B

Problem 5.16 – C

Problem 5.17 – D

Problem 5.18 – A

Problem 5.19 – C

Problem 5.20 – D

Problem 5.21 – A

Problem 5.22 – B

Problem 5.23 – C

Problem 5.24 – A

Problem 5.25 – E

Problem 6.1 – DGH

Problem 6.2 – C

Problem 6.3 – B

Problem 6.4 – A

Problem 6.5 – A

Problem 6.6 – B

Problem 6.7 – C

Problem 6.8 – D

Problem 6.9 – AD

Problem 6.10 – C

Problem 6.11 – B

Problem 6.12 – B

Problem 6.13 – D

Problem 6.14 – B

Problem 6.15 – B

Problem 6.16 – B

Problem 6.17 – A

Problem 6.18 – D

Problem 6.19 – BF

Problem 6.20 – BE

Problem 6.21 – DEF

Problem 6.22 – A

Problem 6.23 – B

Problem 6.24 – D

Problem 6.25 – A

Problem 6.26 – A

Problem 6.27 – C

Problem 6.28 – C

Problem 6.29 – C

Problem 6.30 – D

Problem 6.31 – CE

Problem 6.32 – A

Problem 6.33 – D

Problem 6.34 – B

Problem 6.35 – B

Problem 6.36 – E

Problem 7.1 – B
Problem 7.2 – AD
Problem 7.3 – CE
Problem 7.4 – A
Problem 7.5 – A
Problem 7.6 – C
Problem 7.7 – C
Problem 7.8 – A
Problem 7.9 – A
Problem 7.10 – A
Problem 7.11 – ACD
Problem 7.12 – C
Problem 7.13 – C
Problem 7.14 – E
Problem 7.15 – CDF
Problem 7.16 – D
Problem 7.17 – ADE
Problem 7.18 – ABCE
Problem 7.19 – D
Problem 7.20 – CD
Problem 7.21 – E
Problem 7.22 – B
Problem 7.23 – D
Problem 7.24 – F
Problem 7.25 – CE
Problem 7.26 – CD
Problem 7.27 – A
Problem 7.28 – DE
Problem 7.29 – E
Problem 7.30 – AE
Problem 7.31 – D
Problem 7.32 – BD
Problem 7.33 – C
Problem 7.34 – B

Problem 8.1 – B
Problem 8.2 – CD
Problem 8.3 – C
Problem 8.4 – CD
Problem 8.5 – ACE
Problem 8.6 – AC
Problem 8.7 – ACD
Problem 8.8 – C
Problem 8.9 – D
Problem 8.10 – A
Problem 8.11 – C
Problem 8.12 – BDE
Problem 8.13 – C
Problem 8.14 – D
Problem 8.15 – AD
Problem 8.16 – C
Problem 8.17 – D
Problem 8.18 – E
Problem 8.19 – C
Problem 8.20 – CEFG
Problem 8.21 – D
Problem 8.22 – AE

Problem 9.1 – D
Problem 9.2 – D
Problem 9.3 – A
Problem 9.4 – C
Problem 9.5 – BE
Problem 9.6 – D
Problem 9.7 – AD
Problem 9.8 – C
Problem 9.9 – C
Problem 9.10 – D
Problem 9.11 – B
Problem 9.12 – D
Problem 9.13 – B
Problem 9.14 – C
Problem 9.15 – D
Problem 9.16 – C
Problem 9.17 – E
Problem 9.18 – B
Problem 9.19 – B
Problem 9.20 – B
Problem 9.21 – C
Problem 9.22 – A
Problem 9.23 – C
Problem 9.24 – B
Problem 9.25 – A
Problem 9.26 – C
Problem 9.27 – D
Problem 9.28 – D
Problem 9.29 – AD
Problem 9.30 – A
Problem 9.31 – AD
Problem 9.32 – A
Problem 9.33 – AF
Problem 9.34 – E
Problem 9.35 – B
Problem 9.36 – B
Problem 9.37 – A
Problem 9.38 – C
Problem 9.39 – C
Problem 9.40 – BC
Problem 9.41 – AE
Problem 9.42 – D
Problem 9.43 – E

www.ingramcontent.com/pod-product-compliance
Lightning Source LLC
Chambersburg PA
CBHW060646060326
40690CB00020B/4529